'No historie so meete'

Manchester University Press

Politics, culture and society in early modern Britain

General editors

PROFESSOR ANN HUGHES
DR ANTHONY MILTON
PROFESSOR PETER LAKE

This important series publishes monographs that take a fresh and challenging look at the interactions between politics, culture and society in Britain between 1500 and the mid-eighteenth century. It counteracts the fragmentation of current historiography through encouraging a variety of approaches which attempt to redefine the political, social and cultural worlds, and to explore their interconnection in a flexible and creative fashion. All the volumes in the series question and transcend traditional interdisciplinary boundaries, such as those between political history and literary studies, social history and divinity, urban history and anthropology. They contribute to a broader understanding of crucial developments in early modern Britain.

'No historie so meete'

Gentry culture and the development
of local history in Elizabethan
and early Stuart England

JAN BROADWAY

Manchester
University Press
Manchester and New York

distributed exclusively in the USA by St. Martin's Press

Published by Manchester University Press
Oxford Road, Manchester M13 9NR, UK
and Room 400, 175 Fifth Avenue, New York, NY 10010, USA
www.manchesteruniversitypress.co.uk

Distributed exclusively in the USA by
Palgrave, 175 Fifth Avenue, New York, NY 10010, USA

Distributed exclusively in Canada by
UBC Press, University of British Columbia, 2029 West Mall, Vancouver, BC, Canada V6T 1Z2

British Library Cataloguing-in-Publication Data
A catalogue record for this book is available from the British Library

Library of Congress Cataloging-in-Publication Data applied for

ISBN 0 7190 7294 8 *hardback*
EAN 978 0 7190 7294 9

First published 2006

15 14 13 12 11 10 09 08 07 06   10 9 8 7 6 5 4 3 2 1

Typeset in Scala with Pastonchi display
by Koinonia Ltd, Manchester

Printed in Great Britain
by CPI, Bath

Contents

Figures

Figures 7–11 are from the author's own photographs.

Acknowledgements

This book has been some years in the writing and I have in that time incurred debts to many people for their help and encouragement. I would like to thank all my former colleagues at the universities of Birmingham, Glasgow and Wolverhampton, and my current colleagues at Queen Mary, University of London, for many inspiring conversations and suggestions. Special thanks must go to Richard Cust, who first introduced me to the subjects of this book. The staff and students of the AHRC Centre for Editing Lives and Letters have been instrumental in encouraging me to complete the manuscript, particularly Lisa Jardine, whose energy, enthusiasm and leadership is an inspiration to us all.

Authors of archivally based books invariably owe a great debt to the librarians and archivists who have helped them to access their sources. The British Library and Public Record Office have been invaluable to my research, but this study has depended upon the resources of innumerable local repositories. I would particularly like to thank the staff of the numerous county record offices, city archives and local libraries I have visited, who have been enormously generous with their time and local knowledge. Over the last decade, few long journeys have not incorporated a detour so that I could make such a visit. I have also benefited from conversations with local historians, whose expertise on individuals has been invaluable.

Astrid Wissenburg and Oscar Struijvé know how great a debt I owe them for their practical and moral support, especially since I have been working in London. Finally, my greatest debt is to my partner, Alan Cursue, who has no interest in early modern history but has nonetheless provided constant support and encouragement.

Abbreviations and key to selected references

Archer, *Correspondence*   Bodleian, Eng. lett. b 1 (Simon Archer)

Aubrey, *Brief Lives*   O. Lawson-Dick (ed.), *Aubrey's Brief Lives* (London: Reed International, 1992)

B.L.   British Library

Bodleian   Bodleian Library, Oxford

Browne, *Religio Medici*   Sir Thomas Browne, *Religio Medici and Other Writings*, ed. C.H. Herford (London: J.M. Dent & Sons Ltd., 1906)

Burton, *Leicestershire*   William Burton, *The Description of Leicestershire* (London: John White, 1622)

Burton, *Revised*   Staffordshire County Record Office, D649/4/3 – the manuscript is unpaginated, but the entries are arranged in alphabetical order by place-name

Carew, *Cornwall*   Richard Carew, *The Survey of Cornwall* (London: John Jaggard, 1602)

C.R.O.   County Record Office

Dugdale, *Warwickshire*   William Dugdale, *The Antiquities of Warwickshire* (London, 1656)

Erdeswicke, *Staffordshire*   Sampson Erdeswicke, *A Survey of Staffordshire*, ed. T. Harwood (London: J.B. Nichols & Son, 1844)

Gerard, *Dorset*   *A Survey of Dorsetshire* (London: J. Wilcox, 1732), attributed to John Coker on publication, but now known to be the work of Thomas Gerard

Gerard, *Somerset*   Thomas Gerard, *The Particular Description of the County of Somerset*, ed. E.H. Barnes (London: Somerset Record Society 15, 1900)

Glos. Trans.   *Transactions of the Bristol and Gloucestershire Archaeological Society*

Grey, *Chorographia*   William Grey, *Chorographia or a Survey of Newcastle upon Tine* (Newcastle, 1649)

Habington, *Worcestershire*   Thomas Habington, *A Survey of Worcestershire*, ed. J. Amphlett, two volumes (Oxford: Worcestershire Historical Society, 1895–99)

Hamper, *Dugdale*   William Hamper (ed.), *The Life, Diary and Correspondence of William Dugdale* (London: Harding, Lepard & Co., 1827)

Lambarde, *Kent*   William Lambarde, *The Perambulation of Kent* (London, 2nd edn., 1596)

Leics. Trans.   *Leicestershire Archaeological and Historical Society Transactions*

O.D.N.B.   *Oxford Dictionary of National Biography*

S.B.T.   Shakespeare Birthplace Trust, Stratford-upon-Avon, Warwickshire.

Smyth, *Berkeley* Mss   John Smyth, *The Berkeley Manuscripts*, ed. J. Maclean, three volumes (Bristol and Gloucestershire Archaeological Society, 1883–85)

Smyth Papers   Gloucestershire C.R.O. D8887, vols 1 to 10, catalogued in *Smyth of Nibley Papers* (Gloucester County Library, 1978)

Abbreviations and key to selected references

Stow, *London*   John Stow, *The Survey of London*, ed. H. Wheatley (London: J.M. Dent & Sons Ltd, 1912)

T.N.A.: P.R.O.   The National Archives: Public Record Office

V.C.H.   Victoria County History: this is a project that has published over 200 volumes since 1899. The project is run by the Institute of Historical Research, University of London

Woolf, *Social Circulation*   D.R. Woolf, *The Social Circulation of the Past* (Oxford: Oxford University Press, 2003)

Introduction

A sense of history is one of the characteristics which separates *Homo sapiens* from our nearest relatives with whom we share the vast majority of our genetic make-up. People are fascinated by the past. Any academic historian working in the Public Record Office at Kew or in the network of county and local record offices around the country, as opposed to within the rarefied confines of the British Library, the Bodleian and similar research libraries, cannot but be struck by the extent of historical interest and enthusiasm manifested by the English population. There are people researching the history of their families, houses, villages, towns, jobs and hobbies. The diversity of their interests is matched only by the diversity of their backgrounds. This English obsession with the past is not a new phenomenon of course. In 1605 Richard Verstegan described the 'very natural affection, which generally is in all men to hear of the worthiness of their Ancestors'.[1] What was new in Verstegan's day was that, increasingly, people were interested not simply in hearing about the past, but in reading, researching and writing about it. It was in the Elizabethan and early Stuart period that the study of past became an interest of the many rather than the preserve of the few. It was not that a sense of history suddenly evolved in the second half of the sixteenth century; as we shall see, there is plenty of evidence that the Elizabethan gentleman's interest in the past was shared by his medieval ancestors. Rather, a combination of circumstances combined to equip the late Tudor gentry with the necessary education to explore the past, at the same time as increasing amounts of source materials became available to them. The effects of the printing press and increased literacy on historical research in the sixteenth century may usefully be compared with the influence of computers, and particularly the Internet, four centuries later.

We are accustomed to the idea that religion played a far more significant part in the daily lives of our early modern ancestors than it does for the majority within contemporary society. What is less appreciated is that the past also weighed heavily upon them. Yet the traditions and ideals of their medieval forebears exercised an immeasurable influence on the lives of early modern Englishmen and women. In life an English gentleman surrounded himself with the visual imagery of medieval chivalry, and in death he was arrayed on his funeral monument in a full suit of armour. When he entered a law court or represented his community in parliament, his rhetoric and actions were directed by his understanding of what generations of his ancestors had said and done. A shared reverence for the past underlies the discourse of the opposing factions in the English civil war, however much they differed in their interpretations of the precedents they quoted. An appreciation of the importance placed on history is thus essential to an understanding of late Elizabethan and early Stuart society.

This study is concerned with the importance of history, and especially the history of their own families and localities, to the provincial gentry of Eliza-bethan and early Stuart England.[2] In 1576 The Kentish gentleman Thomas Wotton recommended William Lambarde's *Perambulation of Kent* to his fellow gentry for its usefulness:

> I must needes say, that (the sacred word of Almightie God alwaies excepted) there is nothing either for our instruction more profitable, or to our minds more delectable, or within the compasse of common understanding more easie or facile, then the studie of histories: nor that studie for none estate more meet, then for the estate of Gentlemen: nor for the Gentlemen of England, no Historie so meete, as the Historie of England.[3]

Much has been written about the religious interests of the English gentry from the Reformation to the civil war, but the way in which history impinged upon their lives has been little studied. Existing works dealing with the histo-riography of the period concentrate on the nationally important, published historians. It is also common practice to consider works according to their historical genre, which can obscure common developments across different genres.[4] Two recent works by Daniel Woolf have investigated the consump-tion of history in early modern England and have helped to clarify some of my own thoughts, although he is concerned with a far longer time-span and more socially disparate consumers. My concern, however, is not simply with the role of the Elizabethan and early Stuart gentry as consumers of historical knowledge, but as collectors and producers.[5] My aim is to explore the culture of provincial gentry society in the late Elizabethan and early Stuart period through the church notes, transcripts of documents, heraldic notebooks and other artefacts collected by members of that society and the historical works they produced predominantly for consumption by their families, friends and neighbours. These historical works belong predominantly to the fields of what today would be described as local and family history. Some were published at the time; many more circulated in manuscript form, and many of these have been published by subsequent generations or incorporated into later works. For reasons I shall explain below, I have deliberately cast my net widely and included a catholic selection of works which belong to a variety of genres as defined in conventional historiographical terms. The criteria for inclu-sion have been a degree of historical content and evidence of a work's initial production within the gentry community for consumption predominantly by that community.

In what follows I shall attempt to use these works and the circumstances of their production to examine the significance of history to our ancestors. I shall explore such questions as how an Elizabethan justice viewed the martial exploits of his medieval ancestors, or what an early Stuart gentleman thought were the consequences of the dissolution of the monasteries. My aim is to examine how and why the 'imagined communities' represented in these works were constructed, and how they related to contemporary reality. An 'imagined community' is one where its members will never know all their fellow members, yet are able to conceive of themselves as part of the same communion. One individual may belong to many such communities – the nation, the village, the family – but be unable to gain first-hand knowledge of the whole community because its members are too numerous or because they are separated by space or time. Terms such as nation, village and family are of course themselves socially conditioned and interpreted differently according to the cultural references of those that employ them. The various overlapping communities to which my subjects belonged – antiquarian scholars, the local gentry, the English gentry – had diffuse borders, but this did not make them less influential in informing their views and behaviours. The approach I use to explore the cultural paradigms of my subjects is similar to that adopted by Barrett Beer in his recent study of the Tudor antiquary John Stow. However, by examining a diverse group of authors of both published and manuscript works over an extended period, this book gains a perspective impossible to achieve when studying a single individual. Through a comparative analysis it is possible to discern how the availability of sources, a developing historiographical tradition, financial and practical considerations, and their social and cultural milieu, influenced the imagined communities of individual authors.[6]

Recently historians have placed an increasing emphasis on the importance of cultural artefacts in shaping our understanding of Tudor and Stuart England. Much of this emphasis has been on the culture of the Court and of the metropolis: on court masques, collections of European art and sculpture, the architecture of Inigo Jones, the plays performed at Southwark and in the private theatres of London. Such cultural artefacts, however, impinged rarely, if at all, on the lives of the majority of the provincial English gentry. Other historians have examined popular forms of literature, such as pamphlets and chapbooks. The usefulness of these in illuminating the lives of early modern men and women is limited by the extent to which they were often the products of extreme circumstances, written to shock, titillate or amuse their readers, by and for people who remain largely unknown and unknowable.[7] The works examined here, by contrast, were written predominantly by identifiable individuals, who have left a wealth of material concerning their lives and their antiquarian interests. Letters, notebooks, copies of the documents they saw, and so forth, provide invaluable information which illuminates their works and the context in which they were written. The collections of their contemporaries, who shared their interest in the past but not their compulsion for composition, expand our understanding of how their sense of the past influenced their society.

The term generally used to describe the subjects of this book is 'antiquary'. This has become a perjorative term, with connotations of pedantry and an obsession with the minutiae of the past, and is used to describe someone who exhumes and collects miscellaneous facts without applying scholarly analysis to them or placing them within a wider context. Originally the term was applied to those who sought to recover the antique past from its literary and material remains, but in the period of this study it encompassed those who were interested in the medieval as well as the classical past. Certainly on occasion the works examined here can be antiquarian in this sense, marshalling family and manorial descents, lists of knights and sheriffs, copies of charters, and so forth, with little or no apparent attempt at interpretation. However, as I shall show, to dismiss these works as 'merely' antiquarian is to misunderstand their context and purpose. As used here within the context of the development of early modern historiography, an antiquary is someone who studied the past on a thematic rather than a chronological basis. It is a term that may be applied to those who were at the forefront of developments in historiography, such as William Camden and John Selden. The emphasis in antiquarian works was on the use of primary source materials, which Francis Bacon in his *Advancement of Learning* compared to the remains of a shipwreck:

> Antiquities, or remnants of history, are ... when industrious persons, by an exact and scrupulous diligence and observation, out of monuments, names, words, proverbs, traditions, private records and evidences, fragments of stories, passages of books that concern not story, and the like, do save and recover somewhat from the deluge of time.[8]

It is in large part thanks to the efforts of early modern antiquaries, including the gentry antiquaries who are the subject of this study, that we have as much of the wreckage of medieval England as survives today.

'Local historian' is an anachronistic term to apply to writers in this period, since history was limited to narrative accounts of the past. Family chronicles were described as 'genealogical histories', but what we today label county and urban histories, were by their authors entitled Views, Descriptions, Surveys and Perambulations. Yet the different groups of works shared much in the way of sources, approaches to their material, and overall rationale. To apply the phrase 'local histories' to all antiquarian works written within a local rather than a national context is partly a matter of authorial convenience, but it also reflects my conviction that these authors were increasingly concerned with history and, in particular, with their own, local history. To describe my subjects as local historians also consciously excludes those whose interests were strictly classical, whom contemporaries would also have labelled anti-quaries. A few years ago I thought that there was a clear distinction between county surveys and county histories. The first were predominantly topograph-ical and described contemporary society and the way that the county had been within 'living memory'. County histories, on the other hand, engaged with the medieval past and incorporated documentary evidence. Over the course of researching this book I have come to appreciate that there is no such ready distinction to be made between the authors of county descriptions and county histories, and the content of their notebooks or the subjects of their correspond-ence. Moreover, as the authors of county descriptions revised their works, I found they tended to incorporate increasing amounts of historical material. Thomas Gerard, who wrote a county description of Dorset shortly after his marriage, was writing a far more historical account of Somerset a decade later. The archetypal local historian is a gentleman with antiquarian interests mapping out an area topographically, accumulating historical material and then proceeding to incorporate the one into the other. Many of my subjects never completed all the steps between having antiquarian tastes and becoming a full-blown local historian, and others concentrated on a family rather than a physical locality, but I hope to show that they shared sufficient characteristics to be considered as a group. The careful accumulation of written and physical evidence from the past, and its systematic arrangement, is certainly what we would label antiquarianism rather than history today – but these men did step beyond merely collecting and collating. They recognised that contemporary society was not the same as the medieval and more distant past they glimpsed through the material they collected, and they began tentatively to seek and to advance explanations. It is for this reason that I prefer to label what they were doing as local history rather than antiquarianism.

This is unashamedly a study of the historical interests of the Elizabethan and early Stuart gentry. This is not to suggest that only the gentry were inter-ested in the past; the popularity of chapbook histories and ballads is evidence that such interest transcended social boundaries. It was, however, predomi-nantly the gentry who were in a position to take their interest beyond reading, to engage directly in studying the past through primary sources. It is also overwhelmingly the gentry who provide us with sufficient evidence to put their activities in context. In these circumstances it is inevitable that any study of the early development of local history will be heavily biased towards the gentry. Yet, it is my intention in what follows to go beyond the limits imposed by circumstances, and to argue that the historical interests of the Elizabethan and early Stuart gentry were in many ways distinct from those of university scholars, heralds, citizens of London and provincial towns, and professional writers. This is not to suggest that these groups existed in separate spheres and did not interact. Nor is it possible to draw distinct boundaries around the membership of these groups. To take a single example, in the 1630s William Dugdale was a Warwickshire gentleman studying the history of his county. Towards the end of the decade he was found a place in the College of Arms, which provided him with an income to support his antiquarian studies. In the 1650s Dugdale published his *Antiquities of Warwickshire* (1656), which marks the culmination of his career as a gentleman antiquary. The work also helped to advertise his status as a historian, following as it did his joint publication of the first volume of *Monasticon Anglicanum* (1655) with Roger Dodsworth. From the publication of his *History of St. Paul's* (1658) and his commission to write the *History of Imbanking and Drayning* (1662), Dugdale may be regarded as a professional writer. At the Restoration he returned to the College of Arms and rose to be Garter king at arms, the senior herald in England. Despite his subsequent career for the period covered by this study, Dugdale may be counted as a provincial gentleman and local historian. It is my intention to demonstrate that the historical interests of the gentry were distinct, and that they were shaped by the nature of the society in which they arose. The forms taken by the Elizabethan and early Stuart gentry's interest in their past can thus be used by contemporary historians to understand the society which gave rise to them.

Having hopefully established that it is legitimate to describe the apparently miscellaneous collection of county, urban and family histories, topographical writings, genealogical notebooks and other works that will be discussed here as local history, I should also explain my justification for the period covered. Richard Helgerson has described a generation of writers born in the mid-sixteenth century as having forged through their works a concept of English nationhood.[9] As we shall see, a number of local historians were closely linked with Helgerson's group of writers, and to an important degree they were writing within the national context that their works supplied. However, this book covers a longer period than that which Helgerson devoted to the formation of the Elizabethan concept of England. I begin not with the seismic rupture of the Reformation, but with one of its consequences: the creation of the first generation of English gentry to be educated within the schools that were established to replace the monasteries as centres of teaching, and who benefited from the absorption of humanist learning into secular education. The education they received in provincial grammar schools equipped the Elizabethan gentry to read history and to apply what they read to their own lives. They began to be able to read the deeds and other documents they inherited along with their ancestral lands or acquired with newly purchased property. Maps began to appear that helped them to appreciate how their locality related to the rest of England, as well as how England fitted within the newly expanded world picture. This was the generation that claimed their families and localities as distinct and as having a past that was part of that distinction. I end with the last generation of gentlemen who received their education before the outbreak of the English civil war. The period I have chosen is thus bounded by two events that turned the world of the gentry upside-down: the Reformation and the civil war. I hope to demonstrate that the intervening period produced local historians who strove to use their antiquarian learning to establish a link between their new sense of national and local identity and the world of their medieval ancestors. I believe the events of the civil war and interregnum so influenced the paradigm within which a generation of gentry were raised, that it created a disjunction with previous generations which could never be fully overcome.

Accounts of local history are often weakened by a failure to locate them within a wider geographical, cultural and theoretical context. It may be thought that by concentrating on one aspect of the historiography of a single country over a comparatively short time-frame and concentrating on a single social group, that this work is in danger of lacking that wider context. I am painfully aware that many of the factors I identify as increasing the historical awareness of the English gentry had a wide applicability across early modern Europe. Humanism had a widespread influence on educational structure and content. The religious and political upheavals of the period combined with the discoveries of vast new lands created a disjunction between medieval Christendom and the emerging nation states across the continent. Cartographical developments meant educated people throughout Europe gained greater spatial awareness of their own localities and the wider world. Across Europe emergent nation-states sought to recover their national histories and to link them to a classical past; and they did this co-operatively, knowing about and assisting the endeavours of fellow scholars in other countries. However, while the contributory factors were common and historical research co-operative across national boundaries, the precise conditions within which they operated were different. The butterfly effect of chaos theory may be applied to historiography as readily as to other fields of human endeavour. Differences in initial conditions can have an unexpectedly large influence on consequent results. In Germany the nature of urbanisation, the significance of individual towns, and the lack of a single dominant political power, contributed to make the development of German town chronicles distinct from that of English urban histories – and in Germany family memorials were found within an urban context that does not occur in early modern England. By contrast the French had a tradition of aristocratic family histories going back to the twelfth century, while Dutch historians as well as artists reinterpreted the past to stress the political cohesion of their new republic, not local particularity. This is not to suggest that a comparative study of the development of local history across early modern Europe would be neither possible nor desirable. Indeed, as a study of the development of local history within the imagined community of the English gentry, this book may be viewed as a necessary precursor to such an endeavour. Although Wales and Scotland are spatially connected to England, and to a greater or lesser extent politically linked during the period of this study, the Welsh and Scots form communities that are as separate and distinct from the English as the French, Germans, Italians or Spanish. Hence, they are also excluded from this study.[10]

It is not my intention to provide a comprehensive survey of all local historians for the period studied. Such was the pervasive nature of antiquarian interest among the English gentry that any attempt at such a survey would result in either a dauntingly thick volume or an unsatisfactorily superficial analysis. There is also a problem of evidence. The archives contain many antiquarian manuscripts and collections that are anonymous, while we know little about many Elizabethan and early Stuart antiquaries beyond their names and approximate dates of activity. This includes figures such as the 'Juditious Antiquarie, and great Master of Records' St Loe Kniverton, whose collections were widely used and his expertise praised, but about whom we know practically nothing.[11] I have tried to identify and contextualise a number of these obscure individuals, but it would be a Herculean task to attempt to bring more than a small fraction out of the shadows in which they lurk. Consequently, there is a tendency to concentrate on a few well-documented individuals, and particularly on those antiquaries who formed loosely defined networks and who provide us with correspondence that elucidates their activities. I have attempted to give weight to the full range of gentry local-historical interests and endeavours in this period, and to avoid undue regional bias. I believe that the result is generally applicable to Elizabethan and early Stuart gentry society in England, but, as my subjects themselves found, lack of evidence all too often confounds the desire to be thorough and comprehensive.

It is my aim to locate the antiquaries discussed here firmly within the gentry society which produced them. I am interested in the values and preoccupations which shaped their activities, and how the history they wrote emerged from their researches. Previous studies of Tudor and Stuart historiography dealing with local history have tended to segregate the antiquaries according to the nature of the works they produced. As a result, while F. Smith Fussner in *The Historical Revolution* (1962) recognised the influence of the genealogical and heraldic interests of the gentry on the development of both county and family histories, he did not fully appreciate the links between these two forms of historical writing. He considered these works to belong to two separate and distinct strands within his wider definition of territorial history, namely local and biographical. He ascribed the significant historiographical advances of the period to the field of local history and in particular to the work of the county historians. He was dismissive of family histories, because they remained in manuscript.[12] Stan Mendyk's *Speculum Britanniae* (1989) was concerned with works that fall within a narrow definition of chorographies or regional studies. A significant weakness of Mendyk's study is his failure to appreciate that topographical description was not necessarily a major preoccupation of county historians. William Dugdale's *Antiquities of Warwickshire* had at least as much in common with Sir Thomas Shirley's unpublished family history as with Richard Carew's *Survey of Cornwall* (1602).[13]

The study of early modern local and family history has been significantly hampered by a failure to give sufficient weight to unpublished manuscripts. There is an implicit assumption that, by the sixteenth century, printing had completely supplanted scribal publication and that the copying of manu-scripts passed into history with the Henrician dissolution of the monasteries. Dismissive of family histories, Fussner referred to the 'unexplored' manu-script histories of English towns and counties, but failed to acknowledge the contemporary influence of such works.[14] Elizabethan and Stuart gentlemen frequently produced manuscript treatises that circulated among their friends and acquaintances, and many printed works were initially known in this form. The widespread circulation of manuscripts in this period meant that they could exert an influence on local historians equal to that of published works. When these manuscripts were subsequently published, they are considered in the historiographical surveys, although they are generally regarded as less significant than contemporaneously printed texts. Manuscripts which never achieved publication are ignored. As I hope to show, this leads to a distortion of the account of the development of local history in this period. For example, in the particular genre of county history, Dugdale's *Antiquities of Warwick-shire* has been praised as the 'first of the classical county histories', which established 'new standards of accuracy and method'. With this work, Fussner believed that the 'county history came of age'.[15] It would be churlish to deny the pre-eminence of Dugdale's work, which is undoubtedly more extensive and rigorous than its immediate predecessor as a published county history, William Burton's *Description of Leicestershire* (1622). Yet it is wrong to compare the *Antiquities of Warwickshire* to the work begun by Burton as a law student in the 1590s, and apparently brought to the press for reasons that had as much to do with patronage as scholarship, without considering the extensive amend-ments made to the *Description of Leicestershire* for a second edition. This is particularly important, as we know that Dugdale had read Burton's revised text when he began to write his own county history. Nor should Thomas Gerard's manuscript accounts of Dorset and Somerset, also written in the intervening decades, be ignored. Dugdale had almost certainly read and been influenced by this work. Similarly, his association with Sir Thomas Shirley makes the family historian's careful enumeration of his sources pertinent to a consideration of Dugdale's achievement. The methodical use of documentary evidence in John Smyth's family history of the Berkeleys, which was written some two decades before the *Antiquities of Warwickshire*, led Dugdale himself to describe it as 'a Pattern for some others to follow'.[16] Like Graham Parry I regard the *Antiquities of Warwickshire* as the 'culmination of a tradition', but I would place it within a wider and more varied tradition than that represented purely by the published county histories.[17]

As indicated above, I wish to place works of local history not simply in the correct historiographical context, but also to situate their authors firmly in relationship to the gentry society which moulded them. This is essential for a true understanding of the works, and is required, I believe, because their authors are often quoted by historians as authorities on the period. John Smyth's description of Westminster Hall as 'our cockpit of revenge', for example, provides a useful quote for the historian discussing attitudes to litigation under the early Stuarts. However, this phrase must be understood within the context of a family history written for a limited circulation among those directly interested in the affairs of the Berkeley family. Smyth's concern was with the decline of the manorial courts, which directly affected the income and influence of the family. As a common lawyer, who sent his eldest son to the Middle Temple in his wake, he did not share the dislike of many lay gentlemen for the 'hordes of lawyers, attornies and solicitors' he described. His social background led him to believe that the Westminster courts should be the legal forum for the gentry, while the 'country malice' of the 'inferior sort' should be addressed in local courts. The language he used in expressing this view is significant because it was intended to arouse the Berkeley family to assert their authority in Gloucestershire. Yet Smyth's occasional use of a vivid phrase means that his work is more often quoted than analysed.[18] Like the *Lives of the Berkeleys*, all local histories were influenced by their authors' cultural assumptions, their purposes in writing, and the image of gentry society they wished to convey. Without some understanding of this, their use as historical sources is fraught with difficulty.

In the introduction to *The Social Circulation of the Past*, Daniel Woolf explained his belief that in order to understand the historical consciousness of the past and why the English interest in national history developed in the way it did, historiographers had to adopt a new approach. If we continue to examine historical texts from the perspective of the polemical purposes to which they were put, even examining a wider variety of works will not produce a different picture, just a more detailed one. He accordingly adopted a different approach – that of looking beyond the texts to the ambient cultural noise of the society that produced them. It would fit neatly into a historical narrative if I could say that reading Woolf's work galvanised me into examining the works of local historians from the perspective of their cultural milieu. However, the groundwork of this book was laid long before *Social Circulation* was published, although it was informed by Woolf's earlier essays that pointed in the same direction. While writing my thesis on the development of county history in the Midlands, I found the standard historiographical works inadequate to explain the shape and content of the works I was studying. The need to place local histories in a different explanatory context became obvious to me at that time, and this book is the culmination of that insight.[19]

The first section of this book begins with an overview of the development of local-history writing in England, from its medieval and Tudor beginnings through to the period under discussion. This explores the historiographical context within which the Elizabethan gentry began to explore and express their interest in the past. It also demonstrates that this gentry interest in the past was not newly minted in the late sixteenth century, but was something that medieval historians had been aware of and exploited. This is followed by a discussion of the scholarly environment in which that interest developed. Although the development of local history demands that we look to the regions for an understanding of what was happening, it is important not to lose sight of the role of national and metropolitan influences, such as the universities, inns of court and College of Arms. Having surveyed the national scene, I shall turn to the consideration of regional networks and discuss some representative examples in detail. This discussion will concern not only local historians but also the members of the local gentry, who, in various ways and degrees, encouraged, supported and assisted their endeavours. This section concludes with a discussion of the sources used by local historians.

The second part of this book is concerned with the major historiographical strands represented in local history: genealogical, didactic and topographical. Each strand is examined in turn, through an exploration of the historiographical tradition and the intentions of the antiquaries. I shall also demonstrate how the interests, reactions and concerns of their contributors and readers influenced the content of the works. The genealogical content of local history demonstrates the importance of lineage to late Elizabethan and early Stuart society and to the gentry's sense of their identity and status. True gentility in this period, however, was held to derive from both lineage and personal virtue. The behaviour expected of a gentleman was addressed by the didactic content of the works. In this respect they may be related to other forms of advice literature, which, as we shall see, promoted a similar model of gentility to their readers. Finally, I will consider the relationship between developments in cartography and local history in this period, and how they were shaped by the expectations of their gentry consumers.

The interests and motivations of the late Elizabethan and early Stuart antiquaries examined in this study had a lasting influence on the subsequent development of local history. More than three centuries after the publication of the

Antiquities of Warwickshire, the dead hand of the seventeenth-century squire was seen by local historians such as W.G. Hoskins as casting a genealogical blight on their chosen field of study. The preoccupation with land ownership, pedigrees and heraldry that they identified was indeed the lasting legacy of the early modern practitioners of local history. This study is an attempt to explain how the gentleman and his manor house, rather than the villager and his cottage, became and remained the focus of local history in England until the late twentieth century.[20]

NOTES

1 R. Verstegan, *Restitution of Decayed Intelligence in Antiquities* (Antwerp, 1605) p. 3v.

2 In the context of early modern England it is not possible to define 'the gentry' precisely: see F. Heal and C. Holmes, *The Gentry in England and Wales, 1500–1700* (London: Macmillan, 1994), pp. 6–19. My inclusion of individuals from the urban elite might be disputed, but culturally they were often more closely linked to the provincial gentry than to their urban neighbours.

3 W. Lambarde, *The Perambulation of Kent*, (London, 2nd edn., 1596), hereafter Lambarde, *Kent*, p. ix.

4 Notable works include: F.J. Levy, *Tudor Historical Thought* (San Marino, CA: Huntingdon Library, 1967); A.B. Ferguson, *Clio Unbound* (Durham, NC: Duke University Press, 1979); D.R. Woolf, *The Idea of History in Early Stuart England* (Toronto: Toronto University Press, 1990); S.A.E. Mendyk, *'Speculum Britanniae' Regional Study, Antiquarianism, and Science in Britain to 1700* (Toronto: Toronto University Press, 1989).

5 D. Woolf, *Reading History in Early Modern England* (Cambridge: Cambridge University Press, 2000); D.R. Woolf, *The Social Circulation of the Past* (Oxford: Oxford University Press, 2003), hereafter Woolf, *Social Circulation*.

6 B. Anderson, *Imagined Communities* (London: Verso, 2nd edn., 1991); C. Geertz, *The Interpretation of Cultures* (London: Fontana Press, 1993), chapter 2; B.L. Beer, *Tudor England Observed* (Stroud: Alan Sutton, 1998).

7 For example: R.M. Smuts, *Court Culture and the Origins of a Royalist Tradition in Early Stuart England* (Philadelphia: University of Pennsylvania Press, 1987); K. Sharpe and P. Lake (eds), *Culture and Politics in Early Stuart England* (London: Macmillan, 1994); D. Howarth, *Images of Rule* (London: Macmillan, 1997); M. Spufford, *Small Books and Pleasant Histories* (London: Methuen, 1981).

8 F. Bacon, *The Advancement of Learning and New Atlantis*, (ed.) A. Johnston (Oxford: Clarendon Press, 1974), p. 72; S. Piggott, *Ancient Britons and the Antiquarian Imagination* (London: Thames & Hudson, 1989), chapter 1.

9 R. Helgerson, *Forms of Nationhood* (Chicago: University of Chicago Press, 1992).

10 J. Gleick, *Chaos* (London: Sphere Books, 1987); F. Du Boulay, 'The German town chroniclers', in R. Davis and J. Wallace-Hadrill (eds), *The Writing of History in the Middle Ages* (Oxford: Clarendon Press, 1981), pp. 445–69; M. Keen, *Chivalry* (New Haven: Yale University Press, 1984), pp. 32–3; M. Westermann, *The Art of the Dutch Republic 1585–*

1718 (London: George Weidenfeld & Nicolson, 1996), chapter 4.

11 B.L., Harley 4928, fo. 146 – the phrase is Sir Thomas Shirley's; he used Kniveton's collections for Derbyshire and Nottinghamshire in his family history.

12 F. Fussner, *The Historical Revolution* (London, Routledge & Kegan Paul, 1962), pp. 175, 179–84.

13 Mendyk, *Speculum Britanniae*, pp. 1–8.

14 Fussner, *Historical Revolution*, p. 181; H. Love, *Scribal Publication in Seventeenth-Century England* (Oxford: Clarendon Press, 1993).

15 J. Simmons (ed.), *English County Historians* (Wakefield: EP Publishing, 1978), p. 8; Mendyk, *Speculum Britanniae*, pp. 102–3; Fussner, *Historical Revolution*, p. 182.

16 W. Dugdale, *The Baronage of England* (London, 1675), Preface; W. Hamper (ed.), *The Life, Diary and Correspondence of William Dugdale* (London: Harding, Lepard & Co., 1827), p. 189, hereafter Hamper, *Dugdale*.

17 G. Parry, *The Trophies of Time* (Oxford: Oxford University Press, 1995), p. 241.

18 John Smyth, *The Berkeley Manuscripts*, J. Maclean (ed.), three volumes (Bristol and Gloucestershire Archaeological Society, 1883–85), vol. 1, p. 242, hereafter Smyth, *Berkeley Mss*.

19 Woolf, *Social Circulation*, pp. 3–8; J. Broadway, *Antiquarianism and the Development of County History in the Midlands 1586–1656* (Ph.D. thesis, University of Birmingham,

Chapter 1

The development of local history
in England before 1660

Local history as a distinctive genre of written history can hardly be said to exist before the fifteenth century. The conditions were not auspicious for its development, since it was – and to a large extent remains – dependent upon a local readership. In the medieval period, the lack of a literate lay readership militated against the development of the genre. Local and family traditions almost certainly thrived in a vibrant oral culture, but only occasional clues as to its nature and extent survive. After the demise of the Anglo-Saxon chronicle at the end of the twelfth century, history in all forms was almost entirely written in Latin. This effectively removed it from the local, vernacular sphere and enshrined it within a scholarly environment. In the fifteenth century, rising literacy among the mercantile classes in London created the preconditions necessary for the development of local history, and led to the appearance of the earliest chronicles of the city. More widespread literacy in the sixteenth century led directly to the explosion of interest in local history which is the subject of this study.

While it did not constitute a distinctive genre, local history did form an important element in numerous medieval works. Monastic chroniclers would occasionally give particular emphasis to local events or to those involving individuals associated with their house either as members or patrons. Such material was introduced to emphasise or illustrate a particular point or to establish a claim for the significance of local people or institutions on the national stage. Accounts of monasteries and bishoprics and lives of saints, kings and leading nobles were often local in character, because they concerned an individual or an institution associated with a particular place. As a consequence medieval works provided a rich seam of material for later local historians. An example is the monastic chronicle of 'Florence' (now known as John) of Worcester. This was a general chronicle of more than purely local interest – it was copied by John Stow in 1572 and published two decades later by William, lord Howard of

Naworth, with a dedication to lord Burghley, although none of these men had Worcestershire connections – but it included a wealth of material relevant to Worcester that did not appear in other chronicles. It was an invaluable source for the history of the early bishops of Worcester. The chronicle also included eyewitness accounts of events in the city during the civil war of King Stephen's reign (in the twelfth century). It was quoted extensively by Thomas Habington when writing his own history of Worcestershire in the seventeenth century. Similarly, the *Compilatio* of Henry Knighton, fourteenth-century canon of St Mary's abbey, Leicester, contains little original material beyond what concerns Leicester and its abbey, making it of interest primarily to local historians. Its appearance in a notebook interleaved with extracts from William Camden's *Britannia* represents the most compelling evidence that the Jacobean herald William Wyrley began work on a history of Leicestershire.[1]

The origins of the genealogical interests of local historians may be traced in medieval works which sought to flatter or particularly interest patrons. Elaborate pedigrees were produced, drawing on the deeds contained in monastic archives. Monastic chronicles were also used to record genealogical information. The twelfth-century chronicle of Walden abbey is an important source for the life of its founder, Geoffrey de Mandeville, earl of Essex. Robert of Gloucester's verse chronicle of the following century appears to have been a monastic production designed to flatter Sir Warin of Bassingbourne, who appears more prominently that his importance merits. The genesis of family history may also be traced within noble households, which, like monasteries, housed literate scribes. The origin of the medieval romance 'Fouke le Fitzwarin' lies in a verse account of family history and traditions produced within the household of the Fitzwarines of Shropshire. The proximity of the Welsh border suggests the influence of the Welsh bardic tradition in the verse's production, and it is probable that the poem was initially performed before the household as the climax of a feast. Such celebrations of family history might have constituted a common form of entertainment, but oral transmission leaves few traces for subsequent historians.[2]

In addition to the existence of a literate lay readership, the development of local history depended upon an awareness of locality. An understanding of contemporary topography was required before an interest could develop in how the landscape had been formed and altered. The descriptions of ecclesiastical and urban topography found in the works of William of Malmesbury, Gervase of Canterbury and Lucian of Chester stand witness to the development of this interest in the twelfth century. In the reign of Henry II a Welsh churchman in the service of the English crown wrote topographical accounts of Ireland and Wales. Giraldus Cambrensis (c.1145–1223), a royal chaplain, accompanied Prince John on his expedition to Ireland. Following this experience, Giraldus wrote *Topographica Hibernica*, a record of the natural history, inhabitants and folk-tales of Ireland. Subsequently, he accompanied the Archbishop of Canterbury on a preaching tour through his native Wales in support of the third Crusade, and wrote up his impressions in *Itinerarium Cambriae*. Both manuscripts were well known to later antiquaries; they were translated into English and published in the 1580s. From this early stage there was a link between the interests of the topographer and the historian, since Giraldus also wrote ecclesiastical lives and similar works. Parallels may clearly be drawn with William Fitzstephen's *Descriptio Londiniae*, a topographical account of London from the same period, which formed a preface to his life of Thomas à Becket. It became well known four centuries later when it was appended by John Stow to his *Survey of London* (1598). The *Descriptio*, though short, is the most detailed and graphic account of London surviving from this period, celebrating the city for its 'abundant wealth, extensive commerce, great grandeur and magnificence'.[3] The main emphasis of the work is on the secular rather than the ecclesiastical government of the city, and an account of its sports. Although Fitzstephen mentions that the saint had ennobled the city by his birth there, he makes little attempt to link his preface with the body of his work. The *Descriptio* was written to reflect the author's own pride in his city. Three centuries later such civic pride was to be a significant force in the growth of urban chronicles – one of the earliest distinctive forms of local historical writing. This development in turn influenced monastic writing in the period before the Reformation. Henry Bradshaw (d. 1513), for example, incorporated an account of the foundation of Chester into his verse chronicle of the life of St Werburgh (printed in 1521) and was reputed to have composed a paean to the city in Latin.[4]

Ironically, one of the most influential works on the development of local history produced by a monastic chronicler was the *Polichronicon*, a 'universal' history written by Ranulf Higden (d. 1364), a Benedictine monk of Chester. Despite the work's status as a encyclopaedic history covering a wide range of topics, its inclusion of a wealth of local material and of a geographical description of England ensured its significance in the development of local history. The work was influenced by the topographical surveys of Geraldus Cambrensis. Higden remarked upon the Roman remains at Chester and gave a careful account of the course of the Roman trunk roads – subjects that were to be important to later antiquaries, He also recorded folklore from the Isle of Man. The *Polichronicon* was of particular use to historians of Chester – in the early seventeenth century David Rogers placed it second in his list of sources after Bradshaw's life of St Werburgh – but it also had a wider application for local history. The importance of the *Polichronicon* was increased by its popularity. The Latin manuscript enjoyed an unusually wide distribution (over 120 manuscripts survive) and by 1387 it had been translated into English by John de Trevisa (1326–1412), the vicar of Berkeley, Glos., for his patron Thomas, lord Berkeley. Trevisa produced a comparatively free translation of Higden's Latin, including a number of asides that cast light on fourteenth-century life and manifest his interest in relating the general to the local. Hence, in giving examples of towns sharing the same name he goes from Carthage in Africa and Cartagena in Spain to Newport in Wales and Newport in the parish of Berkeley, 'or again, Wootton-under-Edge and Wootton Bassett, or yet again, Wickwar, Wickpain, and Wick in the parish of Berkeley'. In 1480 Caxton compiled selections from Trevisa's translation of the first book of Polichronicon and published it as the *Description of Britain*. This was one of the earliest historical works to be printed by Caxton, who printed the whole of Trevisa's translation two years later. The popularity of the work is apparent from the subsequent production of further editions by Wynkeyn de Worde and Peter Treveris. In the seventeenth century John Smyth drew attention to the work of his predecessor in the Berkeley service, quoting Trevisa's dedication to his translation of the *Polichronicon* in full in his own *Lives of the Berkeleys*. References to Higden's work are common in the works of local historians, while transcriptions from the Latin manuscripts or Trevisa's translation are frequently encountered among their notes.[5]

In the fourteenth and fifteenth centuries the tradition of monastic chronicles declined, and by the advent of the Wars of the Roses only St Albans retained its importance as a centre of national historical writing. As their role as chroniclers of national history diminished, monastic writers became increasingly important as producers of local history. The motivating factor behind this development was not a desire to further a new form of history, but the need to defend monastic institutions against critics by documenting their antiquity and the historical basis of their rights and privileges. Predominant among these monastic pioneers of local history were Thomas Elmham of St Augustine's, Canterbury; Thomas Burton of Meaux, Yorkshire; and John Whethamsted of St Albans. The chroniclers' narrow focus on the concerns of their monastic institutions made them rich, but limited, sources for later local historians. The extensive legacy of 'old Manuscripts, Leiger-Books, and other Records of credit', available at Canterbury as a result of the historical tradition at St Augustine's, was of great use to Lambarde, Somner and other Kentish historians, and was one of the factors encouraging the strong antiquarian tradition in the county. Similar lesser works abounded, such as the history of St Peter's, Gloucester, written by Walter de Frocester and used by John Smyth as a source for his *Lives of the Berkeleys*. This group of monastic histories included the Crowland chronicle, which was written in the fifteenth century although it purported to be much earlier in origin. In the period covered by this study the Anglo-Norman genesis of Crowland was universally accepted, and it was utilised as an important source by local historians for the poorly documented period following the Norman Conquest. The use of history in defence of their institutions did not ultimately save the monasteries from the depredations of Henry VIII, but did ensure the preservation of their history in the written record, and the institutional bias in favour of the monastic in the surviving records influenced the development of local history.[6]

The fifteenth century also witnessed the advent of the peripatetic topographer and historian. It is not that medieval chroniclers necessarily spent their time cloistered within the monastery walls, observing the world predominantly through written records; although Bede rarely left Jarrow, historians such as William of Malmesbury, Giraldus Cambrensis and Matthew Paris were widely travelled. Nevertheless, with William Worcestre (1415–?1482) we encounter a man for whom antiquarian study became a motivating force for his travelling rather than an interesting adjunct. For around twenty years Worcestre was secretary to Sir John Fastolf of Caister castle, Norfolk, and consequently spent a great deal of time seeking evidence for use in lawsuits (a common spur to the development of antiquarian interests). Born in Bristol, educated at Oxford, employed by a Norfolk landowner and required to attend to his master's affairs in London and elsewhere, Worcestre's life was a peripatetic one. Following Fastolf's death in 1459, Worcestre became embroiled in lawsuits with the Paston family relating to his former master's will. In the final years of his life, however, once the lawsuits were settled, he was able to indulge his interest in topography and local history. We are provided with an insight into that interest through his *Itinerary*, a commonplace book recording notes made on his travels, particularly two journeys he made in the summers of 1478 and 1480, and other miscellaneous materials, such as a description of the siege of Caister in 1469. In 1478 he travelled from Norwich via Southampton and Bristol to Cornwall and from thence to London, while two years later he journeyed to Bristol via Kingston and Oxford. The contents of his *Itinerary* have been judged by his editor as consistent with a project to write a topography of Britain illustrated by historical material, anticipating John Leland and his successors. It is possible that he produced more of this than the surviving manuscripts reveal, but if he had hopes of completing such a project in his retirement, he did not have time to bring them to fruition.[7]

Worcestre's notes are distinctive for their detailed descriptions of the dimensions and architecture of buildings, which are more extensive than those to be found in later itineraries. During a five-week stay in his native city in the late summer of 1480 he compiled a detailed perambulation of Bristol, which anticipates the later urban surveys by Hooker of Exeter, Stow of London and Somner of Canterbury. He visited and described almost all the town's eighteen parish churches and fourteen religious houses and hospitals, measuring widths and lengths by pacing, and heights by counting steps. Unlike later local historians, he showed no interest in armorial glass, although he counted and described the arrangement of windows. The sole window for which he described the stained glass was that in St Mary's Chapel on Bristol Bridge, commemorating the burgesses that had been the chapel's benefactors. This is indicative of the way in which Worcestre associated himself with the urban elite of Bristol rather than the local gentry. Such self-identification with a particular social group was to become an important factor influencing the content and emphases of local history. The perambulation of Bristol provides interesting hints about the culture in which Worcestre undertook it. He was evidently given freedom of access to parish churches and religious houses, as parish priests, monks and friars sanctioned his pacing around their buildings, and produced books and documents for him to examine and copy. Two master masons troubled to give him details of the measurements and architecture of the local churches they were working on. The story of a supposed Jewish synagogue was told to him by 'many people', and the appearance of this same tradition sixty years later when the Tudor antiquary John Leland made his own survey of Bristol, suggests the existence of a vibrant oral historical culture. Finally, the history of the Knights of St John of Jerusalem, which he copied from a board hanging in the Temple church, indicates that a more literate, public interest in the past also thrived in Bristol.[8]

Despite the interest of his manuscript, Worcestre cannot be considered a significant influence on the subsequent development of local history. The *Itinerary* was not published until the eighteenth century and does not appear to have been widely known before that time. After Worcestre's death the manuscript passed to Robert Talbot (c.1505–1558), a prebendary at Norwich cathedral, who added a historical account of the building of the cloisters at Norwich and various marginal notes taken from the *Registrum Primum* of the cathedral. It subsequently found its way into the hands of Henry Aldrich (d. 1593), a fellow of Corpus Christi College, Cambridge, who added further notes. After his death it was lodged in the library of Corpus Christi, where it was available to those scholars who could gain access to the college library. Extracts from Worcestre's notes on Norfolk familes were copied by Sir Henry Spelman, but transcripts of his manuscript did not circulate widely. Sir Simon Archer and William Dugdale, for example, when working on the history of Warwickshire in the 1630s, do not appear to have seen the notes taken by Worcestre in 1479 from a fourteenth-century manuscript compiled by the receiver-general to the earl of Warwick.[9]

The sort of pride in the place of his birth and his family's influence which led William Worcestre to describe Bristol in such detail, led to the growth of the urban chronicle and the development of civic annals. The most numerous of the chronicles were naturally enough dedicated to London, by far the largest and most important city in late medieval England. The dominance of accounts of civic elections, council ordinances and commerical agreements in these chronicles, betray their origins as a product of the civic elite. The mayoral annals of provincial towns are similar. Robert Ricart's *Kalendar* of the mayor of Bristol, for example, dates from the year before Worcestre's description of the city and preserves in detail the involvement of the mayor and councillors in such ceremonies as that of the boy bishop performed at the church of St Nicholas in December.[10] While these works were instigated by and celebrated the urban elite, they were also popular among the increasingly literate middle class. Written in the vernacular, they were accessible in a way that the monastic chronicles in their learned Latin were not. As the fifteenth century progressed, the readership which embraced the *Brut* – a chronicle written in the vernacular– also consumed urban chronicles which circulated in manuscript and are to be found copied into contemporary commonplace books. By the time the first Tudor came to the throne of England, a readership for urban history was firmly established.

An increase in literacy among the landed gentry similarly encouraged the production of dedicated literary works by those seeking patronage, and, in this context, family history was particularly useful as a vehicle for erudite flattery. An example is the account of the Berkeleys written in 1489 by John Newland, abbot of St Augustine, Bristol. The abbey had been founded by Robert Fitzharding and endowed by Henry II with the confiscated lands of Robert de Berkeley, whose daughter married Fitzharding's son. The Berkeleys remained closely associated with the monastery until the Henrician dissolution, and various members of the family were buried in the church, where a Berkeley chapel was built in the fourteenth century. Newland's account was intended to flatter the newly created marquess of Berkeley and to encourage his generosity towards the abbot's own building plans. In his account, Newland perpetuated the 'old tradition' of the family that they were descended from the royal house of Denmark. This work was used as a source by John Smyth, the subsequent historian of the family, who observed that some of his fellow antiquaries believed that the royal descent of the Berkeleys was 'a meere fiction, either of this, or some other flatteringe Abbot, to pallyate and comply with theire founders'. The tradition certainly predated Newland. It was to be found in Ricart's *Kalendar* and in two earlier pedigrees found by Smyth in the Berkeley archive. The earliest pedigree, dated 1351 and attributed by Smyth to Trevisa, may be the original source of the tradition, since the earlier chronicle of Robert of Gloucester correctly ascribes a Saxon descent to Harding. Through Smyth, both knowledge of Newland's work and the circumstances of its production were preserved. The probable fate of such works was to disappear into the archive of the family concerned, to be forgotten or lost.[11]

In William Worcestre's contemporary John Rous (1411–92), the worlds of ecclesiastical scholarship, noble patronage and urban self-awareness combined within a single man. As a result Rous was to have a greater influence on the development of local history than Worcestre, since his works were more accessible to his contemporaries and to later scholars. Rous was a chantry priest at Guy's Cliff near Warwick, which had been founded by Richard Beauchamp, earl of Warwick. The Beauchamps were also associated with the collegiate church of St Mary, Warwick, where the Chapel of Our Lady (commonly known as the Beauchamp chapel) was built to house the tomb of Earl Richard and consecrated in 1475. Rous is credited with the creation of a library in a small room over the south porch at St Mary's, and his association with the town was important for his prestige. From the evidence of Worcestre's *Itinerary* and of itinerant monks such as John Boston and Andrew Boorde, it is easy to envisage how Rous's manuscripts became known when scholars and curious travellers examined the contents of the library at Warwick, or enquired about the existence of chronicles or other works of interest at the Guy's Cliff chantry. Had Rous been marooned in a remote hermitage, his influence would have been far less, but Warwick was proud of its scholar and his memory was preserved.[12]

Of the various manuscripts ascribed to Rous by John Leland in the mid-sixteenth century, few survived the hazards of dispersal and fire. His *Roll of the Earls of Warwick* is, like Newland's pedigree of the Berkeleys, an example of how family history could be used to flatter the descendants of a founder in order to encourage further benefactions. A similar pedigree roll was created in the mid-fifteenth century for Ralph le Boteler, lord admiral and chamberlain to Henry VI, who took the title baron Sudeley from the estate he inherited in Gloucestershire. Richard Neville, earl of Warwick, had acquired the Beauchamp lands by marriage, while Ralph le Boteler was descended from the de Sudeleys in the female line. In both cases the purpose of the pedigree roll was to flatter a powerful man and to demonstrate the legitimacy of his possession of his estate and title. The manuscript of the Rous roll survived in two versions, both elaborately illustrated with portraits and heraldic badges. The earlier English version is Yorkist in tone and dates from shortly after the dedication of the Beauchamp chapel. The Latin version, by contrast, is biased towards the Lancastrians and was clearly written after 1485. To censor Rous, as some critics have done, for the apparent fluidity of his political allegiances, is to misunderstand the purpose of his history. It was a form of Neville propaganda reflecting the interests of his patron. Rous undertook another work, *Historia Regum Angliae*, at the instigation of his friend John Seymour, who was seeking appropriate models of princes and kings as founders of cities and churches to provide subjects for statues to fill niches in St George's chapel, Windsor. Initially begun in the reign of Edward IV, the *Historia* was completed after Henry Tudor's assumption of the throne and dedicated to the king. It should be viewed as a royal family history – a context in which propaganda value was more appreciated than academic objectivity. The work is predominantly remembered today for its account of Warwickshire villages depopulated in the fifteenth century. Rous listed fifty-eight such villages, and for twelve he consulted the hundred rolls to compare their present state with how it was in the reign of Edward I. His account of Fulbrook included his own observations of the effect of enclosure on the village and the decay of the 'noble square tower for the castle' and 'splendid gate-house' erected in the early fifteenth century. His modern editor has written of Rous's mental horizon as extending little further than a bird's eye view of Warwick and its environs. It was this characteristic that made Rous an important figure in the development of local history.[13]

The particular strength of antiquarian culture in Elizabethan and early Stuart Warwickshire owed a good deal to the survival of the Rous manuscripts. These works were abstracted and copied by eager antiquaries, who also attempted to relocate manuscripts which had been dispersed at the Dissolution. The English version of the Warwick roll was copied by the herald Robert Glover in Elizabeth's reign, and by William Burton in 1613. Dugdale copied the Latin version in 1636, and this formed an important source for his account of the earls of Warwick. Burton and Dugdale also used Rous' *Historia Regum Angliae*. Extracts from the Corpus Christi, Cambridge, transcript of this are to be found among Sir Simon Archer's notes, although both Burton and Dugdale used the copy in Sir Robert Cotton's library. Cotton also possessed a book on the life of Richard Beauchamp, earl of Warwick, by Rous.[14] Among the Rous manuscripts that John Leland saw at Warwick in the reign of Henry VIII was *De Antiquitate Verovicensis*, a history of the town of Warwick. In April 1629, Archer wrote to Cotton about this work, which he had been told was in Cotton's library. The following year he wrote again, entreating Cotton to have a copy made for which he would willingly pay. He also made approaches to Richard James, Cotton's librarian. Unfortunately, Archer was misinformed and, presumably as he discovered eventually, Cotton did not have the manuscript. Archer's notebooks reveal that his search for Rous manuscripts led him to Sir Kenelm Digby, and then in 1634 he learnt that a clothier from the Stroud area of Gloucestershire had allegedly acquired some of the books from the St Mary's library by marriage, and that others were believed to have passed into the possession of Mr Spicer of Stone, Worcs. and Henry Ferrers of Baddesley Clinton, Warwickshire. Ferrers was himself a notable antiquary of the previous generation, related to Archer by marriage. Among the projects he began, but never completed, was a history of the earls of Warwick. Since Ferrers was friendly with Glover, who had copied the Warwick roll, and exchanged antiquarian material with him, it is likely that Rous provided a direct inspiration and model for the proposed project. Although Warwickshire antiquaries continued to search for further Rous manuscripts, as Dugdale lamented in the *Antiquities of Warwickshire*: 'most, I suppose, are perish'd, or in such obscure hands, that it is not known to me where they can be seen'.[15]

When in 1629 Sir Simon Archer sought to obtain a copy of John Rous's *De Antiquitate Verovicensis* from Sir Robert Cotton, in exchange he offered copies of his own manuscripts of the sixteenth-century antiquary John Leland (c.1503–52). Leland is an important figure in the development of local history, not only as an author, but also as a preserver of the literary heritage of medieval England. As the monastic houses came under threat from Henry VIII and his religious policies, Leland obtained a commission from the king: 'to peruse and dylygentlye to searche all the lybrayes of Monasteryes and collegies of thys your noble realme, to the entent that the monumentes of auncient wryters, as wel of other nacyons as of your owne provynce, myghte out be brought of deadly darknesse to lyvelye lyght.' This scheme was not without precedent. In the early fourteenth century, a group of Oxford Franciscans had visited ninety religious houses and compiled a union catalogue of their books, known as the *Registrum Anglie de Libris Doctorum et Auctorum Veterum*. Leland was associated with the circle of Anne Boleyn, for whose coronation he helped to devise the principal pageants. His survey may be associated with the attempts of certain reformers within that circle to urge the conversion of monasteries to 'places of study and good letters' in preference to dissolution. For a few years from 1533, Leland toured the country examining and listing the contents of monastic libraries. By 1636, however, Henry VIII's adherence to a policy of wholesale dissolution was clear, and in that year Leland's interest turned from recording to rescue. He petitioned Cromwell that his terms of reference be extended to the collection of manuscripts to be deposited in the royal library. In his petition Leland expressed a particular concern that foreign scholars were acquiring monastic manuscripts and 'putting them abroad as monuments of their own country'. Such national as well as urban or local pride was to be an important motivating force in the subsequent development of local history.[16]

In addition to the preservation of manuscripts, Leland's survey of monastic libraries gave rise to his dictionary of British writers *De Viris Illustribus*, which became better known to later historians through the medium of John Bale (1495–1563). According to Bale, Leland gave him permission to use his work for the former's own *Illustrium Majoris Britanniae Scriptorum Summarium* (1548), and the more extensive *Catalogus* (1557). This bibliographical work was of tremendous importance to later scholars, who were alerted to the existence of certain works and encouraged to trace their existing whereabouts. At the same time, as in the case of Archer and John Rous, references by Leland and Bale to some earlier authors in their works might lead subsequent antiquaries to spend weeks, months and even years in a fruitless search for lost manuscripts.

According to his own account, in 1539 Leland began a project intended to provide a comprehensive topographical and historical account of Henry VIII's realm. In 1546 he prepared a report on the result of his travels in the form of a

New Year's Gift for the king, which was subsequently published by Bale as *The Laboryouse Journey and Serche of John Leylande for Englandes Antiquityes* (1549). In this he described how he had:

> so traveled in your domynions both by see coastes and the myddle partes, sparynge neyther labour nor costes by the space of these vi yeares past, that there is almost neyther cape nor baye, haven, creke or pere, ryver or confluence of ryvers, breches, washes, lakes, meres, fenny waters, mountaynes, valleys, mores, hethes, forestes, woodes, cyties, burges, castels, pryncypall manor places, monasteryes, and colleges, but I have seane them, and noted in so doynge a whole worlde of thynges very memorable.[17]

He intended that his work would enable a detailed map of the country to be produced, which would be supplemented by a comprehensive topographical history of England and Wales, dividing it into as many books as there were counties, with an additional six books to cover the islands. This would have been accompanied by his biographical dictionary of British authors, in four volumes. Leland also proposed to write three books *De Nobilitate Britannica*, indicating the close affiliation between topographical and genealogical history throughout their evolution. It was Leland's intention to have his description prepared for the making of the map within twelve months, but it was not to be. Only a year after the writing of his report Leland apparently suffered a mental breakdown, and the works he had planned never came to fruition.

Like Worcestre's *Itinerary*, Leland's account of his travels provides some indications of the extent and nature of historical interest in Tudor England, particularly among the gentry who provided him with hospitality on his journeys. In Cornwall Mr Arundel of Trerice discussed his pedigree with Leland, and Mr Trelawney told him of the descent of the lordship of Cartuther. In Gloucestershire Mr Tracy of Toddington told him about the building of Sudeley castle, while Sir William Berkeley of Beverstone was his informant concerning Thomas, lord Berkeley's, involvement in the Hundred Years War, and Mr Wicks of Dodington maintained 'with some justification' that the Berkeleys of Dursley were as old a family as the Berkeleys of Berkeley. While Shakespeare's contemporaries took an obsession with pedigree and lineage to new heights, Leland's manuscripts indicate that its roots were firmly established in previous generations. Furthermore, it is possible to trace links between Leland's informants and later local historians, which strengthens our perception of a continuity between the historical interests of the Tudor gentry and those of their Elizabethan and early Stuart descendants. At Deene, Northants., Leland's informant was Mr Brudenell, whose grandson was to become a notable catholic antiquary in Charles I's reign. We find among Leland's notes a reference to a stone marking the meeting point of the boundaries of the four counties of Gloucestershire, Worcestershire, Warwickshire and Oxfordshire. The stone stood on the land of John Palmer of Upper Lemington in Todenham,

Glos. – a gentleman pensioner of Henry VIII whose family came from nearby Compton Scorfen, Warwickshire Palmer had purchased the manor in 1541, and it was his son who told the antiquary that this stone rather than the more famous Rollright stones, marked the county boundaries. A generation later, Edward Palmer, John's grandson and either the son or nephew of Leland's informant, was recommended by William Camden as 'an industrious Antiquary'. The manor of Upper Lemington lay beside the Fosse Way and Edward Palmer gave Camden some of the Roman coins which had been ploughed up on his land. Physical reminders of the past, such as a boundary stone and antique coins appear to have stimulated a continuing interest in the history of their newly acquired manor among the Palmer family. Curiosity about physical artefacts was not a new phenomenon in the Tudor age – the work of Worcestre and Leland bear witness to the interest they aroused and the explanations attached to them by popular imagination in previous generations. What was important for the development of local history was that increasingly the English gentry were equipped with an education that enabled them to provide a context for such artefacts.[18]

During Leland's lifetime his published topographical works were limited to two Latin poems, both of which were accompanied by prose commentaries on the people and places mentioned. The *Genethliacum* (1543) celebrated Prince Edward through an exposition of the topography of his principality of Wales, duchy of Cornwall and earldom of Chester, while the *Cygnea Cantio* (1545) presented a swan's-eye view of the Thames between Oxford and Greenwich, with a commentary that was almost five times as long as the poem itself. Through the latter work Leland became a source for the first Elizabethan county history, William Lambarde's *Perambulation of Kent* (1576). Although Lambarde used *Cygnea Cantio* as a source, he did not take Leland's use of a river to traverse territory as a model for the structure of *Perambulation*. However, Leland's method was imitated by William Camden for his *Britannia* (1586), and subsequently Michael Drayton followed these examples for his topographical poem *Poly-Olbion* (1612), as did a number of local historians for their own county histories. The reasons for the popularity of using rivers to provide structure to topographical works will be discussed in chapter seven.

Despite the paucity of his published works, Leland had a significant influence on the subsequent development of local history, as his manuscripts circulated widely after his death and were well known to later antiquaries. Several sixteenth-century copies of the *Itinerary* are extant, including one made by John Stow. William Burton inherited Leland's *Collectanea* and *De viris illustribus* in 1612 from his uncle Thomas Purefoy, and also acquired eight volumes of the *Itinerary*. Sir Simon Archer had acquired a copy of part of the same work by 1626. The earliest surviving letter from William Dugdale to Archer talks of his copying 'that peece of Leland which you lent me', and of leaving transcripts with Burton for correction. Three years before, in 1632, Burton had confirmed an earlier promise to donate his Leland manuscripts to the Bodleian, but wrote that 'I cannot prefixe the definitive time, by reason of the present use which I nowe have, and hereafter shall have of them'. By 1641 a further volume had come to his attention and he was able to obtain a copy.[19] After Burton's death, only seven of his eight volumes of the *Itinerary* passed to the Bodleian, as one volume had been lent and lost. (As we shall see when considering their use of sources, the loss or maltreatment of their manuscripts was an occupational hazard of early modern antiquaries.)

The comprehensive nature of Leland's material was a significant factor in ensuring its popularity among local historians, and hence its widespread copying and circulation. Although actual itineraries did not survive for the whole country, his extensive collections covered all of England and Wales and provided material on a wide variety of subjects. Somerset was one of the most extensively described counties, and Thomas Gerard was able to make good use of Leland in his *Description of Somerset*. (As we shall see, his failure to use Leland for his earlier *Survey of Dorset* helps to date the period at which he came into contact with the antiquarian circle surrounding Burton and Archer.) The manuscript of the *Description of Somerset* was preserved in the collection of Christopher, lord Hatton, whose library contained five volumes of the Tudor antiquary's works. Leland's manuscripts were also of interest to family historians, such as the Lincolnshire royalist Gervase Holles who used the *Collectanea* in his *Memorials of the Holles Family*. Despite its popularity, the *Itinerary* was not universally regarded with approval or indeed recognised as the work of Leland. In 1626 Sir Simon Archer sent a copy of the volume in his custody to Edward Gwynne of Gray's Inn, a noted genealogist whom he had consulted concerning his own pedigree. Gwynne, who had a copy of Leland's plan for his topographical work, dismissed 'these silly Journalls voyde of Antiquitie but what they drawe from vulgar Relacion', believing that the work was that of 'some laborious Trivialist rather than great Leland'.[20]

An important contemporary of Leland was the future archbishop Matthew Parker (1504–75), who as chaplain to Anne Boleyn was also associated with those who hoped to turn the monasteries into powerhouses of secular education. As vice-chancellor of the university, he was appointed by Henry VIII to the commission to survey the property of the Cambridge colleges and so, like Leland, he was in a position to attempt to mitigate the effects of the king's spoilation on the literary heritage of the monasteries. Parker's interest in historical texts was predominantly ecclesiastical. He sought texts that could be used to support the antiquity of an independent English church, and employed agents to scour the country in search of manuscripts. Yet, by preserving copies of important medieval chronicles and making them available to a wider readership through publication, Parker also influenced the development of local history. Moreover, his nourishing of scholarly and literary talent within his household, and his patronage of antiquaries within the wider community, helped to encourage the Elizabethan expansion of antiquarian research. The future historian of London John Stow, for example, received encouragement from Parker, and was involved in the editing of *Flores Historiarum* (1567) and the chronicles of Matthew Paris (1571) and Thomas Walsingham (1574) for publication.[21]

The dissolution of the monasteries represented a watershed in the evolution of local history writing in England. The monastic tradition was brought to an abrupt end. While much of the vast storehouse of documentary evidence compiled and preserved by the medieval monasteries was lost or destroyed, a significant amount of material passed into lay hands to form part of the raw material for subsequent generations of local historians. The changes in educational provision necessitated by the loss of the monasteries and the increasingly fluid market in land also had an indirect influence on the development of local history. Elizabethan gentlemen would have both the education and the access to documents that they needed to research their own pedigrees and the histories of their manors. In the years when Leland was compiling his *Itinerary*, the stage was being set for the development of a lay tradition of local-history writing among the English gentry.

The scheme of publications outlined by Leland in his *New Year's Gift* represented a blueprint for the next generation of local historians. His activities can be defined as having three main aims: the preservation of the records and artefacts of the English past; the exploitation of that material to the greater glory of England and her monarch; the mapping of the realm. These aims were not unique to Leland. He was not solely or directly responsible for the preservation and publishing of medieval chronicles or the mapping of English towns and counties. As a topographer he had predecessors, and printers such as William Caxton had demonstrated that there was a market for medieval chronicles. Nevertheless, through the medium of Bale and the *Laboryouse Journey*, Leland did provide a public manifesto for the development of local history and cartography.

Among the first to pick up Leland's baton was Laurence Nowell, who in 1561 acquired a copy of *Cygnea Cantio*, with its appendix explaining the derivation of place-names occurring in the text. To this he prefixed a transcript of the similar appendix from *Genethliacon Edwardi*. This collation of Leland's material reflects Nowell's particular interest in Anglo-Saxon place-names. The following year he drew up a list of English parishes and transcribed a number of Anglo-Saxon texts and Giraldus Cambrensis' *Itinerarium Cambriae*. In 1563 he wrote to Sir William Cecil (subsequently Lord Burghley), whose manuscripts he had examined in the previous year, proposing the mapping of individual English 'provinces' as well as the country as a whole. Over the following years he continued to transcribe excerpts from a wide range of texts, selecting material relating to place-names and setting it out cartographically. By 1567 he had completed several county maps and one of the whole British Isles. He was also the first antiquary to attempt the compilation of an Anglo-Saxon glossary.[22]

Although he published nothing, Nowell influenced the development of local history through the use of his manuscripts by later antiquaries. These included his friend and pupil William Lambarde, who by the 1560s was working on what he termed a 'topographical dictionary' of England and Wales. In 1571 he described this as a storehouse from which he hoped to draw material sufficient to furnish histories for all the English counties. Lambarde was a Lincoln's Inn lawyer with an estate near Greenwich, and he chose Kent as the first county for which he would write a history. His work circulated in manuscript and was read by both Archbishop Parker and Lord Burghley. When it appeared in print as the *Perambulation of Kent* in 1576, it was the first English county history to be published. In the preface to the work, Lambarde listed the main subjects he intended to cover in his topographical history: the bounds of the counties; the administrative divisions within them; the cities, market towns and boroughs; castles, religious houses and schools; ports, havens, rivers, lakes and bridges; hills, parks and forests; and finally the 'singularities' of the county. This outline has clear parallels with the material collected by Leland, and it mapped out what were to become the predominant areas of interest for subsequent topographers. The work proved successful. It was updated by Lambarde for a second edition in 1596, and there was a third, undated edition and others in 1640 and 1656.[23]

Although Lambarde had, like Leland, initially conceived the idea of covering the entire country as an individual enterprise, as he proceeded he was forced to recognise his limitations:

> And, as touching the description of the rest of the realm, knowing by the dealing in this one that it will be hard for any one man (and much more for myself) to accomplish all, I can but wish in like sort that some one in each shire would make the enterprise for his own country, to the end that by joining our pens and conferring our labours (as it were) *ex symbolo*, we may at the last by the union of many parts and papers compact a whole and perfect body and book of our English antiquities.[24]

This suggests that Lambarde was contemplating a co-operative scheme akin to that which produced the *Chronicles* (1577; revised 1587) associated with Raphael Holinshed. The *Chronicles* had initially been a project of the queen's printer Reginald Wolfe for producing a 'universall cosmographie' with 'histories of every knowne nation'. Wolfe had inherited Leland's manuscripts and he himself worked on the English, Scottish and Irish portions. On his death in 1573 the work was scaled down to a history and geography of the British Isles, and completed by a number of scholars under the leadership of Holinshed.

After Holinshed's own death in 1580, the role of editor for the second edition was taken by John Hooker. Hooker was a native of Exeter, where he served as chamberlain from 1555. He had produced a description of the city by 1559. This text survives in various manuscript versions, and was published in a joint volume with Hooker's *The Order and Usage of the Keeping of a Parlement in England* (1575). In 1584 he published a *Catalogue of the Bishops of Excester* and *A Pamphlet of the Offices and Duties of Everie Particular Sworne Officer of the Citie of Excester*, both of which he had referred to in the *Description* of the city a decade earlier. Condensed versions of these works and his translation of Giraldus Cambrensis' account of Ireland formed part of his personal contribution to the *Chronicles*. Following the death of Sir Peter Carew in Ireland in 1575, Hooker turned his hand to biography and wrote a book on the life of his former patron. Although Hooker lived for more than a decade after the appearance of the second edition of the *Chronicles*, the effort he had expended as editor, advancing age, and family demands, all prevented him from completing further works from his extensive collections.[25]

As Lambarde was associated with the same scholarly circles as the contributors to Holinshed's *Chronicles*, it is probable that this enterprise acted as a direct inspiration to his own suggestion for a co-operative scheme. William Harrison's *Description of Britain*, which provided the chorographical part of the *Chronicles*, may also have encouraged Lambarde to set a more comprehensive and scholarly chorographical work before the reading public. Harrison was not a great traveller or researcher in the mould of Leland. John Stow described the *Description* as 'for the most part drawn out of John Leyland (borrowed of myself)' and presented as 'the labours of another (who was forced to confess he never travelled further than from London to the university of Oxford)'.[26] The first book of the *Description* was based on the atlas of a general map of England and Wales and thirty-four county maps published by Christopher Saxton in 1579. These maps, despite a number of deficiencies, realised Leland's aim of mapping the country. By enabling the educated gentry to place their own localities within a wider context, they provided a spur to the development of local history. Harrison's style is engaging and his work contains much interesting material, but it was not a work calculated to deter Lambarde from pursuing his own scheme.

Whether Lambarde's scheme ever progressed beyond its first tentative proposal is not known. Unlike the Holinshed collaborators, who were concentrated in London, a scheme to compile a history of the English counties would have required the organisation of a dispersed group of scholars. Some of Lambarde's London colleagues could have become involved. John Hooker might have undertaken the history of Devon, to which he did turn his attention towards the end of his life, but his involvement in Holinshed absorbed most of his time. The herald William Smith compiled a brief account of

Cheshire, which could have fitted into the scheme, and the genealogist James Strangeman might have tackled Essex. Yet, for the most part the enterprise would have been dependent upon local gentlemen of antiquarian interests. We know the names and background of a few gentlemen who undertook the necessary groundwork for the compilation of a county history in the first decades of Elizabeth's reign. Laurence Bostock made collections of church notes for Cheshire, composed verses on the Norman earls of Chester, and wrote a history of the barons of Halton. Robert Kemp, a Norfolk gentleman, was collecting church notes, as was Henry Purefoy, whose family was associated with Leicestershire and Warwickshire and who had acquired some of Leland's works (later to be bequeathed to William Burton). Our knowledge of these men depends almost entirely on the survival of their work in the collections of later antiquaries.[27] Archival deposits provide the researcher with ample evidence of extensive antiquarian activity in this period, but many records are of uncertain origin. Although the identity of many antiquarian gentlemen is lost to us, there is sufficient evidence to suggest that Lambarde could have found collaborators in the majority of English counties. The logistics of organising and co-ordinating such a project in Elizabethan England would, however, have been enormous. Moreover, the emphasis of the majority of collections was genealogical and heraldic. Lambarde's outline of his subject lacked the emphasis on gentry families and land ownership that many contemporary antiquaries would have wanted.

The years immediately following the publication of the *Perambulation of Kent* saw Lambarde advancing in his legal career. In 1579 he became a bencher of Lincoln's Inn and a justice of the peace in Kent. Aware of the importance of his new role, he collected the material for a new work *Eirenarcha: or of the Office of the Justices of the Peace* (1581). This was an immediate success, which was reprinted seven times over the following thirty years. As his career progressed and he became a master in Chancery in 1592 and Master of the Rolls Chapel in 1597, his antiquarian interests became increasingly focused on legal matters. Although he revised the *Perambulation of Kent* for the second edition in 1596, any ideas he had entertained of acting as a general editor of a series of county studies covering the whole country had been abandoned several years before.

As Nowell and Lambarde had taken upon themselves and developed Leland's scheme, the Kentish antiquary in his turn ceded way to another scholar: William Camden. Like Leland, Camden was an enthusiastic traveller in pursuit of antiquities, an enthusiasm he developed at Oxford and continued during vacations as a schoolmaster at Westminster. In 1577 the Flemish map-maker Abraham Ortelius visited London and encouraged the young schoolmaster to publish a chorography of Britain, which would fill a gap in his own knowledge. Ortelius was engaged in producing maps of Europe, both contemporary and historical, and in compiling a glossary of European place-names. His aim was to persuade an English antiquary to identify the contemporary, Roman and Anglo-Saxon place-names of Britain. A decade earlier, Ortelius had met the Welsh historian Humphrey Llwyd in Antwerp. Llwyd had subsequently provided him with both maps and a short historical and geographical description of Britain. This, translated by Thomas Twyne and published as the *Breviary of Britayne* (1573), was the first attempt at a British chorography. Llwyd's collaboration with Ortelius was short-lived, since he died in 1568. A reference by John Hooker in 1584 to 'someone (then living) pretending ... to set foorth a generall description of the whole realme of England, and also a Topographicall and a particular discourse of everie province, citie and towne' may refer to a project Llwyd had planned to undertake, if he had lived. In 1577 Lambarde's established reputation as an authority on Anglo-Saxon place-names would have made him an obvious candidate to replace Llwyd, but his family ties and the demands of his career militated against it. Consequently, he made his material available to the younger man and assisted Camden in his task. Nevertheless, there is evidence that Lambarde continued to toy with the idea of his greater project until the summer of 1585, when he read the manuscript resulting from Camden's research. It was then that he finally ceded the field to Camden, writing that he might not now 'dwell in the meditation of the same things that you are occupied withal'.[28]

The work that Camden had produced was published as *Britannia, Sive Florentissimorum Regnorum Angliae, Scotiae, Hiberniae, et Insularum Adjacentium ex Intima Chorographica Descriptio* in 1586, a small volume of over 500 pages of closely packed Latin text with no illustrations. The first draft of the work had focused predominantly on the history of Britain as a Roman province, which reflects its genesis as the project encouraged by Ortelius. In this respect it drew inspiration from Flavio Biondo's *Italia Illustrata* and paralleled similar undertakings among continental scholars in France and Germany to uncover their Roman past. However, the work was never wholly concerned with Roman Britain. From the beginning Camden was interested in both the prehistoric and the early medieval history of Britain. Subsequently, under the influence of his numerous contacts within the antiquarian community, Camden incorporated increasing amounts of non-Roman material into successive drafts, and this process continued as *Britannia* was expanded in the six editions that appeared during Camden's life.[29]

The *Britannia*, subsequently described as an 'Atlas wourcke of All Brytaine', was of seminal importance in the development of local history, as it provided the provincial gentry with a national framework within which they could locate their own interests.[30] Camden himself also acted as a figurehead for the growing interest in antiquarian research. As we shall see in the next chapter, he was an influential member of the Elizabethan Society of Antiquaries, which was formed around the time of *Britannia*'s initial publication. He also corresponded with a number of local historians and gentlemen-collectors, from whom he received material for his subsequent editions. His correspondence and the acknowledgements he included in the text of *Britannia* are important sources of information concerning the extent and nature of local antiquarian interest. Some informants, such as the Appleby schoolmaster Reginald Bainbrigg, or the Midlands gentleman Edward Palmer, were interested in Roman artefacts. Others, such as the Somerset gentleman Sir Thomas Lyte, were predominantly interested in their own pedigrees. Still others, such as Sampson Erdeswicke in Staffordshire, Henry Ferrers in Warwickshire and William Claxton in Durham, developed a wider interest in the past of their native counties. The catholic hagiographer (writer on the lives of the saints) Nicholas Roscarrock, living at Naworth castle with Lord William Howard, provided information both about the Roman antiquities that he and his patron found in Cumberland, and the saints of his native Cornwall.

To the modern observer one of the most striking features of the early editions of *Britannia* is the absence of maps, which did not appear until 1607. We are so accustomed to have topographical and spatial information presented to us in rich detail, that it is difficult to grasp how novel and exciting the first accurate, comprehensive maps of England must have been to our sixteenth-century ancestors. The publication of Saxton's maps in 1579 enabled the literate gentry to 'see' their own county for the first time, and to relate it to the rest of the country. At the same time, purchasers of the five-volume *Civitates Orbis Terrarum* (Cologne, 1572) by George Braun and Frans Hogenberg, could compare the bird's-eye views of the eleven British cities included with their continental counterparts. The appearance of such visual representations was an important influence on the development of local history, not least in encouraging local antiquaries to produce more accurate and detailed maps incorporating their own intimate knowledge of place-names and topography. Initially access to such maps was the preserve of the wealthy few, but the enthusiasm with which they were greeted ensured that the supply grew and became less exclusive. Although a complete atlas remained an expensive item, individual uncoloured maps of a particular county or of the country as a whole were within the means of most gentlemen. With the publication of the 1607 edition of *Britannia* and the appearance of John Speed's *Theatre of the Empire of Great Britain* (1611), which combined cartography and history in a single work, the importance of maps for a complete understanding of history was established.

While the publication of *Britannia* and the appearance of Saxton's maps encouraged the development of local history in general, it was in the particular field of county history that they were most influential. While Lambarde's pioneering work had provided a model for county studies, it was only with the advent of the *Britannia* that a comprehensive framework was available within which individual local historians could fit their own work. The importance of *Britannia* as a model was attested by Sampson Erdeswicke in a covering note attached to the copy of his work sent to Camden. Erdeswicke, a Stafford-shire recusant, had assisted Camden with his research and been encouraged by him to compose a treatise bringing together his knowledge of the history of Staffordshire and Cheshire. He wrote:

> Sir, haveinge disposed with my selfe to take a further veiw of the shires of Stafford and Cheshire (according to promise) I have sett downe what I have found or can yett learne and have thought it a very comodious way to follow the Rivers (as you have done) And therefore to omitt the seatinge of both the shires and adjoyneinge them to their neighbouringe Counties (that matter beinge by you very well disposed).[31]

From this it is clear that Erdeswicke saw his own *View of Staffordshire* as an adjunct to Camden's *Britannia* and clearly expected that his potential readers would be familiar with the latter work. The work was primarily concerned with genealogy and heraldry, which were Erdeswicke's primary interests. Its topographical form appears to be entirely due to Camden. Without *Britannia* as a direct model it is hard to believe that Erdeswicke would have chosen to present his material in the form he did. The bulk of the work is composed of genealogies showing the descent of manors and discussions concerning the arms borne by Staffordshire families. The buildings mentioned are predomi-nantly manor houses and castles, while churches are noted mainly for their monuments. Although there is some discussion of place-names and descrip-tions of topographical features, this is essentially a description of Stafford-shire as a collection of gentry families gathered within a particular locality from which they drew a degree of common identity. As such it reflected the primary interest of the majority of late Elizabethan local historians in a way that Lambarde's work did not.

Genealogy was also an important element of Richard Carew's *Survey of Cornwall* (1602), although this was not evident to the readers of the modern edition from which much of it was omitted – reflecting academic disdain for genealogy. This work was less directly modelled on *Britannia* than Erdes-wicke's *View of Staffordshire*. Nevertheless, it was *Britannia* which inspired Carew to describe his native county in more detail to his antiquarian friends in the capital. The survey was begun in 1589 and it is clear from the preface to the published version that Camden was one of the friends to whom Carew gave a manuscript copy of the work. The first part of the book provided a general description of the county, covering the climate, geology, industry, education and pastimes. The second part comprised a section on Cornish history, followed by a description of the hundreds parish by parish. Unlike Erdeswicke, Carew did not perambulate the county following the rivers in imitation of Camden – a perfunctory examination of the map of Cornwall with its numerous creeks and inlets provides a good reason for abandoning such a model. The tone of the work is also different. As it describes and extols the merits of Cornwall and the Cornish gentry, the reader is reminded of the extent to which the county was on the periphery of Elizabethan England, and how few of Carew's acquaintances in London would have ventured so far.

In comparison London must have been very familiar to many of those who read John Stow's *Survey of London*, since the city was home to a significant proportion of the reading public, and many provincial readers would have had occasion to visit the capital at some time in their lives. In his dedication to the lord mayor of the city Stow referred particularly to Lambarde's *Perambulation of Kent* and to the 'sundry other able persons' who had 'essayed to do somewhat for the particular shires and counties where they were born or dwelt'. As a Londoner Stow was concerned to ensure that his own native city should not be omitted from this project. Moreover, he hoped that works such as his would provide material for Camden to 'increase and beautify' the *Britannia* for the benefit of foreign scholars. Here again, Camden's work is seen as the equivalent of a map of the whole country, which is sufficiently detailed to satisfy the curiosity of foreign scholars, while the indigenous reader would have a desire or need for more detailed local information.[32]

The structure of Stow's *Survey of London* was very different from the civic annals and chronicles that had emerged in the fifteenth century and which, having spread to provincial towns, remained popular throughout Elizabeth's reign. The work was based on the observations Stow had made as he perambulated the streets of London and visited its churches and principal buildings. The results of this perambulation were then supplemented by documentary material taken from his extensive collections and numerous other printed and manuscript sources. There are many parallels between Stow's account of London and Worcestre's of Bristol a century before, but the *Survey* noticeably lacks the concern with the physical appearance of buildings and their dimensions that was displayed by the earlier work. A number of churches were dismissed by Stow in a sentence, because they contained no monuments of note. As Erdeswicke and Carew had memorialised the county gentry, Stow's work did the same for former mayors of London, aldermen and great merchants.

Stow's comments in the dedication to the *Survey of London* and the examples of Erdeswicke and Carew, both of whom were associated with Camden, indicates that Lambarde's scheme for a comprehensive collection of county studies remained alive at the end of the sixteenth century. A number of potential contributors to a collaborative endeavour can be identified within the circle of the Society of Antiquaries. In the last years of his life John Hooker compiled a *Synopsis Chorographical* of Devon. On his death this passed to the legal antiquary Sir John Doddridge, with the intention that it should be prepared for publication, although this never happened. William Wyrley, who had assisted Erdeswicke with his research in Staffordshire, apparently began work on a history of his native county of Leicestershire. However, Wyrley's predominant interest in heraldry and genealogy, indicated by his publication of the *True Use of Armorie* (1592), was confirmed by his entry into the College of Arms in 1604. Subsequently, any remaining interest in county history was overwhelmed by his professional duties. When describing the border towns of Dudley and Tamworth in his *View of Staffordshire*, Erdeswicke explicitly referred to his hope that Henry Ferrers of Baddesley Clinton would produce an account of the neighbouring county of Warwickshire. It is unclear from Ferrers' surviving manuscripts how far he proceeded with any such account, although his collections did provide a valuable resource for the next generations of antiquaries in Warwickshire.[33]

There are two East Anglian authors who may be considered as potential contributors to a co-operative account of the country, although, unlike the other antiquaries mentioned, neither can be linked directly to Camden and the Society of Antiquaries. The first is an anonymous gentleman, who in the first years of the seventeenth century compiled chorographical accounts of Norfolk and Suffolk. These took the form of a general introduction followed by an alphabetical gazetteer, incorporating material from *Britannia*, other printed and manuscript sources and the author's own observations. While many contemporary collections of church notes record only heraldic and genealogical information, this author also described the monuments. It has been suggested that the Chorographer utilised questionnaires to obtain material, but the evidence is inconclusive. The second East Anglian author was Robert Reyce, the core of whose *Breviary of Suffolk* dates from 1603. Reyce was inspired by Carew's *Survey of Cornwall* to provide 'a plaine and familier description of the Country', which was informed by his own interest in genealogy and history. The work circulated widely among the local gentry, and was altered and expanded over three decades as Reyce produced further copies. He also produced a collection of Latin records relating to East Anglia and compiled brief accounts of royal, noble and gentry figures associated with Suffolk. In a further indication of the strength of antiquarian interests in Elizabethan East Anglia, Great Yarmouth produced *Greate Yermouthe: a Booke of the Foundacion and Antiquitye of the saide Towne* by Henry Manship, a *History* by his son, also Henry, and a brief *Description and first procreation ... of Great Yarmouth* (1599) by Thomas Nash, which was memorably subtitled 'the praise of the red herring'.[34]

The city of Chester and the county palatine represented another area with a vibrant antiquarian culture. The extensive genealogical and heraldic collections of a number of local gentlemen are known to us because they were copied into the vast collections of the herald Randle Holme and his successors, which are preserved in the British Library. A history of Chester was begun by archdeacon Robert Rogers, and subsequently expanded by his son David. The manuscript compiled by David Rogers in 1609 shows the influence of contemporary trends in local historiography and of such works as Stow's *Survey of London*. The later additions, however, indicate the continuing importance of the annalistic form to urban communities. The Rogers' contemporary William Webb, a clerk in the mayor's court at Chester, wrote a similar work, which dwelt heavily on the antiquity of the city's institutions. Subsequently, Webb was inspired by Stow's account of London and by the maps of Cheshire-born John Speed to expand his work. In 1621 he produced a county history, which included an itinerary of each hundred. Like Stow, Webb placed an emphasis on worthy individuals, explaining: 'Nothing doth more illustrate and dignify a country, a city, a nation, or a people, than a well ordered, a long continued, and a thoroughly maintained government, together with the fame, valour, greatness, and noble virtues of the governors.'[35] By the seventeenth century the idea of a county study as envisaged by Lambarde, with its emphasis on topographical detail, was increasingly subordinated to that of a county history, celebrating the memory of the governing classes.

Although Lambarde's model for county studies was modified, his idea of a co-operative history of the country was a tenacious one, which re-emerged regularly. It might be said to have found its ultimate expression in the Victoria County History. By contrast, the last decade of the sixteenth century witnessed the final attempt of a single antiquary to produce individual accounts of all the English counties. John Norden was by profession a surveyor, and his county descriptions originated from the maps he produced, rather than from an exploration of Roman Britain, an obsession with the genealogy and heraldry of gentry families or local pride. He conceived the idea of a *Speculum Britanniae* – a survey of all the counties with maps and descriptions – in 1591, and obtained official backing from the Privy Council. The first part of the work was published in 1593 as *An Historicall and Chorographicall Discription of Middlesex*, dedicated to Lord Burghley. Two years later, Norden produced a manuscript dedicated to the queen, entitled 'A Chorographical Discription of the severall Shires and Islands, of Middlesex, Essex, Surrey, Sussex, Hamshire, Weighte, Garnesey, and Jarsay'. The enterprise was, however, overly ambitious. Although the Privy Council was interested in obtaining more accurate maps and information concerning the location of gentry houses, the state of towns and so forth, there was considerably less interest in providing financial backing. Only one other volume, *Hertfordshire* (1598), appeared in Norden's lifetime, although he completed surveys of Essex, Cornwall, Northamptonshire and Norfolk. Increasingly, he became dependent on being able to secure work surveying gentlemen's estates, and his larger ambitions came to nothing. Norden's works lacked the genealogical material that interested his contemporaries. Although the Chorographer of Norfolk and Suffolk imitated their structure, the majority of local historians and their gentry readership were uninterested in such rigidly topographical studies.

Throughout our period, the market for county histories was comparatively modest, and publication was a way of obtaining kudos rather than money. The popularity of *Britannia* led a few printers and booksellers to take a chance with related works of more local interest in the last years of Elizabeth's reign. This resulted in the appearance of a second edition of the *Perambulation of Kent* in the author's own lifetime – an achievement that uniquely identifies Lambarde among early modern county historians. John Stow's *Survey of London* also achieved a second edition in 1603, indicating both the size of the reading public in London and the enthusiasm within the country as a whole for a description of the capital city. By the reign of James I, the willingness of the book trade to publish local history was waning. There were no further editions of Stow's work, for which the market had presumably been exhausted. The intended second edition of Carew's *Survey of Cornwall* never materialised. For the majority of the book-buying public, Camden's *Britannia* and John Speed's *Theatre of the Empire of Great Britaine* (1611) provided them with all that they needed, or could afford, in terms of topographical history. The first part of Drayton's topographical poem *Poly-Olbion* (1612) did not sell well. Like Leland's topographical poems, *Poly-Olbion* had extensive historical notes, supplied by the legal historian John Selden. The comparative failure of a work by a well-known poet must have discouraged potential publishers from taking a chance with other works. Drayton himself had considerable difficulty in finding anyone willing to publish the second part of the poem, which eventually appeared in 1622.[36] Only one county history was to be published in the reigns of the first two Stuart kings, while other genres of local history, such as town and family histories, remained entirely in manuscript. Histories of provincial towns inevitably lacked the mass-market appeal of Stow's work, while the interest in family histories was even more circumscribed. If we consider the books published in this period, local history is hence largely absent. The fruits of local research, however, may be found in polemical works. Examples include Brian Twyne's *Antiquitatis Academiae Oxoniensis Apologia* (1608) in support of the claims of the University of Oxford and Sir Henry Spelman's *De non temerandis Ecclesiae* (1613) on the sacrilege of lay ownership of Church property.

The single county history published in this period was William Burton's *Description of Leicestershire* (1622). Burton was the elder brother of Robert, author of the *Anatomy of Melancholy* (1621). While the importance his brother's contacts with the book trade and the influence of sibling rivalry cannot be discounted, the appearance of Burton's work in print was largely due to the accident of the king's favourite having been born in Leicestershire. A manuscript preface dated 1604 suggests that the work should be included among those directly inspired by the appearance of Carew's *Survey of Cornwall*, which Burton may have seen in manuscript. He was certainly moving in anti-quarian circles by 1602, when his improved version of Saxton's map of Leicestershire was published in Amsterdam. According to Burton's later account, his county history 'after it had slept a long time, was on a sudden raised out of the dust, and by force of an higher power drawn to the press'. The *Description of Leicestershire* was dedicated to the then marquess of Buckingham, and Burton referred in his introduction to the encouragement of the poet Sir John Beaumont, another Leicestershire gentleman and member of Buckingham's circle. Like the works of the East Anglian Chorographer, the *Description of Leicestershire* took the form of a general description of the county, followed by an alphabetical gazetteer. Burton's work, however, includes far more historical material than either the Chorographer's works or Carew's *Survey of Cornwall*, and also includes legal material, reflecting Burton's training as a barrister. Novel features of the work were the inclusion of details concerning the incumbents and patrons of local churches and engravings of the heraldry found within. Like Stow in the *Survey of London*, Burton omitted physical descriptions of existing buildings, although he described Roman remains in a detail reminiscent of William Worcestre. The *Description of Leicestershire* was also noticeable for its inclusion of digressions on a number of topics, from leprosy and embalming to earthquakes, which reflected the breadth of Burton's reading but had no obvious place in the history of an English county.

In the introduction to the *Description of Leicestershire*, Burton referred to his kinsman Augustine Vincent, a record-keeper at the Tower of London and a herald, 'whose labours also in this kinde for the Countie of Northampton, ere long will come to light'.[37] No such history of his native county remains among Vincent's surviving papers or is known to have circulated in manuscript. It is possible that there was at this stage some notion among Burton's circle of reviving the idea of a co-operative series of county histories, and that Vincent had been nominated to tackle Northamptonshire. However, the demise of the Society of Antiquaries in the early years of James I's reign, the death of key figures such as Camden in 1623 and Vincent in 1626, and the political preoc-cupations of Sir Robert Cotton and John Selden, meant that there was no central focus for such an enterprise. Burton himself had retired to Leicester-shire shortly after being called to the bar of the Inner Temple on the grounds of ill health, and he was not in a position to act as such a focus.

The absence of county histories from the published works of the early decades of the seventeenth century belies the extent to which local gentlemen continued to harbour a desire to ensure that their native counties should not, in Burton's phrase, 'lye obscured with darknesse'.[38] This ambition seems to have been particularly acute in Devon, a county remote from the rest of England where the antiquarian gentry had the goad of Carew's work to encourage them. Sir William Pole may have been directly encouraged by Carew and the antiquarian circles of late Elizabethan London to undertake a history of the county. Much of the material he collected was lost at the time of the civil war, and it is uncertain how far he progressed towards authorship. His collections were, however, well known and used by other antiquaries. Neither Tristram Risdon nor Thomas Westcote were from the same elite section of Devonshire gentry society as Pole, so their friendship enabled these men to benefit from his privileged access to the records of his fellow magistrates. Both men used Hooker's *Synopsis* as the basis for their own accounts. Risdon's *Survey of Devon* was compiled over a long period from 1605 to 1630, while Westcote's own *View of Devonshire* was dated 1630. The enthusiasm with which these works were received by the local gentry is evidenced by the large numbers of copies which survived into the following centuries. It is indicative of how manuscript circulation could generally satisfy the demand for local history.

A further West Country antiquary inspired by Carew's example was Thomas Gerard from Trent (on the southern border of Somerset close to the town of Sherborne), who in 1618 married Anne Coker of Mappowder, Dorset. In the final years of the reign of James I, Gerard wrote a *Survey of Dorsetshire*, drawing on his own travels in the county and the papers of his own and other gentry families. In his work he followed the example of Camden in using the rivers to traverse the county and referred to Lambarde's *Perambulation of Kent*, but it is clearly Carew who most influenced his work. He makes no reference to Burton's more recent *Description of Leicestershire*. The compilation of the survey coincided with the heralds' visitation of the West Country, conducted by Henry St George and Sampson Lennard, and it may have been contact with the antiquarian St George that encouraged Gerard to write the *Survey*. Certainly, Gerard's contacts with wider antiquarian circles appear to have increased between the compilation of the survey and the writing of his *Particular Description of Somerset*, for which about half the manuscript survives dating from the year before his death. By the time he wrote the *Description*, Gerard had read Burton's work on Leicestershire and gained access to manuscripts in the possession of the herald Sir Richard St George, Henry's father and Sir William Pole. He also benefited from the friendship of an older Somerset antiquary Thomas Lyte, a noted genealogist. Lyte's father Henry is known as a botanist who published one of the early English herbals, but he also had antiquarian interests. In the patriotic fervour surrounding the Spanish Armada, Henry Lyte wrote *The Light of Britayne; a Recorde of the honorable Originall and Antiquitie of Britaine* (1588), in which he supported the myth that the Britons were descended from Trojans fleeing the destruction of Troy. His son Thomas was a respected antiquary, acknowledged by Camden for his assistance with the account of Somerset in *Britannia*. However, he retained his father's attachment to the mythical British past, which had been criticised by Polydore Vergil in the mid-sixteenth century and abandoned by the majority of scholars in the succeeding decades. In 1610 Thomas Lyte presented James I with an elaborate illuminated royal pedigree, which traced the king's descent from Brute, the legendary Trojan founder of Britain. The Lytes had been settled at Lytescary for some twelve generations, and his friend's family papers and knowledge of his own and related pedigrees was invaluable to Gerard in researching his county history.

At the opposite end of the country, John Denton compiled an *Accompt of the Most Considerable Estates and Families in the County of Cumberland From the Conquest Unto the Beginning of the Reign of K. James.* Denton was a lawyer, and the basis of his work was legalistic, concerned with the descent of land and manors. Its content is close to that of Erdeswicke's *View of Staffordshire*, although it includes less heraldry. It is probable that Denton was directly inspired to begin compiling his account of Cumberland in the last years of Elizabeth's reign by seeing a copy of Erdeswicke's work that circulated among antiquarian lawyers in London. Denton's original manuscript does not survive, and later copists are known to have reorganised the work, so its original structure may have been closer to Erdeswicke's model. The emphasis on rivers in the initial topographical description and occasional phrases in the text, lends credence to this view. As the Cumberland Crown agent for the discovery of concealed lands, Denton was familiar with the records in the Tower of London. He enjoyed access to the diocesan records at Carlisle through his kinship with the bishop, Henry Robinson, and he was also described by a hostile witness as having 'insinueated himelf into as many of the gentlemen's evidences in his countrie as wold give him any creditt'. Denton's work represented the triumph of the genealogical over the topographical – a county represented entirely through its landowning gentry.[39]

While the influence of *Britannia* and Saxton's maps stimulated the production of county and urban histories, the undoubted Elizabethan interest in genealogy did not immediately result in the production of family histories. Although eminent Elizabethans such as Lord Burghley and Sir Christopher Hatton had elaborate and ornate versions of their pedigrees produced by the heralds, the immediate successors of John Rous were not employed to produce family histories to equal the Warwick rolls. In the seventeenth century, however, a renewed interest developed in writing genealogical history. By 1613 Thomas, earl of Arundel, had commissioned Sir Robert Cotton to write a history celebrating his ancestors. Sir John Hayward, whose history of Henry IV had incurred the wrath of Elizabeth I, also became involved in the project, but no great account of the Howard family was produced. The richly illuminated volume eventually commissioned by Arundel, recording the Howard descent from the reign of King Edgar, was in the tradition of the heraldic pedigree.[40]

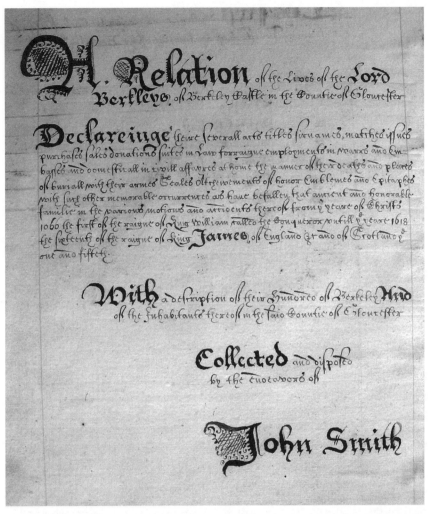

Figure 1 Title page from a manuscript copy of John Smyth's *Lives of the Berkeleys*

It fell to the lot of a family of less-eminent rank to be the subject of the first English genealogical history. In 1609 John Smyth, man-of-business to Henry, lord Berkeley, composed a eulogy on the family history from the time of the Norman Conquest to celebrate the final settlement of a long-running lawsuit. This eulogy formed the basis of what became the *Lives of the Berkeleys* (see figure 1), a three-volume manuscript presentation copy of which was produced for Lord Henry's grandson and successor, George, lord Berkeley, in 1630. Lord Henry's first wife Katherine was great-aunt to the earl of Arundel, and Smyth's professional duties brought him into contact with members of the

Howard family in the first decades of the seventeenth century, while through his antiquarian research and involvement with the Virginia Company he also encountered Sir Robert Cotton and other members of Arundel's circle. These contacts may have encouraged Smyth to develop his family history beyond the model of the extended pedigree, such as the one produced by Abbot Newland, which he found among the Berkeley muniments.[41]

A more certain link may be traced between Smyth and a subsequent family historian, for Sir Thomas Shirley was a grandson of Henry, lord Berkeley, and his assistance was acknowledged by Smyth in the text of the *Lives of the Berkeleys*. In 1632 the catholic Sir Thomas commissioned an immense pedigree of the Shirleys of Staunton Harold, Leics., from their Anglo-Saxon ancestor Sewale to the current head of the family, his elder brother Sir Henry Shirley. This pedigree, measuring 11ft. 9in. by 29ft. 2in. and lavishly illustrated with drawings of coats of arms, monuments, family deeds and seals, was the first substantial product of Shirley's antiquarian researches. In the following years, Shirley compiled a far more extensive *Genealogicke Historie* of the family, which dealt with the main line and subsidiary branches of his family. Like Smyth's work, the *Genealogicke Historie* utilised the full range of antiquarian sources to celebrate the achievements of Shirley's ancestors and the persistence of their line.[42] Among the sources used by Shirley in the production of his family history were the papers of Sir Edward Vernon of Sudbury, Derbys. In 1615 Sir Edward's man of business John Harestaffe produced a rhymed annal of the Vernon family to celebrate the conclusion of litigation over their estates, which represents a clear parallel to Smyth's eulogy of the Berkeley family.[43]

Shirley was a member of the informal circle of local historians that gravitated around William Burton during the reign of Charles I, as he became the most active focus of local historical activity in the period. By the end of 1628 Burton was corresponding and exchanging documents and visits with the Warwickshire antiquary Sir Simon Archer, whose primary interest was his own pedigree. Burton had by this time completed a revised version of his history of Leicestershire and was anticipating going to London to be on hand to correct the proofs. Once this was done, he intended to turn his attention to writing a similar history for Warwickshire. Unfortunately, the printer went bust, and in 1631 Burton was distracted by the need to find another publisher. A letter from Shirley led Burton to believe that he would take over the history of Warwickshire, a county where his family had held land for several centuries, but Shirley quickly made it clear that his interests were at that time strictly genealogical.[44] Despite his disappointment concerning Shirley, Burton did not abandon the idea that another antiquary should undertake the history of Warwickshire with the aid of his own notes on the county. In September 1634 he mentioned the matter in a letter to Archer, in which he also referred to a gentleman 'about Worcestershire Description, but his name I could never yet heare'. The Worcestershire antiquary was Thomas Habington, the catholic son of Elizabeth I's cofferer, who had been involved in the hiding of fugitives after the Gunpowder Plot. Habington had begun working on the history of Worcestershire a decade later, when his involvement in a long and complicated Exchequer lawsuit had forced him to spend extended periods in London. He subsequently visited the churches of Worcestershire, making a comprehensive collection of the arms displayed therein. The first letter from Habington preserved among Archer's correspondence was written in the very month that Burton confessed to not knowing his name, and it reveals that Archer had already lent Habington a book that had helped him to trace the descent of Worcestershire manors. This letter also indicates that Habington was encouraged to draw together his researches into a coherent whole by Sir Robert Berkeley, a local landowner and justice of the King's Bench.[45] Berkeley had been one of the select group among whom Smyth had circulated the *Lives of the Berkeleys*, and Smyth's papers show that he did a good deal of work on the judge's pedigree in 1636. Smyth was also acquainted with Burton, whose family had a long association with the Berkeleys.[46]

Many gentlemen used scribes and copyists to assist them with their antiquarian research and it was as a prospective assistant to more socially elevated antiquaries that William Dugdale was drawn into Burton's circle in the 1630s. Dugdale was a young gentleman of modest fortune, whose house at Blythe Hall in north Warwickshire was within a few miles of Burton's home at Lindley. In 1635 Dugdale was engaged in copying various manuscripts belonging to Archer, and in drawing up an elaborate presentation copy of the latter's pedigree. The following year he was engaged in copying Rous's roll of the earls of Warwick and researching the history of the county in the cathedral archive at Lichfield. Although his correspondence reveals that from this time he was actively directing the course of the research into Warwickshire history, it was the socially superior Archer who was envisaged as being the prospective author by other members of their antiquarian circle. In his revised introduction for his work on Leicestershire, Burton, as reported to Archer by Dugdale, 'doth mention Sir Christopher Hatton, yourselfe, and Mr. Abington, for the intended descripcion of Northamptonshire, Warwickshire and Worcestershire'.[47] Habington was to continue to regard Archer as the prospective historian of Warwickshire throughout his life, although how far the former was ever enthusiastic about becoming an author is doubtful. Unlike Burton, who had retired from public life on the grounds of ill health, and Habington, who was excluded by his religion, Archer was an active justice of the peace. His correspondence with Burton makes it clear that Archer did not put himself forward when Shirley proved unwilling. The introduction of Dugdale may have been intended by Burton to provide Archer with the secretarial support he would need to undertake a county history, but it was the younger man who immediately began to drive forward the research. Archer had the social contacts that opened the studies of the local gentry to their research, but his interest remained predominantly focused on his own pedigree and the part of the county in which his own lands were situated. Although traces of drafts written by Archer can be identified in Dugdale's final text, the older man seems to have cheerfully ceded the role of author to the younger.

The Northamptonshire antiquary Sir Christopher Hatton was, like Archer, actively involved in public life, and could hardly have contemplated undertaking a county history without considerable secretarial and research assistance. One of the antiquaries that Hatton used to assist him in acquiring his extensive collection of manuscripts was the genealogist Richard Gascoigne, a Yorkshire gentleman of slender means. According to Dugdale's later recollection it was through Gascoigne that he and Archer met Hatton during a visit to London, although they had a number of other mutual acquaintances who could have effected the introduction. From the outset Hatton recognised the value of Dugdale's drive and enthusiasm. When Archer returned to Warwickshire, Dugdale remained in London, taking advantage of Hatton's contacts to gain access to the extensive records available in the capital. The surviving correspondence reveals how Hatton considered that the bulk of the work for the history of Warwickshire was to be undertaken by Dugdale, with Archer's role being the financing of the project. Encouraging Archer to procure for Dugdale a copy of Domesday, the pipe rolls and aid rolls for Warwickshire, he assured him: 'had I such a Helper as hee in Northamptonshire, I would not rest a yeare from the presse, and with content to all lovers of these studies'.[48] In the event Archer was unable or unwilling to undertake the entire financing of the project, and Dugdale lacked the resources to continue his research in the capital unaided. Archer approached Hatton with a view to seeking a post for Dugdale, and Burton approached Sir Henry Spelman, but in the early months of 1638 no position had been found and Dugdale was in need of a patron who would support his antiquarian researches.

It was at this juncture that a formal co-operative association for the pursuit of local history was formed. On 1 May 1638 Dugdale joined Hatton, Shirley and the Kentish antiquary Sir Edward Dering in forming this new antiquarian group, signing an agreement entitled *Antiquitas Rediviva*.[49] The purpose of the group was to identify and preserve medieval documents and to systematise the collection of a range of historical information. They were to collect rolls and books of arms, create a list of confirmations of arms and make a collection of seals, which would enable Dering to draw up a new system of armory. They were also to collate records of female heirs, knights, and the mayors, aldermen and sheriffs of London, York and other towns. The document noted their personal interests in Northamptonshire, Kent, Warwickshire and Huntingdonshire (where Shirley held the manor of Bottulph Bridge), but the main thrust of the envisaged research was not the production of a series of county histories. Genealogy and heraldry were of far more interest to this particular group than topography, although Dering did produce an account of the Weald. At this time Dugdale wrote to Archer explaining that he could no longer continue with the projected history of Warwickshire. When Archer failed to take up the suggestion that he should himself complete the work, Hatton agreed to provide support, on the understanding that control of the project passed to Dugdale. Archer seems to have made no objection, and he continued to support Dugdale's work, both by providing him with the products of his own research and by encouraging the participation of other local gentlemen. For Hatton, however, the completion of the history of Warwickshire was less important than the collection of heraldic records. Moreover, once a position in the College of Arms was secured for Dugdale in September 1638, genealogy and heraldry also became the focus of his professional antiquarian life.

The emphasis of the *Antiquitas Rediviva* on the systematic collection of records was symptomatic of the direction in which early Stuart local history was developing. There was an increasing emphasis on written records rather than personal observation or oral reports. The interest in writing county histories had not disappeared, but while earlier antiquaries such as Leland and Norden had envisaged undertaking the description of the whole country, their Stuart counterparts increasingly found the task of writing a comprehensive account of even a single county to be overwhelming. There were more and more printed sources, original records and transcripts available, while potential readers were increasingly well-informed and demanding. Burton was revising his *Description of Leicestershire* throughout the 1630s, and his final manuscript was far lengthier than the small volume of his first edition. It included a comprehensive set of pedigrees and a wealth of historical material, although his fellow antiquaries were often sceptical about the accuracy of his transcripts. Burton continued to encourage other local historians to produce accounts of their own counties. With Habington this eventually bore fruit, but in other cases he was less successful. The catholic, Thomas, lord Brudenell, was inspired by Burton to begin work on a history of Northamptonshire. Brudenell was also friendly with Hatton and Shirley and shared the latter's predominant interest in genealogy, especially that of his own family. Although his extensive collections included a wealth of relevant material and he had access to Hatton's own collections, his county history did not progress beyond a few pages on the villages in the hundred of Corby.[50] Walter Chetwynd collected material for history of Staffordshire over a number of years and helped Burton with his own work, but he did not proceed to composition.[51] In eastern England, John Layer devised an ambitious draft for a history of Cambridgeshire, but the surviving manuscript covers only the history of the borough and University of Cambridge and most of the county south of Ely. Like Archer, Layer was a justice of the peace and his public duties must have distracted from the time he could devote to his antiquarian researches, although he did find time in the mid–1630s to make a comprehensive survey of the county's parish churches. Layer's interest in his public role is reflected in other treatises he wrote on the duties of justices, constables, churchwardens and other officers.[52] Gervase Holles collected a considerable amount of material for the history of Lincolnshire in the early 1630s when the inheritance of the family estate and marriage led him to reside predominantly in Grimsby. Towards the end of the decade, however, his time was increasingly absorbed by public duties and the writing of the county history of Lincolnshire did not progress. Other antiquaries limited themselves to an account of only part of a county, such as the Kentish historian Sir Roger Twysden's *Discourse Concerning the Weald*, and John Smyth's *Description of the Hundred of Berkeley*.

By contrast with his less-ambitious peers, the Yorkshire antiquary Roger Dodsworth was not content simply to tackle the history of the largest English county. He also intended to write an English baronage and an account of the English monastic houses. Dodsworth was encouraged in his researches by the Fairfax family. Charles, third son of lord Fairfax, was a keen antiquary, who worked alongside Dodsworth and who compiled a collection of pedigrees and notes concerning the various branches of his family, entitled *Analecta Fairfaxiana*. In 1635 Dodsworth secured a pension of fifty pounds per annum from the family to support his work on monastic foundations. (As a parliamentary general, Charles' nephew, Thomas Fairfax, was to show his respect for learning by his concern to guard the Bodleian from the depredations of his soldiers after the fall of Oxford in 1646.) Dugdale was introduced to Dodsworth around 1635 by Samuel Roper, a Lincoln's Inn lawyer who was related to Dugdale by marriage and through whom he also met Dodsworth's fellow Yorkshireman Richard Gascoigne. Dodsworth took notes from Hatton's collection in the same year. Although only the *Monasticon* ever completed the transition from research notes to coherent work, Dodsworth's extensive collections were a valuable resource for his fellow antiquaries, both during his lifetime and beyond.[53]

In 1640 Dugdale and the arms painter William Sedgewick made a tour of cathedrals and churches from London to York and from Norwich to Chester, making a record of the monuments they found. According to Dugdale's later account, this journey was prompted by Hatton's clairvoyance in foreseeing the destruction of church monuments that was to occur in the following years. More prosaically, the tour may be seen as part of the scheme for a comprehensive collection of arms envisaged in the *Antiquitas Rediviva*. Although numerous local historians had made collections of church notes for their own counties, and London was well covered by John Stow, a comprehensive study was lacking. John Weever had intended such a work, but the published volume of *Ancient Funerall Monuments* (1631) covered only London, Canterbury, Rochester and Norwich. Weever complained that he had encountered difficulties with some churchwardens, who would not let him view monuments because he lacked a commission such as Leland had obtained from Henry VIII. Dugdale, by contrast, had his official position as a herald to support his entitlement to record the arms and pedigrees he found. (Similarly, Robert Sanderson was a prebend at Lincoln when he made a survey of monuments there in 1641, and Habington was accompanied on some of his expeditions to collect church notes by Nathaniel Tomkins, prebend at Worcester and son of the cathedral organist.) Although Dugdale's account of the reason for the cathedral tour in 1640 was written with the benefit of hindsight, political events did begin to affect antiquarian research at this time. By the spring of 1640 work had begun in earnest on the recording of a collection of charters and their seals in a volume that today consists of 128 vellum folios. The project was referred to in a letter from Dugdale to Archer, who was asked to bring some of his 'choicest' deeds with him when he attended the Short Parliament. In the event Hatton's collection includes no charters provided either by Archer, who went on to support parliament in the civil war, or Dering, who was vocal in support of church reform in the Long Parliament. In normal times shared antiquarian interests overcame religious differences, so that the godly Archer and Dering could co-operate happily with the catholic Habington and Shirley and the Laudian Hatton and Burton. As the Long Parliament began its attack on the Laudian church and the king's prerogative, the times were far from normal.[54]

It is symptomatic of the way in which antiquarian interests overcame religious differences in the 1630s that Burton entrusted the revised text of his *Description of Leicestershire* in 1638 to Sir John Lambe, dean of the Court of Arches, while arranging for the puritan Simonds D'Ewes to write the preface. By the time the final revision of Burton's manuscript was completed in 1642, Lambe had appeared as a delinquent before the Long Parliament in which D'Ewes played an active part. The reluctance of printers to take a chance on works of local history was now compounded by the distractions of political and religious unrest, and Burton's work failed to achieve publication. The potentially wider interest in Canterbury as the capital of the English church may explain why a printer was found to publish William Somner's *The Antiquities of Canterbury* (1640). This was reputedly the second history of the city to be written, but the earlier work associated with the schoolmaster John Twyne was untraceable half a century after his death. Somner was registrar of the ecclesiastical courts of Canterbury and his work was dedicated to Laud, who was shortly to be impeached by parliament. However, apart from the preface, there was little that was controversial about Somner's work, which was written as a perambulation of the city similar in style and content to Stow's *Survey of London*. Having published his account of Canterbury, Somner intended to proceed to a history of the county, but abandoned the project when overtaken by the 'impetuous storm' of civil war. In November 1642, Habington sent the manuscript of his account of Worcestershire to Archer, explaining that he had completed the work shortly before his house was 'ransacked & (to use the newe wourd) plundred' by soldiers. Although Archer expressed his joy that the work had not perished in 'these distracted times', the civil strife prevented not only publication of such works but even the wide circulation in manuscript that had occurred previously.[55]

The detrimental effects of the political strife of the 1640s on antiquarian discourse may be seen in the history of John Trussell's *Touchstone of Tradition*, an ambitious history of the city of Winchester. Trussell was an alderman and steward to the bishop of Winchester, although his family ties were to the Midlands. Despite the demands of his professional life, which included twice serving as mayor, he was also recognised as an antiquary and poet. In 1636 he contributed a poem to the *Annalia Dubrensia*, celebrating Robert Dover's revival of the Cotswold Games, and published *A Continuation of the Collection of the History of England* covering the period from the reign of Edward III to the end of the Wars of the Roses. He had already started to work on a history designed to 'enritch and illustrate' the city of Winchester and an early draft on the city's origins, dedicated to John, marquess of Winchester, was lent by him to Sir John Oglander, an antiquary on the Isle of Wight. The original dedication of the third section of the *Touchstone of Tradition* indicates that it was begun around 1636. However, as Trussell later explained, the strained relations between the marquess and the city, and his own unpopularity on account of his reforming zeal led him to put the manuscript to one side in favour of compiling an account of the city's benefactors. By 1642 he had returned to his abandoned manuscript and increased its intended scope. The four sections of the work were dedicated respectively to the marquess of Winchester, the bishop Walter Curll, the mayor, and a collection of local dignitaries, including the earl of Southampton as high steward, and viscount Ogle as governor of the castle and city. The manuscript was again revised in 1647, by which time the marquess of Winchester was a parliamentary prisoner and the bishop had fled the city after it fell to the parliamentary forces. Two of the four 'props' that Trussell had hoped would support his work with their patronage had foundered, one was visibly in danger, and only the mayor remained to provide a 'cornerstone' to his work. Although, as a subject, Winchester, the ancient Saxon capital, might have held the wider potential to persuade a printer to publish the work, the advent of the civil war ensured that the work remained a little-known manuscript.[56]

While the civil war inevitably interrupted communications between antiquaries in different parts of the country, it did not prevent the study of local
history. Indeed, the anonymous compiler of an uncompleted history of
Cheshire recounted that he took up his long-neglected studies during the war
because the times were unpropitious for any other activity. William Blundell
wrote an account of the Isle of Man after spending some time there in exile
from his Lancashire estate. Dugdale accompanied the king to Oxford in 1642
and spent much of his time there until the city fell in 1646, pursuing his
researches in the Bodleian and college libraries. He was also able to examine
the records of Worcester cathedral during a visit to the royalist garrison there.
Sir Wingfield Bodenham began compiling material for a history of Rutland
while a prisoner in the Tower between 1644 and 1647, during which time he
relied heavily on the assistance of Fairfax's pensioner Dodsworth. Despite the
difficulties documented by Trussell, town histories also continued to develop
during this unsettled period. The *Survey and Antiquitie of the Town of Stamforde*
(1646) was written by Richard Butcher, who, as town clerk, held a position
often associated with the compilers of annalistic town chronicles. According to
the dedication, the work was written in response to a suggestion from wealthy
London citizens who originated in Stamford.[57] William Grey, by contrast, was
a wealthy merchant of Newcastle-upon-Tyne, although his business interests
had been affected by the war when he published his *Chorographica, or a Survey
of Newcastle upon Tine* (1649). This brief pamphlet and other works, such as
Richard Hollingworth's *Mancuniensis* on Manchester and Nathaniel Bacon's
work on Ipswich, seem to be symptomatic of the way in which, at a time of civil
strife, some citizens turned to a new form of urban history, less dominated by
the often-divided civic authorities. These works also referenced *Britannia*, and
were part of the wider antiquarian project to expand that work.

Antiquarian discourse was resumed with enthusiasm as soon as parliament's
victory brought the civil war to an end. Despite having supported opposing sides
in the conflict, local historians still resumed their previous friendships. As the
royalist Dugdale wrote to the parliamentarian D'Ewes: 'your discourse with
me of Antiquities can affoard noe matter of exception to these jealous times'.[58]
Nevertheless, the antiquarian environment was changed by the passage of time
and as a result of the conflict and its aftermath. Of those who had signed the
Antiquitas Rediviva in 1638, Dering was dead, while Hatton and Shirley had fled
abroad. Burton, Habington, Spelman, Smyth and Layer all died between 1640
and 1647. Former royalists such as Dugdale had their freedom of movement
restricted, while others, including Somner, Brudenell and Oglander, suffered
periods of imprisonment. D'Ewes was expelled from the House of Commons
by Pride's Purge and retired to his Suffolk estate, where he died two years later.
Archer, still involved in public duties, was distracted by his role as executor to
the royalist Sir Thomas Puckering, whose daughter and heir was kidnapped

and carried abroad by a persistent suitor in 1649. By contrast, obtaining the office of sequestrator in Herefordshire and a moiety of the bishop's palace provided Silas Taylor with the opportunity to begin his researches into the history of Herefordshire. To this end, he was reported to have 'ransacked' the archives of Hereford and Worcester cathedral and to have removed various documents, including an original Saxon grant of King Edgar.[59]

Despite the difficulties experienced by individuals, antiquarian discourse and co-operative research did resume. Dodsworth's association with Fairfax was particularly useful at this juncture, as he was able to move freely and to visit prisoners in the Tower. He also made efforts on Dugdale's behalf to secure him passes allowing him to travel to London. In 1649 a scheme was mooted for Dodsworth to publish an English baronage in co-operation with John Vincent, who had inherited the papers of his father Augustine, the former herald and putative historian of Northamptonshire. In 1652 the council of state gave Dodsworth free access to the records in the Tower. Among Dugdale's new correspondents in this period was William Vernon, a gentleman from a Cheshire family who resided at Shakerley, Lancs. The notes of Randle Holme, a Chester herald painter, show that Vernon was known as an antiquary by 1636, although his surviving correspondence with Dugdale begins in 1647. Vernon was researching the history of Cheshire, and Dugdale put him in touch with other antiquaries, eased his access to public and diocesan, records and obtained for him a good transcription of the Domesday text for Cheshire.[60] While Dugdale and Vernon continued to work on county histories, other local historians turned to different fields. Somner pursued his interest in Anglo-Saxon and did not resume his intended history of Kent. After a period of imprisonment the royalist Gervase Holles left England and settled in Holland, where he received those of his papers that had not been lost when his house in Grimsby had been plundered by parliamentary troops. At such a distance from Lincolnshire and from the archives he would need to consult for a county history, he set about writing a history of his family. At this time, a genealogical history, which could serve as an inspiration and conduct book for his children, was in any case a more satisfying form for Holles. In Somerset Sir Edward Rodney also set about writing a family history following the death of his only son. In this case the work could stand as a reminder to his five daughters of the significance of their paternal family and as a lasting memorial to the family name.[61]

The loss of income from Crown and ecclesiastical appointments forced a number of local historians to seek new sources of income during the interregnum. Somner, who had shown more diligence in his historical research and archery practice than ecclesiastical administration under Laud, was fortunate to secure the stipend of the Anglo-Saxon lecture at Cambridge established by Spelman. Dugdale was obliged to compound for his estate after the fall of

Oxford, and lost his official income as a herald. He continued his loyalty to his patron Hatton, visiting the latter in France in 1648, but his precarious position necessitated a search for new patrons and sources of income. Assisting Dodsworth with the preparation of the *Monasticon Anglicanum* provided Dugdale with work that interested him, while also bringing him to the notice of his friend's patrons. At the same time he returned to the history of Warwickshire, which would reinforce his reputation as an antiquarian scholar once published and might attract further patronage. In this he was assisted by Archer, who once more used his local influence to gain access to documents and to encourage members of the local gentry to pay for the engraving of maps and illustrations for the work. In 1653, Archer also suggested that Dugdale should arrange to have printed one of the manuscripts in their possession, such as Erdeswicke's *View of Staffordshire*, Webb's history of Cheshire or 'any other manuscript that may yield you profit'. Dugdale took up the idea of publishing Webb's manuscript in conjunction with the herald William Smith's account of the same county, a copy of which was in the possession of Daniel King, a Chester engraver and herald painter who had transferred his business to London. King was prepared to supply engravings of maps and views of the county for the work, and Dugdale approached his contacts among the Cheshire gentry in the hope that they would support the undertaking. Although he recognised that Vernon's work would be superior to that of Webb and Smith 'if he do accomplish it', he thought that age and infirmity would prevent its completion. Three years later the proposed volume with some further additions by King and the puritan cleric Samuel Lee appeared as the *Vale Royal of England* (1656) under King's name.[62] In 1655 the first volume of *Monasticon Anglicanum* was at the press, when Dodsworth died. In his will he asked the historian John Rushworth, who had served Fairfax as secretary during the war, to ensure that publication was completed. It was apparently Rushworth who insisted that Dugdale's name should appear with Dodsworth's on the title page. Hence, although his work in assisting Dodsworth may have yielded Dugdale little immediate financial benefit, it enhanced his reputation as a scholar. Finally, the *Antiquities of Warwickshire* was published in 1656, to great acclaim. Dugdale's work was far more comprehensive and exhaustive than any previous county history. It combined topographical description with detailed genealogies and extensive descriptions of heraldic monuments and stained glass. It also included erudite digressions on the monastic orders of medieval England and other subjects of more relevance to a county history than the digressions that appeared in Burton's first edition. A new standard had been set against which subsequent works would be judged.

The publication of the *Antiquities of Warwickshire* stimulated renewed interest in the writing of county histories. Acknowledging the work's status as an aspirational standard, Somner wrote: 'I wish I could in the same way bring you as well acquainted with our County. But whilest I heartily wish it, I find it vaine to hope it: neither my selfe, nor (I believe) any other, being able, though ever so willing, to give so faire an account either of this or any other County.'[63] The last years of the interregnum did see a flush of works published relating to Kent: a new edition of Lambarde's *Perambulation* in 1656; Thomas Philipot's *Villare Cantianum* (1659), which was actually the work of his father John, formerly Somerset herald; and Richard Kilburne's *Survey of Kent* (1659). None of these works reached the new standard established by Dugdale. In March 1660, when the Wiltshire gentry met to select their MPs, 'it was wished by some that this Country (wherein are many observable Antiquities) were surveyed in imitation of Mr. Dugdale's Illustration of Warwickshire'. The task being considered too great for one man, it was agreed that William Yorke, a lawyer, and John Aubrey should divide the county between them with three other gentlemen acting as assistants. Other gentlemen approached Dugdale to write a history of their counties, including Norfolk, Cheshire and Leicestershire.[64] In view of Dugdale's continuing relationship with Hatton it is possible that he would have undertaken a history of Northamptonshire, if the Restoration had not returned him to the College of Arms. This interest in producing county histories in the mould of the *Antiquities of Warwickshire* did not end in 1660. In Cheshire Sir Peter Leycester took forward the research begun by William Vernon, which eventually formed the core of his *Historical Antiquities* (1673), and Walter Chetwynd the younger continued his father's work on Staffordshire. Robert Thoroton's *Antiquities of Nottinghamshire* (1677) was directly modelled on Dugdale's work and the elder antiquary's encouragement was influential in persuading Thoroton to publish his research. As late as the third decade of the eighteenth century, William Hals was writing a county history of Cornwall that mirrored the interests and concerns exhibited by local historians a century before.

The successive editions of Camden's *Britannia* had led to the cornerstone of late Elizabethan topography being moulded by the antiquarian interests of its readers and contributors. Since the *Antiquities of Warwickshire* did not go through an equivalent process of revision, it stood as a monument to the early Stuart concept of local history. It did not reflect the way in which scientific interests and curiosity about the natural world increasingly affected antiquarian research from the 1650s. The year after its publication, Dugdale undertook a commission from the company responsible for draining the Great Level to write a history of land drainage. The resultant *History of Imbanking and Drayning* (1662) contains one of the first ever attempts at landscape archaeology, combining geological observations with an examination of recovered artefacts. This passage reflects the influence on Dugdale of Thomas Browne, a Norwich physician and author of *Religio Medici* (1643). In *Hydriotaphia – Urne Buriall* (1658) Browne combined a traditional literary approach to his subject with Baconian experimentalism, while his later account of funerary urns found at Brampton, Norfolk, is a fine example of an early archaeological report. The Wiltshire antiquary John Aubrey was one of the original members of the Royal Society. Another member was the herald Elias Ashmole (1617–92), whose engraving of a flint axehead had appeared in the *Antiquities of Warwickshire* and who later married one of Dugdale's daughters. The Lancashire antiquary Christopher Towneley was responsible not only for the compilation and transcription of many volumes of historical records, but also for the preservation of the papers of the astronomers Jeremiah Horrocks, William Crabtree and William Gascoigne. The scientific revolution of the seventeenth century hence influenced antiquarianism as it did other intellectual pursuits. Local history was, however, increasingly seen as a field distinct from the disciplines of topography and archaeology, and as being practised by people who were not greatly influenced by natural philosophy. The continued importance of the gentry and the descent of manors in local history for more than three centuries reflects the success of the Elizabethan and Stuart gentry in creating a genre in their own image, and the continued attachment of their descendants to that image.[65]

NOTES

Antiquaries as a group are well served by the *Dictionary of National Biography*, and this chapter is heavily indebted to this invaluable resource; individual references are given only where an article is quoted directly. For county historians the most comprehensive source is C. Currie and C. Lewis (eds), *A Guide to English County Histories* (Stroud: Alan Sutton, 1994), which also covers some urban historians. An overview of urban history is also provided by Peter Clark, 'Visions of the urban community: antiquarians and the English City before 1800', in D. Fraser and A. Sutcliffe (eds), *The Pursuit of Urban History* (London: Edward Arnold, 1983), pp. 105–24. No similar work is available dealing with family historians.

1 A comprehensive survey of medieval historiography is provided by A. Gransden *Historical Writing in England*, two volumes (London: Routledge & Kegan Paul, 1974–82); Birmingham University Library, misc. 7/i/16. Roger Twysden published Knighton in *Historiae Anglicanae Scriptores Decem* (London, 1652).

2 Gransden, *Historical Writing in England*, vol. 1, pp. 432–8.

3 John Stow, *The Survey of London*, H. Wheatley (ed.) (London: J.M. Dent & Sons Ltd., 1912), hereafter Stow, *London*, p. 501.

4 C.S. Lewis, *English Literature in the Sixteenth Century* (Oxford: Clarendon Press, 1954), pp. 122–3.

5 British Library, hereafter B.L., Harley 1944, fo. 3v; Gransden, *Historical Writing in England*, vol. 2, pp. 43–4; M. Collins, *Caxton: Description of Britain* (London: Sidgwick & Jackson, 1988), p. 68; Smyth, *Berkeley Mss*, vol. 1, p. 343.

6 A. Gransden, *Legends, Traditions and History in Medieval England* (London: Hambledon, 1992), chapter 14; N. Battely, *The Antiquities of Canterbury* (London, 1703), preface to the first part; Smyth, *Berkeley Mss*, vol. 1, p. 292.

7 J.H. Harvey (ed.), *William Worcestre Itineraries* (Oxford: Oxford University Press, 1969).

8 F. Neale, 'William Worcestre: Bristol churches in 1480', in J. Bettey (ed.), *Historic Churches and Church Life in Bristol* (Bristol and Gloucestershire Archaeological Society, 2001), pp. 28–54; J. Chandler, *John Leland's Itinerary* (Stroud: Alan Sutton, 1998), p. 179. Worcestre also recorded notes on Sheen Syon near Brentford originating from Nicholas Burton of Bristol: Harvey (ed.), *William Worcestre Itineraries*, p. 335.

9 Harvey (ed.), *William Worcestre Itineraries*, pp. 209–21.

10 L. Toulmin Smith (ed.), *The Maire of Bristowe is Kalendar by Robert Ricart* (Camden Society, new ser. 5, 1872).

11 Smyth, *Berkeley Mss.*, vol. 1, p. 12.

12 T. King, *The Collegiate Church of St Mary, Warwick* (Andover, Hampshire: Pitkin Pictorials Pitkin Guide, 1994); D. Douglas, *English Scholars* (London: Jonathan Cape, 1939), p. 156.

13 C. Ross, *The Rous Roll* (Gloucester: Sutton, 1980); Gransden, *Historical Writing in England*, vol. 2, pp. 320–1; Gransden, *Legends, Traditions and History in Medieval England*, pp. 326–7.

14 In the *Antiquities of Warwickshire* Dugdale mentions only the Latin version of the *History of the Earls of Warwick* belonging to Robert Arden of Park Hall, and Cotton's copy of the *Historia Regum Angliae*, as Rous's surviving works. Presumably he regarded the English version of the Warwick roll and other manuscripts as copies and not distinct works.

15 W.T. Collins, 'A manuscript book of Rolls in Shakespeare's Birthplace Trust Record Office', *Warwickshire History* 4(2), (1978), p. 69; S.B.T. DR473/293, fos 79–81; B.L., Cotton, Julius C3, April 1629 and 30 Oct. 1630; S. Archer, *Correspondence*, Bodleian, Eng. lett. b 1, hereafter Archer, *Correspondence*, fo. 21; Warwickshire County Record Office, hereafter C.R.O., CR1059/2; William Dugdale, *The Antiquities of Warwickshire* (London, 1656), hereafter Dugdale, *Warwickshire*, p. 185.

16 Chandler, *John Leland's Itinerary*, pp. xiii, 1–2; J.D. Austin, *Merevale Church and Abbey* (Studley, Warwickshire: Brewin Books, 1998), appendix F; E.W. Ives, *Anne Boleyn* (Oxford: Blackwell, 1986), pp. 274, 310.

17 Chandler, *John Leland's Itinerary*, p. 9.

18 Chandler, *John Leland's Itinerary*, pp. 66, 81, 170, 191, 328, 374; W. Camden, *Britannia* (Newton Abbot: David Charles, facsimile of 1695 edn., 1971), p. 240; T. Fuller, *The Worthies of England* (London: F.C. & J. Rivington, 1811), pp. 387–8.

19 Hamper, *Dugdale*, pp. 151–2: November 1635; L. Toulmin Smith (ed.), *The Itinerary of John Leland in or About the Years 1535–1543* (London: Centaur, 1964), vol. 1, pp. xxii–xxviii; S.B.T., DR37/Box 87/82.

20 Northants. C.R.O., FH4017 and FH2664; A.C. Wood (ed.), *Memorials of the Holles Family 1493–1656* (London: Camden Society, 3rd ser. 55, 1937), p. 18; S.B.T. DR37/Box 87/82.

21 Woolf, *Reading History in Early Modern England*, pp. 55–6; Beer, *Tudor England Observed*, pp. 9, 12.

22 R. Flower, 'Laurence Nowell and the discovery of England in Tudor times', in E.G. Stanley (ed.), *British Academy Papers on Anglo-Saxon England* (Oxford: Oxford University Press, 1990), pp. 1–27; Currie and Lewis, *A Guide to English County Histories*, p. 10.

23 R.M. Warnicke, *William Lambarde: Elizabethan Antiquary 1536–1601* (Chichester: Phillimore, 1973).

24 Quoted in Currie and Lewis, *A Guide to English County Histories*, p. 12.

25 Lewis, *English Literature in the Sixteenth Century*, pp. 303–5.

26 Stow, *London*, p. 311.

27 D. MacCulloch, 'Henry Chitting's Suffolk collections', *Suffolk Institute of Archaeology and History* 34 (1980), pp. 103–4; B.L., Egerton 3510, *passim*.

28 John Vowell, alias Hooker, *A Catalogue of the Bishops of Excester* (London: H. Denham, 1584), p. Aii; Warnicke, *William Lambarde*, p. 26.

29 F.J. Levy, 'The making of Camden's *Britannia*', *Bibliothèque d'Humanisme et Renaissance* 26 (1964), pp. 70–97; W. Rockett, 'The structural plan of Camden's *Britannia*', *Sixteenth Century Journal* 24 (1995), pp. 829–41.

30 Thomas Habington, *A Survey of Worcestershire*, J. Amphlett (ed.), two volumes (Oxford: Worcestershire Historical Society, 1895–99), hereafter Habington, *Worcestershire*, vol. 2, p. 124.

31 B.L., Harley 1990, fo. 10. Only a fragment of Erdeswicke's parallel account of Cheshire survives.

32 Stow, *London*, pp. xxiii–xxiv.

33 According to Burton, who knew Wyrley, the *True Use of Armorie* was Erdeswicke's work which he allowed Wyrley to publish in his own name; Sampson Erdeswicke, *A Survey of Staffordshire*, T. Harwood (ed.) (London: J.B. Nichols & Son, 1844), hereafter Erdeswicke, *Staffordshire*, pp. 333, 523.

34 C.M. Hood, *Chorography of Norfolk* (Norwich: Jarrold & Sons, 1938); D. MacCulloch (ed.), *The Chorography of Suffolk* (Suffolk Record Society 19, 1976); A. Hassell-Smith and D. MacCulloch, 'The authorship of the chorographies of Norfolk and Suffolk', *Norfolk Archaeology* 36 (1974), pp. 327–41; C.G. Harlow, 'Robert Reyce of Preston, 1555–1638', *Proceedings of the Suffolk Institute of Archaeology* 32 (1973), pp. 43–70.

35 B.L., Harley 1944; G. Ormerod, *The History of the County Palatine and City of Chester*, three volumes (1875–82), vol. 1(1), p. 142.

36 R. Hardin, *Michael Drayton and the Passing of Elizabethan England* (Kansas: Kansas University Press, 1973), pp. 63–6.

37 J. Nichols, *History of Leicestershire*, four volumes (1795–1815), vol. 3(1), p. xx; Burton, *Leicestershire*, To the Reader.

38 William Burton, *The Description of Leicestershire* (London, 1622), hereafter Burton, *Leicestershire*, To the Reader.

39 J. Denton, *An Accompt of the Most Considerable Estates and Families in the County of Cumberland*, (ed.) R.S. Ferguson (Cumberland and Westmorland Archaeological Society, 1887), p. 14; Currie and Lewis, *English County Histories*, pp. 92–3.

40 K. Sharpe, *Sir Robert Cotton* (Oxford: Oxford University Press, 1979), p. 209; C. White, *Anthony van Dyck: Thomas Howard, the Earl of Arundel* (Santa Monica, CA: Getty Museum, 1995), pp. 4, 17.

41 Berkeley Castle, Select Books 2 – see I. Jeayes, *Descriptive Catalogue of the Charters and Muniments of Berkeley Castle* (Bristol, 1892).

42 Leics. C.R.O., P99/1–55; B.L., Harley 4928; Northants. C.R.O., FH269 & FH270.

43 J. Cox, 'The rhymed chronicle of John Harestaffe', *Journal of the Derbyshire Archaeological and Natural History Society* 10 (1888), pp. 71–147.

44 Archer, *Correspondence*, fos 18–28, 53, 62, 76.

45 Archer, *Correspondence*, fos 106, 108.

46 Gloucestershire C.R.O. D8887, vols 1 to 10, catalogued in *Smyth of Nibley Papers* (Gloucester County Library, 1978), hereafter *Smyth Papers*, vol. 1, fos 55, 58, 77.

47 Hamper, *Dugdale*, pp. 151–6.

48 Hamper, *Dugdale*, pp. 170–1. Dugdale's account of this period in his autobiography is unreliable.

49 L.B. Larking, 'On the Surrenden charters', *Archaelogia Cantiana* 1 (1858), pp. 50–65.

50 J. Wake, *The Brudenells of Deene* (London: Cassell & Company, 1953), pp. 106–7.

51 H.E. Chetwynd-Stapylton, *The Chetwynds of Ingestre* (London: Longmans, Green & Co., 1892).

52 W. Palmer, *John Layer (1586–1640) of Shepreth, Cambridgeshire* (Cambridge: Cambridge Antiquarian Society Octavo Series 53, 1935).

53 N. Denholm-Young and H. Craster, 'Roger Dodsworth (1585–1654) and his circle', *Yorkshire Archaeological Journal* 32 (1936), pp. 5–32.

54 John Weever, *Ancient Funerall Monuments* (London, 1631), To the Reader; L.C. Lloyd and D.M. Stenton (eds), *Sir Christopher Hatton's Book of Seals* (Oxford: Oxford University Press, 1950); Hamper, *Dugdale*, pp. 202–3.

55 D. Williams, 'William Burton's 1642 revised edition of the Description of Leicestershire', *Leicestershire Archaeological and Historical Society Transactions*, hereafter *Leics. Trans.* 50 (1974–75), pp. 30–6; Hamper, *Dugdale*, p. 200; Shakespeare Birthplace Trust, hereafter S.B.T., DR37/Box 87/103.

56 Hants. C.R.O., W/K1/11–13.

57 Richard Butcher, *The Survey and Antiquitie of the Towne of Stamford* (London, 1646), p. A3.

58 Leics. C.R.O., DE2191; Hamper, *Dugdale*, p. 204.

59 O. Lawson-Dick (ed.), *Aubrey's Brief Lives* (London: Reed International, 1992), hereafter Aubrey, *Brief Lives*, pp. 292–3.

60 B.L., Harley 2037, pp. 194–5; Hamper, *Dugdale*, pp. 251–3, 266–8.

61 Gervase Holles, *Memorials of the Holles Family 1493–1656*, ed. A.C. Wood (London: Camden Society, 3rd ser. 55, 1937); B.L., Additional Manuscripts 34239.

62 Hamper, *Dugdale*, pp. 272–3; B.L., Additional Manuscripts 6396, fo. 17.

63 Hamper, *Dugdale*, p. 309.

64 D. Tylden-Wright, *John Aubrey* (London: HarperCollins, 1991), p. 124; J. Broadway, *William Dugdale and the Significance of County History in Early Stuart England* (Stratford-upon-Avon: Dugdale Society, Occasional papers 39, 1999), p. 20.

65 C. Webster, 'Richard Towneley (1629–1707), The Towneley group and seventeenth century science', *Transactions of the Historical Society of Lancashire and Cheshire*, 188 (1966), pp. 51–76.

Chapter 2

◆

The national context of local history

This book is primarily concerned with the influence of the provincial gentry on the development of local history. There were, however, a number of external forces which shaped the way in which the late Elizabethan and early Stuart gentry approached the past. It is these external forces that are the subject of this chapter. The potential for education to influence historical understanding, and the way in which it might equip – or fail to equip – fledging antiquaries, is easily appreciated. Similarly, the skills and attitudes of those with control of public records are clearly of relevance to this discussion. A local gentleman might indulge his interest in the past for several years among his own papers. Nevertheless, in time, that interest was likely to develop and to lead him to think of tracing the records of his family and lands in the 'national' archives of the Tower and Rolls Chapel. More prosaically, a lawsuit might force him to become acquainted with the legal records of the king's courts in Westminster. Less immediately obvious among the external forces influencing the development of local history may be the significant role played by the heralds, since in the twenty-first century the denizens of the College of Arms are little more than a harmless anachronism. In the period of this study, the heralds were an active instrument of royal policy and frequent visitors into the provinces from London. As such, they acted as important conduits for historical understanding and research. It is not necessarily obvious why the inns of court should have had any significant influence on the development of local history. The inns of court were, however, both an important educational institution for the English gentry and a focus for their continued association with the capital. Many local gentlemen retained links with their Inns long after their education was completed, and they stayed there or in the vicinity when in London and were drawn thereby into antiquarian circles. This chapter concludes with an examination of the Society of Antiquaries, which sprang up in the wake of the publication of *Britannia*, flourished for some twenty years and then disappeared almost without trace. A purely metropolitan society with a closed membership holding its meetings in private might be thought to have had little influence on the provincial gentry. Yet, there is evidence that the society was known about beyond its self-selected membership, and that it did become a focus of local historical writing.

History as a distinct subject had little place within the formal educational system of early modern England. The curriculum had evolved from that introduced at the time of the Roman occupation, and was dominated by the teaching of Latin and the study of classical texts. As a consequence of the Reformation, the ecclesiastical domination of education had been greatly diminished and was gradually replaced by the intervention of the state. English had begun to replace Latin as the language of religious education, but the classics continued to dominate secular learning. Within the classical model, history was considered as a branch of literature and its subjects were the classical civilisations of Greece and Rome. The national history of Britain or the medieval history of Europe had no place within the formal curriculum. The Elizabethan curriculum of the Free Grammar School in Leicester was typical of the period. There the prescribed classical authors were Cato, Aesop, Cicero, Terence, Ovid and Horace, suggesting that even classical history was little taught at this level. At university the traditional course in the arts included studies in the trivium (grammar, logic and rhetoric), the quadrivium (arithmetic, geometry and music), and in moral and natural philosophy and metaphysics. Tutors could add to the course prescribed by the statutes, and the study of classical historians such as Livy, Florus and Suetonius were quite common. At Oxford a history lectureship was established in 1621 by William Camden, while Sir Fulke Greville founded a similar lectureship at Cambridge six years later. These lectureships were concerned with classical not national history.[1]

In considering the role of history in formal education it is important to remember Francis Bacon's division of history between history proper, or perfect history, and antiquarianism, or history defaced. Since the role of the universities was to produce churchmen, diplomats, statesmen and civil lawyers, history as a guide to action, morality and the welfare of the state was their proper concern. Hence, although Matthew Parker was appointed master of Corpus Christi, Cambridge, and vice-chancellor of the university in the reign of Henry VIII, this important antiquarian scholar and promoter of Anglo-Saxon studies did not attempt to alter the nature of history teaching at Cambridge. Although he regarded Corpus Christi as the safest repository for his medieval books and manuscripts, the historical scholarship that Parker sponsored was concentrated within his own household. It is also in the context of history as a guide to action through precept that William Camden founded a chair in civil history at Oxford. The first incumbent was not one of the many young antiquaries known to Camden, but the classicist Degory Whear, who subsequently lectured for twenty-four years on Roman history from the *Epitome* of Lucius Annaeus Florus. The text for Whear's lectures was prescribed by Camden, and he performed the role that his patron had intended: to lecture 'on civil history, and therein make such observations as might be most useful and profitable to the younger students of the university, to direct and instruct them in the knowledge and use of history, antiquity and times past'. It was not that British history was incapable of providing appropriate models for the young, but that, in Bacon's words, 'it hath pleased God to ordain and illustrate two exemplar states [Greece and Rome] of the world for arms, learning, moral virtue, policy and laws'. Moreover, more recent history could represent a political quicksand, as the Cambridge lecturer Isaac Dorislaus found to his cost. Lecturing on the *Annals* of Tacitus, Dorislaus, who was born in Northern Holland, drew parallels between the events recorded by the Roman historian and the Dutch revolt against Spain. His impolitic support for rebellion against 'legitimate' authority led to his suspension. As Sir John Hayward had found when he entered the *First Part of the Life and Raigne of Henrie the IIII* (1599) on the Stationers' Registers, a combination of recent British history and Tacitus could also lead to trouble from the authorities. As the work was dedicated to the earl of Essex, in the fervid atmosphere of the last years of Elizabeth's long reign its account of the deposition of Richard II was interpreted as condoning the act. This led to Hayward's examination by the Council and his imprisonment until the accession of James I. It was a brave, or foolish, lecturer who introduced recent history into their formal teaching.[2]

Although the formal curriculum could have done little to foster the development of local history, the general increase in education among the gentry was an important factor in increasing their active engagement with the past. While the set texts might be religious and classical, the ability to read English and Latin enabled gentlemen (and some gentlewomen) to pursue more catholic interests in their subsequent reading. Quantifiable evidence concerning the prevalence of history reading among the late Elizabethan and early Stuart gentry is difficult to establish. Studies of the book trade provide data on how many books were printed, while inventories, accounts and library lists give some indication of who bought them. There is, however, no direct relationship between these measures and the distribution and dissemination of books. A single copy may have had many readers, as it was read aloud to a group or lent, sold or bequeathed. Marginal notes, diaries and commonplace books provide us with less-quantifiable evidence, but they do sustain the impression that there was a widespread interest in the historical works among the gentry. This impression is strengthened by the success of certain works, which by their cost or subject matter suggest a predominantly gentry readership.[3]

The extent to which individual schoolmasters or tutors may have influenced the subsequent reading habits of their pupils is impossible to assess. We know that Elizabeth I read Livy under Roger Ascham, and William Camden was clearly an important influence on Sir Robert Cotton, his pupil at Westminster. Camden also taught Godfrey Goodman, the future bishop of Gloucester, who established a lending library for the clergy and gentry within his diocese and worked for many years on a volume of church history. We know little about less-celebrated teachers. Philemon Holland, who translated Camden's *Britannia* into English in 1610, was at the time usher at Coventry Free School. Among Holland's pupils in Coventry was George, lord Berkeley. In November 1613 George received the gift of a copy of Speed's *History of Great Britain* from Smyth, his grandfather's man of business. It is likely that the choice of appropriate book for the twelve-year-old boy was influenced by his schoolmaster, who is credited with a translation of Speed's *Theatre of the Empire of Great Britain* into Latin, although the gift was also in keeping with the antiquarian Smyth's own interests. We may assume that Reginald Bainbrigg, the schoolmaster at Appleby, Westmorland, shared his interest in Roman antiquities with his pupils and showed them the collection of inscribed stones that he arranged in his house and garden. Perhaps he was accompanied on his expeditions along the line of Hadrian's Wall in 1599 and 1601 by an interested pupil or former pupil, just as Cotton accompanied William Camden on his antiquarian expeditions. The comparative obscurity of early modern schoolmasters and our knowledge that actual teaching was often in the hands of an unknown deputy means that we can say little more than that the particular scholarly interests of individual teachers were likely to have influenced the pupils they taught.[4]

While the gentry's interest in the past was stimulated by increasing access to education, the experience of university education could clearly help to develop this into outright antiquarianism. University education was far more common among local historians as a group than among the whole body of Elizabethan and early Stuart gentry. The emphasis on history as literature and on its didactic potential within the formal syllabus did not prevent future local historians from gaining an insight into other ways of studying and interpreting the past. The evolution of the tutorial system and the availability of additional facilities within the vicinity of the universities provided students with an opportunity to pursue a broad-based education beyond the confines of the formal curriculum. Richard Holdsworth, a tutor at Cambridge from around 1613 until the civil war, drew up 'Directions for a Student in the Universitie', which included a reading list of around forty books for those who attended the university not to obtain a degree but 'to get such learning as may serve for delight and ornament and such as the want whereof would speak a defect in breeding rather than scholarship'. The list covered a variety of topics, including natural philosophy, classical and English literature, classical and modern history, modern languages, travel and geography, morality and divinity, manners and courtesy, and heraldry. It included Speed's *History of Great Britain* (1611), Camden's *Remains* (1605), William Martyn's *Historie and Lives of the Kings of England From William the Conqueror Unto the End of the Raigne of Henrie the Eight* (1615), Samuel Daniel's *Collection of the History of England* extended by John Trussell (1636), and Thomas Fuller's *History of the Holy Warre* (1639). When we examine the evidence concerning the books owned by students, it supports the implication of this list that recent developments in historiography were known and appreciated within the universities.[5]

There were a number of college fellows who were actively interested in the preservation and study of manuscripts. One notable example at Oxford was Thomas Allen of Gloucester Hall, who during a long life acted as a special tutor to all who showed some interest in mathematics and science. Allen had a sizeable collection of manuscripts which covered history as well as mathematics, astronomy and philosophy. He was tutor to Robert Burton, the author of the *Anatomy of Melancholy* (1621) and brother of the Leicestershire historian. It is possible that William Burton knew Allen from his own time at Oxford, but more likely that their acquaintance arose from his brother's interest in mathematics. Allen lent Burton a fourteenth-century manuscript of the ordinances of the Knights Hospitallers. He also provided him with copies of church notes that he had collected. Allen's family came from Staffordshire, and Erdeswicke writes of him in his survey of the county as 'a man of Oxford, so well known for his virtue, knowledge, and learning, that he needs not any commendation of mine'. Given the two men's shared antiquarian interests and local associations, Gloucester Hall's reputation during Elizabeth's reign for sheltering recusants, and their mutual friendship with Camden, it would be surprising if they did not exchange manuscripts. Unfortunately, the relative paucity of evidence concerning Erdeswicke's sources makes this impossible to substantiate. After Allen's death a number of his manuscripts were inherited by another of his former students, the polymath Kenelm Digby, under whose auspices they continued to be available to antiquarian scholars.[6]

The role of a university education in developing a sense of spatial and cultural identity within the late Elizabethan and and early Stuart gentry will be discussed in chapter seven. Here it is important to emphasise the practical advantages of membership of a university, for however brief a period, to the aspiring local historian. Firstly, the universities were significant as repositories for medieval books and manuscripts. To be a member of the university was to be enabled to access this material. Although the Bodleian would grant admittance to 'gentlemen strangers' who were not Oxford men, the college libraries were jealously guarded and it was extremely difficult for outsiders to gain admittance. Secondly, important links with other scholars, collectors of manuscripts and useful future contacts were forged within the colleges of Oxford and Cambridge. Erdeswicke, for example, met the future lord chancellor Thomas Egerton, while at Brasenose College, Oxford, in the mid-1550s. This association was maintained as Egerton moved on to Lincoln's Inn, where he became friends with William Lambarde and Francis Thynne. It was through such personal contacts as these that Erdeswicke was able to establish his reputation and pursue his interests as a local historian despite his status as a convicted recusant. Two decades later a similar circle developed at Christ Church, Oxford, around Sir Philip Sydney. This included William Camden, Richard Carew and the geographer Richard Hakluyt.[7]

The emphasis that William Dugdale placed in his autobiography on his father's education at Oxford and the MA to which he was himself recommended during the civil war suggest that he considered it a disadvantage not to have been sent to university during his education. At school in Coventry his historical interests may have been stimulated by Philemon Holland. For the future local historian the reading of 'Littelton's Tenures, and some other Law-books, and History' subsequently set by his father may have been of equal practical value to a university career. However, Dugdale lacked the social contacts that such a career would have brought him, and in his early career he benefited from the graduate Burton's contacts with the wider antiquarian community.[8]

The heralds represent the professional antiquaries of the Elizabethan and early Stuart period, but their importance in the development of historiography is often overlooked. With the exception of Camden, who entered the College of Arms after he had become a noted scholar, they are considered predominantly as narrow genealogists, who were willing to be less than scrupulous when faced with the desire of the English gentry for pedigrees than reflected their status. However, the importance of genealogy in encouraging the early historical interests of many antiquaries, and the significance of the College of Arms as a repository of historical records, made the heralds an important element in the development of local history. By going out into the provinces in the performance of their duties at visitations and funerals, the heralds played a vital role in the formation of antiquarian networks which fostered the development of local history and provided a link between antiquarian activity in the regions and the metropolis.

Camden was not the only herald whose scholarly standards were respected by his contemporaries. In 1583 Robert Glover, Somerset herald, conducted the visitation of Staffordshire, and three years later he wrote and emblazoned the Erdeswicke pedigree at the request of Sampson Erdeswicke. (Some years before, Glover had stayed with William Claxton during the compilation of the visitation of Durham and later produced an extended Claxton pedigree – perhaps this was an accepted return for hospitality.) In the *View of Staffordshire*, Glover is described as 'the only sufficient man in his time for armory and descent in this land'. Although he died in 1588, his influence was felt by later antiquaries, who made use of the careful pedigrees that he had assembled. Thomas Gerard referred to him as the 'judicious' herald 'whom I dare trust'. A generation later, John Aubrey recorded, that 'I have heard Sir Wm. Dugdale say, that though Mr. Camden had the Name, yet Mr. Glover was the best Herald that did ever belong to the Office'. Erdeswicke's contemporaries among the Staffordshire gentry also benefited from the heraldic expertise and assistance of Robert Cooke, Camden's predecessor as Clarenceux. In 1591 Richard Broughton wrote to Richard Bagot, a noted local genealogist, describing Cooke as 'my verie good and auncient frendlie acquayntance ... by whose help these twentie yeres I have had many favours in his office, and private helps in knowledge'.[9]

The formal occasions for contact between the provincial gentry and the heralds were provided by visitations of counties, to ensure that arms were being used correctly, and heraldic funerals. Other occasions for contact arose when a family wished to obtain a new or altered grant of arms or to commission a heraldic pedigree. These contacts were often stimulated by an alteration in a family's circumstances, such as a rise in status, the inheritance of new land or the descent of an estate to a distant branch of a family. The herald might be commissioned to produce a pedigree in keeping with the family's higher status, to justify their quartering of a new coat of arms or to bolster the position of a new heir. The experience of having a herald working on a family's pedigree seems frequently to have acted as a stimulus to further genealogical interest. It is common to find a heraldic pedigree that has given rise to a succession of copies in the family archive, prepared for different branches of the family or recording additional information. An example of this is found in Durham, where a pedigree was prepared for the Bowes family of Aske by Edmund Knight, Norroy herald (d. 1593). This was a cadet branch of the Bowes family, who had inherited Aske by marriage to a co-heir, and the pedigree was apparently prepared to celebrate the status achieved by Sir George Bowes (d. 1580), who played a prominent role in the suppression of the Northern Rebellion. A booklet based on the pedigree relates to his brother Robert (d. 1597), an Elizabethan diplomat. It includes the epitaph of Robert's wife Eleanor (d. 1623) taken from Easby church, near Richmond, showing a prolonged interest in these records within the family.[10]

For William Burton, forced by ill health to retire from London, his contacts in the College of Arms were essential to his antiquarian interests. In 1608 he wrote to the herald Nicholas Charles for his help concerning the pedigree of Thomas, marquess of Dorset. Dorset had died in 1530, but his tomb at Astley, Warwickshire had recently been opened. It was intended to set up a new epitaph, for which an accurate exposition of his pedigree was required. Charles also provided Burton with church notes from Kent, Oxfordshire and Buckinghamshire, and copies of pedigree rolls belonging to the herald were copied by Burton into a collection that he later presented to Sir Simon Archer.[11] The assistance available to local historians from members of the College of Arms went beyond the heraldic and genealogical. William Le Neve, who became Clarenceux in 1635, had a wider interest in history than that required by his professional role. He was the author of 'A Short Account of the Life and Actions of King Edward III, and of his son Edward, Prince of Wales'. He also assisted various local historians with reference material, including Burton and Habington when increasing age and infirmity restricted the latter's movements. Although the majority of references to Le Neve by local historians refer to heraldic records such as his ordinary of arms, he also possessed other useful sources such as a cartulary (a volume into which charters and other legal documents were copied, to provide a convenient record) of Wymondham Priory, Leics.[12]

Like the colleges of Oxford and Cambridge, the College of Arms guarded its library against outsiders and personal contacts were essential for securing access. In 1568 the duke of Norfolk as earl marshal had laid down regulations specifying that a special room should be set aside for the library, which no outsider might enter unless accompanied by a herald. Although the demise of the duke shortly thereafter put the implementation of his reforms in abeyance, they were revived in 1597, and henceforth access to the library was carefully regulated. The Lancashire antiquary John Weever was fortunate to make the acquaintance of the herald Augustine Vincent when he settled in Jacobean London after travelling abroad. According to the preface of Weever's *Ancient Funerall Monuments*, he embarked on the collection and publication of a record of British funeral monuments: 'having seene ... how carefully in other Kingdomes the Monuments of the dead are preserved'. In this endeavour he was encouraged by Vincent, who gave Weever access to his own extensive collection of church notes and also provided him with 'free accesse to the Heralds Office, to write out such antiquities as I could finde for my purpose'. The assistance of a herald who was accustomed to the library would also have been a benefit to the outsider. The oldest extant catalogue was compiled by Sampson Lennard in 1618. Even with the gradual appearance of such aids, finding items of interest in this continually evolving collection represented a significant challenge.[13]

The benefits of the relationship between the heralds and local historians were not all bestowed by the former on the latter. The frequent squabbles between members of the College of Arms concerning their respective authorities and perquisites did not increase their standing among the gentry at large, especially when they resorted to abusing each other publicly through printed treatises. Nor did the cost of heraldic visitations and funerals endear them to those that had to bear the expense. While no gentleman would want his right to bear arms publicly impugned, the trouble and cost of attending the heralds to prove what no one doubted, was considered an unreasonable imposition by many local gentlemen. The expense of the heraldic funeral was even more burdensome and also placed considerable strictures on participants. (Smyth wrote a detailed account for Lord Berkeley of his wife's funeral in Coventry in 1596, because protocol forbade her husband's attendance.) Consequently, an influential section of those gentry entitled to a coat of arms turned increasingly to night burials and other methods of avoiding the need for a heraldic funeral. In these circumstances it was advantageous to the heralds to have sympathetic contacts in the provinces, who could provide them with a comfortable lodging and good company on their journeys and could defend them against their provincial critics. A sympathetic local landowner could also encourage the co-operation of their neighbours with a visitation. The influence of one local antiquary may be seen in the 1575 visitation of Durham, when nearly one-third of the pedigrees entered appear to have been registered during the herald's stay with William Claxton at Winyard.[14]

Local genealogists were also in possession of local knowledge, which could assist the heralds in their work. A collection of church notes could reveal that members of a gentry family had in the past been buried in a church remote from their current residence. Or it might contain the description of a monument which had since been defaced or removed. A gentleman might also be able to provide the herald with information from his own knowledge of the community, knowledge which was difficult to obtain elsewhere. In Augustine Vincent's copy of the 1619 Visitation of Leicestershire, there is a note added to a pedigree of the Hartop family:

> I doe doubt whither Hartop may be justified so long of Burton Lazars, which was an hospitall for Lazers and in the Crown for most part since the Dissolucion: and only fermed by them and long dwelt upon by Valentine Hartop uncle (as I take it) to Sir Edward the baronet which Valentine had issue Sir William and William had issue Thomas, whoe lately purchased the lordship of Burton in fee & were all three familiar acquaintance of mine.[15]

This note is unlikely to be contemporaneous with the visitation, since the manuscript remained in the hands of Vincent and his son John, and was consulted by a number of antiquaries before it was given to the College of Arms in 1684. Nevertheless, it does demonstrate the sort of local knowledge about the status of manors and the relationships within and between gentry families that a herald unfamiliar with the community would lack.

Naturally, a number of heralds had familial links to a particular county, and their antiquarian interests might range beyond the limits of their professional interests. The earliest county history of Cheshire, for example, was written by the herald William Smith. The lack of a clear distinction in the early modern mind between the personal and the professional make the collections of heralds difficult to evaluate. Several almost certainly deserve to be considered local historians independently of their professional role, but evidence of antiquarian activity involving future heralds can be difficult to interpret. The miscellany of East Anglian items preserved in a volume that formerly belonged to Henry Chitting suggest that he developed an interest in the history of his native county beyond the purely heraldic before he became a herald in 1618. There is, however, evidence that various members of the College of Arms had informal connections to the office before they acquired a patent from the king. Two letters to the herald painter Richard Scarlett suggest that William Wyrley was working on pedigrees for members of the College of Arms some six years before his appointment as Rouge Croix pursuivant. Similarly, the presence of 'Herald Neve' among the proposed members of Edmund Bolton's *Academ Roial* in 1617 suggests that William Le Neve was recognised as a herald before his formal appointment in 1622. There is also confusion concerning the status of deputies. Roger Dodsworth was never a formal member of the College of Arms, but he did deputise for Richard St George in the 1620s in the ordering of funerals and the preparation of funeral certificates in Yorkshire. In the year of Dodsworth's death, John Hopkinson was appointed deputy by William Riley. Since the survival of such documents as Hopkinson's deputation is rare, it is impossible to assess the extent to which local historians acted in a semi-official basis in their own regions.[16]

Despite the good relations between the heralds and local historians, the latter were concerned to avoid impinging on the purlieu of the College of Arms. In the first book of the *Survey of Cornwall* Carew wrote:

> I had also made a more paynful, then perfect collection of most of the *Cornish* Gentlemens names & Armes: But because the publishing thereof might perhaps goe accompanied with divers wrongs, to my much reverenced friends the Heralds, by thrusting my sickle into their harvest; to a great many [of] my Countrymen, whom my want of information should be forced to passe over unmentioned; and to the truth it selfe, where my report (relying upon other mens credits) might through their errour intitle me the publisher (though not the author) of falshood: I rather thought it fit altogether to omit it.

Echoing Carew, Gerard explained in the *Survey of Dorsetshire* that he had excluded pedigrees 'especiallie of moderne Families, because in my Opinion it is not fitt they should be divulged for that they might breed Emulation amongst Gentlemen' and he included the arms of the gentry only in blazon for the information of his friends the heralds and 'such as have Insight in that Facultie'. For similar reasons Burton limited the pedigrees and arms in his first edition to those of extinct families and friends 'upon whose kindnesse I have presumed'. Even this timid approach led to a rebuke from the heralds: 'our approbation grounded upon your bare assertion, without any proffe in your booke to give us satisfaction, may lay upon us such an aspertion and stayne of our reputation as we dare not with our safeties give way to it.'

The wealth of pedigrees in Burton's planned second edition, however, shows that the heralds' disapproval was not shared by the local gentry – they wanted their pedigrees included. This discrepancy between the wishes of their neighbours and the complaints of the heralds created a dilemma for local historians. Burton decided to please his neighbours, while Thomas Westcote sided with the heralds. Westcote had collected the pedigrees of 300 local families, which he might have incorporated into his history of Devon. He explained why he had not included them, using the analogy of a child, that, once burnt, learns to fear fire: 'I am not now so improvident altogether, though I was sometime, as you know, in such a business somewhat too bold, rashly to intrude myself into their sacred profession, to whom it belongs'. The concern of the heralds was in truth perhaps less with the potential inaccuracies of the genealogies produced by local historians, as with the authority of such material when it appeared in print. It has been noted that many of the Warwickshire elite failed to co-operate with the 1682–83 visitation of the county. Indeed, why should they bother once more to produce their evidences for Clarenceux's deputy, when their pedigrees had been published by the local historian who subsequently became Garter king at arms? Within a few years the practice of heraldic visitations was abandoned altogether.[17]

There were two predominant forms of public record that were of interest to local historians. The first were the legal and administrative records of Chancery, the Exchequer and so forth. The second were the ecclesiastical records held in diocesan archives. A local historian wishing to peruse such records was faced by a daunting task. There were difficulties to be overcome in both locating records and gaining access to archives. Vast numbers of legal and administrative records were held in the Tower, others were in the four treasuries of the Exchequer and the Rolls chapel at Westminster, while still others were in the offices of the Six Clerks and other officials. Despite the elaborate precautions that were taken involving multiple locks on the doors of the depositories, with the keys held by different office-holders, the preservation of the records was in a parlous state. The buildings in which they were kept were often damp, the records were in great disorder and they were frequently eaten by vermin. Moreover, members of the privy council, the Crown's legal officers and others were inclined to remove the records that they needed for a particular purpose and to never return them. The ecclesiastical archives were subject to similar problems, which were exacerbated in dioceses where the bishop was in dispute with the dean and cloister. During the period of this study, written records became increasingly important to the functioning of civil and ecclesiastical government and of the legal system, while demand for access to those records from the literate public also grew. In this environment the various officers with responsibility for the keeping and locating of public records played an important role, and it is possible to identify some individuals whose antiquarian interests were of use both to their immediate employers and the wider public.

One such individual was Thomas Talbot, a clerk in the records office of the Tower in the reign of Elizabeth I. Talbot was the younger son of a Lancashire gentry family, and was probably educated at Trinity College, Cambridge. He appears to have been working among the records of the Tower by 1573, and became clerk of the records before 1580. He was assiduous in collecting and abstracting records, and his extracts were widely used by antiquarian scholars. In *Britannia*, Camden paid tribute to him as a diligent researcher and as a 'master of our antiquities'. Talbot was a founder member of the Society of Antiquaries, and his discourses '*Of Sterling Money*' and '*Of Antiquity of Shires*' survive. His extensive abstracts and collections from the records in his charge continued to be used after his death, so that his name and expertise as an antiquary were well known to later generations of researchers. Some of his transcriptions preserved records that were subsequently lost, while others simply made the records that they contained more accessible to researchers who did not enjoy his daily access to the Tower records.[18]

Among Talbot's fellow members of the Society of Antiquaries, was Arthur Agard, who trained as a lawyer before gaining a place as a clerk in the Exchequer. He ended his life as deputy chamberlain in the Exchequer and keeper of the Exchequer records. Like Talbot, Agard was a respected antiquary, who produced a substantial collection of abstracts from records. Several of his discourses for the Society of Antiquaries also survive. His most significant contribution to antiquarian research was, however, an attempt to bring order to the Exchequer records. He later recorded how he spent a whole summer sorting out two chests of records kept in the Chapter House of Westminster cathedral. He also produced various calendars of the Exchequer records. In 1610 he completed a compendium of the records in the four treasuries of the Exchequer with the assistance of Sir Robert Cotton and Sir Walter Cope, the chamberlain of the Exchequer and himself a member of the Society of Antiquaries. Although a number of the calendars prepared by Agard were subsequently lost and some records reorganised, the manuscript catalogue he prepared was still being annotated by his successors in 1696. In 1611 Agard and George Austen compiled a catalogue of the treaties of peace and commerce made between England and other countries on the orders of Robert Cecil. Agard described the reasons for the production of the compendium of Exchequer records as 'for the King's service, and for answeringe of the Subject that repayreth to search'. The value of both his catalogues to the legal profession is indicated by their inclusion in the *Repertorie of Records* (1631), published by the attorney Thomas Powell. They were also of great value to local historians, whose access to the public records was limited by time, distance and expense. With the assistance of the catalogues they could identify which of the four treasuries should hold the records they were interested in, and whether there was a manuscript calendar available.[19]

In addition to making finding aids to the public records for which they were responsible, the keepers could also act as a clearing house for information concerning the whereabouts of other records. Like Agard, Scipio Le Squyer was a deputy chamberlain in the Exchequer, who spent much of his time compiling, finding aids and assisting lawyers, antiquaries and others to locate records. Among John Smyth's memoranda for business in London in Michaelmas term 1638, is a reminder to conduct a 'serch with Mr. Squire from 1 EI downwarde out of his abstracts: for my discription of B: hundred, eyther legall or historicall'. Through his various contacts, Le Squyer was able to compile information concerning the whereabouts of monastic records dispersed at the Dissolution. Two lists survive, detailing who had possession of a number of monastic cartularies. The first, dating from between 1618 and 1623 (George Villiers is described as a marquess) listed fourteen cartularies relating to twelve separate monastic houses. The second list was compiled five to ten years later, and added a further eighteen cartularies. The circumstances which led to the compilation of these lists is unclear. They do not include all the cartularies Le Squyer would have known about. Some of those in the office of the King's Remembrancer in the Exchequer and in Cotton's library are included – others are omitted. Whatever their purpose, the lists show how the keepers of the public records could acquire information about records in the possession of provincial gentlemen or other archives and act as conduits for that information.[20]

Despite the role of patronage in influencing public appointments, there is evidence of an attempt to provide the public records with keepers who were qualified for the role and would encourage the introduction and maintenance of order in the archives. William Bowyer apparently impressed William Cecil with his abilities as bailiff of the borough of Westminster before being preferred to the post of keeper of the records in the Tower. He was later credited with being the first keeper who attempted to bring order to the records under his charge. Bowyer produced digests of the parliament, close, charter and foreign rolls for the reigns of King John to Edward IV, making these records far more accessible. He also attempted to secure custody of the parliamentary and chancery records that were stored in the Rolls chapel, but this administratively sensible move was stymied by the master of the Rolls. In 1597, Thomas Egerton, the lord keeper and friend of Erdeswicke, appointed William Lambarde as keeper of the records in the Rolls chapel, and in 1600 Lambarde became deputy keeper of the records in the Tower. The following year he presented the queen with an account of the Tower records, his *Pandecta Rotulorum*. Robert Bowyer was secretary to Thomas Sackville, earl of Dorset, through whose influence he obtained his father's former post of keeper of the

Tower records. In 1610 he became clerk of the parliaments. His subsequent efforts in bringing order to the parliamentary records led to the recovery of the Lord's journal for 1536. In 1616 John Smyth contemplated purchasing the keepership of the Tower records from Bowyer. The value of the office was reputed to be as much as £200 per year, and the asking price was over £1,000, plus an unspecified composition with the master of the Rolls. Nothing came of this venture, whether because the price was too high or because Smyth at the time lacked a patron to assist him in securing the patent, we do not know.[21] Despite the failure of the Gloucestershire local historian to secure the post, it is apparent that in this period the men appointed to be record-keepers and clerks were increasingly interested in establishing what was to be found in the archives and how they should be preserved and exploited. This trend was followed by the parliamentary authorities during the civil war, who appointed the great legal antiquary John Selden to the office of keeper of the Tower records.

There were strong links between the records office of the Tower of London and the College of Arms, with several record-keepers also being appointed as heralds. Augustine Vincent established a reputation as a scholar and antiquary while working in the Tower records office, before entering the College of Arms in 1616. In the preface to the *Baronage of England* William Dugdale mentioned Vincent's own interest in such a project, 'for the effecting whereof, he had no small advantage by his free access to the Publick Records in the Tower of London, being then a Clerk in that Office'.[22] Sir John Borough, who trained as a common lawyer at Gray's Inn, assisted Francis Bacon by providing archival material for his *History of Henry VII* during 1621, when Bacon was exiled from London. The following year he visited Venice, where he acted for Sir Robert Cotton in the purchase of manuscripts. In 1623 he was appointed keeper of the records in the Tower, and a few months later he was appointed a herald-extraordinary through the favour of the earl marshal. In December 1623 he succeeded to the position of Norroy king of arms. This rapid promotion illustrates both Borough's reputation as an authority on historical records and the importance of patronage. It is a reflection of the growing importance of antiquarian scholarship within the college that Borough eventually became Garter king at arms, the senior herald, in 1634. At around the time of Borough's appointment as keeper of the records, William Ryley obtained one of the clerkships under him. Ryley's rise was less meteoric than his superior, but it followed a similar trajectory. He had trained at the Middle Temple before entering the Tower records office, and in 1633 he followed Borough to the College of Arms on his appointment as Bluemantle poursuivant. In 1641 he was promoted to be Lancaster herald. Both Borough and Ryley accompanied the king to Oxford, but in 1643 Ryley obtained a royal warrant to return to London in order to protect the Tower records during Borough's absence.

He served as clerk of the records under John Selden, and was proposed for the replacement post when the keepership was abolished in 1651. At the Restoration he and his son became deputies to the new keeper, William Prynne.[23]

We know little about the keepers of ecclesiastical archives, although there are occasional references to them among the papers and correspondence of local historians. Dugdale mentioned 'Mr. Lathom, who is a lover of antiquities and Official to the Deane', who promised him access to the Dean's Register at Lichfield. In Somerset Sir Edward Rodney discussed the records of Wells cathedral with Dr Ralph Barlow, the dean and godfather to Rodney's son, and Dr Pearce, a prebendary of the cathedral. Two local historians, Dodsworth and Somner, were the sons of ecclesiastical registrars, and Somner was himself appointed a registrar at Canterbury cathedral by Laud. For the most part, however, those responsible for the day-to-day management of ecclesiastical archives are buried in obscurity. What is apparent is that gaining access to these records was comparatively straightforward, although officials of rival jurisdiction could experience difficulties – as reported by John Hooker, chamberlain of Exeter. Knowledge of what the archives contained was, however, limited. In 1638, when he had been researching the history of Leicestershire for three decades, Burton admitted that he had not used the wills at Leicester because he had not known they were available. If he had known of them, he was sure his friend Sir John Lambe, the dean of Arches, would have secured his access. Even known recusants were able to use the ecclesiastical archives without any apparent problem. A certain respect for the scholarly activities of recusant antiquaries is suggested by the permission granted to Erdeswicke in 1575 to go home and fetch his books before being committed to the custody of the bishop of Worcester. Subsequently, Erdeswicke made use of the records held at Lichfield. For Habington the cartularies of Worcester cathedral were an invaluable resource, not only for his treatise on the church of Worcester from its foundation to the Reformation, but also for his wider county history. He must have made many visits to the cathedral registry, and in February 1638 he offered to accompany Archer there, 'wheare I am acquaynted with the Clarkes'.[24]

Not all the local historians considered in this study negotiated the maze of early modern public records in person. Some relied on extracts from the records, which circulated widely but were of varied quality. Others utilised scribes, in the way that modern academics employ research assistants. However, some understanding of the organisation of the records was necessary to locate what was required and contacts among those responsible for their upkeep were useful, even for those who never ventured into the archives themselves.

While the value of antiquarian interests and expertise to the early modern herald is readily appreciated, their usefulness to common lawyers may be less immediately apparent. Yet the number of practising lawyers who were members of antiquarian circles, and the high incidence of legal training among subsequent local historians, are highly suggestive of a link. The most prominent legal antiquary was John Selden, but, among local historians, William Lambarde, William Burton, John Smyth and Sir Simonds D'Ewes were all barristers. Many other local historians had attended one of the inns of court as part of their education, although some like Sir Edward Rodney may have 'only saluted the Law a farre off' and misspent their time.[25] A brief consideration of the nature of legal training and the conduct of litigation in this period will serve to indicate why an aptitude for antiquarian research could be useful for an early modern lawyer or a gentleman embroiled in litigation.

The changes experienced by the legal profession in the Tudor period stimulated an interest in antiquarian research among many common lawyers. The fundamental force for change was the increase in litigation and the consequent growth in the size of the legal profession. The increase in the number of common lawyers enhanced the influence of the inns of court, necessitated changes in the nature of legal training and allowed the development of specialisation. At the same time, the legal profession developed a more rigid structure, with the division between attorneys and counsellors gaining greater definition. Attorneys followed the procedural aspects of a suit, while counsellors presented the legal arguments in court. At the end of the sixteenth century, a call to the bar of one of the four inns of court became the sole qualification for practice as a counsellor in the royal courts. The status of Gray's Inn, Lincoln's Inn and the Inner and Middle Temples as educational establishments was thus greatly enhanced.[26]

During the same period the inns of court were increasingly seen as institutions where young gentlemen with no intention of becoming practising lawyers could acquire a useful smattering of legal knowledge. Shortly before his execution in 1572 Thomas, duke of Norfolk, advised his son and heir, Philip, earl of Arundel, that after a year or two at Cambridge: '[if] you spend your time in some house of the law, there is nothing that will prove more to your commodity, considering how for the time you shall have continual business about your own law affairs; and thereby also, if you spend your time well, you shall be ever after able to judge in your own causes.'[27] Attendance at an inn also provided an opportunity to make invaluable personal contacts among leading lawyers and fellow students, and to take advantage of the varied educational and social facilities of the capital. In his family history, written shortly after the Restoration, Sir Christopher Guise described his time at the Middle Temple some twenty-five years before: 'in the law I made no progresse, butt pleased myselfe with poetry, some mathematickes, and a little history'. Between 1620 and the civil war, more than half the Warwickshire justices had attended an inn for part of their education. The opportunity for foreign travel as a means of completing a gentleman's education was available to only a small minority of the wealthy and well connected in this period. For the remainder, the inns of court provided a more accessible finishing school. While many students had little interest in pursuing serious legal study, it must have required great will-power to remain totally unaffected by the immersion in a legal atmosphere that the communal life of the inns represented.[28]

In the Tudor period the written word became an increasingly important element in legal training and practice. The invention of printing had made it possible for legal practitioners to have ready access to written authorities, such as the summation of medieval land law known as Littleton's *Tenures* (which Dugdale's father made him read) and the 260 volumes of year-books that were published by 1560. By the end of Henry VIII's reign the medieval year-books, which were apparently produced by relatively minor legal practi-tioners, had been replaced by a new form of law report produced by influential counsellors and judges. The most important of these, such as the collections of Dyer, Plowden and Coke were published, while a number of others circu-lated in manuscript. Increasingly in the practice of common law, arguments based on reason were superseded by arguments based on authority. This increased significance of the written word enhanced the value of documentary evidence in litigation and encouraged lawyers to learn how to locate and use that evidence effectively. As medieval and Tudor records became increasingly important in legal practice, the ability to locate, understand and exploit those records became a valuable skill.[29]

There are several local historians, whose antiquarian interests emerged during their exposure to the legal world of London. For those students who were intending to pursue a legal career, the training was long. Before advancing to the degree of barrister the majority of students were required to have been members of their inn for a minimum of seven years, and substantially longer periods of training were not uncommon. This long period of training required students to spend a great deal of time in the capital, immersed in an environ-ment which was placing increasing emphasis on the use of written records and with access to the repositories of the public records. During this period they frequently became involved in the conduct of the legal affairs of their families. William Burton began collecting copies of records relating to his own manors as a law student, and the *Description of Leicestershire* had its origins in this period of his life. John Smyth's studies at the Middle Temple were supported financially by the Berkeley family. In return he acted not only as Lord Berkeley's solicitor, but also spent many hours searching among the records for material relating to Berkeley manors. Much of this material was subsequently included in the *Lives of the Berkeleys*. Some six decades later Thomas Estcourt copied notes on Wiltshire history into his legal commonplace book while studying at Lincoln's Inn. Among Estcourt's friends during this period was Sir Robert

Atkyns, the future historian of Gloucestershire. In contrast Thomas Habington's antiquarian interests were not apparently stimulated by his sojourn at
Gray's Inn in the 1580s, but developed when he 'indured a most troulesome
Sute which exceeded in leangthe the Seyge of Troy' in the Exchequer in the
reign of James I. Obliged to remain in London during the law terms to ensure
that his case was properly conducted, he passed his time gathering material
relating to Worcestershire from the Exchequer records. The volume of litigation in this period led many provincial gentlemen like Habington to become
involved in cases before the Westminster courts. As a result of spending part
of his education at one of the inns, a gentleman might well have more experience of these courts than a provincial attorney, who was likely to have learnt his
trade by apprenticeship. Consequently, gentlemen with a smattering of legal
knowledge frequently became involved in the day-to-day conduct of their legal
affairs. This stimulated an awareness of the significance of medieval records
in many, and a wider antiquarian interest in a significant proportion.[30]

For a gentleman engaging in litigation, an understanding of the significance of the records in his muniment room could facilitate the management
of his legal affairs. For a law student it was increasingly possible to build
a career on the possession of antiquarian skills. The term that Smyth and
others most often used to describe his role was 'solicitor'. Originally this term
described not a class of legal practitioners, but one of the activities that an
apprentice at law performed. In 1600 the role of the solicitor in this limited
sense was described as 'to put the attorneys in remembrance of their business
and to pay them, without the doing of which things they would not look to
the cause'. In the seventeenth century, the term came to be used in a wider
sense to describe someone who took overall responsibility for the preparation
and conduct of legal business on behalf of another. This was the role Smyth
performed for lord Berkeley, preparing legal cases and briefing barristers in
much the same way as a modern solicitor. John Selden was similarly described
by Aubrey as having been solicitor to the earl of Kent. The role of solicitor to
a great landowner was particularly appropriate to someone like Selden, who
was excellent at preparing evidence but 'no eminent practiser at Barre'. This is
not to suggest that antiquarian skills were not useful to practising barristers.
The success of such legal figures as Sir Edward Coke, Sir Robert Berkeley, Sir
Randolph Crewe and Sir John Doddridge is evidence that antiquarian skills
were useful in all branches of the law.[31]

The Elizabethan Society of Antiquaries brought heralds, record-keepers
and antiquarian lawyers together into a single body. The society was founded
around the time of the first publication of Camden's *Britannia*, and appears to
have remained active until 1608. The society met regularly in London during
the law terms. The meetings were usually held in the heralds' office in Derby
House and occasionally in the house of William Dethick, Garter king at arms.

Members of the society ate together and the introduction of uninvited guests was prohibited. At each meeting it was customary for two questions to be propounded, for consideration when the society next met, and all members were expected to contribute.[32] The majority of papers prepared for presentation at the meetings have not survived, but there are over a hundred discourses identified as written for the society. These relate to thirty-eight separate meetings. The propounded questions examined a range of subjects of antiquarian interest: the currency, heraldry, origin and privileges of various offices and institutions; the antiquity of English cities, castles, towns and so forth.

The precise membership of the society is not known, but the majority belonged to professions requiring some expertise in the use of historical records: heralds, keepers of the public records, and lawyers. An exceptionally high proportion of the known members were graduates, but there are no clerics who were indisputably members. Two lawyers, William Hakewill and Francis Tate, were among those who served as registrar for the society, while the surviving papers suggest that Arthur Agard was its most active member. The majority of members were metropolitan or at least resident in London during the law terms. The local historians who form the subject of this study had little direct involvement in the society. Sir Henry Spelman, James Strangeman and Richard Carew were members, but have left little or no evidence of their contributions to meetings. Little is known about Strangeman, but as land and office holders in their respective counties both Spelman and Carew had responsibilities which would have kept them from being frequent attenders. Carew and Spelman did not begin to correspond until after the demise of the society. The way in which their correspondence was initiated shows that, though both were members, their paths did not cross at meetings sufficiently to establish a close acquaintance. Noted local historians visiting London during the law terms may have been invited to attend a meeting. Erdeswicke is known to have been invited to a meeting in 1598 and a copy of an invitation directed to Richard St George exists among the papers of Henry Ferrers. It seems likely that the county histories of Staffordshire and Cornwall originated as a form of discourse for the society from members unable to attend regularly, but this is conjectural.[33]

It is difficult to gauge the influence of the society on those antiquaries who were not members. Its meetings were private, although the discourses presented apparently circulated in manuscript. Several discourses survive among the antiquarian papers of Sir Christopher Hatton, and others can be identified in the volumes left by Sir Matthew Hale to the library of Lincoln's Inn. (Hale was one of John Selden's executors, which may explain the presence of the society's discourses among his papers.) This suggests that the society had an indirect influence on later generations of antiquaries, even before the publication of their discourses by Thomas Hearne in the eighteenth century. However, the circulation of the discourses does not appear to have been as extensive as that of many other contemporary treatises. The questions propounded by the society also influenced the published works of its members. Stow's digression on the currency in his section on the Tower of London in the *Survey of London*, for example, can be linked to the society's consideration of sterling money in 1590.[34] The existence of the society is evidence of how various factors encouraging the development of scholarly antiquarian activity coalesced in the capital in the last twenty years of Elizabeth's reign. The extent to which this development met with official approval is uncertain. A petition for the incorporation of the society as an academy endowed with a library to be donated by Sir Robert Cotton did not receive the approval of the queen. Like her Stuart successors Elizabeth was suspicious of the potentially subversive ideas that could arise from discussions concerning the origins of institutions and the extent of their rights and privileges. No incorporation was forthcoming.

According to Spelman, the society flourished for around twenty years, but declined as leading members died or left London. In 1614 some former members attempted to revive the society. The attempt was abandoned, when it was learnt that James I 'took a little Mislike of our Society, not being informed that we had resolv'd to decline all Matters of State'. In view of the role played by Sir Robert Cotton and John Selden in Jacobean parliaments, the king's concern is not difficult to understand. Shortly afterwards the catholic antiquary Edmond Bolton proposed the establishment of a royal academy, whose membership would include antiquaries, heralds, scientists, poets, scholars and royal officials. The relative absence of lawyers from Bolton's list of 'essentials' or working members of the academy has been seen as representing a decline in antiquarian interests at the inns of court. This is not the case. The continued interest of leading legal figures in antiquarianism is demonstrated by the presence of Hakewill, then the queen's solicitor; Sir James Ley, attorney to the court of Wards; and Sir John Davies, among those named by Spelman as attempting to revive the Society of Antiquaries in 1614. Bolton's list was far from comprehensive. It was biased towards his personal friends, fellow catholics and sympathisers, and men from the gentry circles in Leicestershire, Herefordshire and Worcestershire with which he was associated. It is possible that the minimisation of the role of legal figures was intended to allay the king's fears concerning the subversive potential of antiquarian research. In the event, Bolton's proposal came to nothing, and the revival of the Society of Antiquaries had to await the coming of another age. In the meantime the interests reflected by the society were increasingly pursued by local historians in the provinces.

NOTES

1 H. Jewell, *Education in Early Modern England* (London: Macmillan, 1998), chapter 2; M. Curtis, *Oxford and Cambridge in Transition 1558–1642* (Oxford: Clarendon Press, 1959), pp. 86–94, 120.

2 M. McKisack, *Medieval History in the Tudor Age* (Oxford: Clarendon Press, 1971), chapter 2; J.H.M. Salmon, 'Precept, example, and truth: Degory Wheare and the *ars historica*', in D. Kelley and D. Sacks (eds), *The Historical Imagination in Early Modern Britain* (Cambridge: Cambridge University Press, 1997), p. 28; Francis Bacon, *Essays Including His Moral and Historical Works* (London: Frederick Warne, 1885), p. 178.

3 For an exhaustive exploration of this subject, see Woolf, *Reading History in Early Modern England*.

4 *Smyth Papers*, vol. 2, fo. 48; vol. 3, fo. 8; F. Haverfield, 'Notes on Reginald Bainbrigg of Appleby, on William Camden and on some Roman inscriptions', *Transactions of the Cumberland and Westmorland Antiquarian and Archaeological Society, New Series* 11 (1911), pp. 343–78.

5 Curtis, *Oxford and Cambridge in Transition*, pp. 131–3; for examples of student book ownership, see *Smyth Papers*, vol. 5, fos 32–3, 35; V. Larminie (ed.), *The Undergraduate Account Book of John and Richard Newdigate, 1618–1621* (London: Camden Society, 4th ser. 39, 1990).

6 Burton, *Leicestershire*, p. 85; B.L., Egerton 3510, fo. 20; Erdeswicke, *Staffordshire*, p. 17.

7 J. Butt, 'The facilities for antiquarian studies in the seventeenth century', *Essays and Studies* 24 (1938), pp. 64–7; L. Knafla (ed.), *Law and Politics in Jacobean England* (Cambridge: Cambridge University Press, 1977), pp. 42, 48.

8 Hamper, *Dugdale*, p. 7.

9 J. Verasanso, 'The Staffordshire heraldic visitations: their nature and function', *Midland History* 26 (2001), pp. 128–43; Robert Surtees, *The History and Antiquities of the County Palatine of Durham*, four volumes (1816–40), vol. 1, p. clii; Erdeswicke, *Staffordshire*, p. 333; Gerard, *Somerset*, p. 79; Aubrey, *Brief Lives*, p. 52; A.G. Petti (ed.), *Roman Catholicism in Elizabethan and Jacobean Staffordshire* (Collections for a History of Staffordshire, 4th ser. 9, 1979), p. 51.

10 Durham C.R.O., D/St/C1/1/2.

11 Warwickshire C.R.O., CR2598/1; B.L., Egerton 3510, fos 76, 81, 86v, 91; S.B.T., DR37/Vol. 44.

12 Archer, *Correspondence*, fo. 331; Staffordshire C.R.O., D649/4/3 – the Burton manuscript is unpaginated, but the entries are arranged in alphabetical order by place-name – hereafter Burton, *Revised*, General Introduction; Smyth, *Berkeley Mss*, vol. 1, pp. 175, 208, 214, 226, 268; E.M. Thompson (ed.), *Correspondence of the Family Hatton*, two volumes (London: Camden Society, 1878), vol. 1, pp. 4–6.

13 T. Woodcock and J. Robinson, *The Oxford Guide to Heraldry* (Oxford: Oxford University Press, 1988), p. 145; J. Weever, *Ancient Funerall Monuments* (London: T. Harper, 1631), To the Reader.

14 McKisack, *Medieval History in the Tudor Age*, p. 151; Heal and Holmes, *The Gentry of England and Wales*, pp. 28–9; C. Gittings, *Death, Burial and the Individual in Early Modern England* (London: Routledge, 1984), chapter 8; Smyth, *Berkeley Mss*, vol. 2, pp. 388–91; Surtees, *The History and Antiquities of the County Palatine of Durham*, vol. 1, pp. 5–6.

15 College of Arms, Vincent 127, fo. 32.

16 MacCulloch, 'Henry Chitting's Suffolk collections', pp. 103–28; College of Arms, Vincent 94, fos 353, 359; E.M. Portal, 'The Academ Roial of King James I', *Proceedings of the British Academy* (1915–16), pp. 189–208; W.T. Lancaster (ed.), *Letters Addressed to Ralph Thoresby* (Thoresby Society, 1912), pp. 198–201.

17 Richard Carew, *The Survey of Cornwall* (London, 1602), hereafter Carew, *Cornwall*, p. 65; Gerard, *Dorset*, pp. 127–8; Burton, *Leicestershire*, To the Reader; Nichols, *History of Leicestershire*, vol. 2(2), p. 842; Thomas Westcote, *A View of Devonshire in MDCXXX*, G. Oliver and P. Jones (eds) (Exeter: W. Roberts, 1845), p. 455; P. Styles, *Studies in Seventeenth Century West Midlands History* (Kineton, Warwickshire: Roundwood Press, 1978), pp. 108–49.

18 B.L., Harley 2223; B.L., Cotton, Vespasian D, XVII.

19 Agard's catalogue is printed in F. Palgrave (ed.), *The Ancient Kalendars and Inventories of the Treasury of His Majesty's Exchequer*, three volumes (1836), vol. 2, pp. 311–35; McKisack, *Medieval History in the Tudor Age*, pp. 85–93.

20 R. Ovenden, 'Scipio Le Squyer and the fate of monastic cartularies in the early seventeenth century', *The Library, Sixth Series* 13 (1991), pp. 323–37; Glos. C.R.O., D8887/13611, fo. 19v.

21 *Smyth Papers*, vol. 5, fo. 22. George, lord Berkeley, was a minor in 1616.

22 Dugdale, *The Baronage of England*, preface.

23 D.R. Woolf, 'John Selden, John Borough and Francis Bacon's *History of Henry VII*, 1621', *Huntingdon Library Quarterly* 47 (1984), pp. 47–53.

24 Hamper, *Dugdale* pp. 159–60; B.L., Additional MS 34239, fos 6v–7; Nichols, *Leicestershire*, vol. 2(2), p. 843; J. Dasent (ed.), *Acts of the Privy Council 1575–7*, thirty-two volumes (London: Stationery Office, 1890–1907), p. 18; Society of Antiquaries, Mss 99, fo. 40; Archer, *Correspondence*, fo. 209.

25 B.L., Additional MS 34239 – Rodney was a student at the Middle Temple, before becoming involved in the marital escapades of his kinsman Sir William Seymour and Arbella Stuart.

26 W.R. Prest, *The Inns of Court under Elizabeth I and the Early Stuarts* (London: Longman, 1972); W.R. Prest, *The Rise of The Barristers* (Oxford: Clarendon Press, 1986).

27 D. Starkey, *Rivals in Power* (London: Macmillan, 1990), p. 192.

28 G. Davies (ed.), *Autobiography of Thomas Raymond and Memoirs of the Family of Guise of Elmore, Gloucestershire* (London: Camden Society, 3rd ser. 28, 1917), p. 119; A. Hughes, *Politics, Society and Civil War in Warwickshire* (Cambridge: Cambridge University Press, 1987), pp. 347–51.

29 C. Stebbings (ed.), *Law Reporting in Britain* (London: Hambledon, 1995).

30 Glos. C.R.O., D1571/F115 – Estcourt died in 1668; Habington, *Worcestershire*, vol. 1, p. 35.

31 Smyth, *Berkeley Mss*, vol. 2, p. 333; J. Hunter, *Three Catalogues* (London: 1838), pp. 120–1; J.H. Baker, 'Solicitors and the law of maintenance 1590–1640', *Cambridge Law Journal* (1973), pp. 72–3; Aubrey, *Brief Lives*, p. 271.

32 J. Evans, *History of the Society of Antiquaries* (Oxford: Oxford University Press, 1956); McKisack, *Medieval History in the Tudor Age*, chapter 7; L. Van Norden, 'Sir Henry

Spelman on the chronology of the Elizabethan College of Antiquaries', *Huntingdon Library Quarterly* 13(2), (1949–50), pp. 131–60.

33 R.J. Schoek, 'The Elizabethan Society of Antiquaries and men of law', *Notes and Queries* 199 (1954), pp. 417–21; T. Hearne (ed.), *A Collection of Curious Discourses*, two volumes (1771) includes the surviving discourses presented at the meeting; Elizabeth K. Berry, *Henry Ferrers: an early Warwickshire antiquary* (Dugdale Society, occasional papers 16, 1965), p. 28.

34 Stow, *London*, pp. 48–53.

Chapter 3

The development of
regional networks

I n his description of the decline of the Elizabethan Society of Antiquaries,
Sir Henry Spelman referred to 'many of the chief Supporters hereof either
dying or withdrawing themselves from London into the Country'.[1] Despite
the importance of contacts on a national level for individual local historians, it
was within the regions that the shape and content of local history was forged.
These were works that grew out of the gentry society in which their authors
lived; they described a largely idealised and nostalgic version of that society and
articulated the concerns of a significant section of the English gentry before
and in the aftermath of the civil war. This chapter will explore the regional
networks that supported the development of local history and how an individual's social and religious status influenced membership of such networks.
This I will do by looking at specific local historians, who occupied different
social strata within the gentry and represented a variety of religious views.

In tracing networks of local historians, the extent and richness of the available evidence varies greatly. The most straightforward evidence is to be found
in their correspondence. The survival of a large volume of correspondence
concerning antiquarian matters written to and by the Warwickshire antiquary
Sir Simon Archer is extremely useful in tracing antiquarian activity in the
Midlands from around 1628 and is supported by an extensive family archive
held at the Shakespeare Birthplace Trust. A large proportion of William
Dugdale's correspondence was published in the nineteenth century and, in
combination with the detailed footnotes of the *Antiquities of Warwickshire*, can
be used to recreate the social and intellectual setting in which that work was
created. The archive of John Smyth in the Gloucestershire County Record
Office is dominated by the legal and estate affairs of the Berkeley family, but
does include a number of letters which cast light upon his antiquarian activity.
Again this information is supported by other documents and the extensive
footnotes in his works, which acknowledge the sources of those documents

he used from outside the archive at Berkeley castle. For the majority of local historians, little or no correspondence survives, and other forms of evidence must be used.

The reconstruction of manuscript networks for local history may be approached from two directions.[2] Firstly, there are the copies of local histories, or extracts from them, found in gentry collections and commonplace books. Occasionally these include notes indicating their provenance. The alternative approach is to identify where and how local historians obtained their sources. By the end of the period covered by this study, it was becoming usual for local historians to acknowledge the sources of the documents they used in footnotes. This was often supplemented in the text by appreciative comments concerning the kindness of local gentlemen for allowing them access to their archives. In earlier works footnotes were not used and there is often no indication within the text concerning the source of a quoted document. In these cases we are largely reliant on any manuscript notes that survive. Antiquarian notebooks can be a fascinating resource, but they must be analysed with caution. It is not unusual for a notebook to include a title page giving a date of compilation, but this can be misleading, as such records were compiled over several years and added to intermittently thereafter. The title page may alternatively have the date not of original compilation, but of copying (see figure 2). The blank pages of a manuscript prepared for one purpose might then be used for rough notes or pedigrees collected much later. Therefore it can be difficult to date when a local historian had access to a particular source. In a volume recording the arms of the northern gentry, apparently begun in the 1640s, Christopher Towneley acknowledged the use of Erdeswicke's records for the pedigree of Aston of Aston, Cheshire, and of a collection compiled by Robert Glover in 1584. He appears to have access to the Erdeswicke material through a copy retained by the Astons, but it is not recorded where he saw the Glover manuscript. The source of his list of the Yorkshire gentry in 1590 is not acknowledged, but may be presumed to have been derived from Dodsworth's manuscripts. In addition to providing information about their access to sources, antiquarian notebooks also contain marginal notes indicating other contacts, such as companions on visits to certain churches, or informants who could verify particular information. A volume of church notes compiled by Burton records not only his own expeditions to particular churches with the appropriate date, but also the heraldic notes provided by other antiquaries, local gentry and clergy.[3]

Even the footnotes in the best-referenced antiquarian works of this period do not allow us to trace with certainty the precise sources used. Many medieval sources, such as Domesday, the *Nomina Villarum*, monastic registers and the works of medieval authors, are referred to simply by name and do not indicate whether an original or transcript was used. In the absence of other

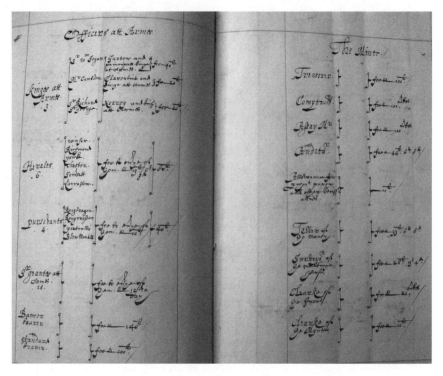

Figure 2 Extract from a Book of Officers, dated 1627 on the title page
but copied from an earlier manuscript, as the list of heralds shows.

evidence, it is impossible to be sure on the basis of the use of a particular
source that a local historian had contact with the owner of the original. It has,
for example, been posited that Thomas Gerard was acquainted with William
Burton, because he quoted excerpts from Leland's *Itinerary* in his account of
Somerset. However, we know that Burton allowed other antiquaries to make
transcripts of the Leland manuscripts, and that these circulated within the
antiquarian community. No relationship between Gerard and Burton can be
supported on this evidence alone. Indeed, given that Gerard refers to Burton
and the *Description of Leicestershire* on various occasions in his text without
mentioning any friendship between them, it seems unlikely that they knew
each other. This conclusion is supported by the lack of any reference to Gerard
in Burton's church notes in relation to his research into the arms of Polydore
Vergil at Wells cathedral. Both Burton and Gerard had access to documents
in the possession of the herald Richard St George. Henry St George, Richard's son, was involved in the visitation of the western counties in the early
1620s, and Gerard referred to his friends among the heralds in his *Survey of
Dorsetshire*.[4] It is entirely possible that it was through the heralds that Gerard

saw a copy of the Leland manuscripts. Alternatively, since a copy of Gerard's account of Somerset found its way into Hatton's archive, it is possible that the contact was through Dugdale. Unlike Burton, Dugdale did have links with the West Country, but unfortunately we know little about his antiquarian activities before Gerard's death in 1634.

In what follows I have adopted the approach recommended by Gervase Holles, of affirming nothing that I have not seen warranted by record. If it seems likely that two antiquaries knew each other or were aware of each other's work, I suggest the possibility. However, I make no assumptions on the basis that it seems likely or even inevitable that they knew each other. The case of Thomas Habington and Thomas, lord Brudenell sounds a warning against any complacency concerning the likelihood that men of similar interests moving within a particular social circle must become aware of their affinity. Habington and Brudenell were both catholics and members of a network of recusant families within the Midlands, linked by ties of religion and marriage. Brudenell was married to Mary, the daughter of Sir Thomas Tresham. Another of Tresham's daughters was married to William Parker, lord Monteagle, whose own sister was married to Habington. Yet Habington tells us that when he enquired among the heralds concerning the family of Sir John Blacket, 'they toulde mee the Lord Brudenell as an heyre quartered hys Armes, whereuppon addressinge mee to hys Lordship, hee showed mee hys petegree'. This demonstrates the role of the heralds in facilitating contacts between antiquaries, and reminds us not to assume that a local historian's interests and preoccupations were inevitably known to all his acquaintances.[5]

A further note of caution must be sounded in relation to the use of local historians' references to identify their contacts and sources. Footnotes identify the owner of the document in question, but that does not necessarily mean that the local historian was personally acquainted with the owner or had direct access to the document. Occasionally, it is obvious that things are not as they appear. From Dugdale's footnotes it would appear that Thomas Dilke of Maxstoke castle, Warwickshire, provided access to his papers for the *Antiquities of Warwickshire*. The date 1609 would appear to be a misprint, since Dugdale was only four years old. From some of Burton's surviving notes, however, we discover that the date relates to when he took notes from the Maxstoke castle muniments, and that Dugdale seems to have used these notes, not the originals. It is likely that Dugdale also used Burton's notes taken in 1607 from the papers of Thomas Astley of Wolvey, but the evidence in this case is more equivocal. Furthermore, although documents were invariably referenced by antiquaries as belonging to men, access was often controlled by a woman. In 1627 Theophila Coke was provided with a large number of documents from Berkeley castle archive for use in a court case concerning the manor of Portbury. Had a local historian consulted these papers, the footnote reference would certainly have been either to Theophila's brother, lord Berkeley, or to her husband. Nevertheless, Smyth's letter listing the papers he was sending, makes it clear that he was entrusting them to Theophila's personal care. Women would often control access to the papers of the heir to an estate while a minor. When Sir John Preston died, Dugdale heard that the wardship of his heir had been awarded to Mrs Morgan. She intended to live at Weston, Warwickshire and Dugdale hoped 'to imploy some freind to her touching those old evidences which I desire to see'. Widows might also control the papers of their late husbands. One pedigree noted by Burton was taken from a book compiled in the fifteenth century, belonging to 'Johane Willington of Hurley widow'. Such women played an important role in genealogical research, which is concealed from us by the footnotes of antiquarian works.[6]

The role of servants in controlling access to their employers' archives is unrecognised in antiquarian footnotes, and a number of important relationships have almost certainly gone unrecorded. However, the dual role of John Smyth as both historian and man of business to the Berkeleys enables us to gain some insight into the role of stewards and other servants in local historical research. As their man of business, Smyth was responsible for the Berkeley muniments and acted as a repository of legal knowledge about their estates. As such, he would have been a useful contact for local historians and for gentlemen with land that was or had been part of the estate of the Berkeleys and their ancestors, whatever Smyth's personal interest in antiquarian research. This is suggested by a letter he wrote to Arthur Gregory of Stivichall, Coventry in 1599. Gregory was a fellow lawyer who had served as coroner in Coventry, and feodary for Warwickshire. Like many of his contemporaries he was obsessed with his pedigree and had managed to persuade the College of Arms to allow him to quarter the coats of Marmion and Segrave with his own, although he did not represent the main line of descent. In 1580 he purchased part of the manor of Caludon, a former Segrave manor, from lord Berkeley, who was also descended from this medieval family. Gregory's researches into the Segrave pedigree were utilised by Smyth in his own research into lord Berkeley's feudal rights, while Gregory hoped to trace deeds relating to his manor of Alspath in the Berkeley archives. In relation to this, Smyth wrote:

> for the deedes your letter mentioneth; of my creditt; I will not be unmyndfull theirof: and I have occasion of other busines of my lo: to ransacke every corner in his study, as soone as certayne gentlemen (with whom he is nowe on huntynge) are gone: And besides within theis ten dayes I goe to Berkley castle to search for evidence their: where I am in good hope to satisfy both you and my selfe. And of my faith your note shall not depart my pockett.

In return for such dedication to Gregory's interest, Smyth was hoping for some practical recompense. The jury's verdict had gone against Smyth in a case which he had been pursuing for lord Berkeley at the Coventry assizes. Smyth had no intention of accepting the verdict, but intended to 'persecute them to the end of the world for their perjurye'. As part of this persecution, he wanted Gregory to prosecute a Coventry lawyer who had opposed the Berkeley case, for having allegedly accused Gregory of forgery: 'Hee said openly that you had corrupted the Priors booke, which nowe remayneth in the Exchequer'. Smyth urged Gregory to 'lett him speedyly bee arrested'.[7] This letter shows how relationships could be built upon mutual antiquarian and legal interests.

Through his involvement in one particular local lawsuit, it is possible to see how Smyth utilised his position as a respected legal historian within his local community to advance his own research. The case revolved around the question of whether the township of Hill was within the parish of Berkeley, and who held the right of presentation. The appropriation of the church and vicarage of Berkeley belonged to the dean and chapter of Bristol, who claimed the rights to the tithe of Hill and the choice of incumbent. This was opposed by the lord of the manor, Edward Fust, who had installed his own candidate as vicar. In 1635 Edward Chetwynd, dean of Bristol and vicar of Berkeley, applied to the Berkeleys for permission to ask Smyth, their 'worthy, wise and carefull Steward', to search for evidence on his behalf in the archives of Berkeley castle and to entrust him with 'such parcells of Evidences and Records as ... [he] shall finde, and in his wisdome thinke meete to have communicated and produced'. This was granted and, following the receipt of written instructions, Smyth delivered various pieces of evidence to Chetwynd. At the same time Smyth instructed his clerk, while in London on legal business, to inspect for Edward Fust some deeds relating to the manor of Hill. These deeds were in the possession of Sir Robert Poyntz, whose father had sold the manor to Fust's father. Smyth noted that in this way he would find out what was in the deeds belonging to Poyntz. He subsequently used these deeds in his account of Hill in the *Description of the Hundred of Berkeley*. In his account of Berkeley in the *Description*, Smyth also mentioned the case, which had gone against Chetwynd, 'but unjustly, as I and others then conceived: and not unlikely therefore to come about heereafter, if Doctor Chetwind live a yeare about, which in his owne opinion hee is not like to doe'. (Chetwynd died in May 1639).[8]

Not all Smyth's involvement with the antiquarian research of the local gentry revolved around lawsuits, as may be seen through an examination of his relations with Roger Kemys of Wickwick in Frampton Cotterell, Glos., and his son Arthur. Roger Kemys was a prominent local gentleman and justice of the peace, who served Henry, lord Berkeley as receiver and constable of Berkeley castle. He appears to have been the owner of a royal pedigree from William the Conqueror to Elizabeth I, which may have been his own compilation. In 1606 Kemys took notes on the heraldry to be found in thirteen churches in the vicinity of his home and in the parlour of the manor house at Codrington. The following year he incorporated these into a 'Collectione of some Antiquitie of the County of Gloucester with the Armes of Sonderye knightes, esquires and Gentlemen of the said County collected in the year of our Lorde 1607. parte out of A Booke of Mr Smyths of Nyblye And part of my owne collection'. The emphasis of the volume is heraldic, including not only the church notes but coloured drawings of 178 contemporary coats of arms arranged to reflect the social hierarchy of the county, and fifty-seven drawings taken from a four-teenth-century roll of arms belonging to Sir Thomas Seymour of Frampton Cotterell. The non-heraldic content included an *inspeximus* of Kingswood Forest; a copy of an inquisition from the reign of Edward II; and some tax-collector's accounts from the reign of Henry III. Kemys continued to collect material after the initial compilation of the notebook, and Smyth, who was spending much of his time in London at this period, was a useful source. In 1608 Kemys had occasion to write to Smyth on matters to do with the Berkeley estate, but he appended a personal note to his friend: 'I pray you forget not Wykewyke in your serches'. In his turn Smyth was able to use Roger's papers in his own work. Although Roger Kemys died in 1610, his antiquarian inter-ests were continued by his son, who added notes taken from Selden's *Titles of Honour* (1614) to the notebook. Arthur also appears to have been responsible for a detailed pedigree of the various branches of the Kemys family, for which he was able to draw on his father's researches. This pedigree was drawn up around the time of the 1623 visitation of Gloucestershire, but contains far more detail than that prepared for the College of Arms. Smyth also continued to enjoy access to the Kemys family papers. It is indicative of the time-span over which he compiled the *Lives of the Berkeleys* that both Roger and Arthur Kemys are acknowledged as having provided sources.[9]

When we examine the list of those who provided Smyth with material for his research, two main groups predominate. The first were local Gloucester-shire landowners, who were either connected with the Berkeleys as tenants and office-holders, or were members of the extensive kinship circle which Smyth joined through his marriage in 1609 to Mary Browning, the daughter of a local family of minor gentry. The second group of contributors repre-sented those whose descent from the Berkeleys or connection to them by marriage was recorded in Smyth's text. The membership of the two groups overlapped, as Smyth's extensive genealogies show how many local gentry families could trace a link to the Berkeleys through their pedigrees. While the kinship of Richard Berkeley of Stoke Gifford and his son Sir Maurice would have come as little surprise, Smyth's work showed how other contributors, including his father-in-law John Browning, Anthony Kingescote of Kinges-cote, William Basset of Uley and William Try of Hardwicke, were also related to the Berkeleys. Smyth's position as the Berkeley man of business undoubt-edly gave him access to a number of documents through his professional life, and many local landowners may have assisted him with a view to their own advantage rather than any particular interest in genealogy and local history. Nevertheless, Smyth's archive does reveal that his interests were shared to some extent by a number of his neighbours. Edward Trotman of Cam was related to Smyth by the Browning marriage and addressed him as cousin. Like the Brownings, Trotman was a member of the parish gentry, risen from the clothiers and yeomanry of the vale of Berkeley. He acquired a grant of arms in 1616. Four years before he had sent Smyth two letters concerning his extended pedigree, including the details of a number of marriages contracted by female relatives and the names of 'your young fry of kyndred'. Richard and Sir Maurice Berkeley were part of the network among whom Smyth circulated the three volumes of the *Lives of the Berkeleys* in 1636–37. Richard Berkeley was himself a scholar, who translated the *Commentaries* of the sixteenth-century French soldier Blaise de Montluc for his son John, who fought in Germany with Gustavus Adolphus, and composed a Calvinist treatise on *The Different State of the Godly and the Wicked* for the guidance of his younger children. Having read Smyth's work, he sent a number of corrections and requests for clarification. In a subsequent letter, he recorded his personal recollections of various members of the Berkeley family mentioned in Smyth's text. Three letters from his son record his enthusiasm as he acknowledged receipt of each volume of the *Lives*. He also sent Smyth material concerning the manor of Bradley from among the 'ould writings' left at his house by his father, material which was subsequently incorporated into the *Description of the Hundred of Berkeley*. Sir Maurice's clerk Henry Poole also wrote a fulsome letter in praise of the *Lives*.[10]

As a family historian Smyth was able to take advantage of the wider Berkeley kinship circle beyond Gloucestershire in pursuing his research. This circle included the antiquaries Sir Thomas Shirley, whose mother was a daughter of Smyth's first master Henry, lord Berkeley, and Sir Edward Dering, whose family had made a match with a descendant of a fourteenth-century lord Berkeley. The assistance of both men was acknowledged by Smyth, and that of Dering was particularly important, as tracing the descendants of Berkeleys that had married or settled at a distance from the family's main estates was a challenging task. Another member of the extended Berkeley kinship network with an interest in local history was the judge Sir Robert Berkeley. Sir Robert was the younger son of a Worcester clothier Rowland Berkeley, whose wealth had allowed the family to establish themselves within the gentry community of Worcestershire at the end of the sixteenth century. Both Rowland and Sir Robert were friends of Thomas Habington, who included the judge among the 'nobility' of the county to whom his history was dedicated. Sir Robert had an interest in local history which went beyond his own family and county, as indicated by a letter of 1641 in which Dugdale wrote to Archer that he was 'glad to heare that Justice Berkley is such a favourer of these neglected studyes'. Nevertheless, it was in his own pedigree and the potential of genealogy and heraldry to bolster his family's claim to status within Worcestershire society that most interested Sir Robert. Rowland Berkeley died in 1611 and was given a heraldic funeral. Three years later Sir Robert erected a fine marble tomb to his father and another for himself in a chapel at Spetchley, Worcs. A copy of Rowland Berkeley's funeral certificate is to be found among Smyth's papers (see figure 3). This showed his descent from Richard Berkeley of Dursley in the mid-sixteenth century, but in the *Lives* Smyth traced the family's descent from Thomas, fourth son of James, lord Berkeley in the fifteenth century. In June 1636 Smyth delivered a copy of this revised pedigree to Sir Robert, who like Smyth and his son John was a member of the Middle Temple. With the pedigree were instructions from Smyth to send it to lord Berkeley with an explanation of its provenance and 'to desire it may bee approved by his lord-ship, or reformed if hee find it in any thinge mistaken: And after to have his leave to attend him as a kinsman'. The following month Sir Robert received the first volume of Smyth's manuscript to read. From his letter acknowledging the receipt of 'your painfull and judicious' history, it becomes clear that a number of deeds, subsequently used as a source for the *Description*, were copied by Smyth's clerk in July 1636 on behalf of Sir Robert. This relationship between the man of business and the judge, facilitated by their mutual interest in gene-alogy, was intended by both sides to be mutually beneficial. A further volume of the *Lives* was delivered to Sir Robert by Smyth's eldest son, John, whose career the judge undertook to forward.[11]

The wide extent of the Berkeley estates and the nature of Smyth's respon-sibilities as a man of business meant that he became part of regional anti-quarian networks outside Gloucestershire. Smyth was himself born in Leicestershire, where his uncle had been appointed by the Berkeleys as rector of Hoby. George, lord Berkeley, sold his remaining estates in Leicestershire in the 1630s, but Smyth retained an interest in the county through family connections and his acquisition of the right to appoint the rector of Hoby. Among Smyth's antiquarian compositions was a history of the Berkeley manor of Melton Mowbray, Leics., which survives only in a draft form. The Burtons held land in the tenure of the Berkeleys, and William Burton's father Ralph had consequently become their ward when he inherited his lands as a minor. An account of the lawsuit over Ralph Burton's refusal to marry as his guardian wished was provided by his son for inclusion in the *Lives of the Berkeleys*. Smyth also quoted verbatim an extract from the *Description of Leicestershire* in his own work. William Burton was a contemporary of Smyth's at Oxford and it is likely that they met there, when Burton would have paid his respects to Thomas Berkeley. As students at the inns of court, they undoubtedly moved in the same antiquarian circles in London. The Berkeley connection was strong

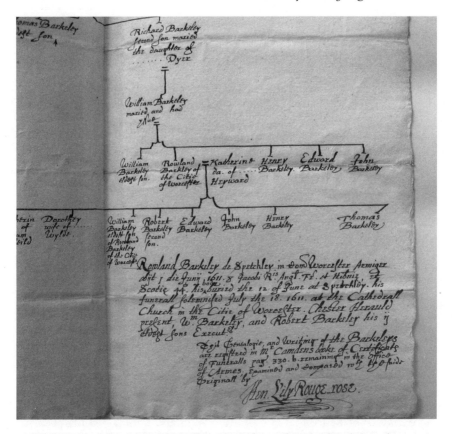

Figure 3 Part of a copy of the funeral certificate of Rowland Berkeley, 1611

within Burton's circle in Leicestershire. Among 'some few of my friends', whose pedigrees Burton included in the *Description of Leicestershire*, was Sir Henry Berkeley of Wymondham, who acted as the steward of George, lord Berkeley in Leicestershire. In the *Lives* Sir Henry was described as Smyth as 'a true lover of his noble race, whose encouragements have much furthered these collections'. A less-obvious Berkeley connection was Henry Duport of Shepshed, who provided Burton with church notes for Hatherne in 1611, and whose pedigree was prepared for inclusion in Burton's second edition. (In 1640, Henry Duport died without leaving a male heir, which may explain the omission of his pedigree from the 1642 manuscript.) Duport's interest in heraldry was apparently shared by the vicar of Shepshed, Robert Palmer, whose church notes for Ashbourne, Derbys., taken in 1620 and 1624 appear in Burton's collections. Henry Duport's father Thomas had been one of Smyth's predecessors in the service of Henry, lord Berkeley, and guardian of Burton's father. He had also acquired the lease of the grammar school in

Wotton-under-Edge, which Smyth purchased from his sons in 1608. Some of the details included by Smyth concerning Thomas Duport's experiences in the service of the Berkeleys suggest that he benefited from Henry's recollections of his father.[12]

From the 1590s until the last years of his life Smyth spent a sizeable portion of his time in London, living in lodgings in the vicinity of the inns of court, and spending his days in Westminster Hall or the repositories of public records. There are few indications in his copious surviving archive of the nature of the antiquarian contacts he made during that period. He lacked the social and professional standing required to be admitted to the Society of Antiquaries, but had some form of acquaintance with several of its members. The origin of the *Lives of the Berkeleys* lay in the period when he was most constantly in London and was presumably influenced by contacts such as Augustine Vincent. It is tempting to suggest that Smyth was himself an influence on John Harestaffe, who was in London during the same period pursuing the legal settlement of the disputed descent of the Vernon estate. The similarity of the occasions for which Smyth composed the first account of the *Lives of the Berkeleys* and Harestaffe his chronicle of the Vernons is suggestive, since both were a celebration of the conclusion of a lawsuit that had threatened the prosperity of the family concerned. These lawsuits had led both Smyth and Harestaffe to spend every law term in London over several years, and it may be reasonable to assume that such constant attendance in Westminster Hall would have led them into an acquaintance. A later connection is known through Sir Thomas Shirley, who used the Sudbury evidences for his account of his own family. It may be more than coincidence that Harestaffe revised and transcribed his poem in 1635, at the same time that Smyth was having a copy of the *Lives of the Berkeleys* prepared for circulation.[13]

While both Smyth and Burton moved in the same antiquarian circles in London as law students and were subsequently linked through their mutual connection to the Berkeley family, what we know of Burton's network of regional contacts reveals the difference in their social status. For Smyth his professional status made him an influential figure within a limited area in the south of Gloucestershire and within the wider ambit of the Berkeley influence. Although a wealthy man, he did not enjoy a high status within Gloucestershire society as a whole. Local worthies such as Sir William Throckmorton, Richard and Sir Maurice Berkeley and John Dutton of Sherborne recognised his usefulness in legal and practical matters, but did not consider him their social equal. Although he served in a number of minor posts within the county administration, such as escheator, subsidy collector and commissioner of sewers, Smyth never obtained the more prestigious appointment of justice of the peace. While William Burton did not serve as a justice, this was due to the weakness of his constitution and his desire for the retired life of a scholar, rather than any lack of social status. Although Burton did not play an active political role within gentry society, the circle that supported his antiquarian research reflected the status he nevertheless enjoyed.

In part, Burton's status derived from his family's long association with the region and the close kinship ties which he enjoyed with various leading members of local society. The Burton ancestral manor was in Fauld, Staffs., where Burton wrote the *Description of Leicestershire*, and he could trace his pedigree through family documents back to the reign of Richard I. The family had acquired their land in Lindley, Leics. in the mid-sixteenth century through the marriage of Burton's great-grandfather to the eldest of the daughters and co-heirs of John Herdwick. By this marriage the Burtons became incorporated into a kinship circle based on the Herdwick inheritance of manors in Leicestershire and Warwickshire. Another Herdwick daughter had married into the Dineley family of Charlton, Worcs., and in 1599 Burton was taking notes from the records of his 'cosin' Dineley. In this family Burton found kinsmen not merely sympathetic to his interests, but themselves enthusiastic about genealogy and heraldry. Henry Dineley of Hanley, Worcs., was described by Habington as 'a gentllman excellent in armory'. The pedigree included on the funeral monument of his elder brother Francis Dineley (d. 1624) was devised by Henry. It incorporated the fruits of his own research and contradicted what Camden had written of the family's origins. Through the Herdwick marriage the Burtons also became related to the Purefoys of Drayton, Leics., and Caldecote, Warwickshire. It was from his Purefoy kinsmen that Burton inherited Leland's manuscripts and a collection of church notes from the beginning of Elizabeth's reign. In 1603 he consulted the Purefoy manuscripts, when compiling his volume of records relating to Lindley. He included their pedigree in the *Description of Leicestershire*, and updated it in 1642, including a description of the tomb of George Purefoy (d. 1628). The family's continuing antiquarian interest is attested by the access that Dugdale and Archer enjoyed to the papers of William Purefoy of Caldecote, and his promise in 1636 to speak to lord Brooke on their behalf 'concerninge such old evidence and matters of Antiquitye that he hath'. Furthermore, in the *Antiquities of Warwickshire* Dugdale described William's rebuilding of their manor house 'with a fair structure of brick and stone, where the Armes and matches of his Family are in severall pieces of sculpture, very exactly represented'.[14]

Through his mother, Burton was linked to a second kinship circle centred on Leicestershire, which was significant for the level of education among its members and their links with a national scholarly network. Dorothy Burton was the daughter of William Faunt of Foston. Her brother Arthur was the Jesuit author of eleven theological works. Her niece married the elder son of Francis Beaumont, a justice of the Common Pleas, whose brothers were the dramatist Francis Beaumont and the poet Sir John Beaumont. Through her mother, Dorothy was descended from the Vincent family of Pekleton, enabling Burton to claim kinship with the herald Augustine Vincent. In the preface to the *Description of Leicestershire*, Burton acknowledged the encouragement he had received from both Vincent and Sir John Beaumont. He also received assistance from his Faunt relatives, being given access to the personal letters written by his Jesuit uncle in order to write an account of his life. Further assistance came from Sabeian Staresmore and his son Francis, who were cousins of Burton through his Vincent great-grandfather. In 1606 Burton recorded the eight coats of arms displayed on the parlour ceiling of their house at Frolesworth, Leics., and presumably examined the family's papers at around the same time. In 1615 Francis, a justice and deputy lieutenant, was in possession of a list of rectories and impropriations in Leicestershire with the names of their patrons. Since the list he had was incomplete and inaccurate, he did not forward it to Burton, but promised to let him have 'one more perfect' as soon as he was able. The information included by Burton about the status of Leicestershire churches and their patrons is one of the innovative features of the *Description of Leicestershire* and may be traced in part to the assistance he received from Francis Staresmore.[15]

One consequence of Burton's status for his career as an local historian was that members of his social circle had generally held their manors for several generations; had extensive collections of family papers; and could supplement their documents with evidence from funeral monuments and heraldic displays in their homes. This abundance of evidence enabled Burton to prepare detailed genealogies of the friends who allowed him to examine their evidences. These included Henry, lord Grey of Groby, Leics.; Thomas Astley of Wolvey, Warwickshire; and Sir Thomas Burdet of Bramcote, Warwickshire. The detailed pedigree of the Astleys appeared in the *Description of Leicestershire* under the account of Broughton Astley, although two of the branches of the family were settled in Warwickshire and the other in Northamptonshire. Similarly, the pedigree of Sir Thomas Burdet was included under the family's ancestral manor of Newton Burdet and an updated pedigree was prepared for the second edition. Although few of Burton's notes and little correspondence survive, it appears that those 'friends' whose pedigrees were included in the first edition were gentlemen whose papers he had personally examined. If we assume that pedigrees were prepared for the second edition on a similar basis, this would suggest that there were comparatively few significant gentry families in Leicestershire that did not allow Burton access to their papers. While the lack of references in the text and other evidence makes it impossible to be certain, it appears that Burton's second edition received the same sort of support among the Leicestershire gentry that Dugdale's footnotes show was achieved by him in Warwickshire. This would have been prompted by Burton's status as a published author of a county history, bolstered by his social position.

As with Smyth, although to a lesser degree, those who assisted Burton with his research could also derive benefits from the association. An example of this is the case of Richard Chamberlain of Astley castle, Warwickshire. In 1600 the church tower at Astley fell down, demolishing part of the church. As impropriator, Chamberlain undertook the rebuilding with the support of a collection from the county, although he foreshortened the church, making the choir into the nave, and a small chapel into the chancel. In the course of this restructuring in 1608 it was necessary to move the monument to Thomas Grey, marquess of Dorset. As a result 'at the curious desire of some, and earnest motion of others', the coffin within the vault was opened. Among the witnesses was Burton, who described the well-preserved state of the body and used this as the starting point for a digression on embalming in the *Description of Leicestershire*. The intention was to restore the monuments at Astley with new epitaphs and to this end, as we have seen, Burton wrote on Chamberlain's behalf to the herald Nicholas Charles seeking clarification of elements of the Grey pedigree and their dates of death. In the event, the monuments were not restored, but were seen by Dugdale decades later, lying discarded in the belfry of the church and an old outhouse. It seems that the interest in the restoration of the church was supplanted by a desire to remodel the living quarters of Astley castle to provide a modern level of comfort. Although in this instance his assistance was not utilised, the importance of heraldry to the gentry in this period for the decoration of their homes and their funeral monuments, made the knowledge of local historians such as Burton about local families and their coats of arms invaluable. The papers of Sir Edward Dering provide an example of the sort of help that might be sought by a gentleman, who had an interest in the associations of a coat of arms and wished to convey the right image, but was not concerned with the science of heraldry. In this case Sir John Skeffington wrote to Dering on behalf of his 'brother Bayly', asking him to select one of the enclosed coats of arms for him to present to the heralds, and to provide 'some words of art' to explain his choice.[16]

Finally, within the hierarchical society of Elizabethan and early Stuart England, Burton's social status bestowed upon him a certain automatic respect from his fellow gentry and from those lower down the social scale. Combined with his reputation as a published author, this enabled him to take advantage of a network of clergymen and others, who were encouraged to assist his research because of the potential influence he could wield on their behalf. Burton's church notes include many that are ascribed to individuals who cannot now be identified, and who are likely to belong to this group. One who can be identified was the mathematician Edmund Gunter, who provided church notes for Magdalen, Oxford, as a student in 1605. Another was William Gregory, who was born in Warwickshire and educated at Oxford before becoming rector of Chelvey, Somerset. In 1630 Burton asked Gregory to compare the arms of Polydore Vergil preserved at Wells cathedral with what was recorded in Leland. Although he knew little about the science of heraldry, Gregory made a special trip to Wells and did his best, with the help of his equally ignorant friends, to describe what he saw. In 1632 Burton was asked by Sir Simon Archer to help him convince Robert Palmer of Overton, Leics., that he was interested in Palmer's records purely in order to understand how the Archers had come to dispose of a manor that they had held from the thirteenth to the sixteenth century. Palmer had refused Archer's own request because there were rumours that he intended to attempt to reclaim the land. Burton's status as a member of the local elite and a published author was sufficient to reassure Palmer and persuade him to allow Archer access to his records.[17]

Richard Carew was also a member of the protestant elite, who enjoyed contacts with a national scholarly network and a high status within his own county. As we saw in chapter two, he was a member of the Society of Antiquaries, although he would have been able to attend their meetings only infrequently. Unlike Burton, Carew did not retire to his study to enjoy the life of a scholar. His antiquarian studies were pursued in tandem with an active role in the civil administration of Cornwall, as a justice of the peace, deputy lieutenant and MP. His official positions gave him access to various local records and an entrée into gentry houses, garrisons and other places of interest, but they also absorbed a great deal of his time. Similarly, his involvement as a county representative in disputes over pilchard fishing and tenancy rights in the duchy of Cornwall gave him valuable source material for local history, but at the expense of much time and effort. Camden described Carew as being in the process of writing a 'full description' of Cornwall in 1586, although the *Survey of Cornwall* did not appear until 1602. Carew then described it in the dedication as 'long since begun, a great while discontinued, lately renewed, and now hastily finished'. The planned second edition never appeared.[18]

The Carews were a widespread family of Norman origin, whose branches were found in Cornwall, Devon and across the Bristol Channel in South Wales. In 1564, at the age of eight, Carew inherited an estate at Antony, which had been in his family for four generations following a marriage with a Courtney heiress in the late fifteenth century. In the *Survey* Carew described all Cornish gentlemen as being cousins. In his own case through his mother, wife and other close relatives he was linked to seven prominent Cornish families: Godolphin of Godolphin, Erisey, Arundell of Tolverne, Godolphin of Treveneague, Edgcumb, Arundell of Trerice and Cosworth. He was more distantly related to the Carnsews, Grenvilles, Hills, Killigrews and St Aubyns. He was also a distant cousin of Sir Walter Raleigh, as he reminded the lord warden of the Stannaries in his letter of dedication in the *Survey*. When he was called upon to dispute with Sir Philip Sidney before the earls of Warwick and Leicester while at Oxford, he was advised by Sir Peter Carew 'the elder of that name, and the eldest of our stock (a Gentleman, whose rare worth my pen is not able to shaddow, much lesse with his due lineaments to represent)'.[19] Carew also acknowledged the assistance he had received in compiling the *Survey* from Sir Francis Godolphin, William Carnsew the elder, William Carnsew the younger and William Treffry. These names almost certainly represent only a few of the Cornish gentlemen who assisted his labours, as his manuscript and its author circulated widely within Elizabethan Cornish gentry society.

In terms of wealth and length of pedigree Sampson Erdeswicke, Thomas Habington and Sir Thomas Shirley were the social equals of William Burton and Richard Carew, but their status within gentry society was to an extent undermined by their overt catholicism. Richard Bagot's description of Sampson Erdeswicke as a gentleman of 'good knowledge and experience' in matters of genealogy shows that it was possible for a catholic antiquary to be accepted by his fellow enthusiasts.[20] Yet there was a great difference between achieving recognition from other antiquaries, and being so accepted within the local community that gentlemen would happily invite you into their private studies. The alternatives of allowing a catholic to borrow your papers or visiting them in their own home might be equally awkward for the gentlemen, who might not be overtly hostile to recusants, but at the same time would not relish too close an association. With each generation the marriages of the English gentry became increasingly segregated along religious lines, weakening the kinship ties of catholic local historians with their protestant neighbours and making it more difficult for them to rely on the claims of cousinage to encourage co-operation with their research. For a family historian such as Shirley this was not so important, as the bulk of his material came from the papers of his immediate family. Aspiring county historians like Erdeswicke and Habington required far greater access if their works were to be comprehensive.

The political situation during the period in which Erdeswicke was compiling his history of Staffordshire was particularly fraught, coinciding as it did with the period of the Armada and heightened suspicion of the catholic minority. Richard Bagot, who respected Erdeswicke's genealogical expertise, was a deputy lieutenant responsible for ensuring that he was taken into custody at times of political tension. Another deputy lieutenant was Sir Walter Aston, whose son Edward allowed Erdeswicke to examine his evidences. While the situation might be socially awkward, being remanded into the custody of local office-holders such as Bagot provided Erdeswicke with an opportunity to view their papers. Similarly, he may have seen a deed belonging to Sir Walter Harcourt mentioned in the *View of Staffordshire*, on the occasion when his family's case of pistols were delivered to Harcourt as captain of the lances in 1585.[21] Although divided by religion, Erdeswicke and the leading protestant gentry in Staffordshire and Cheshire were linked by ties of kinship and a shared history that had only recently been ruptured. Where circumstances brought Erdeswicke into immediate contact with his fellow gentlemen, he seems to have been granted access to their papers quite readily. Nevertheless, the majority of his contributors were fellow catholics, such as Brian Fowler of St Thomas, Stafford; William Macclesfield of Meere; Richard Biddulph and John and Philip Draycot.

The social isolation imposed by his religion made Erdeswicke dependent to an extent upon the assistance of others who were not so hampered. His friendship with members of the College of Arms makes it likely that the heralds took advantage of his local knowledge in conducting their visitation of Staffordshire in 1583. In return Erdeswicke would have acquired indirect access to a large amount of material. He was also able to utilise the kinship circle of William Wyrley, who initially acted as Erdeswicke's assistant, and subsequently established himself as an authority on genealogy and heraldry in his own right before his entry into the College of Arms in 1604. His association with Erdeswicke and travels around the Midlands collecting church notes caused suspicion, and led to Wyrley being denounced to the Warwickshire recusancy commissioners in 1592, but he was not himself a catholic. He was close to his cousins, the Wyrleys of Hampstead, who were staunchly Protestant. His cousin John Wyrley was suggested by Richard Bagot as a potential recusancy commissioner in 1594, but died shortly thereafter. John was succeeded by his son Humphrey, whose sister Dorothy subsequently married Wyrley. John Wyrley's deeds and those of his uncle Robert Moseley had been transcribed by Wyrley in 1592. Two years later Erdeswicke wrote to another of Wyrley's cousins, William Comberford of Wednesbury, about his pedigree. In this letter there is the first mention of the *View of Staffordshire*. Inviting Comberford to visit Sandon for a few days, Erdeswicke asked him to bring his evidences to fill in the gaps in the pedigree 'for that they will doe well to be sette downe for proofes to furnishe the booke withall'.[22] Significantly, the Comberfords were a catholic family, and consequently had no objection to visiting Erdeswicke at Sandon.

In the preface to the *Survey of Worcestershire* Habington wrote of that 'some fewe of our Gentellmen have assysted me with theyre private evydences which I requyred with settinge out theyre familyes', but indicated that in the majority of cases he had been obliged to rely on public and ecclesiastical records. Later he complained that 'scarce any one healpethe with evydences'.[23] A comparison of Habington's work with Burton's revised text or Dugdale's *Antiquities of Warwickshire* reveals the effect of this lack of access on what he was able to write. The pedigrees and accounts of gentry families are fewer and less detailed, and the descents of manors less full and connected. As the son of Elizabeth I's cofferer, who had entertained the queen herself at Hindlip during her progress to Worcestershire in 1575, Habington was born into the highest stratum of gentry within the county. Although Hindlip was a new house, built by his father as an expression of his increased status, the family had held land in Worcestershire since the thirteenth century and were linked to their neighbours by the usual ties of kinship. However, the family's reputation for militant catholicism set them apart from their protestant neighbours, and their social intercourse was predominantly conducted with fellow adherents of the old religion. The majority of those 'fewe of our Gentellmen' who assisted Habington with access to their records were members of this community of catholic gentry: Russell of Little Malvern, Wintour of Huddington, Talbot of Grafton, Throckmorton of Feckenham, Lyttelton of Hagley, Blount of Soddington and Sheldon of Beoley. Also within this catholic circle was William Bell, clerk of the peace in Worcester, who made the oration to Elizabeth I on her visit to the city in 1575. His will, written in 1580, represented a combination of family history, justification of his catholic faith and testamentary instructions. In it he proudly traced his family's association with Worcestershire back to the reign of Edward I, although their ancestral manor had been sold in Henry VIII's reign.[24]

Although the catholics predominate, a number of other gentlemen showed themselves to be interested in Habington's researches. Nathaniel Tomkins was a member of the Worcester cathedral clergy and son of the organist, Thomas Tomkins. He shared Habington's antiquarian interests, writing a memoir of Sir John Packington and observations on the Worcestershire section of Camden's *Britannia*. He was responsible for the preservation and restoration of some of the monuments in the cathedral, and presumably assisted Habington's access to the archive there. He also accompanied Habington on his tours of local parishes to collect church notes. We have seen how Sir Robert Berkeley shared Habington's antiquarian interests. There was a long-standing friendship between the two families, who held land in close proximity to each other. Habington described Rowland Berkeley, the judge's father and himself a justice of the peace as 'my ancient friend', who 'left me not (where this world forsooke me) in my stormy troubles'. The family was also sympathetic to the old religion and Sir Robert Berkeley's only son converted to catholicism. Another friend who shared Habington's interest in genealogy and heraldry was Sir Edmund Harewell, 'Shyreefe of thys county, an expert Justyce, a rare Commissyoner and learned Gentellman'. Harewell was the preferred candidate of the Worcestershire catholics for the parliament of 1604 because of his sympathy for their cause. The unusual triptych, erected by him at Besford following the death of one of his infant sons, reveals his interest in heraldry and genealogy. Lacking an heir and obliged to sell Besford and to retreat from public life, Harewell had little reason to conceal his true religious beliefs and converted to catholicism before his death. As Habington informs us, he was himself 'an eye witness in hys extreme agonies'.[25]

Not all the gentlemen who assisted Habington in his researches were necessarily sympathetic to his religious position. Arthur Salwey, a justice who allowed Habington to consult his evidences, was a lawyer who held a post in Elizabeth's Exchequer. He was commended by Habington for his industriousness, both in the service of the community as a justice and of his own family in re-establishing their fortunes. He was related by marriage to Erdeswicke, who mentioned him in the *View of Staffordshire* and may also have had access to his personal papers. Although Arthur and his son Humphrey, a parliamentarian in the civil war, were not sympathetic to catholicism, they were interested in establishing their family's claim to status through ancient lineage. This presumably encouraged them to provide Habington with access to their papers, to the end that his work would support that claim. A similar interest in establishing his claim to a pedigree appropriate to his wealth and status seems to have motivated William Mucklowe of Areley, whose family, like the Berkeleys, was newly risen from the Worcester cloth trade. In 1634 Habington worked on the Mucklowe pedigree, using their court rolls and other documents, and subsequently arranged for it to be drawn up in colour by a herald painter in London. By providing Habington with access to his papers, Mucklowe gained an authoritative basis for his claim of descent from the medieval Mutlowes of Shropshire, and to the use of their arms. As recorded in the *Survey of Worcestershire,* he subsequently had these arms painted on the wall of Areley church. Similarly, Nicholas Lechmere of Hanley castle suggested some improvements to Habington's account of his family 'more expressely alliancing us to some noble houses'. In this case, Habington provided Lechmere with a copy of what he proposed to write about the family, and Lechmere added material from his own evidences. His association with Habington did not extend to allowing the antiquary free access to his papers.[26]

There is little evidence of support for Habington's antiquarian research among his protestant kinsfolk. None of the families into which the three daughters of his uncle Richard Habington married are known to have provided any assistance to his work. In the *Survey of Worcestershire* he described the funeral monument of his cousin Mary and her husband Richard Barneby of Bockiston, but he did not include an account of the Barneby descent, as they came from Yorkshire. The inclusion of his uncle and cousins and their marriage alliances on the inscription of his father's funeral monument indicates that Habington was keen to stress their kinship, but there is no evidence that this desire for alliance was reciprocated. However, a more distant kinsman was prepared to assist Habington, because it was to his advantage. In October 1641 Habington wrote to his 'cousin', Thomas Hall of Easbury in Hallow, seeking information about who owned the manor before his family acquired it, and in exchange offered information about its medieval owners. Four days later Hall responded with the information Habington required from his own documents. From this letter it is clear that Hall wanted through his co-operation to acquire some useful information about his rights in Easbury, as he explained that he 'shuld be glad to understand the tenure, yf you wilbe pleased to doe me so much favour'. His father had been embroiled in a lawsuit at the end of Elizabeth's reign, concerning the tenure of Easbury, and Hall with Habington's assistance hoped to ensure himself against further challenges to his rights.[27]

Antiquarian research held a special appeal for many catholic gentlemen, as it allowed them to dwell upon the medieval past of religious uniformity. The number of recusants among the local historians considered in this study far exceeds their representation among the gentry as a whole. Generally, catholic local historians were drawn from the social elite of their counties, suggesting that antiquarian sociability may have been more difficult to establish across the religious divide at lower levels of gentry society. Nevertheless, once established, there appear to have been few interruptions to discourse within antiquarian circles that could be attributed to religious differences. Although individual antiquaries on occasion expressed opposition to catholicism or extreme protestantism, their personal opinions do not seem to have prevented them co-operating with adherents of religious positions that they opposed. Yet, the social isolation from which the study of the past could be a refuge did place limits on the scholarship of recusant antiquaries. The studies of the protestant gentry were, on the whole, closed to them, and they often relied on a few close associates who shared their antiquarian interests, when they needed to access sources. As the catholic minority became increasingly marginalised in the course of the seventeenth century, the ability of a catholic to write comprehensive local history became increasingly circumscribed.

For some catholics this social isolation arrived earlier. Despite some difficulties resulting from their recusancy, Erdeswicke and Habington seem to have maintained comparatively amicable relationships with the local gentry, and to have experienced harassment only at times of heightened tension. In Lancashire, where catholics represented a far higher proportion of the population as a whole, the tensions were greater, and there was apparently far less possibility of peaceful co-existence with their protestant neighbours. The family of William Blundell had held land in the vicinity of Little Crosby since the thirteenth century, and enjoyed correspondingly close kinship ties with their protestant neighbours, but this did not save them from persecution. William was imprisoned with his father at Lancaster in 1590 for harbouring a priest, was then briefly released on licence following the death of his father, and then rearrested and held at the Gatehouse in Westminster for two years. When his house was searched once more in 1598, he escaped and took refuge with a kinsman near Wrexham in Wales. During the remainder of Elizabeth's reign, Blundell spent the majority of his time moving between catholic safehouses. For two years he lived in Staffordshire, moving between six safehouses there. It is possible that Blundell met Erdeswicke during this time, although, as the

Staffordshire antiquary was reputed to have gone mad before his death in 1601, it is unlikely that such a meeting would have been very fruitful. However, this prolonged sojourn within a community where an interest in genealogy and heraldry had been encouraged by Erdeswicke's researches, may have had an important influence on Blundell's intellectual interests.[28]

In 1611 a hoard of Anglo-Saxon coins was found in the catholic burial-ground that Blundell had established for his tenants and neighbours. Blundell's careful investigation of the coins shows that he owned or had access to a range of recent and medieval sources typical of a gentleman with fairly keen historical interests. All his sources were available in print, however, suggesting that Blundell was not part of an antiquarian circle that exchanged manuscripts. He did prepare an account of the coins for limited circulation in manuscript and copperplate print, but, given the location of the find, this was a pious as well as a historical study. It was probably intended for circulation among a catholic rather than an antiquarian circle, like the sectarian ballads Blundell also composed. In this it resembles family histories, which were circulated among family members regardless of their level of interest in history generally. Blundell's reference in his account to a catholic gentleman and friend living about thirty miles away, who provided him with local information about St Oswald may indicate the existence of a circle of local catholic gentlemen with antiquarian interests. The clandestine nature of much of catholic sociability in this period leaves comparatively few traces and, without locating copies of Blundell's work or references to it, it is impossible to be sure of the extent of its circulation. The absence of references to William Blundell as a possible source of local knowledge or of extracts from the Little Crosby records in the notes of contemporary or later antiquaries in Lancashire or Cheshire, suggests that his interests were not known outside his immediate, catholic circle. Blundell's antiquarian interests were inherited by his grandson William, as were his strong catholic convictions. The grandson was wounded fighting for the royalists in the civil war, had his estate seized, and spent considerable periods exiled from his home until the Restoration. His active support for the king may have encouraged the younger Blundell's acceptance into royalist circles despite his religion. Certainly, in 1646 and 1648 he spent some time on the Isle of Man, where James, earl of Derby had retired, and was accepted into the gentry community there. He produced the first extensive topographical study of the island, in which he was assisted by John Greenhalgh, the earl's appointee as governor of the island and himself a former royalist officer. The isolation of the beleagured royalists brought them for a short period closer to some of their catholic neighbours, but it was a temporary respite. Blundell's work did not gain him access to wider antiquarian circles after the Restoration.

In Warwickshire Sir Simon Archer, a justice of the peace and member of a long-established family, enjoyed a similar position to Burton in Leicestershire and Carew in Cornwall, and was able to exploit his kinship ties and social status to aid his antiquarian research. By contrast, William Dugdale was a comparatively new member of Warwickshire gentry society and his financial position placed him firmly among its lower strata.[29] What strikes the reader of Dugdale's correspondence is the amount of time that he spent travelling the country, making transcripts of records, researching pedigrees, and carrying messages from one gentleman to another. This peripatetic lifestyle continued after Dugdale became a herald, was maintained throughout the civil war and interregnum, and continued on into old age. When he was not visiting his far-flung network of antiquarian acquaintances, he maintained contact through letters, and remained a conduit for information. Throughout his peripatetic career Dugdale was an important catalyst in the promotion of local history in England.

It is a characteristic of the Midlands' gentry that their familial ties crossed county boundaries. Although Dugdale is inextricably linked with Warwickshire, his marriage to Margery Huntbach also gave him an interest in Staffordshire. Margery's family lived in the vicinity of Wolverhampton and her sister subsequently married a tradesman from the town – a marriage Dugdale opposed because of its threat to his family's social status. Throughout his career Dugdale maintained close links with Staffordshire. He visited the county in 1635, when he made notes on the arms at Bushbury and Brewood. In 1636 he spent Easter in Staffordshire and arranged to return at Whitsun to meet John Langley, the steward to Sir Richard Leveson of Trentham. He was also invited to view the evidences of the Wrottesleys and the archive at Dudley castle. The Wrottesleys of Wrottesley were one of the oldest Staffordshire families, while his invitation to Dudley castle came from Humble Ward, husband of Frances, granddaughter and heir of Edward, lord Dudley. Given Dugdale's status as a relatively minor Warwickshire gentleman and the similar status of the Huntbachs, the apparent ease with which the antiquary was admitted into the society and evidence-rooms of the Staffordshire elite owed much to his association with Burton. It was hoped that Burton, who had written the *Description of Leicestershire* while living on his Staffordshire estate, would write a similar account of his ancestral county. In June 1636 Dugdale reported to Archer: 'Mr Burton tells me that if the booke of Staffordshire pen'd by Mr Erdswicke, which I am promised, be to any purpose, he will presently fall in hand with the descripcion of that countye, for he hath allreadye more than the one halfe thereof compleate.'[30] At this time Dugdale was not only acting as a research assistant to Archer, but was also gathering material for Burton, and this association opened the muniment rooms of Staffordshire to him.

Although Dugdale's meeting with Langley was forestalled, on his Whitsun visit he found so 'many rare antiquityes' at Dudley castle that he was able to do no more than sort through what was there. A more detailed perusal required a further visit, which also enabled him to make Langley's acquaintance. The documents at Trentham under the steward's control included the register of Lilleshall, subsequently an important source for the *Antiquities of Warwickshire*. Letters between Langley and Dugdale survive for the period 1642 to 1660, but these clearly represent only a fraction of the whole exchange of correspondence, which was of course supplemented by regular meetings. Early in 1637, Dugdale completed a transcript of Erdeswicke's *View of Staffordshire*. His interest in and knowledge of the history of Wolverhampton is reflected in the additions that he made to Erdeswicke's account of the town. The transcript was lent to Burton, and Dugdale continued to collect notes on Staffordshire history.[31] At some point the baton of potential historian of Staffordshire passed from Burton to Walter Chetwynd of Ingestre and his son (also called Walter) and Burton's notes passed to the latter after Burton's death. All three men benefited from the industrious Dugdale and his indefatigable search for historical records.

Before settling in Warwickshire, Dugdale's father had been tutor at Oxford for several years to William Paulet, a grandson of William, first marquess of Winchester. The Paulets' ownership of Maxstoke priory had influenced John Dugdale's decision to settle nearby at Shustoke, and the association with these noble patrons was maintained by his son. In April 1637 Dugdale mentioned an intended visit to Wiltshire to visit his father's former pupil in a letter to Archer. The evidence of the church notes he collected for Burton in Wiltshire and neighbouring counties, and the notes he made in his almanacs, indicate that these visits were a regular occurrence. Throughout his life Dugdale's antiquarian interests were melded to his need to acquire and retain patrons. It is in this light that his initial contact with Burton and subsequent relationship with Archer should be viewed. From 1637 Hatton became his most important and consistent patron, and was instrumental in securing him his initial appointment within the College of Arms. The relationship continued even during the hiatus of Hatton's exile under the Commonwealth, when Dugdale visited him in France. Dugdale's role was partly to undertake practical antiquarian research for Hatton, by seeking and transcribing records; organising the collection of copies of seals; arranging his library; and undertaking with an arms painter the 1640 survey of funeral monuments. Through his career as a herald and as a scholar, Dugdale also lent lustre to Hatton's image as a patron of letters and learning – describing him in the dedication to the *Antiquities of Warwickshire* as a 'principal Maecenas of learning'. Twenty years later, Hatton's son rushed to inform Dugdale when the post of Garter became vacant, and urged his somewhat reluctant client to accept the position and the knighthood that accompanied it. Although Dugdale's protestations should not be taken entirely at face value, it seems quite reasonable that a man of seventy-two might feel some reluctance to accept a post that would require him to abandon the comforts of his Warwickshire home to live in London. For Hatton, however, it was important for his status that his client should be appointed by the king to this most prestigious of heraldic posts.[32]

Although Hatton was the most important of Dugdale's patrons, the antiquary also maintained a series of other relationships with influential families. One such was with Sir Randolph Crewe, the chief justice of King's Bench, removed for his opposition to the forced loan. Although Crewe had risen to prominence through the law from a background in trade, he believed in the importance of lineage and was proud of the long heritage of the Crewe name. This is exemplified by his comments in his prologue to the Oxford peerage case of 1625: 'Where is Bohun, where's Mowbray, where's Mortimer? &c. Nay, which is more and most of all, where is Plantagenet? They are entombed in the urns and sepulchres of mortality. And yet let the name and dignity of De Vere stand so long as it pleaseth God.'[33] Sir Randolph was also interested in local history. He possessed a copy of William Smith's description of Cheshire, and he provided material for the *Antiquities of Warwickshire* before his death in 1646. His younger son, John Crewe of Utkinton, Ches., was a friend of the Cheshire historians William Vernon and Sir Peter Leycester. In 1653, John Crewe paid Dugdale three pounds for the cost of engraving of the monuments at Wixford, Warwickshire, where Thomas de Crewe had been a notable figure in the fifteenth century. He also gave him two pounds for searches in the Tower on his behalf, although these had been largely unsuccessful. In his letter of acknowledgement, Dugdale attempted to interest Crewe in the project to publish the volume of Cheshire history that eventually became Daniel King's *Vale Royal*. At this time, Dugdale's financial position was particularly difficult, and the support of men such as Crewe for his publishing projects and their commissions for research were important in enabling him to continue his work. The relationship continued after the Restoration, when Dugdale had been restored to the College of Arms. In 1663 Crewe paid for an engraving of his father's portrait to be included in Dugdale's *Origines Juridiciales* (1666). This coincided with Dugdale's heraldic visitation of Cheshire, which provided him with an opportunity to visit his patron.[34]

While a visit to Cheshire required a special journey, Dugdale's patrons in Northamptonshire could be visited on his journeys to and from London. In addition to Hatton and lord Brudenell, Dugdale was also associated with Geoffrey Palmer of Carlton and Sir Justinian Isham of Lamport. In 1657 Dugdale was busy transcribing the Leland volumes that Burton had bequeathed to Oxford for Hatton. In August of that year he also spent successive nights at Carlton and Lamport. Geoffrey Palmer was a lawyer, who was to become attorney-general after the Restoration, and would subsequently publish the law reports of his father-in-law Sir Francis Moore. It is probable that Palmer began editing the reports during his enforced retirement during the interregnum, and employed Dugdale as a research assistant. For Isham, Dugdale acted as a conduit for news, and in the autumn of 1657 he hoped to acquire gold coins that had belonged to the recently deceased Sir Simonds D'Ewes through Dugdale's agency. Isham also shared the general gentry interest in his pedigree, which Dugdale fuelled by unearthing copies of references to Isham's family from the public records.[35]

Dugdale's career as an antiquary and herald was characterised by continual movement between London and the provinces, with comparatively little time spent at his estate in Warwickshire. In the early years this peripatetic lifestyle was undoubtedly dictated in large part by his need to maintain close ties with potential patrons and to pursue commissions which enabled him to support his own researches. It is also clear that Dugdale was a sociable man, who enjoyed his career contacts with cultured and wealthy people. Although after the Restoration he did employ a number of deputies in the provinces, he did not hand over the conduct of visitations to others as previous heralds had often done. For Dugdale the pursuit of antiquarian interests enabled him to become a significant member of a sociable network that covered the Midlands and north of England and included a number of gentlemen whose social status was far above his own.

As the son of the registrar of York minster, Roger Dodsworth's social position was initially far below the Yorkshire elite, but he benefited from growing up in an environment that encouraged his antiquarian inclinations. In his twenties he began extracting records from the minster's archives and compiling pedigrees of local families. He also began collecting church notes, and in 1609 he examined the evidences of his uncle, Simon Bigod of Shacklethorpe. Following his marriage in 1611 to Holcroft Rawsthorne, a comparatively wealthy widow, and his move to her house at Hutton Grange, near Preston, Lancs., he continued to pursue his interest in Yorkshire history. His wife's family were the Heskeths of Rufford Old Hall, an elite Lancashire family, and through his mother-in-law he was linked to the Stanleys, earls of Derby. Although his wife died within a decade, his marriage provided Dodsworth with a physical base and a social position from which to pursue his antiquarian interests for the rest of his life. The eighty-five volumes of manuscripts that now remain in the Bodleian library stand as testimony to the extensive and peripatetic nature of his research.[36]

Dodsworth made contacts in London early in his antiquarian career. In 1615 he took notes from a book belonging to Jacob Chaloner, a London arms painter, and by 1618 he had gained access to Cotton's library. It is likely that his ready admittance into metropolitan antiquarian circles was assisted by his ability to reciprocate with access to the important ecclesiastical archives at York. It may have been through his London contacts that Dodsworth made the acquaintance of Charles Fairfax, the seventh son of lord Fairfax, a keen antiquary who was called to the bar in 1618. Dated transcripts show that Dodsworth had access to his friend's documents by 1625, and Dodsworth transcribed many of the papers in the Fairfax family archive at Denton and at Menston, where his friend established his home after his marriage. Sir Ferdinando Fairfax, Charles' elder brother, also told Dodsworth what he knew about their family. The Fairfax family became Dodsworth's principal patrons and, as we saw in chapter one, this association with a leading parliamentarian family was very useful for Dodsworth and his contacts during the civil war and interregnum. In 1646 Ferdinando Fairfax appointed his brother to intervene in a dispute over the Clifford estates, which gave Charles and Dodsworth access to the extensive archive at Skipton castle. The advantage that Dodsworth gained from this opportunity is shown in a letter to Sir Simonds D'Ewes written in 1647, which also shows the value of Dodsworth's research to his friends who could not travel north during the war. D'Ewes was interested in the pedigree of the Tempests, and Dodsworth wrote: 'I am att Skipton Castle ... where I find many fine antiquities of [the Tempest] family. I went a fortnight since to the heire in hope to see the evidence, who told me they were all plundered by my Lord of Newcastle's people'.[37]

When examining the long list of people that gave Dodsworth access to records during the compilation of the *Monasticon Anglicanum*, the reader is struck by their social, geographical, political and doctrinal range. Beyond his immediate family, his early contacts in Yorkshire were predominantly among the godly. In 1619 the religious controversialist and vicar of Leeds, Alexander Cooke, lent him a volume from Kirkstal Abbey; the godly gentleman Francis Bunny of Newland, near Wakefield, lent him a cartulary of Holy Trinity, Pontefract; and the widow of Sir Stephen Proctor allowed him access to two couchers of Fountains Abbey. This suggests that Dodsworth's own religious background was within godly circles, which certainly flourished in York during the archepiscopate of Matthew Hutton. Among the early sources that he used was a list of Yorkshire fees in the possession of the feodary (local representative of the Court of Wards), suggesting that his links to the registry at York helped him to acquire access to officials and their records. Through his marriage, Dodsworth gained links to Lancashire gentlemen, such as Sir Ralph Assheton, Sir Charles Gerard of Halsall and Thomas Standish of Duxbury. In the 1620s his association with the Fairfax family helped him to gain access to a far wider section of Yorkshire gentry society. His sources included the deputies lieutenant Sir William Lister and Robert Rockley, and the prominent ironmasters Sir Francis Wortley and Sir Gervase Cutler. Some gentry who allowed him to view their evidences had names that went back to the Norman Conquest, such as John Mauleverer and Sir Thomas Vavasour. In contrast, the family of Francis Burdett of Birthwaite had acquired their estate within living memory. Despite Dodsworth's association with Calvinist circles, there was a high proportion of catholic families among his sources. His praise for the paternalism of Sir Peter Middleton is symptomatic of how local historians attempted to rise above doctrinal differences. As well as ranging widely in Yorkshire and Lancashire in search of monastic sources, collecting church notes along the way, Dodsworth also travelled north to Levens Hall and Sizergh Castle in Westmorland, and south to Cheshire, Derbyshire, Nottinghamshire and Rutland. In 1629 he journeyed as far as the border with Scotland, to visit William, lord Howard, at Naworth castle. Lord Howard was, of course, a link back to the London circle of Sir Robert Cotton and Sir Henry Spelman. From the late 1630s the influence of this wider antiquarian community in locating and acquiring access to monastic records for Dodsworth is apparent. Yet, it was Dodsworth and Fairfax's own contacts in the north of England that made the *Monasticon Anglicanum* possible.[38]

Unlike the other local historians considered in this chapter, Dr Thomas Browne of Norwich was a polymath whose interests were not concentrated on genealogy, heraldry and the law. A medical doctor, he was celebrated as the writer of *Religio Medici* (1643), a confession of his Christian faith. In *Pseudodoxia Epidemica, or Enquiries Into Very Many Received Tenets and Commonly Presumed Truths, Which Examined Prove But Vulgar and Common Errors* (1646), he sought by Baconian enquiry to discern the truth behind folklore. He was also a collector of coins, fossils and other artefacts. His interest in the natural world and experimentation look forward to the post-Restoration generation of antiquaries, such as Robert Plot, who would be influenced by the Royal Society. Yet his account of the monuments in Norwich cathedral, published posthumously, linked him to the previous generations of local historians, and his antiquarian collection included the manuscript of the anonymous chorographer of Norfolk. In the dedication to *Hydriotaphia, Urne Buriall; or a Discourse of the Sepulchrall Urnes Lately Found in Norfolk* (1658) Browne made it clear that he considered himself engaged in the same work of erecting a 'new Britannia' as Dugdale and his circle.[39] In 1656 Browne, whose father's family came from Cheshire, wrote a dedicatory epistle to King's *Vale Royal of England*, indicating that he was by this time associated with those engaged on this project. Through *Hydriotaphia* and other sources it is also possible to trace the outline of the circle of scholarly gentry that surrounded Browne in Norfolk. A generation after Sir Henry Spelman departed the county to live in London, the Norfolk gentry retained their interest in genealogy and heraldry. This traditional antiquarianism was combined with a new 'scientific' interest in archaeological remains, which was encouraged by the frequency with which well-preserved finds were discovered.

Living as he did in Norwich and practising his profession among the leading gentry families of Norfolk, Browne was well placed to act as the centre of a scholarly network. The circumstances that led Browne to settle in Norwich are not clearly understood, but it was at least partly at the instigation of Sir Charles Le Gros of Crostwight and Nicholas Bacon of Gillingham, who were impressed by the circulating manuscript of *Religio Medici*. From his arrival in Norwich in 1637, Browne was accordingly recognised as a scholar, although he did not publish anything for several years. His marriage in 1641 to Dorothy Mileham augmented his existing acquaintance in Norfolk with connections among other local families: Knyvett, Townshend, Astley, Pettus, Paston, Tenison and Le Gros. Twenty years later he dedicated *Hydriotaphia* to Thomas Le Gros, the heir of his former patron, whom he described as 'no slender master of Antiquities'. In the same year he published *The Garden of Cyrus* (1658), a work intended to show how the number five pervaded the horticulture of antiquity and plant and animal life in general. This idiosyncratic work he dedicated to Nicholas Bacon, whom he described as having 'been so long out of trite learning, that it is hard to find a Subject proper for you'.[40]

Browne's status as a scholar within Norfolk gentry society is confirmed by such evidence as Sir Hamon L'Estrange of Hunstanton sending him an eighty-five-page manuscript 'Observations on the Pseudodoxia' in 1654, although the two men were not at that time acquainted. Sir Hamon was brother-in-law and ward to Sir Henry Spelman, who lived at Hunstanton during his guardianship. Although Spelman had settled in London in 1612 to pursue his antiquarian studies, he remained closely associated with Norfolk until his death in 1641, and remained an influence on the intellectual life of the county at the time when Browne settled in Norwich. Sir Henry passed on an interest in the past both to Sir Hamon and to his own sons: Sir John, who maintained the family association with Norfolk, and Clement, who penned a long preface to a new edition of his father's *De Non Temerandis Ecclesiis* in 1646. Among Browne's friends was Sir Ralph Hare, a neighbour of Spelman's who had been moved by the latter's analysis of the deleterious effects of the lay appropriation of church wealth, and had restored the impropriatium of Stow Bardolph. Sir Ralph also owned land at Brancaster, where Roman coins were frequently found. Another friend was Sir William Paston of Oxnead, whose travels in the years immediately preceding the civil war took him as far as Cairo and Jerusalem. He was known for his 'Museum' with its 'infinite variety of the most choice and admired Rarities'. As reported by Browne, these rarities included items recovered from funeral urns dug up on ground at Buxton belonging to his 'worthy friend' Roger Jegon (son of a Jacobean bishop of Norwich and, through his mother's subsequent remarriage, stepson to Sir Charles Cornwallis, memorialist of Henry, prince of Wales). Sir William Paston's son Robert, later earl of Yarmouth, was a fellow of the Royal Society and instigated a correspondence between Browne and John Evelyn. Following the finding of urns at Brampton in 1667, he, in concert with Browne, 'had the Curiosity to open a Piece of Ground in his Park at Oxnead'.[41]

The frequency with which well-preserved Roman remains were found in Norfolk doubtless stimulated the gentry's interest in amateur archaeology. Knowing of Browne's interest in this field, it was natural that they should turn to him as the local expert for an explanation of their finds. In his account of the Brampton urns, we find Browne being sent word of the finding of the first urns during the digging of ditches, and then hurrying to the site. There he 'used all Care with the workmen' to try to recover the urns undamaged. Where Browne could not attend in person, accounts of the finding of remains and samples were sent to him by his acquaintances. While some were motivated predominantly by the hope of finding something valuable and reaping a financial benefit, within Browne's circle it was intellectual curiosity that drove their research. The workmen employed by William Masham must have expended considerable effort in breaking through five layers of brick and stone, some of which required 'hard blows'. The pot recovered intact through the 'great Care of my worthy Friend' was of scholarly rather than monetary value.[42]

The development of local history in the Elizabethan and early Stuart period, and particularly the appearance of the first county histories, have frequently been interpreted as evidence of a strong sense of and pride in a local identity based on the county. This interpretation is supported by the examples of Lambarde's *Perambulation of Kent* and Carew's *Survey of Cornwall*, since both Kent and Cornwall were believed to exhibit other features associated with the idea of a cohesive, self-conscious county community. Yet Lambarde and Carew achieved publication because of their close ties with the centre of antiquarian scholarship in London, rather than any local enthusiasm for their work. If the manuscript of Erdeswicke's account of Staffordshire had found its way into print at the end of Elizabeth's reign, the picture would have looked rather different, since Staffordshire exhibited few of the attributes of county communities delineated by Alan Everitt.[43]

The idea of a county community undoubtedly had a symbolic importance to the English gentry, even in counties where it had little social or economic reality. It represented, in Peter Laslett's phrase, a medium of political consciousness, which provided a vehicle for the expression of collective concerns and aspirations and for mediation between the individual and the state. The county was one of several imagined communities to which the English gentry belonged.[44] Local historians addressed their county histories to the gentlemen of their shire, and considered their neighbours as forming the natural readership of their works. At the same time, they saw their works as representing an image of the county and its gentry to the world. Yet an analysis of the networks on which local historians relied to obtain their sources reveals the variety of factors which influenced their neighbours to assist with their researches. As we have seen, these factors included ties of kinship, mutual advantage and religious affiliation. A sense of county community may also have played a part, but does not appear to have been a decisive factor. Moreover, when we consider the importance of contacts between local historians in different parts of the country, and the influence exerted by London, the localism of antiquarian activity in the provinces becomes less convincing.

Ironically, local history was in many ways the product of the nationalism of the age. It is impossible to separate its development from the chorographical and cartographic shaping of the national consciousness described by Richard Helgerson.[45] Such national consciousness had become an increasingly important element in European culture during the Renaissance, and Camden's *Britannia* was symptomatic of the production of chorographies of the Roman provinces which forged links to the classical past, bypassing Italy. The Reformation and the break with Rome encouraged interest in a national past, while the accession of James I and the possibility of the union of his kingdoms intensified issues concerning national identity. The attention focused on what defined the English and made them different from the other nations of Europe, inevitably also drawing attention to regional differences. A young Cornish law student travelling to London would pass through country that little resembled his native soil. Arriving at the inns of court, he would find that some of his fellow students spoke with accents that were barely less foreign to him than that of a Breton sailor. In these circumstances the importance of what united the English gentry, and a natural desire to describe their own native landscape and communities and to claim their place on the national stage, helped lead to the growth of local history.

NOTES

1 Van Norden, 'Sir Henry Spelman on the chronology of the Elizabethan College of Antiquaries', p. 135.

2 Local historians undoubtedly worked within overlapping, open-ended networks, not circles or spheres: J. Scott-Warren, 'Reconstructing manuscript networks: the textual transactions of Sir Stephen Powle', in A. Shepard and P. Withington (eds), *Communities in Early Modern England* (Manchester: Manchester University Press, 2000), pp. 18–37.

3 Cumb. C.R.O., D/Lons/L12/4/1/3; Lancs. C.R.O., DDM 11/71; B.L., Egerton 3510.

4 B.L., Egerton 3510, fos 113, 119; T. Gerard, *A Survey of Dorsetshire* (London: J. Wilcox, 1732), attributed to John Coker on publication, but now known to be the work of Thomas Gerard. Hereafter Gerard, *Dorset*, p. 128.

5 Holles, *Memorials of the Holles Family*, p. 3; Habington, *Worcestershire*, vol. 1, p. 518.

6 Staffs. C.R.O. D(W)1744/73; Dugdale, *Warwickshire*, p. 728; *Smyth Papers*, vol. 9, fo. 40; Hamper, *Dugdale*, p. 260; Staffs. C.R.O. D649/1/1, Part 2. See also Society of Antiquaries Mss 145, fos 128v–9 for evidence of Habington's use of female informants.

7 Glos. C.R.O., D8887/6942, fo. 11; S.B.T., DR10/1952.

8 *Smyth Papers*, vol. 3, fo. 61; vol. 2, fo. 77; vol. 10, fo. 34; Glos. C.R.O., D8887/13611, fo.

12; Smyth, *Berkeley Mss*, vol. 3, pp. 99, 223.

9   Glos. C.R.O., D421/Z11 – both pedigrees are in poor condition; D885; *Smyth Papers*, vol. 7, fo. 80; Smyth, *Berkeley Mss*, vol. 1, p. 131, vol. 2, pp. 173, 283.

10 *Smyth Papers*, vol. 1, fos 70–4, vol. 2, fo. 89, vol. 7, fos 100–1; Badminton Muniments FmS/C3/3–4; Smyth, *Berkeley Mss*, vol. 1, pp. 15, 245–7, vol. 3, p. 110.

11 Smyth, *Berkeley Mss*, vol. 1, pp. 311, 312, 354; vol. 2, pp. 87, 200, 202, 404; Habington, *Worcestershire*, vol. 1, pp. 32, 370–3; Hamper, *Dugdale*, p. 202; *Smyth Papers*, vol. 1, fos 55, 75, 77; B.L., Additional MS 33588, fos 58–9.

12 B.L., Additional MS 33588; Smyth, *Berkeley Mss*, vol. 1, pp. 206, 210, 213; Burton, *Leicestershire*, To the Reader; B.L., Egerton 3510, fos 39v, 88; Staffs. C.R.O., D649/4/2; Glos. C.R.O., D8887/13616. In his will Smyth left a ring to Sir Henry Berkeley's wife.

13 J. Cox, 'The Rhymed Chronicle of John Harestaffe', *Journal of the Derbyshire Archaeological and Natural History Society* 10 (1888), pp. 71–147.

14 Staffs. C.R.O., D(W)1744/73; Habington, *Worcestershire*, vol. 1, pp. 180, 269–70; Burton, *Leicestershire*, p. 94; Burton, *Revised*, Drayton; B.L., Egerton 3510, pp. 8, 23, 28v, 40; B.L., Additional MS 6046; Hamper, *Dugdale*, pp. 155–6; Dugdale, *Warwickshire*, p. 799.

15 Burton, *Leicestershire*, To the Reader, pp. 104–8, 110; B.L. Egerton 3510, fo. 48v; D(W) 1744/73.

16 Burton, *Leicestershire*, pp. 51–2; Warwickshire. C.R.O., CR1598/1; Dugdale, *Warwickshire*, p. 75; West Kent C.R.O., Dering Mss, 232.

17 B.L., Egerton 3510, fos 79, 119; Archer, *Correspondence*, fos 68, 85.

18 F.E. Halliday, *Richard Carew of Antony* (London: Andrew Melrose, 1953); A. Rowse, *Court and Country* (Brighton: Harvester, 1987), pp. 242–77; J. Chynoweth, N. Orme and A. Walsham (eds), *The Survey of Cornwall by Richard Carew* (Devon and Cornwall Record Society New Series 47, Exeter, 2004).

19 Carew, *Cornwall*, p. 102v.

20 G. Wrottesley, 'A history of the Bagot family', *New Collections for a History of Staffordshire, New Series*, 11 (1908), p. 87.

21 B.L., Harley 506, fos 112v–117v; Erdeswicke, *Staffordshire*, p. 114; Petti, *Roman Catholicism in Elizabethan and Jacobean Staffordshire*, p. 16.

22 Society of Antiquaries, Mss 99, fos 31–2v, 44v, 58v–62, 63v–64v.

23 Habington, *Worcestershire*, vol. 1, p. 35; vol. 2, p. 50.

24 Francis Bel, *The Testament of William Bel* (Douai, Belgium: publisher not given, 1632): Bell actually died several years after writing his will.

25 Habington, *Worcestershire*, vol. 1, pp. 49–52, 378; vol. 2, pp. 281–2, 447; T. Nash, *The History and Antiquities of Worcestershire*, two volumes (1781), vol. 1, p. 352; F.T.S. Houghton, 'Notes on triptychs at Besford (Worcs.) and elsewhere', *Birmingham Archaeological Society Transactions*, 49 (1923), pp. 66–76.

26 Habington, *Worcestershire*, vol. 1, pp. 345, 381–2; vol. 2, pp. 198, 286; Erdeswicke, *Staffordshire*, p. 202; Worcs. C.R.O., 989-9:429; E.P. Shirley, *Hanley and the House of Lechmere* (London: Pickering & Co., 1883), pp. 51–2.

27 Habington, *Worcestershire*, vol. 1, pp. 17–18, 77–8; vol. 2, pp. 106–7.

28 T. Gibson (ed.), *Crosby Records* (London: Longman's, Green & Co., 1880); M. Blundell (ed.), *Cavalier: Letters of William Blundell to His Friends 1620–1698* (London: Longman & Co., 1933); D.R. Woolf, 'Horizons of early modern historical culture', in Kelley and Sacks, *The Historical Imagination in Early Modern Britain*, pp. 93–132; Woolf, *Social Circulation*, pp. 246–56; M. Sena, 'William Blundell and the networks of Catholic dissent in post-Reformation England', in Shepard and Withington, *Communities in Early Modern England*, pp. 54–75.

29 The importance of Archer in encouraging contributions to the *Antiquities of Warwickshire* is examined in Styles, *Studies in Seventeenth Century West Midlands History*, pp. 1–41.

30 Hamper, *Dugdale*, pp. 154–6.

31 Hamper, *Dugdale*, pp. 157, 161–2; Warwickshire. C.R.O., Z65/5; Erdeswicke, *Staffordshire*, pp. 354–9; B.L., Egerton 3510, fos 75, 75v; Staffs. C.R.O., D868/5.

32 Hamper, *Dugdale*, p. 165; B.L., Egerton 3510, fos 75, 88, 110v, 115v; Warwickshire. C.R.O., Z65/1; Dugdale, *Warwickshire*, p. a4; B.L., Additional MS 29549, fos 76, 78.

33 Quoted in Oxford Dictionary of National Biography, hereafter O.D.N.B., Crewe, Sir Randolph (1559–1646).

34 Dugdale, *Warwickshire*, p. 632; B.L., Additional MS 6396, fos 17, 19; T. Fuller, *The Worthies of England*, (ed.) J. Nichols, two volumes (London: F.C. & J. Rivington, 1811), vol. 1, pp. 193–4.

35 J. Wake and G. Isham, 'Sir William Dugdale in Northamptonshire', *Northamptonshire Past and Present* 2(2), (1955), pp. 8–12; Northants C.R.O., FH114; FH2664; Warwickshire. C.R.O., Z38/1–2.

36 N. Denholm-Young and H. Craster, 'Roger Dodsworth and his circle', *Yorkshire Archaeological Journal* 32 (1936), pp. 5–32; J. Hunter, *Three Catalogues* (London: Pickering, 1838), pp. 57–249.

37 J. Halliwell (ed.), *The Autobiography and Correspondence of Sir Simonds D'Ewes*, two volumes (London: Richard Bentley, 1845), vol. 2, p. 314.

38 J. Cliffe, *The Yorkshire Gentry* (London: Athlone Press, 1969), p. 46 and *passim*.

39 Browne, *Religio Medici*, pp. 93–4.

40 Browne, *Religio Medici*, pp. 93, 169.

41 B.L., Sloane 1839 – L'Estrange sought Browne's medical advice in the last year of his life and their surviving correspondence dates from this time; Heal and Holmes, *The Gentry of England and Wales*, p. 344; Browne, *Religio Medici*, pp. 104, 147; R. Wenley, 'Robert Paston and the Yarmouth collection', *Norfolk Archaeology* 41 (1991), pp. 113–39; E. Phillips, *The New World of English Words* (London: E. Tyler, 1658), dedication.

42 Sir Thomas Browne, *Religio Medici and Other Writings*, ed. C. H. Herford (London: J.M. Dent & Sons Ltd., 1906), hereafter Browne, *Religio Medici*, pp. 102, 142, 146–7.

43 A. Everitt, *The Community of Kent and the Great Rebellion 1640–1660* (Leicester: Leicester University Press, 1973); A. Duffin, *Faction and Faith* (Exeter: Exeter University Press, 1996) raises doubts about the Everitt model with respect to Cornwall.

44 P. Laslett, 'The gentry of Kent in 1640', *Cambridge Historical Journal* 9 (1947–49), pp. 148–64.

45 Helgerson, *Forms of Nationhood*, chapter 3.

Chapter 4

Sources for local history

I t is a characteristic of early local historians that they were not willing to sacrifice substance in favour of style. They preferred to overburden their readers with evidence rather than to omit sources from their works. Habington justified transcribing four deeds into his account of one Worcestershire manor on the grounds that they were short and 'cannot bee tedyous to any but suche whose tast cannot relyshe nor stomacke digest antiquityes'. Similarly, Lambarde included the Saxon will of Byrhtric of Mepham, 'though happily some other man may say, that I do therein (and in many others also) nothing else but *Antiquiora Diphtera loqui*'. There was an implicit assumption that some at least of their readers would appreciate the depth of their research. Gerard concluded entries in the *Description of Somerset* with blazons of the arms of local families:

> or as manie of them as by my seeking in old rolles and bookes, Churches, Windowes, Tombes, and antient seales have come to my knowledge, which though to manie that understand it not may seeme a needles labour, yett it may be a pleasure to some and will seeme right well for the amending of divers grosse errours in Armoury.[1]

This list of sources for just one aspect of local history helps to explain why many antiquaries became overwhelmed by the collection of evidence and failed to make progress on its assimilation and presentation. It was not unusual for local historians to undertake immense programmes of research that occupied many years. Dugdale wrote that in preparing the *Antiquities of Warwickshire*: 'I have spent the chiefest of my time for much more than twenty years, diligently searching into the vast Treasuries of publique Records, besides a multitude of Manuscripts, originall Charters and Evidences in private hands'. John Smyth described the *Lives of the Berkeleys* as the 'gleanings of forty years vacant hours'. When the *Description of the Hundred of Berkeley* was published in the late nineteenth century, a reviewer complained of the 'wearisome amount of profitless items' it contained, reflecting the comprehensive nature of Smyth's research if not his skill as an editor.[2] While the subject of the sources used by local historians may seem somewhat dry and unexciting, it is essential to an understanding of what they wrote and why.

The absence of modern referencing standards in the sixteenth and seventeenth centuries means that a certain amount of detective work is required in order to identify the written sources used by local historians. In completed works, marginal references are of varied quality and quantity, although these improved over time, partly due to pressure from within the antiquarian community. Exasperated comments concerning the impossibility of verifying what another antiquary had written appear with regularity in correspondence. In 1655 Thomas, lord Brudenell, cautioned Dugdale that he should 'be sure you printe youre authorities plainely'.[3] For local historians who never produced a fair manuscript of their work or whose referencing was minimal, information about the sources they used can be gleaned from their notebooks, copies made of their collections by later antiquaries, and correspondence. Printed sources such as chronicles were referenced by the name of the author. Where an author was associated with more than one work, a title might also be given. Manuscript chronicles were also referred to by the name of the author, with possibly the name of a library or current owner. For public records it was usual to give the name of the source (more or less equivalent to the modern Public Record Office class) and the regnal year. For legal records the court, regnal year and term was given. Since no established convention existed, it became common to include an explanation of abbreviations used in the margins at the end of the text. Gradually the inclusion of chapter, page or folio references increased. However, many records were used in abstracted form or as copies from the original in which such information was lost, so this did not become general in the period under discussion. Initially no references were given to the papers of the local gentry. In his *View of Staffordshire* Erdeswicke quotes at length from a number of documents, without indicating whether the sources were in his possession or had been copied from the papers of one of his neighbours. In some cases this information can be determined from the surviving evidence of his researches. Half a century later Dugdale gave the names of the owners of documents he had consulted but no further information. It is doubtful that Dugdale expected his readers to have either the desire or the means to follow in his footsteps and examine the private papers he had used. For family historians the situation was rather different, since their readers might have practical reasons for wanting to trace a record to which they referred. Consequently, references to family papers in such works tend to be quite detailed. Shirley did not use marginal references, but gave a list of the sources he had used as an appendix. For papers belonging to his family he gave the name of the house in which they were located and described how the relevant box was marked.

In the period covered by this study using the public records held in various depositiories around London was a difficult, time-consuming and expensive business. In part this was a result of the haphazard manner in which medieval records had been preserved. Before the fourteenth century, individual officers of the Crown had been responsible for the care and conservation of documents relating to their offices. These officers stored those records not required on a daily basis where they could, often utilising monasteries as depositories. Later the Tower of London became the major record office for the Exchequer and Chancery records. In 1377 the master of the Rolls acquired a chapel in Chancery Lane, which was used to accumulate Chancery records before they were transferred to the Tower. By 1500 the transfer of important records from the Rolls chapel to the Tower had ceased. By the same date the Exchequer remembrancers, clerks of the pell and auditors of receipt were also retaining their records in their offices. The officers of the new courts established in the sixteenth century such as Star Chamber, Requests, Augmentations, Wards and First Fruits and Tenths all did the same. However, the Tower continued to receive legal records. In addition there were spasmodic transfers of administrative records from the Exchequer, Chancery and other offices to the Tower. This confused situation made it difficult to work out where a particular record should be. A memorandum survives among Archer's papers advocating a search in 'Mr Agar's office in the nether end of Westminster Hall up the stayres where the talleyes be' for a *Quo Warranto* of Edward III's reign, as well as in the Exchequer, Mr Osborne's office and the courts of Augmentations and First Fruits. This indicates the amount of time his helpers might spend simply locating the records for him.[4] The haphazard storage of the public records was added to the dangers of damp, mice, mildew and official carelessness, which threatened the survival of all records and made the work of researchers more challenging.

The most important of the Exchequer records was the Domesday Book. For those localities covered, the survey provided a firm starting point for genealogies and manorial histories. Since Domesday recorded the names of the tenants-in-chief and sub-tenants before and after the Conquest, it was theoretically possible for local historians to trace the descent of a manor from that point to their own day. In reality, there was usually a gap of several generations between Domesday and the next reliable source of evidence for a manorial descent. From the publication of Lambarde's *Perambulation of Kent*, Domesday was used as a source by local historians, and Erdeswicke included a summary of its contents for Staffordshire at the end of his *View* of the county. As local history became more genealogical in content, the importance of Domesday increased proportionately. Comparatively few local historians consulted the Exchequer volumes directly – most relied upon transcripts of varying quality (see figure 4). In 1647 Dodsworth was clearly responding to criticism of his

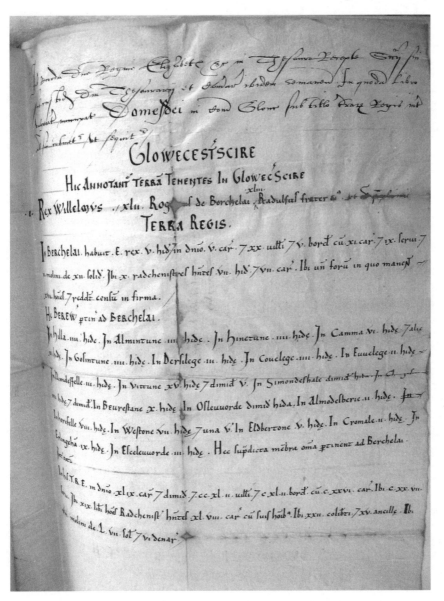

Figure 4 Copy of excerpt from Domesday Book for Gloucestershire

own transcription standards from D'Ewes when he wrote: 'I cannot endure to be told of vast omissions, when I have not left out one word that I liked, in any record, in all my life. As for transcribing Records *literatim & verbatim*, let them that list undertake itt, I disclayme itt.'[5]

Domesday transcripts might be of an entire county, or more limited extracts relating to one or more manors. As a law student Burton made extracts from Domesday relating to his ancestral manor of Lindley and to Ibstock, a manor in the same hundred where the Herdwicks also held land. By the time the *Description of Leicestershire* was published, he had clearly acquired further extracts, but as late as 1634 he was hoping to get a full copy of Domesday for Leicestershire 'by the Lord Treasurer's favour'. Three years later Dugdale and Archer were attempting to gain access to a copy of Domesday made by a previous lord treasurer, James Ley, earl of Marlborough, a former member of the Society of Antiquaries. When this endeavour failed, Hatton urged Archer to finance the procuring of a copy for Dugdale in London. Dering owned a transcript relating to Kent by 1638, and after the civil war Dugdale obtained a copy for Cheshire on behalf of Vernon.[6] Gerard's account of Somerset stands out because of its failure to make significant use of Domesday, indicating that no transcript for the county was in general circulation. As a consequence his descents of manors generally start from entries in the plea rolls in the reign of John, or a thirteenth-century inquisition *post mortem*. This was not as great a disadvantage as it might appear, as few manorial descents could be traced with any certainty between Domesday and the late twelfth century.

In addition to Domesday the Exchequer contained a number of surveys and collections of records compiled by medieval treasurers and their offi-cials. These included the twelfth-century *Black Book of the Exchequer*, the *Red Book of the Exchequer*, *Testa de Nevill* and *Kirkby's Quest* from the thirteenth century; and the *Nomina Villarum* of Edward II's reign. Such compilations mitigated to an extent the loss of many original medieval records through their haphazard storage, and extracts from these records circulated widely in antiquarian circles. An invaluable record for local historians was the *Valor Ecclesiasticus*, which was held in the office of First Fruits. This general survey of church property conducted on the eve of the Reformation represented an ecclesiastical Domesday. Importantly, the form of the entries was standard-ised, providing a consistent record. Although the *Valor* originally covered the whole of the country, a number of returns were subsequently lost or damaged. The lost returns were in part supplied by the summary *Liber Valorum*, also held in the office of First Fruits. The *Liber* preserved the names of dignitaries and benefices with their values, but not the particulars available on the original returns. Archer had a complete copy of the *Valor* for Warwickshire along with the contemporary chantry certificates, while the Chorographer of Norfolk and Suffolk had a mid-Elizabethan updated abridgement. In early Stuart Here-fordshire someone with antiquarian interests copied details on the founders of religious houses in the county and a list of their valuations into a notebook, a book that also contained extensive genealogical information. Hatton's exten-sive collection of records included a copy of the *Liber*.[7]

The correspondence between Archer, Dugdale and Hatton in the late 1630s provides a valuable spotlight on how the public records were used for local history. In 1637 Hatton advised Archer to 'procure' Dugdale 'Domesday, the Aid Rolls, the Pipe Roll, and such general records as will adorne the History'. The pipe rolls contained the annual accounts returned by sheriffs to the Exchequer, the earliest of which dated from 1130. The aid rolls related to the collection of feudal aids (medieval taxes). At this time Dugdale was spending much of his time among the Exchequer records, copying the register of the College of Warwick. He was also busy extracting Warwickshire material from the plea rolls – records of common-law actions in the Exchequer, Common Pleas and King's Bench, surviving from the twelfth century. When he had the opportunity, Dugdale intended to compare the records of knight's fees taken from the transcript of a taxation of Henry VI's reign with the original. Six months later, Dugdale was hoping Hatton's abstracts of the patent and charter rolls in the Tower would be sufficient for his needs, and that the Warwickshire feodary's records would provide the inquisitions. There were, however, inquisitions in the Exchequer that were not in the Tower, which they had to have 'or we shall be lame' and which he hoped to have abstracted, as this would be cheaper than copies. By the end of 1638 Dugdale had extracted the substance of the Leger Book of Coventry from the Exchequer and was about to 'fall upon the Roules in Chancery Lane from H.7th tyme downwarde, wherin I have the promise of much furtherance of an antient Clarke who hath allredy carefully and exactly abstracted them'.[8] From this correspondence it becomes apparent why Dugdale at this time despaired of being able to complete the task he had set himself in undertaking a comprehensive study of the history of Warwickshire.

Dugdale's reference to the ancient clerk, who had abstracted the Chancery rolls, acts as a reminder of the usefulness to local historians of personal contacts among the record-keepers, as discussed in chapter two. His friendship with Vincent, for example, meant that Burton had extensive access to the Tower records – with which he had become familiar during the course of his legal training. This is evidenced by his claim to D'Ewes in 1638 that 'all the records for Leicester county, which are in the Tower, I have perused so many as are kalendered; and all in the Rolls till 17 Elizabeth.'[9] The difficulties associated with consulting the numerous public records meant that many provincial antiquaries were dependent upon contacts in the city to obtain transcripts. These transcripts were necessarily of varying reliability. Some commissioned the transcripts directly from clerks in the record office concerned, while others used the services of their legal representatives, law students among their acquaintances, or others willing to undertake the work for a fee. Transcripts and extracts from the public records had legal as well as antiquarian value, as indicated by the volumes left by Sir Matthew Hale to the library of Lincoln's

Inn. This collection includes various transcripts compiled for Hale for use in his legal career, and several volumes that he inherited as John Selden's executor. Among the various volumes of records compiled by Smyth was one containing all the offices or inquisitions *post mortem* and of *ad quod damnum* for Gloucestershire between 1225 and 1537, which he compiled in 1603 while a law student. This volume is one of several pieces of evidence that Smyth, in London during the period when Stow and Carew were publishing their histories, contemplated writing a county history before circumstances took his antiquarian labours in a different direction. In subsequent decades it became a valuable resource for his antiquarian contacts in Gloucestershire.[10] Among John Denton's surviving manuscripts is a carefully extracted volume of the fines levied in Cumberland and Westmorland between 1208 and 1498. This formed the basis for his *Accompt of the Most Considerable Estates and Families in the County of Cumberland,* although it may initially have been compiled for professional rather than antiquarian reasons. In 1637 Habington was preparing to turn from his history of the diocese and abbey of Worcester to a wider county history. In a letter to Archer, he explained that 'because none can wade into so greate a deapthe without knowledge of the Recordes of the Tower & courtes of lawe so far as they concearne thys Shyre', he wanted to employ Dugdale to transcribe the relevant records for him. Less-fortunate gentlemen were reliant upon third-hand copies of transcripts from other antiquaries' notes or that had been prepared for a court case. The Warwickshire antiquary Sir Simon Clarke possessed two volumes containing records of the land held by knight service or *in capite* of the king from the reign of Henry I to 1476 taken from the Tower records. These were borrowed by Archer in 1630, who promised to let Burton see the copies he had made. Such repeated copying of transcriptions led inevitably to the incorporation of errors. It was with good reason that Dugdale advised Archer that 'to depend on any men's collections or transcripts without comparinge them with the originalls will but deceive you'.[11] Unfortunately, for many provincial gentry comparing a transcript with the original was beyond their resources of time and money.

As is the case today, many of the public records of most use to local historians were not located in London, but were to be found nearer to home. The nature and availability of such records depended upon the structure of local institutions and the attitudes of office-holders. The status of a local gentleman might open the way to certain records, but others might be guarded by officers suspicious of a local historian's motives and fearful of encroachments upon the privileges of their institutions. In 1630 the Herefordshire gentleman Townshend Hereford, a kinsman of Sir Simon Archer, saw 'an ancient Manuscript of the Customes of the Citie of Hereford', but he was not allowed to read more than a few lines 'because it was the misterie of their gobernment and the ground of the Charter'.[12] Such suspicion meant that writing urban history was largely restricted to aldermen and town officials. The most useful of the local officers for those interested in genealogical research was the feodary, who maintained the feudal rights of the Crown within their jurisdiction. (The value of escheators, who conducted inquisitions *post mortem*, was limited by their annual appointments, although Dodsworth's notes do show him using a book of Yorkshire tenures in the possession of a local escheator.) Burton warned that offices and inquisitions 'are very incertaine, sometimes cleane contrary to truth', as local juries had a vested interest in defending local rights against the encroachments of the Crown. Consequently, these sources were useful for identifying the particular area of land that someone held, but the nature of the tenure and other details had to be treated with caution. Three of the men who held the office of feodary in Warwickshire during the period of this study were linked to Archer, and all gave considerable assistance to the research for the *Antiquities of Warwickshire*. The Elizabethan feodary Arthur Gregory compiled a large volume of copies of deeds and inquisitions. His son John, Archer's cousin, had 'vowed never to lend it out to any, bycause one that borrowed it of him cut two leaves out', but he allowed Archer and Dugdale to transcribe this and other documents at his house.[13] Humphrey Colles of Hampton in Arden was an assiduous collector of records, while Edward Chamberlayne of Astley castle compiled a book of escheats which was extensively used by Dugdale. The records available from a feodary varied considerably from county to county. In 1630 Townshend Hereford approached the Herefordshire feodary to see whether he had a record similar to Colles' abridgement to assist him in tracing his pedigree – in this case the answer was no. In contrast George Raymond of Thornbury, the Gloucestershire feodary, was described when appearing in the court case over Hill as a witness for Chetwynd, as having 'taken great pains in seeking out records to find what parishes, hamlets and villages are within the county of Gloucester, and to find out the tenure and owners thereof'. Such a contact was of obvious use to Smyth, who was also involved in the case and interested in the material collected by Raymond for inclusion in the *Description of the Hundred of Berkeley*.[14]

Having a keen antiquary as a local office-holder could be both a blessing and a curse, as is demonstrated by the example of Sir Edward Dering. Dering was lieutenant of Dover castle between 1629 and 1635, during the wardenship of Theophilus, earl of Suffolk. During his tenure various records found their way from Dover to Dering's house at Surrenden. In 1636 the lord warden was obliged to write to Dering about his failure to return all these documents to Dover. Despite Dering's protestation of innocence, some of the castle records do appear to have been given by him to Cotton and never returned to their rightful place. The volume known as the Dover Domesday book was particularly mentioned by Suffolk. Regarding this volume, Dering wrote:

being torne and defaced and unbound, I took care to have it renewed as it is, resolving to have added to the end thereof the names and arms of your Lordship's honourable, and some royal predecessors in office with their Lieutenants, but I could not get the painters down this summer nor could I get Mr. Somerset's help in perfecting the catalogue.

Dering never completed the intended work and also failed to return the volume. While his stated intention was to preserve and beautify the Domesday (while enhancing his own status by including his arms among the rest), he actually diminished the archive that had been in his care.[15]

At the end of the *Lives of the Berkeleys* Smyth listed the various depositories of public records he had used in the course of his research:

I have taken into hand year after yeare most of the Records in the Tower of London, between the first and last whereof some parts of each of 34 years were spent; And what records and books I have turned over in the offices belonging to the kings bench, Rolls chapple, Chancery, Common pleas, Exchequer, Treasury, pipe and pell offices, and other places there, let my marginall vouchers, and my books of the lord Berkeleys tenures declare.[16]

Considering the practical difficulties and expense of working in these offices, the list is testimony of the dedication of Smyth and his contemporaries to using as many 'authentic' records as possible.

Large volumes of ecclesiastical records of relevance to the researches of local historians were to be found in diocesan archives. Further records lay in the muniment rooms belonging to the dean and chapter of each cathedral. Somner's *Antiquities of Canterbury* was 'chiefly collected from old Manuscripts, Leiger-Books, and other Records of credit, exhibited to me for the most part by the Treasury of our Cathedral'.[17] The three great surveys of their manors, compiled by medieval bishops of Worcester in the twelfth, thirteenth and fifteenth centuries, were the most important of all the documentary records used by Habington. Dugdale also made extensive use of these sources, which he examined during a visit to the royalist garrison at Worcester during the civil war. He had earlier acquired access to the records at Lichfield through the good offices of a cathedral official, while Hatton's influence had ensured his entrance to the Lambeth archive of the archbishop of Canterbury. John Hooker was less successful, possibly because of the antagonism between the corporation of Exeter and the cathedral over their respective privileges. Dedicating his *Catalogue of the Bishops of Excester* to the current incumbent, he complained of the lack of assistance he had received: 'some being more suspicious than needed; some ... not unlike Aesops dogge, who would neither eate haie himselfe, nor yet suffer the oxe to do it'.[18]

For the modern genealogist, parish registers and wills are generally the most important classes of ecclesiastical documents. These records were surprisingly little used by early local historians. In 1638 Burton told D'Ewes: 'For wills and testaments at Leicester, I never saw any of them'. Nor did Habington use the wills available at Worcester. Parish registers and wills were used by Archer in researching his own pedigree and Dugdale searched the archepiscopal records at Lambeth for Warwickshire wills from the reign of Edward III to 1558. The more generalised use of these records for local history, however, did not occur until later.[19] The problems of locating wills in the absence of finding aids presumably militated against the widespread use of this material, particularly given the complexity of jurisdiction in relation to the proving of wills. In 1639 Smyth, who knew more than most about the land owned by his fellow gentry in the vale of Berkeley, was unsure whether the will of one William Hill had been proved at Gloucester or London.[20] Those wills that were incorporated into the text of local histories almost invariably came from the copies found among a family's private papers. The parish registers were a comparatively new source for local historians, their compilation having been required only since 1538. Archer acquired transcripts of entries in various parish registers relating to his research into his own pedigree. In 1635 Dugdale asked Archer to 'peruse the register of Tanworth Church, for findinge out the births mariages and deaths' of the ancestors whose arms he quartered.[21] Several factors militated against the wider use of parish registers as a source for local history. The limited time-span covered, and the dependence on the diligence of individual ministers for their compilation, limited their usefulness. The problems of gaining access were also considerable, as applications had to be made to individual ministers. The introduction of Bishop's Transcripts in 1598 came too late to be of much use to the early local historians. The potential value of the parish registers was, therefore, outweighed by the difficulties of using the source.

In contrast to parish registers and wills, monastic registers and cartularies were among the most used and most useful sources for local history in this period. They provided information not only about the monastic houses them-selves, but also about their benefactors and tenants. They recorded leases made to local landowners by the monasteries and the pious gifts of the gentry. They also preserved the names of those who kept the monks' manorial courts, sent their sons to be educated, or retired themselves to the seclusion of the cloister for their final years. These registers were consequently of immense value in researching the history of the medieval nobility and gentry, and of those yeoman families who had advanced into the gentry through acquiring the lands of their former landlords at the time of the Dissolution. These documents had great value as legal documents recording entitlement to land and perquisites. Accordingly, they were not destroyed as were so many of the contents of monastic libraries, but preserved by the new owners of the land. They often passed to those who acquired the site and primary estate of a monastic house. Thus, the Leighs retained the records of Stoneleigh Abbey, Warwickshire, and the Trenthams those of Rocester Abbey, Staffs. The

Shirleys acquired the register of Breedon, Leics., through their purchase of the priory church, and the Proctors of Fountains Hall, Yorks., possessed two couchers (large breviaries: a breviary being a book containing psalms, hymns, lessons, etc. used in religious services), from Fountains Abbey. The dean and chapter of the six cathedrals created from former monasteries inherited the records of their predecessors. The records of other monastic houses were more difficult to locate. A number of cartularies (volumes into which charters and other legal documents were copied) remained in the possession of the Crown even after the lands were sold, and these were to be found among the public records in the Exchequer. The lands of the priory of St Thomas the Martyr, Stafford, passed into the possession of the bishop of Lichfield, who subsequently granted the land to his recusant nephew Brian Fowler. The cartulary passed into his hands, and access to it was widespread among local historians. George, earl of Shrewsbury, acquired the cartulary of Monk Bretton, Yorks., along with part of its former lands, in 1580. This passed in turn to his daughter Mary, and in the reign of Charles I was in the possession of her second husband, William Armine of Osgodby, Yorks., where Dodsworth saw it. A further Monk Bretton cartulary was owned by Sir Francis Wortley, who also held some of the former monastery's land. It is unclear how the register of Merevale, Warwickshire, came to be owned by Richard Chamberlain of Chilvers Coton, Warwickshire, who allowed Burton and Dugdale to examine it. The manor and site of the abbey had been granted to the Devereux family at the Dissolution, and remained in their hands until after the civil war. It is possible that the cartulary was in Chamberlain's possession by virtue of his office as clerk of the Court of Wards. It was not unusual for such records to be transferred from the public records into the private archive of an office-holder. Cartularies were useful to Chamberlain in determining types of tenure and other legal questions, both within the Court of Wards and in his wider legal practice. A Warwickshire cartulary was particularly valuable, as much of his private legal practice derived from the local gentry. A number of local historians and heralds possessed monastic cartularies and registers, which related to their own and their neighbours' lands. As landowners and antiquaries they were well aware of the dual value of the records as both historical and legal evidence.

For Dodsworth's work on the *Monasticon Anglicanum*, monastic records were obviously of primary importance. He owned at least eight cartularies himself and consulted many others. In addition to those in private hands, cathedral archives and the office of the remembrancer of the Exchequer, he had access to several in Cotton's library. The muniments of a number of Yorkshire houses were held in St Mary's Tower, York. They were examined by Dodsworth before its destruction during the civil war, when many of the records rescued from the tower passed into the hands of his colleague Charles Fairfax.

The legal significance of monastic records meant that they were frequently copied, and in many cases it was a copy rather than the original that was examined by Dodsworth and Dugdale. Such copies often contained modifications, introduced either as a result of scribal error or deliberate falsification. Despite Dugdale's warning to Archer concerning the dangers of relying on copies, the compilers of the *Monasticon* did not undertake the comparison with originals or collation of various transcripts that would have improved the accuracy of their collection. As well as inaccurate transcriptions, many completely spurious deeds also found their way into the *Monasticon*, despite Sir Roger Twysden's warning that the text included forgeries. Such deficiencies reveal the limitations of contemporary antiquarian practice in the handling of medieval documents.[22]

In his *Survey of Worcestershire* Habington expressed a greater confidence in the reliability of public records than private papers, writing of being 'forced to private evidences being destitute of publique Records'.[23] Other local historians seem to have been equally happy using private papers and public or ecclesiastical records, and Habington's apparent prejudice may be no more than a recognition of his limited access to private evidence. Certainly, deeds, marriage settlements, wills and other private papers remaining in the custody of a gentry family provided the most straightforward evidence for tracing their descent. A wealth of material was available to Smyth in the archives of Berkeley castle, including a fifteenth-century cartulary of Berkeley charters. Shirley was able to use a large number of documents from among his own papers and those of his father and brother. Archer was able to trace his pedigree back to the reign of Henry II, through the deeds and other documents preserved at Tanworth. Edward Gwynne's commendation of the 'wondrous and generous care' of Archer's ancestors, who had been 'so tenacious of theyre nobilitye in the preservation of theyre profes', suggests that this was relatively unusual.[24] Nevertheless, the studies of most gentlemen's houses contained some documents relating to their estates, pedigrees or public service that was of potential interest to a local historian.

Among the private papers of a local gentleman, an antiquary was liable to encounter a pedigree produced for the family by a member of the College of Arms. In 1635 Habington agreed that Archer was right not to rely on such pedigrees, as they 'are often farced with untruthes'. The families to which such pedigrees belonged, however, were often attached to the fables they propagated. This required local historians to tread warily in their treatment of the family's descent. Sir Charles Smith of Wootton Wawen was the owner of just such a spurious pedigree. He was also an important potential source of material for the history of Warwickshire and Leicestershire. At the end of the sixteenth century the Smith family had realised that the extravagant coat of arms awarded to their ancestor Sir John Smith in the reign of Henry VIII indelibly marked them out as 'new men'. Accordingly, a spurious narrative was concocted, which professed to prove that the family were descended from the heir of the Carringtons of Cheshire, obliged to change his name to Smith in order to avoid persecution under Henry IV. This forgery was accepted by the heralds, who allowed the family to adopt a coat of arms based on that of their supposed Carrington ancestors. The suspicions of later antiquaries were aroused by the changes in the arms borne by the Smiths. When raised to the peerage in 1643 Sir Charles Smith chose the title lord Carrington, reflecting his attachment to the spurious family pedigree. Dugdale was not convinced by the family history, but he had no desire to upset lord Carrington, who had allowed him and other local historians considerable access to his papers. Consequently, he inserted the spurious Carrington descent into the *Antiquities of Warwickshire*, as 'what I have seen attested by Sir William Dethick sometime Garter principall King of Armes, and Robert Cooke Clarenceux'. Hiding behind the authority of his predecessors as heralds, Dugdale included the information that lord Carrington wanted to see.[25]

Wills were among the most potentially useful sources for local historians, since they provided evidence not only of family relationships and land ownership, but also of personal attachments, religious and institutional affiliations. As we have seen, local historians did not conduct general searches for wills among the ecclesiastical archives, but were dependent upon such wills as were preserved among the papers of the local gentry. Unfortunately, as wills were concerned with property, local historians were often unable to gain access to this valuable source. In this respect family historians were generally more fortunate than those with wider interests, as they enjoyed unfettered access to the surviving wills in their family archive. Wills were particularly useful for providing evidence of the charitable acts of the local gentry, which might otherwise go unrecorded. Wolstan Dixie provided evidence for Burton of the 'divers considerable sums in Acts of charity & piety' disposed of by Sir Wolstan Dixie, a former mayor of London, taken from his uncle's will. (His founding of a free school at Bosworth, Leics., led Stow to include Dixie among those citizens who acquired honour by their charitable acts in the *Survey of London*.) With the assistance of Gervase Holles, Dugdale was able to revive the memory of Sir William Holles, who had paid for the erection of the cross in Coventry a century before. Habington regretted the loss of the will of Mr Newport of Droitwich, which meant that he was unable to record his pious and charitable acts. In contrast Smyth used the will of William, marquess Berkeley, as evidence of his selfishness and lack of consideration for his family and posterity. However, as Stow repeatedly warned in the *Survey of London*, the evidence of wills alone was unreliable, since not all charitable bequests were carried out: 'executors of our time having no conscience (I speak of my own knowledge) prove more testaments than they perform'.[26]

Family archives also included manorial court rolls, rentals and other estate records. In addition to the original records, copies were frequently made. These were in many cases more useful to a local historian, as a number of related documents would be copied into a single volume. For example, when the manor of Chalgrave, Beds. passed from Jane Cheney to her great-nephew Thomas, lord Wentworth, in 1614, he acquired the originals of all deeds relating to the manor from 1564, when the manor had been settled on Jane by her husband. At the same time a cartulary was compiled containing copies of the deeds and lord Wentworth's agreement that he would produce the originals 'uppon reasonable request'.[27] It was a common practice of landowners, especially those with some legal training, to copy deeds and other material relevant to their estates into a single volume for ease of reference. In the case of local historians like William Burton, the compilation of such notebooks is often cited as the first indication of antiquarian interest. For many gentlemen, however, such collections had a purely practical purpose. The Cobbe family of Sharnbrooke, Beds., possessed such a volume, containing copies of deeds, surveys, taxation records and other information relating to their two manors within Sharnbrook. The volume also contained a genealogical account of the recent generations of the family, showing dates of birth and marriage alliances, which apparently dates from the time of the heralds' visitation of Bedfordshire in 1634 and contains the information required to update the pedigree presented at the previous visitation. The genealogical details suggest that the volume was compiled by John Cobbe, town clerk of Bedford, whose professional role may explain the presence in the volume of lists of justices of the peace for Northamptonshire and Bedfordshire and sheriffs for Bedfordshire. The Cobbes were of merchant stock and had acquired their manors by purchase in Elizabeth's reign. The absence of copies of medieval deeds, court rolls and so forth in the volume suggests that John Cobbe had access only to material relating to his family's period of ownership of the manors, although it is possible that a companion volume of earlier material has been lost. The volume was a practical, working document, compiled over a number of years and with blank pages left between different sections for later additions. Although there was almost certainly no antiquarian impulse behind its compilation, it demonstrates the type of useful information that such sources could hold for local historians, both in respect of the family concerned and their manors, and also with regard to the wider history of the locality.[28]

The frequency of contemporary lawsuits over manorial rights and claims to land meant that access to relevant documents was often restricted. Burton himself was cautious regarding evidence relating to his own manors. His notebook, entitled *Antiquitates de Falde et Coton*, bears the following inscription on the title page: 'This booke is only proper to the heyre, & is not to be perused of any or to be lent to any man, because it contayneth copyes of evidences'. Brian Manning's research into the disputes of Sir Robert Cotton and his son with their tenants suggests that the stealing of court rolls and other manorial records was not unusual. This led to suspicion of the motives of those seeking to examine such muniments for antiquarian purposes. Once again, family historians had an advantage, as the records of the manors in which they were most interested were likely to be in their own archives. Smyth expended much effort on analysing the evidence of medieval estate records and accounts remaining in the Berkeley archive, and his extensive use of this material is a distinct feature of his work. Smyth's work as an estate steward presumably stimulated his interest. His own contributions to the Berkeley archives listed at the end of the *Lives of the Berkeleys* included rent rolls and surveys. These documents were of interest to subsequent historians, but were originally compiled because of their usefulness to the Berkeleys in exploiting their estate. Stow also showed an interest in accounts and similar material. He included a fourteenth-century household account for Thomas, earl of Lancaster, the inquisition of Hugh Despenser and other records in the *Survey of London*, to show the grand households maintained by the medieval nobility in London. The majority of local historians, however, were more concerned with the martial exploits of the medieval gentry and their possession of land, rather than in calculating how many sheep they owned or how many barrels their cellars held.[29]

The importance of the local gentry in the political and administrative life of the country was often reflected in the contents of their private papers. A collection of documents belonging to Richard Berkeley and his son Sir Maurice, who both allowed Smyth access to their papers, is preserved among the Badminton muniments. These include an indexed volume compiled by Richard Berkeley, incorporating documents sent to him and to his grandfather, Sir Richard Berkeley, as deputies lieutenant and justices of the peace during the reigns of Elizabeth, James I and Charles I. Another volume of alphabetically arranged memoranda for justices of the peace includes as appendices various legal opinions, petitions to the Gloucestershire justices, and their response. Both Richard and Sir Maurice Berkeley served as MP for Gloucestershire, and their papers include a number of parliamentary papers, including records of speeches and debates and locally significant documents such as 'Reasons to move the High Court of Parliament not to pass the Bill for the repairing of the bridge near Tewkesbury' from 1621. The collection also preserves a record of the Eyre of the Forest of Dean in 1634.[30] This example illustrates how a gentleman's papers might contain material beyond that which concerned his own family and their lands. Nor were the Berkeleys exceptional in this regard. The surviving papers of local gentry families often provide evidence of their involvement in local affairs over successive generations, as deputies lieutenant, justices, sheriffs, escheators and collectors of parliamentary subsidies. In all these roles they might acquire documents that were of interest to local historians.

The estate and personal records of a local family could provide an antiquary with an invaluable storehouse for local history, but, like many public records, such records suffered from problems of haphazard and careless storage. In 1637 Dugdale reported a visit to the home of Sir Simon Montfort at Bescote, near Walsall, West Midlands. He described to Archer 'the great spoyle of the many rare and antient seales, by carelessnesse, the peeces wherof lye mangled, like chipps, in a huge trunke, and much of the evidence utterly rotted with wett and rayne'. Despite the poor state of the records, Dugdale was able to examine more than five hundred deeds, and found some fine seals. Even the muniments of a local historian such as Henry Ferrers were not immune from the dangers of lackadaisical storage; after his death in 1633 his son Edward warned Archer that the best of his father's collections had been ruined by damp getting into the chest in which they were stored so that 'the greatest parte of them were absolutely lost and were digged out of the chest all rotten, that not a word could be red of them'. Recent records and those relating to property that might be the subject of legal wrangling were the most carefully preserved. Earlier medieval records were more vulnerable, since their practical value was often less. Thomas Selwine was happy to sell his land in Hurst, Glos., and to hand over the related medieval documents, since 'noe man could read my deeds they were growne so old'. In such circumstances the neglect of medieval documents was not surprising, despite the despair it engendered in local historians.[31]

There were two main sources of heraldic records available to local historians. The first were those belonging to the College of Arms. These included records collected during the course of their official activities: visitation records, funeral certificates and grants of arms. The college library and individual heralds also possessed heraldic treatises, medieval rolls of arms and other records, and all of these items assisted their work. The other source of heraldic records was the coats of arms displayed in stained glass and carved in stone and wood in churches, manor houses and on public buildings across the country. Collections of heraldic notes recorded in local churches and manor houses are among the most common forms of evidence of widespread antiquarian activity among the gentry to survive from this period (see figure 5). Some cover a small area – usually that surrounding the collector's home. Many concentrate on the arms of a single family and their alliances. Others cover a wide area and display a more catholic interest. These varied collections are testimony to the strength of interest in heraldry and genealogy in the period.

Of the records in the College of Arms, the pedigrees of local families collected by the heralds during visitations were particularly useful, although the transcriptions that circulated widely contained many errors. In 1639 Dugdale

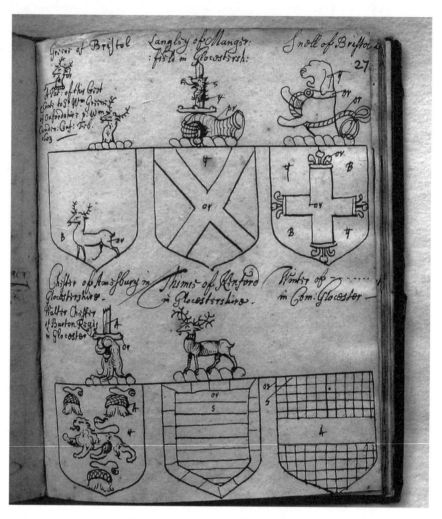

Figure 5 Jacobean heraldic notebook

sent a copy of the visitation of Warwickshire to Archer, which he described as
'taken from a false copye much maymed by often transcribinge as is most of
that stuffe which the Paynters have got togeather, wherwith they please many
better then descents laboured out of authentick Records'. In 1656 he lent a
similar copy to Thomas Ellis. In Hereford there is a copy of the 1569 visitation of the county, supplemented by later information collected by heralds
in the course of their research into pedigrees relating to funerals and grants
of arms. The manuscript shows a particular interest in the Baskerville and
Coningsby families, and the copying of an original record from the College of

Arms suggests it relates to the marriage of Sir Humphrey Baskerville to Elizabeth Coningsby in the reign of James I. The latest event recorded in the pedigrees is dated 1636. Also in Hereford is a rough copy of the pedigrees from
this manuscript, dated 1658. The process of copying manuscripts in this way
led inevitably to the promulgation of transcription errors. Even when an accurate copy of the visitation record was available, the pedigrees it contained were
not necessarily accurate or complete. The printed version of the 1619 visitation of Leicestershire, taken from a manuscript predominantly in the hand of
Camden's deputy, Sampson Lennard, curiously has Burton recorded as 'dead
without issue'. Many families only provided sufficient material to establish
the three generations of gentle descent required by the heralds, rather than
having their full pedigrees recorded. Habington complained that whoever had
presented the Hanley pedigree at the visitation had 'deminished the reputation of thys family in numberinge so fewe discentes who might by a diligent
perusall of theyre evidences have rather shewed the lineall continewance of
thys house fowre hundred years'. The funeral certificates kept by the heralds
supplemented the visitation records, since they included a copy of the
deceased's pedigree and their arms. Both forms of heraldic pedigree were,
however, limited in the information they contained. They were compiled for
the purpose of demonstrating that an individual or family had a right to the
status they claimed. The maiden name and parentage of a wife was often only
recorded if she was an heiress or of significantly higher social status than
her husband. The recording of Christian names was erratic. The details of
childless marriages and of younger children were often omitted altogether.
This made the verification of claims of marital alliance and descent from cadet
branches difficult to either verify or disprove using these records.[32]

The other important class of heraldic record were the medieval rolls of arms.
These were essential sources for identifying coats of arms, as they associated
a particular device with an individual knight at a specific date. Such rolls were
being compiled by the middle of the thirteenth century. Some recorded the
arms borne by the knights at a particular battle or tournament, while others
were a general list of the arms known to the compiler or in use in a particular
locality. Few original medieval rolls of arms survive, and most rolls are known
only from the copies made by Tudor and Stuart antiquaries and heralds.
Wyrley transcribed several rolls in blazon in 1592, including the Caerlaverock
Roll and the Dunstable Roll dating from the first decade of the fourteenth
century. Both were included in a collection made by Burton a decade or so
later. The centrepiece of this collection was Thomas Jenning's roll, containing
over 1500 coats, which Burton probably transcribed from the copy belonging
to the herald Nicholas Charles. In 1628 Burton gave this armorial collection
to Archer. The importance attached to the rolls of arms by local historians is
demonstrated by the clause in the *Antiquitas Rediviva*, which laid down that

Hatton was to 'collect and register all old rolles of armes, and old parchment bookes of armes'.[33]

The armorial rolls assisted in the interpretation of the richest seam of primary material for genealogical research: the evidence of the numerous coats of arms, surrounding the Elizabethan and Stuart gentry in their daily lives. Among the earliest of the armorial notes made by Burton was that concerning the heraldic display to be seen at his home at Lindley in 1597, which he later described in words:

> in the hall, upon the upper end, is carved in a schocheon of wood the coat of Burton's arms, a fess between three talbots' heads, erased Or; and in the chapel chamber the said coat is twice on the East window; first by itself; secondly impaled with, Gules, a saltire engrailed Argent, between four mullets Or, which is Herdwike's coat. And upon the pillars of the bed in the same chamber there is carved on the one side the coat of Burton, on the other the coat of Herdwike. And upon a beam over the South window of the said chamber, without towards the garden side, the coat of Burton impaled with Herdwike is carved again.[34]

The prevalence of coats of arms in everyday use is evidenced by a collection of Elizabethan Essex gentry wills. At the highest social level, Thomas Radcliffe, earl of Sussex, bequeathed his brother '10 pieces of hangings wrought with my arms and with the arms of my house'. At lower levels, coats of arms are mentioned adorning silver and gilt bowls, goblets and jugs, bed coverings and hangings, pillows and carpets. As the practical use of heraldry for identification on the battlefield and in the tiltyard declined, its symbolic importance as an expression of the continuity of the social hierarchy increased. The proscription of religious imagery after the Reformation further emphasised the importance of heraldry within the visual culture of the gentry.[35]

The extent to which the gentry understood the coats of arms surrounding them in their everyday lives is uncertain. The respondents to Archer's questionnaire about the village of Tysoe wrote: 'We have (as we suppose) divers arms in our church windowes, but for want of skill we cannot express them'. In 1630 William Gregory apologised to Burton for not giving him a better description of Polydore Vergil's arms in Wells cathedral 'for want of something towards an herald'. In his *Survey of Dorset*, Thomas Gerard thought that by giving the coats of arms only in blazon he was effectively restricting the information to 'my Friends the Heraulds' and 'such as have Insight in that Facultie'.[36] For the local historian eager to learn the art of blazon, however, there were a number of heraldic treatises available. Of these the most popular were Legh's *Accedens of Armorie* and Guillim's *A Display of Heraldrie*. Edmund Bolton, who proposed the Academ Roial to James I, was the author of *The Elements of Armories* (1610). In 1654 the herald and close friend of Dugdale, Edward Bysshe, published an edition of Upton's fifteenth-century *De Studio Militari*, which had previously been available only in manuscript.

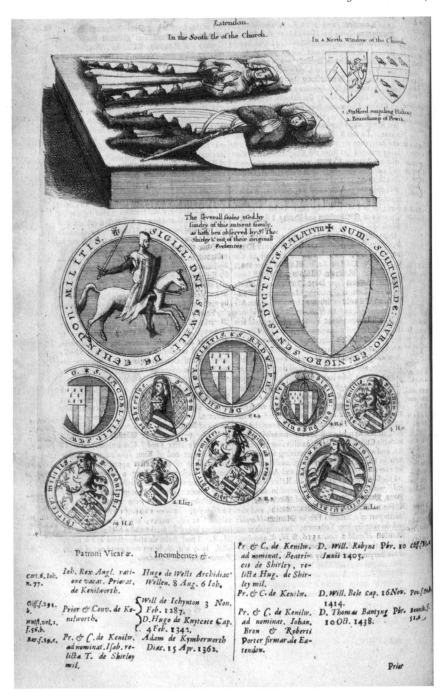

Figure 6 Engraving of Shirley seals from the *Antiquities of Warwickshire* (1656)

The evidence derived from coats of arms was particularly important for the early medieval period, given the scarcity of documentary evidence. The earliest known coat of arms was in use by 1128 and by the middle of the twelfth century rules were beginning to emerge concerning the composition and style of shield devices. These devices also became an increasingly common element in the design of seals attached to important documents. It was a natural development that the device associated with a particular lordship in the minds of its tenants should descend with the lands to the heir. This helped to legitimise inheritance, but could confuse a genealogist when lands did not descend in a direct line. When copying deeds and other documents, local historians included careful copies of the attached seals wherever possible. For families such as the Berkeleys, Shirleys and Archers, the line of descent could be traced through the seals attached to their documents as well as through the contents. Both the *Lives of the Berkeleys* and the history of the Shirley family included drawings of the seals used by different members of the family, which could be used to date documents (see figure 6). According to the *Antiquitas Rediviva*, the task of collecting armorial seals 'with a breviate of the deedes and true dimensions of the seales' fell to Dugdale, although subsequently it seems to have been undertaken by Hatton.[37]

Coats of arms were an important source for genealogical research, because they could provide pictorial evidence of parentage and familial alliances for which no documentary proof existed. However, the evidence was often difficult to interpret, especially when the visual language had been used to assert unjustified claims. The Spencers of Northampton, for example, adopted a coat of arms differenced from the arms of the medieval Despencers by the addition of three scallop shells. This suggested a relationship between the two families, a relationship which did not exist. In 1581 Arthur Gregory obtained permission from the College of Arms to quarter the arms of Marmion and Segrave with his own. This quartering was invalid according to the rules of heraldry, as Gregory, being a lawyer and antiquary, knew full well. Henry Ferrers distrusted any arms granted in the Tudor period, as he believed that since the reign of Henry VII 'armes have corruptly ben used by gentlemen that have risen' and that heralds 'withoute skill' had accepted unsubstantiated claims.[38]

Even where no attempt had been made to deliberately mislead, it was often difficult to interpret the evidence provided by coats of arms. Habington reported that the representative of the senior branch of the Coventry family had expressed a wish that lord Coventry should use the family arms without the difference of a cadet branch. Although lord Coventry declined the invitation, the example illustrated how prominent representatives of cadet branches of other families might adopt the arms of the senior line – to the confusion of genealogists. Erdeswicke noted that the Harcourts of Ellenhall, 'presently after their marriage with the Noels' heir, intruded themselves into Noels' armory'. As Burton explained, it was not unusual for the son of an heiress to adopt his mother's arms, particularly if he was not the direct male heir of his father's family. This had happened in Sir Simon Clarke's family at the beginning of the fourteenth century, when Sir Simon Woodchurch had married the daughter and heiress of Henry Clarke. The descendants of the second son of this marriage had inherited the Clarke lands and arms, placing their own Woodchurch arms in the second quarter. Sir Simon reversed this order and adopted the Woodchurch arms as his own. As in this case, the adoption of the arms of a supplanted family was often accompanied by the assumption of the extinguished surname. Lawrence Stone has investigated the devices for the preservation of a family's surname in the eighteenth century, when he argued that they first came into common use.[39] As local historians became increasingly aware during the course of their research, however, practices designed to maintain the illusion of continuity had been common from within a few generations of the Conquest. The adoption of the arms of the previous owner to indicate the legitimate descent of land had occurred before the use and inheritance of surnames became general. In Elizabethan Staffordshire a dispute arose between Richard Bagot, the genealogist friend of Erdeswicke, and Edward, lord Stafford, over whether the Stafford family were descended from the marriage of an heiress to Hervey Bagot in the twelfth century. In 1590 lord Stafford wrote to Bagot that 'I doe better know the descents and matches of my own lineage than any creature can inform me', referring to his records, pedigrees and particularly to the use of the same arms – from the first baron after the Conquest to himself. In his turn Bagot relied on 'good records and evidence, under ancient seals the four hundred years past'. In the Stafford pedigree he compiled six years later, Erdeswicke recorded that Robert, baron Stafford, had two children: Robert, who died without issue, and Milicent, who married Hervey Bagot. Hervey, baron Stafford, was the son of Hervey and Milicent, and for several generations the arms were differenced to reflect the deviation of the descent from the direct line. In time the arms used by the early barons were readopted by the Staffords.[40]

Despite the difficulties associated with interpreting their evidence, the collection of coats of arms from churches and manor houses was one of the commonest forms of antiquarian activity in our period.[41] John Leland had collected heraldic notes during his travels around England in the 1530s, and his notes alerted later local historians to the location of arms of local families on display in places remote from their main residence. Among Burton's surviving manuscripts is a volume of heraldic notes collated from his own observations and those supplied by others. The volume is divided into five sections, covering the counties of Warwickshire, Leicestershire, Northamptonshire and Staffordshire, with a collection of arms from miscellaneous counties included at the end. The most significant contributors to the volume, aside from Burton, himself were: a Purefoy kinsman, who was collecting church notes in the 1560s; the Northamptonshire antiquary William Belchier, who died in 1609; and Wyrley and Dugdale. The dates included in the text indicate that Burton was himself collecting arms between 1597 and 1642. They also reveal that Burton visited and collected notes in some places several times. For example, his notes for Tamworth are dated 1603, 1615 and 1625.[42]

Church notes included not only coats of arms, either drawn or in blazon, but also descriptions of funeral monuments, their inscriptions and epitaphs. These could be extremely useful for the genealogist. The monument erected to his father by Habington included the family pedigree from the time of their first association with Worcestershire in the reign of Edward I. The various monuments erected by Sir Simon Clarke provided an explanation of their heraldry in their inscriptions. For the pedigree of the Dineleys, kinsmen of Burton, Habington was able to refer his readers to his description of the tomb of Francis Dineley in Cropthorne church. In Winchester cathedral, directly above the memorial to Jane Austen, is a monument erected to the Clerke family of Avington, Hants. in 1622. The inscription details the parallels in names, careers and fortunes of three generations 'grandfather, father and son successively clerks of the Privy Seal'. This family history is supplemented by the family arms and crest, and eight shields showing the alliances of each generation. Such monuments were a product of the gentry's interest in gene-alogy, and their appearance coincided with the development of local history. Although extremely useful, they provided antiquaries with the genealogies of comparatively few families. Medieval inscriptions were generally less inform-ative, although still very useful where they survived. Many had been torn away by tomb robbers, iconoclasts or members of the gentry attempting to claim an extinct family as their own ancestors. Coats of arms recorded only in the 'brytell glasse' of church windows suffered from both accidental damage and deliberate replacement with plain glass to increase light levels. The Chorog-rapher of Suffolk remarked that he had seen the arms of the Howards, dukes of Norfolk, in the windows of the church at Chellesworth 'not long since ... which I find now gone'. The vulnerability of funeral monuments made the church notes of earlier antiquaries particularly useful. In Burton's notes there are several drawings of arms seen by Wyrley in the 1580s, which had disap-peared two decades later. In the *Antiquities of Warwickshire*, Dugdale used notes taken by Burton's source William Belchier and by Henry Ferrers, which recorded monuments and inscriptions which had since been lost. In addition, works such as Stow's *Survey of London* and John Weever's *Ancient Funerall Monuments* provided descriptions of monuments which local historians might not have been able to examine at first hand. Smyth, for example, used Stow's description of St Paul's as his source for the epitaph of Margaret, Countess of Shrewsbury.[43]

While it was possible for any genealogically minded gentry to collect notes on the arms in local churches and manor houses, the identification of the coats was a complicated matter. In 1640 Habington sent copies of his notes on Worcestershire churches to Archer, explaining that 'I have not, lyke Mr Burton, set downe the owners of the Armes, because I want Kalendars & Ordinaryes of Armes to informe mee'. Within a few months he had been provided with an ordinary of arms by the herald William Le Neve. (In an ordinary the arms were arranged according to their design, making this the most useful form of roll for Habington's purpose.) The task of identifying the multitude of arms he had collected took him more than three months.[44]

Local historians carried out careful examinations of local funeral monuments, although they frequently misinterpreted their findings. In Dudley, Erdeswicke measured an effigy and tomb chest. Finding them to be eight feet in length, he concluded that 'the body could be no less, for if it had it could not with conveniency have been laid in it'. Burton accepted the 'great stature' of Sir John Talbot on similar evidence from his tomb at Whitwick, although he treated with some scepticism the local inhabitants' belief that the knight had been a giant.[45] It was erroneously thought that cross-legged effigies had been exclusively reserved for crusaders. This mistaken belief had been perpetuated by Camden in his *Britannia*, and generally went unchallenged by his successors. It still occasionally resurfaces today.[46] It caused Habington some difficulty, when faced with the effigy of a cross-legged child in armour. He concluded that either the child had intended to go on a crusade until death intervened, or that he was 'some renowned chyld who dyd an acte above his age agaynst the Infidells'.[47] Although they were occasionally mistaken in their assumptions, the antiquaries did develop expertise in the interpretation of funeral monuments. Erdeswicke deduced that a decayed monument at Burton was not the original tomb of the abbey's founder, as the use of alabaster, the armour and the design of the shield all argued for a much later date. Dugdale, on the other hand, was inclined to accept the traditional attribution of a tomb at Hill Morton, because it showed similarities in design to the contemporary brass of Edward I's queen at Westminster.[48]

Despite their associated problems, funeral monuments presented one of the most comprehensive sources for local history. Most gentry families of any significance in the history of a locality had left behind some form of funeral monument. For some this remained the only evidence of an association with a particular area. As a result of Humphrey Stafford's forfeiture of his estate (because of his rebellion against Henry VII) and the later abolition of the chantries, the only remaining evidence of the Stafford association with Grafton in Worcestershire was 'a fayre tombe over theyre ashes'. Engravings of the memorials to several generations of the Bracebrigg family in the *Antiquities of Warwickshire*, combined with their pedigree, served to emphasise the 'great improvidence' of the descendant, who sold their estate at Kingsbury at the beginning of the seventeenth century. Such evidence could provide a useful hook for a direct observation on the mutability of human fortunes, intended to encourage the gentry to leave behind them 'an honourable fame'. A reference to the tomb of Francis Clyfton enabled Habington to reflect that the extinguishing of the ancient family of Clyfton showed 'that eavery worldly thinge must have hys peryod'.[49]

Church notes provided evidence beyond their obvious genealogical and heraldic use. The presence of coats of arms in the windows of churches or carved into the stone was often the only surviving clue as to the identity of former benefactors. Burton used such evidence to identify the Cuiley family as either the builders of or significant benefactors to the church at Shepey Magna. In 1632 Roger Smith of Edmondthorpe wished to ensure that Burton's revised text would establish his ancestors' claim to have built the church at Withcock. This claim was based partly on family tradition and partly on the presence of his ancestors' arms in the windows and carved on the chancel walls. In his account of Withcock, Burton ignored the hearsay evidence and relied exclusively on the evidence of the arms to identify the builders of the church. Similarly, the extent to which Steven Gennings, merchant tailor and sometime mayor of London, was responsible for the rebuilding of St Andrew Undershaft, was deduced by Stow from the appearance of his coat of arms over the pillars on the north side of the aisle, in the windows on the south side and on the pews.[50]

A distinctive feature of the development of local history was the gradual marginalisation of oral sources and popular traditions in favour of written records. Daniel Woolf has traced the decline in popularity of oral sources from 1600, and has suggested that in the *Antiquities of Warwickshire* Dugdale wholeheartedly adopted a bias in favour of written evidence. Local historians were undoubtedly influenced by the changes in legal practice in this period, which led to a favouring of documentary evidence and an increasing distrust of oral testimony. John Smyth, who qualified as a barrister and spent much of his life preparing legal cases, used oral evidence sparingly as a historian. One of the best-known sections of the *Lives of the Berkeleys* is the account of the battle of Nibley Green in 1469. Into this he incorporated the folk memory of the 'plaine Country people' living in Nibley and the family tradition reported to him by Charles Hyet, whose grandfather had fought in the battle. Yet in his closing remarks he indicated a distaste for this material: 'But enough of these traditions and reports, wherein I have exceeded my own Inclination because this passage is of most remarkableness in this family'. An increasing distrust of oral sources was characteristic of the development of local history. Echoing Smyth's treatment of Nibley Green, Burton included the oral traditions surrounding the battle of Bosworth in the *Description of Leicestershire* in

1622. This material was omitted in the 1642 version of his text. In his history of Worcestershire, Habington wrote that 'when I walke amounge these slyppery owld storyes I trembell for fear of fallinge into errors'. Although he recognised that written evidence could be contradictory or unreliable, he preferred it to oral accounts. However, tradition could suggest lines of enquiry to a local historian. Habington recorded how 'in Staunton I heard a vulgar report which I slyghted of a marcate in former ages', which he subsequently confirmed by documentary evidence. In Dorset Gerard clearly regarded the tradition concerning the seige and destruction of Woodford castle with some scepticism. In evidence the locals 'will shewe you, not farre offe in the Warren, Gunhill, where they sawe the Ordnance planted'. The tradition allowed him to approximately date the purported seige to 1460, thus helping him in the search for confirmatory evidence.[51]

However, the marginalisation of oral sources can be overstated. Introducing his account of Devon, Thomas Westcote wrote:

> I hope I may intermix a pleasant tale with a serious discourse, and unwritten tradition with a chronicled history, old ancient armories and epitaphs, well near buried in oblivion ... ancient families now extinct, or rather transanimated into others; some etymologies seeming and perchance strange and far fetched; old, new, serious, jovial, curious, trivial: for these and matters of such nature ... may give recreation to a wearied body and mind (that reads for recreation,) with more delight and content for variety.[52]

Since Westcote wrote for scribal circulation rather than publication, entertaining his neighbours was more important to him than satisfying the 'great artists or supercilious criticks' who prevailed upon William Burton to remove some of the lighter material from the *Description of Leicestershire* for the second edition. The role of publication in shaping a text is significant in this respect. Nor should we over-emphasise the significance of oral sources in earlier periods. As early as Bede we find a willingness to use oral testimony combined with a desire to stress the authority of the source and the reason to accept the evidence as reliable. Similarly, later antiquaries would stress that their informants were men of 'good credit'. Oral sources and popular traditions were often used by local historians as starting points for their researches. Occasionally it is possible to see how a local story has shaped their understanding of the documentary or physical evidence, although the original story does not appear in their final text. In this regard it is misleading to compare the contents of Leland's *Itinerary*, which represent the undigested collections of his journeys, with later local histories. An edited version prepared for presentation to the public might have given a less-prominent place to oral sources.

Within certain contexts local historians in the mid-seventeenth century were as willing to use oral sources as Leland had been more than a century before. Dugdale told the story of how John Dudley had acquired the manor of Birmingham 'as by tradition from divers discreet persons I have heard'. The eventual fate of the former duke of Northumberland made him an ideal example for local historians of the over-mighty subject, who respected neither the Crown, the Church nor the nobility of England. Erdeswicke, although admitting that he was himself 'ignorant except by hearsay and report', publicised the idea that Northumberland was the grandson of a carpenter. He criticised the manner of Northumberland's acquisition of Dudley castle, and blamed him for the state of the monuments in Dudley priory. Dugdale perpetuated the idea of Northumberland's lowly birth, while expressing doubts that he was quite so closely related to a carpenter as suggested by Erdeswicke, and emphasised his iconoclastic role. Gerard related the morality tale of how Richard de Hankford procured his own death by pretending to be a poacher in his own park, 'which take as you please as it was delivered unto me'. Although Habington was generally as distrustful of oral evidence as Dugdale, he did use it to remind his readers what was expected of a gentleman. For example, he reported what he had heard 'from a gentellman borne in thys parishe' concerning the former charitable gifts made by users of the river to the hermit at Radston's Ferry. Such uses of oral evidence do not contradict a bias among local historians in favour of written evidence, but oral evidence remained important in certain contexts.[53]

A particularly clear case of the use of oral evidence for the education of the local gentry is Dugdale's account of the Cokeseys of Milcote. At the beginning of Elizabeth's reign the Cokeseys were a wealthy and prominent Warwickshire family. Ludovic Cokesey, however, plotted the murder of one of his wealthy tenants and forged a will in his own favour. Dugdale described this crime, having heard about it in person 'from credible tradition'. The murder was discovered, as 'divine providence ceases not to prosecute such bloody actions' and Ludovic was executed. As is inevitable in such cases, further heinous offences were ascribed to the condemned man. Dugdale incorporated one of these, which included some verifiable facts. Namely, that Ludovic's son and eventual heir had accidentally shot his elder brother with a longbow. The detail that Ludovic had joked about the tragedy was based purely on hearsay, but it helped to emphasise the overall impression of the Cokeseys as a tainted family. It was, therefore, only proper that the male line of the family should die out and that the estate should be sold, not even decently transferred by inheritance to the descendants of the female co-heirs. Although Dugdale would not take it upon himself to state that this was the judgement of God, his opinion was clear. The idea that God wreaked his revenge on a man's heirs was common from accounts of the kings of fifteenth-century England by historians such as Polydore Vergil. Writing in this vein, Smyth used the continuation of lord Berkeley's line, and the failure of the Dudleys', to support his claim that the former had been the innocent victim of the Dudleys' machinations.[54]

An understanding of the oral culture of a locality could also be of practical help in clarifying the contents of medieval documents. The way in which a place-name was pronounced by the locals could reveal an origin obscured by the written form, or help local historians to link the current name with a different spelling found in the records. For example, Dugdale found a record relating to Henley, in 'which Record it is called Hanley, but in truth it ought to have been written Heanley, as the ordinary sort of people doe still pronounce it; for that was its originall name, and occasioned from the ascending ground, whereunto it is so near situate, hean in our old English signifying high'. From Archer's correspondence with Dugdale, we learn how important the knowledge of local names for lanes and pieces of land could be for understanding medieval deeds and other documents. At the same time the gentry could be distanced from the oral culture of an area because of language differences. Richard Carew had a reading knowledge of Greek, Dutch, French, Spanish and Italian in addition to the inevitable Latin, but his knowledge of Cornish was limited. His languages were predominantly learnt from books, and there were no printed grammars for Cornish. His inability to converse with native speakers of Cornish hampered his recording of local oral traditions, and his etymologies of local place-names suffered from his lack of facility with the language.[55]

Popular traditions could also be a means of linking a locality with important events or individuals, particularly in the remote past for which little documentary evidence survived. The Lancashire recusant William Blundell learnt from Camden that verses relating to the seventh-century Northumbrian king St Oswald were inscribed on the porch of Winwick church about thirty miles from his home at Little Crosby. He accordingly wrote to 'a Catholique gentleman and frend of myne whoe had dwelt heretofore nere the saide place' to seek further information. From his friend he learnt that 'the people thereaboute have yet in there mouthes (it may be by tradition)' that Oswald 'being greevouslie wounded in a battell not farre from yt place, vowed yt if hee might wendequicke (or whicke according to there speache) he wolde there builde a Churche'. He also learnt from the same source of a nearby well named for the saint, which had allegedly been a place of pilgrimage. Blundell concluded his account: 'I have thought good to take or rather seeke occasion here to write of ye place of this blessed K. and martir his death, because ye same is by wronge information saide in a late pious booke to have bine at Osetree'. The local pride that prompted the use of popular tradition in this case is obvious. It is noticeable, however, that Blundell received the tradition through the mediation of a gentleman. This is typical of contemporary local historians, who consulted their acquaintances about local stories and traditions rather than seeking out and questioning aged villagers as their successors were to do.[56]

While local historians did not ignore oral traditions which were useful for their purposes or supplemented written sources, they did attempt to extract from them a kernel of truth. Both Dugdale and Habington included in their county histories a story of a crusader, who was miraculously rescued from imprisonment abroad and transported to his own manor. That a knight should build a chapel or found a monastic house to celebrate his safe return from a crusade is not exceptional. Nor is it difficult to understand how this should give rise over the course of time to a tradition of miraculous intervention. In considering the traditions surrounding Sir John Atwood, Habington dismissed the tomb at Wolverley popularly reputed to be that of the knight, since stylistically it dated from no earlier than 1340. However, he accepted the evidence of the chapel founded by Atwood and the 'gyves themselves reserved as a trophy of thys glorious redemption so cleere a testimony, as none but [a] wollfull obstinate [man] can denye itt'. In considering the supposed foundation of the nunnery at Wroxhall by a similarly rescued crusader, Dugdale was more cautious. He included an account taken from a fifteenth-century manuscript, 'which, though some may think wholy fabulous, in respect of the Miracles wherewith it is so much deck't; yett, setting them aside, and well considering the Story, a body of Truth is not hard to be discerned therein'. The morals to be drawn from such stories, concerning gentry piety and faithfulness and the power of God to intervene in human affairs, inclined local historians to include them in their works.[57]

The tendency of local history to be written by members of the community concerned makes personal recollection a distinctive and important source within the genre. John Stow, writing at the end of his life about the city where he was born, littered the *Survey of London* with phrases such as 'in my youth I remember' and 'as I myself have seen in my childhood'. When describing the bone and tooth that had been displayed in St Lawrence Jewry, he drew on his memory of what he had seen 'more than seventy years since'. When he reached the extent of his own memory, Stow was able to draw upon the stories told to him by his father. Since county histories were written by representatives of the gentry communities they described, there was clearly scope for personal recommendations of individuals. Burton referred to the qualities of several recently deceased local notables of his acquaintance in his *Description of Leicestershire*, including Francis Beaumont of Gracedieu, Sir William Skipwith, Henry Noell, and his own uncle Arthur Faunt. This was a less-obvious feature of his second edition, suggesting that a more impersonal style was gaining favour.[58] On occasion, local historians were able to use their own personal recollections to counteract popular traditions, which undermined the integrity of the local gentry. At the time of James I's accession to the throne, the catholic Robert Wintour of Hoddington was the subject of rumours concerning the mysterious death of his father, who drowned in his own moat. The subsequent involvement of Wintour in the Gunpowder Plot and his execution in 1606 gave greater credence to the idea of patricide. In his account of Worcestershire, Habington was concerned not simply to defend the reputation of his co-religionist. An attack on the reputation of one gentleman was by extension an attack on the whole class. Accordingly, Habington reported a conversation he had conducted with a reputable physician from Worcester, who had viewed George Wintour's body after his death and considered that he had died of natural causes. Habington did not limit his defence of Wintour to a straightforward refutation of popular tradition. He presented a positive image of his friend as an honest and brave gentleman. Habington had offered the use of the priest holes at Hindlip for the preservation of Wintour, should the rumours concerning his father lead to a physical threat against him. As one would expect of a man of honour, Wintour responded that 'hee would neaver in thys case obscure hymsealfe, but in the face of the wourld justifye hys innocencye.'[59]

For family historians the temptation to include family traditions in their accounts was great, especially as their readership would expect the familiar stories to appear. In the *Lives of the Berkeleys*, Smyth's presentation makes it clear that the balance of the evidence was in favour of the descent of the family from a Saxon thane rather than a Danish prince. In deference to the feelings of the family, however, he ostensibly came down in favour of the family tradition of royal descent. Family traditions were particularly difficult to ignore, when there was little or no other evidence concerning a particular ancestor. Occasionally Shirley made it clear that he was dependent upon supposition. Of one of his ancestors, he wrote that 'the Historians have not marked any Militarie actions of this Henry yett there is such a pregnant appearance and probabilitie that they seem to establesh a certaine beleefe that he did great services for the king.' Elsewhere his copious references to a wide range of material obscures the lack of confirmatory evidence for some of his statements. It is not clear on what basis – other than a family tradition or simple assumption – he claimed that another ancestor had fought alongside the Black Prince and been knighted after the battle of Poitiers. Shirley's occasional laxity in relation to his own ancestors was not echoed by Dugdale, who wrote of the putative hero of Poitiers: 'Of Sir Thomas Shirley I find nothing memorable but his death'.[60]

Traditional rhymes, sayings and proverbs do not form a significant part of the contents of the majority of early local histories. Risdon recorded a rhyme that related to the popular belief that treasure was hidden in Cadbury Castle, while Burton included some local weather lore and Erdeswicke used a 'vulgar rhyme' to support the claim of Clent to be the place of St Kenelm's martyrdom.[61] These examples indicate the peripheral nature of such evidence in the majority of works, where they were relegated to a confirmatory role. The exposition of the local dialect and the hundred proverbs included by Smyth in the *Description of the Hundred of Berkeley* is without parallel among contemporary works. Smyth was concerned to stress the local nature of the material he included:

> In this hundred of Berkeley are frequently used certaine words proverbs and phrases of speech, which wee hundreders conceive, (as we doe certaine market moneyes,) to bee not only native but confined to the soile bounds and territory therof; which if found in the mouthes of any forraigners, wee deeme them as leapt over our wall or as strayed from their proper pasture and dwellinge place: And doubtles, in the handsome mouthinge of them, the dialect seemes borne of our owne bodies and naturall unto us from the breasts of our nurses.[62]

What this passage obscures is that Smyth was born in Leicestershire, did not live in the vale of Berkeley until his thirties, and thereafter until his old age spent large parts of each year in London and the Midlands. He had to learn the local dialect and sayings as an adult, and it is likely that his accent always marked him out as an incomer. This may account for his unusual interest in this material. His position was akin to that of later collectors of folk history, who were divorced from the communities they observed. That the majority of local historians did not collect this material suggests that the divide between the elite culture of the gentry and the popular culture of the community-at-large identified by historians, was not sufficiently advanced at this time to cause the forensic gaze of the former to be turned upon the latter.[63] The comparative lack of interest in traditional pastimes demonstrated by local historians reinforces this impression. Such attention as they receive is almost entirely within the context of mourning a departed golden age of 'Merrie England' and comparing it with a degraded present. It was a feature of local history that controversial subjects were avoided, which might account for some reticence in the light of the political sensitivities concerning the Book of Sports and suppression of certain pastimes during the interregnum. Nevertheless, the surviving evidence of notebooks and correspondence reinforces the impression that sustained interest in popular culture was not a feature of early local historians.

As discussed in chapter one, certain medieval chronicles and other secondary sources were important to later local historians because of their local provenance and associations. On the whole, however, the development of local history was characterised in this period by an increasing reluctance to accept the uncorroborated evidence of secondary sources. The unreliable use of documents, lack of references and paucity of critical acumen of many chronicles led local historians to view them with suspicion. Smyth wrote: 'I have in these relations proposed myself to be more directed by matter of record than by the vulgar chronicles' and in general there was suspicion of any secondary evidence that was not supported by primary sources.[64] The debunking of Geoffrey of Monmouth's mythology by Polydore Vergil and others was generally accepted among local historians by the end of the sixteenth century, although a few, such as Thomas Lyte, clung to the old fables. The extent to which local historians such as Burton were inclined to explain why 'this forged history of Brute and his progenie' was 'fabulous and improbable' suggests that the old 'fables' of Geoffrey of Monmouth retained currency among their gentry readership. Lambarde, who rejected the 'fonde dreames of doting monkes and fabling friars', still defended Geoffrey as not being wholly unreliable. The martial Britons that Geoffrey of Monmouth had portrayed continued to hold a privileged place in the psyche of English gentry, and he articulated a traditional view of gentility which remained popular.[65]

Despite their disadvantages, chronicles and other secondary sources were useful for their references to individuals in their accounts of military campaigns, court occasions, political intrigues and so forth. In his account of the earls of Warwick, Dugdale explained the origin of some of the more lurid passages in the medieval chronicles in a way, which mirrored the justification of local historians for the continued use of such sources: 'it hath been so usual in our ancient Historians, for the encouragement of after ages unto bold attempts, to set forth the exploits of worthy men with the highest encomiums imaginable: And therefore, should we for that cause be so conceited as to explode it, all History of those times might as well be vilified'.[66] By the same token a local historian could justify including unsupported evidence from a chronicle on the grounds that an account of the heroic exploits, charity and public service of their ancestors would encourage the current generation to emulate them. Despite this, it was preferable to have supporting evidence where possible. In 1650 William Bromley sent Dugdale an extract from Holinshed concerning the exploits of his ancestor during Henry V's campaign in France. Holinshed was useful to local historians, but the mixing of contemporary and later accounts of events without differentiation diminished its authority. The support for the chronicle's evidence provided by the contemporary augmentation to his arms awarded to Sir John Bromley, encouraged Dugdale to include it in his account of the family.[67] Occasionally a secondary source was included despite a lack of supporting evidence, because it suited a local historian's purpose. Dugdale was a supporter of the rights of the Church against the encroachments of many of his fellow gentry. In his account of Long Compton he included a story concerning St Augustine, derived from a manuscript of the fourteenth-century historian John of Tynemouth in the Bodleian. As the source was much later than the reported events, its uncorroborated evidence was suspect. To the modern reader the story of witnesses being raised from their graves also make the story fantastic, but Dugdale may not have viewed it in the same way – he provided John Aubrey with supernatural tales for his *Brief Lives*, and was a friend of the astrologer William Lilly. Moreover its suggestion that the payment of tithes was 'very antient' made it an important source of support for the institution in a community inclined to respect ancient precedent.[68]

The prominence of London in the political, ecclesiastical, legal and social affairs of the country meant that its historian did not lack for references to the city in the general medieval chronicles. Himself a chronicler, Stow was well acquainted with the available sources, particularly the works of Matthew of Westminster, Matthew Paris and Thomas Walsingham, which he had himself edited. He made wide use of a number of secondary sources in the *Survey of London*, but was particularly concerned to correct the 'fables' perpetuated by other writers, such as Robert Fabian and his personal rival Richard Grafton. Generally Stow demolished the fables without deigning to name their authors. An exception is his account of 'Gerrard the giant', where he quoted Grafton's own description of the supposed tooth of the giant, before ridiculing the evidence and the edifice of conjecture that was built upon it.[69] This demolishing of the unreliable evidence of more recent chroniclers stands in stark contrast to the comparatively mild warnings about the need for caution with regard to the evidence of some medieval historians. Stow included a catalogue of alleged archbishops of London during the Dark Ages, which 'I find only to be set down by Joceline of Furnes, in his book of British bishops, and not elsewhere'. How far Jocelin, a Cistercian monk writing at the end of the twelfth century, was to be believed, Stow left 'to the judgement of the learned', although he also provided evidence that 'maketh the matter of archbishops doubtful, or rather, overthroweth that opinion'.[70] We sense a willingness to accord early medieval historians respect, perhaps resulting from the rarity of their work and a belief that sources that had been preserved for centuries in manuscript form had an intrinsic value. Such respect was accorded to the history ascribed to Ingulphus of Crowland, secretary to William the Conqueror, which was universally accepted as genuine in the period covered by this study. Dugdale referred to a Saxon forerunner of the Domesday survey described by Ingulphus 'which Roll Time hath consumed, I believe; for I could never discern that our greatest Searchers after Antiquities had seen it'.[71] Since so little evidence survived from the Saxon period, the lack of confirmatory references to the survey could be overlooked. Once the internal inconsistencies in the work are catalogued, it seems obvious that it is a fourteenth-century forgery, but respect for medieval texts and an appreciation of the problems of scribal copies made early antiquaries less critical than later generations of historians.

As befitted an author whose first published work was an edition of Geoffrey Chaucer, Stow's *Survey of London* reflected his interest in poetry, and he drew on several medieval poems for descriptions of the medieval city. Among the sources he had acquired was part of the collection of John Shirley, who in the fifteenth century had 'painfully' preserved the works of Chaucer, John Lydgate and other medieval poets. These poems were treated by Stow as primary sources for the period of their composition. He quoted from the *Visions of Piers Plowman*, when writing of the provision of bread for the city, and from the *Canterbury Tales* for a description of the Tabard Inn in Southwark. The poem *London Lickpenny*, then attributed to Lydgate, provided a vivid picture of how lively and rich the city appeared to a rural visitor of the early fifteenth century. Stow also provided a detailed description of the monument of John Gower in St Mary Overie, Southwark. Gower's *Confessio Amantis* had been printed by Caxton, but his other poems remained in manuscript. Of these, Stow possessed *Vox Clamantis* and *Cronica Tripartita*, but 'Speculum Meditantis I never saw, though heard thereof to be in Kent'.[72] The same three poets, Chaucer, Gower and Lydgate – with the locally relevant Robert of Gloucester – were singled out by Smyth in the *Description of the Hundred of Berkeley* when writing of the 'honored memory of our old forefathers' and their traditional manner of speech.[73] Of more recent poets, Leland's *Cygnea* was used by Lambarde, and Drayton's *Poly-Olbion* was referred to and quoted by a number of local historians. As we have seen, these topographical poems were closely related in both inspiration and purpose to early prose works of local history, and were treated similarly. The historical works of contemporary poets such as Drayton and Samuel Daniel represented a further poetic source of material. These provided references to individuals that could be incorporated into local histories, and their use paralleled that of prose chronicles.

The most significant of the secondary sources utilised by early local historians were contemporary antiquarian works. The most obvious of these was Camden's *Britannia*, which provided a framework into which local histories could be fitted and also provided an encyclopaedic reference to the rest of the country. Camden's *Annals of the Reign of Elizabeth to 1588* (1615) and his eclectic volume of *Remains* (1605) were also widely utilised. John Foxe's *Book of Martyrs* (1563) provided accounts of local victims of the Marian persecution of protestants, while Francis Godwin's *Catalogue of the Bishops of England* (1601) was a useful source for episcopal history. Local historians might disagree with the conclusions of John Selden's *History of Tithes* (1618), but this did not prevent it being widely used as a source alongside his *Titles of Honour* (1614). When the dissent within the College of Arms became public knowledge through the publication of Ralph Brooke's *Discoverie of Certaine Errours* (1599), criticising the 1594 edition of *Britannia*, some local historians became directly involved. Sampson Erdeswicke penned a response in defence of Camden, while John Smyth contributed his own knowledge of the Berkeley pedigree to Augustine Vincent's *Discoverie of Errours* (1621), a criticism of Brooke's work.[74] Since Burton worked closely with Vincent, it is probable that he was also involved in researching this work, but the absence of acknowledgements in the text makes this impossible to prove. What is clear from textual references and antiquarian notebooks, is that local historians and the wider gentry were acquiring and reading the most recent works of antiquarian scholarship. Even for those who were not directly linked to the wider scholarly community, this meant that they were exposed to the developing sophistication in the use and referencing of sources. The results of this exposure may be seen in the developing expertise in the use of sources by local historians.

NOTES

1 Habington, *Worcestershire*, vol. 1, p. 460; Lambarde, *Kent*, p. 442; Thomas Gerard, *The Particular Description of the County of Somerset*, ed. E.H. Barnes (Somerset Record Society 15, 1900), hereafter Gerard, *Somerset*, p. 3.

2 Dugdale, *Warwickshire*, p. b1; Smyth, *Berkeley Mss*, vol. 1, Dedication; J. Taylor's essay in the *Saturday Review*, 6 February 1886.

3 Hamper, *Dugdale*, pp. 296–8.

4 S.B.T., DR37/Box 86.

5 Halliwell, *Autobiography and Correspondence of Sir Simonds D'Ewes*, vol. 2, p. 312.

6 B.L., Additional MS 6046, fo. 22a; Archer, *Correspondence*, fo. 106; Hamper, *Dugdale*, pp. 163–5, 170–1; Northants. C.R.O., FH4024.

7 Herefs. C.R.O., B56/1, fos 10v–11; Northants. C.R.O., FH106.

8 Hamper, *Dugdale*, pp. 170–1, 176–8, 188–9.

9 Nichols, *History of Leicestershire*, vol. 2(2), p. 843.

10 Smyth, *Berkeley Mss*, vol. 2, p. 412.

11 Cumbria C.R.O., D/Lons/L12/4/1/3; Archer, *Correspondence*, fos 46, 186; Hamper, *Dugdale*, pp. 181–4.

12 Archer, *Correspondence*, fo. 50.

13 Burton, *Leicestershire*, To the Reader; Dugdale, *Hamper*, p. 172; S.B.T., DR10/1409; R. Bearman, *The Gregorys of Stivichall in the Sixteenth Century* (Coventry: Historical Association, Coventry Branch, Coventry and Warwickshire History Pamphlets 8, 1972).

14 Archer, *Correspondence*, fos 48–50; Glos. C.R.O., D908, Box 4.

15 F. Hull, 'The Domesday of Dover Castle – an archival history', *Archaeologia Cantiana* 98 (1982), pp. 67–75.

16 Smyth, *Berkeley Mss*, vol. 2, p. 440.

17 Battely, *The Antiquities of Canterbury*, First Part, Preface.

18 Habington, *Worcestershire*, vol. 2, p. 40; Hamper, *Dugdale*, pp. 21, 160, 176–8, 187–9; J. Hooker, *Catalogue of the Bishops of Excester* (1584), p. Aii.

19 Nichols, *History of Leicestershire*, vol. 2(2), p. 843; Archer, *Correspondence*, fo. 209; S.B.T. DR37/Box 93 has evidence of Archer searching for wills at Hereford and being referred to the Prerogative Court at Canterbury; Hamper, *Dugdale*, pp. 188–9.

20 Glos. C.R.O, D8887/13614, fo. 2.

21 S.B.T., DR37/Box 86; Hamper, *Dugdale*, pp. 153–4.

22 Douglas, *English Scholars*, pp. 38–9.

23 Habington, *Worcestershire*, vol. 2, p. 129.

24 Berkeley Castle Muniments, Select Book 10; B.L., Harley 4928, fos 143–end; S.B.T., DR37/Vol. 46.

25 B.L., Additional MS 28564, fo. 236v; J.H. Round, *Peerage and Pedigree*, 2 volumes (London: Nisbet, 1910), vol. 2, pp. 185, 210–11; College of Arms, Vincent 127, fo. 262; S.B.T., D473/293, fos 44–5, DR37/Box 86; Dugdale, *Warwickshire*, pp. 600–1.

26 Burton, *Revised*, Market Bosworth; Staffs. C.R.O., D649/1/1, Part 2; Stow, *London*, pp. 105, 244; Dugdale, *Warwickshire*, p. 87; Habington, *Worcestershire*, vol. 1, p. 481; vol. 2, pp. 310–11; Smyth, *Berkeley Mss*, vol. 2, p. 147.

27 Beds. C.R.O., MC 16.

28 Beds. C.R.O., AD 997.

29 B.L., Additional MS 31917, fo. 4; R.B. Manning, 'Antiquarianism and the Seigneurial Reaction: Sir Robert and Sir Thomas Cotton and their Tenants', *Historical Research* 63 (1990), pp. 277–88; Smyth, *Berkeley Mss*, vol. 2, pp. 411–12; Stow, *London*, pp. 78–80.

30 Badminton Muniments, Fms/C1/1, FmS/C1/4, FmS/C1/7, FmS/C2/3, FmS/C2/9.

31 Hamper, *Dugdale*, pp. 163–4; Archer, *Correspondence*, fo. 94; Smyth, *Berkeley Mss*, vol. 3, p. 249.

32 Hamper, *Dugdale*, p. 191; Warwickshire. C.R.O, Z13/8, fo. 12; Herefs. C.R.O., B56/1, AN79/1; J. Fetherston (ed.), *Visitation of Leicestershire, 1619* (London: Harleian Society 2, 1870), pp. 56–7; Habington, *Worcestershire*, vol. 2, p. 108; Gittings, *Death, Burial and the Individual in Early Modern England*, p. 168; *Smyth Papers*, vol. 1, fo. 55; Smyth, *Berkeley Mss*, vol. 2, p. 87.

33 A.R. Wagner, *Historic Heraldry of Britain* (Oxford: Oxford University Press, 1939), pp. 24–31; B.L., Additional MS 51047; S.B.T. DR37/Vol. 44; W.T. Collins, 'A manuscript book of rolls in Shakespeare's Birthplace Trust Records Office', *Warwickshire History* 4(2) (1978–79), pp. 69–73.

34 B.L., Egerton 3510, fo. 29; Nichols, *History of Leicestershire*, vol. 4(2), p. 647.

35 F.G. Emmison, *Elizabethan Life: Wills of Essex Gentry and Merchants* (Chelmsford: Essex County Council, Essex Record Office 71, 1978), pp. 2, 7, 20, 23–4, 29, 33, 43, 126–7, 198; P. Styles, 'Sir Simon Clarke', *Birmingham Archaeological Society Transactions* 66 (1945–46), pp. 6–34; N. Llewellyn, 'Claims to status through visual codes: heraldry on post-Reformation funeral monuments', in S. Anglo (ed.), *Chivalry in the Renaissance* (Woodbridge, Suffolk: Boydell Press, 1990), pp. 145–60; P. Coss, *The Knight in Medieval England, 1000–1400* (Stroud: Alan Sutton, 1993), chapter 4.

36 S.B.T., DR37/Box 93; B.L., Egerton 3510, fo. 119; Gerard, *Dorset*, pp. 127–8.

37 B.L., Harley 4928, fos 19–23v; Berkeley Castle Muniments, Select Books 2, vol. 3 – in the printed edition the seals are included for each lord at the point where they are described, but in the original they were collected together.

38 Berry, *Henry Ferrers*, p. 22.

39 Habington, *Worcestershire*, vol. 1, p. 175; Erdeswicke, *Staffordshire*, p. 134; Burton, *Leicestershire*, p. 213; Burton, *Revised*, Abbey Kettleby, Holt: here the change appears to have been part of the marriage agreement; Dugdale, *Warwickshire*, p. 200: Thomas Morgan

required his female heir to marry someone with the surname Morgan; Sir Simon Clarke's ancestors used the common formula 'Clarke alias Woodchurch' for several generations: Styles, 'Sir Simon Clarke', p. 30; L. Stone and J.C.F. Stone, *An Open Elite?* (Oxford: Oxford University Press, abridged edn., 1986), pp. 79–89.

40 G. Wrottesley, 'A history of the Bagot Family', *Collections for a History of Staffordshire* 11, *New Series*, (1908), pp. 85–7; Erdeswicke, *Staffordshire*, pp. 151–2.

41 For example: B.L., Harley 2151, Lansdowne 860A; Northants. C.R.O., ZA8025; Glos. C.R.O. D885; MacCulloch, 'Henry Chitting's Suffolk collections', pp. 103–28; R.E.G. Cole (ed.), *Lincolnshire Church Notes Made by Gervase Holles AD 1634 to AD 1642* (Lincoln: Lincoln Record Society 1, 1911).

42 B.L., Egerton 3510, fos 1, 8, 15, 23, 28v–29, 43v, etc.; this volume seems to have been originally compiled between 1609 and 1612 and may be the source for the collection of Leicestershire church notes in College of Arms, Vincent 127. For Belchier, see E.A.G. Lamborn, 'Belchier's note book: a Midland heraldic manuscript', *Notes and Queries* 193 (1948), pp. 202–5.

43 Habington, *Worcestershire*, vol. 1, pp. 245–6; D. MacCulloch (ed.), *The Chorography of Suffolk* (Ipswich: Suffolk Records Society, 1976), p. 105; B.L., Egerton 3510, fos 29v, 33; Dugdale, *Warwickshire*, pp. 27, 713; Smyth, *Berkeley Mss*, vol. 2, p. 29; Stow, *London*, p. 301.

44 B.L., Additional MS 28564, fo. 226; Archer, *Correspondence*, fo. 331.

45 Erdeswicke, *Staffordshire*, pp. 340–1; Burton, *Leicestershire*, pp. 276–7, 305–6.

46 See *Guardian*, 16 June 2001, Travel Supplement, p. 15.

47 Dugdale, *Warwickshire*, p. 739; Habington, *Worcestershire*, vol. 1, p. 417, vol. 2, p. 193.

48 Erdeswicke, *Staffordshire*, pp. 474–5; Dugdale, *Warwickshire*, pp. 13, 15.

49 Habington, *Worcestershire*, vol. 1, pp. 97, 395; Dugdale, *Warwickshire*, pp. 325, 770–3.

50 Burton, *Revised*, Shepey Magna, Withcock; see also Burton, *Leicestershire*, p. 315; Nichols, *Leicestershire*, vol. 3(1), pp. 520–1; Stow, *London*, p. 131.

51 D.R. Woolf, 'The 'common voice': history, folklore and oral tradition in early modern England', *Past and Present* 120 (1988), pp. 26–52; Smyth, *Berkeley Mss*, vol. 2, p. 115; Burton, *Leicestershire*, pp. 47, 173–4; Burton, *Revised*, Market Bosworth, Lindley; Habington, *Worcestershire*, vol. 1, pp. 159, 187, 213, 268, 375; B.L., Additional MS 28564, fo. 236v; D.R. Woolf, 'Speech, text and time: the sense of hearing and the sense of the past in Renaissance England', *Albion* 18(2) (1986), pp. 159–93; Gerard, *Dorset*, p. 75.

52 Quoted in M. Hansen, 'Identity and ownership: narratives of land in the English Renaissance', in W. Zunder and S. Trill (eds), *Writing and the English Renaissance* (London: Longman, 1996), p. 94, to show the range of sources used by antiquaries.

53 Dugdale, *Warwickshire*, pp. 286–7, 659; Erdeswicke, *Staffordshire*, pp. 337–42; Gerard, *Somerset*, pp. 45–6; Habington, *Worcestershire*, vol. 2, pp. 17–18.

54 Dugdale, *Warwickshire*, pp. 534–5; Ludovic Cokesey was not the first of his family to gain a reputation for violence: C. Carpenter, *Locality and Polity: A Study in Warwickshire Landed Society, 1401–1499* (Cambridge: Cambridge University Press, 1992), pp. 578–9; Levy, *Tudor Historical Thought*, pp. 171–2; Smyth, *Berkeley Mss*, vol. 2, p. 325.

55 Dugdale, *Warwickshire*, p. 597; Hamper, *Dugdale*, p. 247; Rowse, *Court and Country*, pp. 246, 274–5.

56 Quoted in Woolf, 'Little Crosby and the horizons of early modern historical culture', p. 128.

57 Habington, *Worcestershire*, vol. 2, p. 321; Dugdale, *Warwickshire*, p. 489.

58 Stow, *London*, pp. 117, 128, 177, 246; Burton, *Leicestershire*, pp. 42, 77, 87, 105–6.

59 Habington, *Worcestershire*, vol. 2, pp. 112–14.

60 B.L., Harley 4928, fos 44v, 59–60; E.P. Shirley, *Stemmata Shirleiana* (Westminster: privately printed 2nd edn., 1873), p. 26; Dugdale, *Warwickshire*, p. 476.

61 B.L., Additional MS 36748, fo. 20v; Burton, *Leicestershire*, p. 2; Erdeswickee, *Staffordshire*, pp. 389–90.

62 Smyth, *Berkeley Mss*, vol. 3, pp. 22–3.

63 The withdrawal of the literate classes from popular culture was posited by Peter Burke, *Popular Culture in Early Modern Europe* (London: Temple Smith, 1978) and the English context is discussed in R. Hutton, *The Rise and Fall of Merry England* (Oxford: Oxford University Press, paperback edn., 1996), pp. 244–6.

64 McKisack, *Medieval History in the Tudor Age*, pp. 95–125; Levy, *Tudor Historical Thought*, chapter 5; Gransden, *Legends, Traditions and History in Medieval England*, pp. 199–238; Smyth, *Berkeley Mss*, vol. 1, p. 231.

65 Burton, *Leicestershire*, pp. 160–1; Lambarde, *Kent*, pp. 9, 68–70.

66 Dugdale, *Warwickshire*, p. 299.

67 Hamper, *Dugdale*, pp. 241–3; Dugdale, *Warwickshire*, p. 153.

68 Dugdale, *Warwickshire*, pp. 445–6; Aubrey, *Brief Lives*, p. 296–7.

69 Stow, *London*, p. 312.

70 Stow, *London*, pp. 423–4.

71 Dugdale, *Warwickshire*, p. b2.

72 Stow, *London*, pp. 142, 334, 363–4, 368.

73 Smyth, *Berkeley Mss*, vol. 3, p. 23.

74 Staffs. C.R.O., D649/1/1, Part 1; Smyth, *Berkeley Mss*, vol. 1, p. 208, vol. 2, p. 145.

Chapter 5

Genealogical history

In the age of Elizabeth I genealogy was not simply the province of antiquaries and heralds. It was broadly recognised that aristocrats and the gentry had a personal, legitimate interest in promoting and preserving their lineage, and this interest could significantly affect the political, financial and marital fortunes of a family. In 1570 a double marriage was proposed between Mary and Frances – daughters and co-heirs of Henry, lord Berkeley – and Sir Philip and Sir Robert Sidney – the nephews of the earls of Warwick and Leicester. These marriages would have united two competing claims to the ancestral lands of the Berkeley family. The claims, created by the death of Thomas, lord Berkeley, without a son in 1417, had caused one hundred and fifty years of feuding, legal wrangling and occasional bloodshed. The proposed union held the prospect of sparing lord Berkeley what eventually proved to be a further forty years of expensive lawsuits. That it did not happen was due largely to the opposition of his wife, a proud Howard by birth who opposed any connection with the Dudley family as demeaning to her daughters and to their lineage. The execution of her brother (the duke of Norfolk), in 1572, intensified Katherine Berkeley's opposition to the marriages. At the same time, the Dudleys revived their legal claim to the lands in the hope of counteracting Lady Berkeley's influence and persuading her husband to agree to a settlement, but all this manoeuving proved ineffective. The idea of solving the legal tangle by uniting the claims through marriage was only finally abandoned in 1575, when the Berkeleys somewhat unexpectedly produced a male heir.[1]

In the opinion of Katherine Berkeley the descent of the Dudley family did not bear comparison with that of her daughters. The Berkeleys claimed descent from Harding, a putative Danish prince reputed to have arrived in England at the time of the Conquest. They had held the manor and castle of Berkeley since the reign of Henry II. Lady Berkeley herself was the daughter of Henry Howard, earl of Surrey, whose pride in his Plantagenet blood had led directly to his death in the last days of Henry VIII's reign. This pride had been transmitted to his children: Katherine; Thomas, duke of Norfolk, executed for his involvement with Mary, Queen of Scots; and Henry, who was the subject of suspicion in Elizabeth's reign because of his catholicism and felt himself to live 'beneath the compass of his birth', but who was made earl of Northampton by James I.[2] In contrast the grandfather of the prospective bridegrooms, John, duke of Northumberland, had been descended through a younger son from John Sutton, who had been ennobled within recent memory on his marriage to the heir general of the Dudleys. Moreover, it seems that contemporary gossip persistently ascribed an ignoble birth to the duke's father, Edmund Dudley. Although Leland and Naunton acknowledged Northumberland's noble descent, both Erdeswicke and Dugdale promulgated the suggestion that he was descended from a carpenter. Sir Philip Sidney's insistence on his family's lineage in the *Defence of the Earl of Leicester* (1585) suggests the gossip predated Erdeswicke.[3] To Katherine Berkeley, the Dudley brothers and their nephews were representatives of the upstart Tudor aristocracy, and their blood was not fit to intermingle with that of her daughters.

It was in no small part due to the early influence of this proud, educated and imperious woman, that John Smyth was to attach immense importance to the Berkeley lineage throughout his career. In the year of Katherine's death, Smyth drew up a pedigree of the Berkeleys to present to Elizabeth, the new wife of the heir to the barony, Sir Thomas Berkeley, whose birth had finally scuppered the prospect of his sisters marrying the Sidneys. Ironically, Elizabeth was also a representative of the new Tudor aristocracy. She was the only child of George, lord Hunsdon, whose family had risen to prominence as a result of their kinship with Elizabeth I. The link to royalty and the wealth of the bride doubtless helped to overcome any scruples Katherine might have had about the suitability of Elizabeth Carey's pedigree. Although her mother's family, the Spencers of Althorp, claimed a spurious descent from the medieval Despencers, her daughter-in-law's lineage was no more impressive than that of the bridegrooms rejected by Katherine for her daughters a quarter of a century before. In failing health, anxious to see her son settled and not to leave the arrangement of his marriage to her husband, Katherine must have consoled herself that the status of the husband predominated over that of his bride. Thomas would raise Elizabeth by marriage, just as in Katherine's eyes the Sidneys would have lowered her daughters. The pedigree prepared by Smyth for Elizabeth shortly after her marriage was clearly intended to remind the bride of the basis of her new family's claim to status, and how she had been elevated by her acceptance into it. Similar motives may be seen at work in the bequest of William Claxton of 'my signett of goulde and a brod ingraven seale of my armes, and the Pedigree of myne auncestors, drawen in parchment' to his kinsman Lancelot Claxton, who inherited the Winyard estate through marriage to Claxton's granddaughter.[4]

The birth of their brother had reduced the value of the Berkeley daughters in the marriage market. Although they still offered an illustrious pedigree to prospective suitors, their Howard connection was devalued by the political climate, and they were no longer the heirs of a large, if troubled, inheritance. Their eventual marriages reflect the value of a baron's daughter (with connections to the aristocracy) to a landowner who had wealth but not titles. The elder daughter, Mary, finally married in 1584 at the age of thirty. Her husband, John Zouch, was ten years her junior. His family owned Codnor castle, Derbys., which they had inherited by marriage at the end of the fifteenth century to the heir of Henry de Grey. This late marriage reflects the lowering of her mother's expectations for Mary, once her brother had survived the hazards of early modern childhood. The marriage was not a happy one, and John repudiated his wife four years later. Her younger sister Frances was apparently more fortunate in her marriage to Sir George Shirley. The Shirleys were the possessors of an impressive lineage, although they had never risen above the ranks of the upper gentry. They traced their pedigree back to the Saxon Saswalo, had owned the manor of Nether-Ettington, Warwickshire since before the Conquest, and took their surname from an ancestral manor in Derbyshire. The family historian Sir Thomas Shirley was the second son of this marriage. His history of the family paid tribute to the contribution his mother made to his family's lineage: 'the offspring of this high borne Ladye sees himselfe Allyed to the Cheefest Crownes of Christendome and to the Easterne, and Westerne Emperors, As well as to the greatest part of the Illustrious Barrons, Viscountes, Earles and Dukes of England and France.'[5]

Frances died in childbirth in 1595 after ten years of marriage. As they grew up, her children were constantly reminded of the importance of her contribution to the Shirley lineage, by the magnificent funeral monument erected in her honour in the church at Breedon.[6]

An obsession with genealogy was a direct cause of the explosion of antiquarian interest among the English gentry in the late sixteenth and early seventeenth century. Lawrence Stone drew attention to this in the 1970s, but his brief perceptive remarks have not been fully developed by historiographers. In his magisterial study *The Idea of History in Early Stuart England*, Daniel Woolf acknowledged that restoring the reputation of his family was a motivating force behind Sir George Buck's *History of King Richard the Third*. At the same time his observation that 'whatever' Buck's motives the work is one of the most original pieces of historical writing of the period, denigrated genealogy as a serious concern for a historian. In the same work, Woolf observed that Camden added genealogical material to the revised editions of *Britannia*, but Woolf did not discuss the significance of this. Considering wider historical culture in his *The Social Circulation of the Past*, Woolf devoted far more attention to genealogy, but still appeared to regard it as ancillary to history proper. In the development of local history, genealogy played a pivotal role.[7] The extent to which the Elizabethan or early Stuart family in its daily routine looked beyond the confines of the immediate household has been vigorously debated. What is apparent is that for their understanding of society and their sense of status the gentry drew on a concept of kinship that was extended in time and space. It was this wider concept that informed their genealogical research.[8]

As we have seen, it was characteristic of the early local historians to begin by researching their own pedigrees and those of allied families, and only gradually to develop wider historical interests. There is considerable evidence for a wide and active interest in genealogical research among the gentry as a whole in this period. Although many families employed the services of a herald to research and record their pedigree, it was not unusual for a gentleman to undertake the task himself. A notebook compiled by the Essex barrister John Maunsell shows how he examined his own deeds to provide evidence of his descent for the 1634 visitation, and subsequently developed a wider interest in heraldry. Even where a herald produced the pedigree, this does not mean that the members of the family employing him did not take an active interest in the research. Two versions of the Finch family pedigree, drawn up by John Philipot around 1620, survive to this day. The pedigree is a less-elaborate version of the type of 'Lives' written by Smyth and Shirley and includes copies of documents, inscriptions and other primary source material. The original was apparently prepared for Sir Thomas Finch, while a copy was made for his younger brother Sir Heneage Finch at the time of his knighthood and promotion to the rank of sergeant at law. Both copies include additional information – such as details concerning children, and notes taken from the works of Selden and Godwin – indicating that their respective owners supplemented the work of the herald. Similarly, a decorative copy of the 1634 pedigree of the Buckinghamshire family of Ingoldby survives, which has been updated to 1650. From the evidence of the additions and armoury, the copy belonged to the regicide Sir Richard Ingoldby, a younger son. The production of an elaborate pedigree provided a means to celebrate and memorialise an important event in a family's history in a form that could be distributed among its disparate branches. When Oliver St John obtained an Irish peerage in 1620, his brother-in-law, the herald Richard St George, produced an illustrated pedigree book, of which three copies are known to survive. As with the Finch pedigree, once distributed, such copies could be updated to reflect the diverging fortunes of the different branches.[9]

The gentry's obsession with genealogy requires closer examination, if we are to understand the development of local history. The importance of their lineage to the gentry's sense of identity was crucial in dictating what aspects of local history attracted their interest. In a period of social upheaval the English gentry increasingly demonstrated an interest in genealogy, a study predicated on continuity and hierarchy. During the sixteenth century the number of claimants to gentry status increased faster than the growth in the population as a whole. The number of grants of arms made during the reigns of Elizabeth and her Stuart successors is testimony to the respect that newcomers to gentry society accorded to the traditional trappings of gentility.[10] An emphasis on traditional values enabled the new entrants to be absorbed by the gentry community without undue stress. It represented stability and continuity within gentry society in the face of religious, social, political and economic change. Newly risen families acquired a pedigree and coat of arms, and asserted their claim to status through the traditional rhetoric of lineage. Other families, who had been adversely affected by economic change or had undermined their own position by adherence to catholicism, claimed status through the linkage of gentility and lineage. In this way the gentry community could represent a bastion of hierarchy and stability in the face of the threat of popular unrest.[11] This chapter initially explores the definition and meaning of lineage to the gentry of late Elizabethan and early Stuart England. This is followed by a discussion of how these interests can be shown to have shaped the contents of local histories as they developed, encouraging authors to include certain material or causing them to explain its omission. Finally, there is a discussion of how genealogical obsession influenced one of its most obvious manifestations: the rise of family history as a distinct sub-genre within local history.

For Elizabethan and early Stuart antiquaries the study of what Smyth described as 'genalogike history' was not concerned simply with tracing the descents of local families. Their genealogical studies were concerned with lineage, a concept that encompassed more than just pedigree. Lineage linked the inheritance of blood from one's ancestors inextricably with the maintenance of their ancient estate. It was lineage which underpinned the traditional social hierarchy. The importance of a family's lineage depended on a combination of the length of their pedigree and the continuity of tenure of their lands.[12] It was an essentially patriarchal concept of descent. The lineage was enhanced by prestigious marriages and by the acquisition of additional acres, especially when these added manorial lordships to the family's holdings. Equally, it was diminished by unfortunate alliances and the sale of ancestral manors. Female lines of descent might be represented on pedigrees to show how a family acquired certain property, but this did not challenge the essential patrilineal dominance. Heraldry provided the gentry with a pictorial language in which to represent their lineage. A family's coat of arms, their crest and supporters descended from generation to generation along with their ancient manors. It was this panoply of elements which constituted lineage, and helped to provide the English gentry with their sense of identity. It was a mentality in which ancestors played a vital, but passive, role. While heraldry, funeral monuments and – increasingly in this period – portraits, acted as memorials of past representatives of a family, ancestors did not constitute an active presence in this society. The abolition of purgatory at the Reformation may have emphasised the disjunction represented by death, but doctrinal differences are not obvious in this respect among local historians.[13]

The most important element of a family's pedigree was its length. There was some dispute as to whether it was desirable for a family to trace its pedigree in England from before the reign of William I or only from the Conquest. In the *True Use of Armorie*, a Norman pedigree was described as preferable to a Saxon, since 'it is much more honourable to be descended from a most famous nation conquering, then such people by plain feat of Armes subjuged'. The elaborate pedigree which Robert Glover drew up for Erdeswicke in 1586 accordingly traced the Staffordshire historian's descent back to the Conquest. In a similar vein the Berkeleys preferred to identify their progenitor as a Danish prince fighting for the Normans, rather than as a defeated Saxon thane. In the *Survey of Cornwall* Carew 'thought requisite, to lay downe the names of such Cornish Gentleman, as I find recorded to have come in with the Conquerour'. Unsurprisingly, the list included Karrow (alias Carew). Similarly, William Grey listed thirty-seven families in Northumberland 'which hath continued from William the Conquerour unto these late dayes', beginning with the Grays of Chillingham and Horton. In Dorset, Gerard wrote, the Husseys 'surelie for Antiquitie and Birth gave place to fewe' being by 'antient Evidence' able to show descent from an aunt of William I.[14] Nevertheless, in the early seventeenth century a pre-Conquest origin was often considered to bestow particular honour on a lineage. Shirley derived considerable satisfaction from being able to trace his family back in the direct male line to a Saxon thane. Among Archer's notes is an account of the Arden family, which records that the 'house of Arden is *merely* English of the ancient blood of the Saxons'.[15] The Warwickshire polymath Sir Kenelm Digby, whose pedigree could be traced to the thirteenth century, was reputed to have spent £1,200 to procure the scholarly apparatus required to support a claim to Saxon ancestry. As a local historian, Sir Edward Dering was well equipped to fabricate his own evidence in support of a claim to pre-Conquest ancestry. Through a mixture of genuine research and forgery he created a pedigree, which stretched the lineage of his family back to a mythical Saxon thane allegedly killed at Hastings. He then had the arms on the font of Pluckley church recut, and installed brasses in the late medieval style for his ancestors in order to support his revision of his family's lineage and consequent alteration to their arms. Since humans in each generation require two parents, it was clearly possible for the astute gentleman to sustain a claim to both Saxon and Norman descent. Accordingly, in an account of his ancestors compiled in 1639 John, viscount Scudamore, hedged his bets by claiming descent from both Richard, duke of Normandy, and King Harold. A similar claim was made for the Talbots.[16]

It is uncertain how seriously gentlemen who manipulated the evidence of their pedigree intended or expected their claims to be taken. In the earliest French aristocratic family histories, dating from the twelfth century, the narrative would be traced back beyond the available genealogical evidence to a mythical Jesse figure. Similarly, Tudor courtiers were presented with elaborate decorative pedigrees that traced their descent beyond the documentary record, even as far back as Noah and his sons. It was comparatively common for a family on acquiring a manor to modify the monuments in the local church in order to adopt them as symbols of their own status and permanence. The gentlemen, who realised that elaborate coats of arms were a mark of Tudor extravagence, rediscovered the simpler arms of the medieval gentry and claimed them as their own. These expressions of lineage were intended to express status and to represent stability. They were important symbols, and were recognised as such by their observers. Lord Burghley may have paid for the apparatus that showed his descent from Welsh princes and a friend of King Harold, but that does not mean that he believed the fiction he procured. It was an expression of his status, as was the elaborate pedigree drawn up for his colleague Sir Christopher Hatton in 1590. Hatton's pedigree, which traces his descent from a Norman called Yvon, is endorsed as seen and registered by William Dethick, Garter king at arms, whose responsibilities included preserving the appearance of social stability. Likewise, John Hooker lent his antiquarian expertise to the concoction of a pedigree for Sir Walter Raleigh, which provided him with a claim to Plantagenet blood through the female line. The queen's highest servants and closest associates should naturally be of noble lineage – so evidence of this was provided. A form of doublethink was widely practised in early modern England as a means to accommodate social change. This was a generally unpublicised pragmatism. If the Elizabethan Spencers could claim to be the heirs of the medieval Despencers in practice, should their neighbours object to them adopting the heraldic symbols of inheritance? Pedigrees produced to support claims to land and inheritance did not invoke the rhetorical flourishes of the herald's art, and invariably remained within the bounds of genealogical evidence. These legal pedigrees presented Bacon's 'naked and open daylight' of truth, which did not show 'the masques and mummeries and triumphs of the world, half so stately and daintily as candle-lights'. Heraldic pedigrees in this analogy represent the flattering products of candlelight. The Elizabethan and early Stuart gentry appear to have accepted forgeries which reinforced a claim to lineage commensurate with an individual's status. This does not mean that they were unaware of the supposed deception. Sir Thomas Smith's observation that a gentleman could buy the trappings to go with their wealth would not have surprised his readers – though they might have thought it something that was best discreetly ignored.[17]

Among the Elizabethan and early Stuart gentry, it was undoubtedly desirable to be able to sustain some claim to a pedigree originating at or before the time of the Conquest, regardless of whether this depended on the collective turning of blind eyes. As Gervase Holles showed, the desire for a long pedigree retained its appeal, despite the increasing realisation that the necessary evidence was lacking:

> How many have wee that will confidently tell you their sirnames flourished even in the Saxon times, though the understanding antiquary knowes that they can have no record to justify it and that those times had no setled sirnames at all, and very few for above two hundred yeares after the Conquest. How many have wee in Lincolnshire that will affirme themselves to have been gentlemen there ever since the Normans' entrance, when I knowe that there are scarse sixe families in the whole county that can make proofe they had one foot of land there the 20th yeare of K. Henry the third.[18]

Holles felt the lure of the long pedigree as much as his neighbours, writing that he was sure his name had a 'generous originall', although 'we have run some time as it were under the ground in obscurity'.[19] Your neighbours' willingness to accept your Conquest origin was an important signifier of your current status. Some gentlemen were sufficiently secure to rely upon a simple assertion, while the manipulation of evidence extended far down the social scale from Elizabeth's leading courtiers. In 1598, William Wyrley and the arms painter Richard Scarlett were involved in the production of a pedigree for Henry Bellingham, fellow of New College, Oxford. In a letter to Scarlett, Bellingham enquired, 'howe farre the pedigree reaches which you have of Mr Wyrlye, whether it be only of us since we came into Sussex; or whether it ascends higher to the first originall, which we rekon to be from one Alan de Bello Campe, who lived in the conquerours time'. Such prompting no doubt helped the herald to produce a product that pleased the purchaser, even if it did not stand up in the harsh light of truth. The memorial to Walter Bagot of Blithfield, Staffs., who died in 1623, baldly asserted in common with many contemporary funeral monuments that the family 'have continued in the county ever since the Conquest'. Erdeswicke's account of the family supported their claim to have possessed the manor of Bagot's Bromley at the time of Domesday, although there followed a considerable gap in the pedigree to the middle of the twelfth century. The Bagots were, however, a well-connected, prominent local family, whose status was secure and whose assertions were unlikely to be challenged. In contrast Sir Simon Clarke, a relative newcomer to Warwickshire whose estates were newly purchased, went to some lengths to introduce two generations into his family's pedigree, carrying the descent back before 1100.[20] Clarke was a major contributor of documents to the *Antiquities of Warwickshire*, and shared Sir Simon Archer's interest in genealogical research. His status in county society, however, was not as secure as his antiquarian neighbour's.

Occasionally we can detect a dichotomy between what a local historian wished to believe about their pedigree and what the documentary evidence supported. Archer could trace his pedigree back to the reign of Henry II through his own documents. Even so, he sought the assistance of Edward Gwynne – a London lawyer and noted genealogist – in discovering his ancestor's origins. Gwynne obligingly found that Robert l'Archer had lived 'in the tyme of the conqueror' and had been tutor to Henry I. How seriously Archer took this is uncertain. He preserved the results of Gwynne's research, but his own expositions of his pedigree consistently start in the reign of Henry II. Similarly, Sir Edward Rodney admitted that he could not reliably trace his family before the late thirteenth century 'because their roote runnes up into those times which by reason of horrible commotions and civill warres become dark and obscure'. Yet the 'constant tradition' in the family and an earlier pedigree gave names to earlier ancestors, so he repeated them in his history. The family tradition was that the Rodneys had arrived in England in the train of the empress Maud during the twelfth century. His mother had told Rodney of a piece of brass inscribed with a list of manors allegedly given by Maud to his ancestor, which had been used to support their claim. This was presumably an inscription removed from a funeral monument, and its removal might suggest a change in ownership of the manors followed by an attempt to appropriate the monuments of former owners. In any case the plaque had been lost following the suicide of Sir George Rodney in 1601, and 'my father was exceedingly displeased with the loss of it'. Although Rodney lacked evidence to support the story of his family's origins, he could not resist perpetuating it in his family history.[21]

The length of a family's pedigree might be supplemented by marriages to heiresses, who themselves could boast of a considerable lineage. In his *Defence of the Earl of Leicester* Sir Philip Sidney drew particular attention to his maternal inheritance: 'I am a Dudley in blood, that duke's daughter's son, and do acknowledge though in all truth I may justly affirm that I am by my father's side of ancient and always well esteemed and well-matched gentry, yet I do acknowledge I say that my chiefest honour is to be a Dudley.'[22] Although Sidney's mother was not an heiress on her marriage in 1551, by the time that he was writing the *Defence* of his uncle, Sidney expected to inherit the Dudley mantle. Robert, the only legitimate son of the earl of Leicester, had died in 1584, and the marriages of his other surviving Dudley uncle, Ambrose, earl of Warwick, had produced no heir. In the event, Philip's own death in 1586 meant that it was his brother Robert, who inherited the Dudley lineage on the deaths of the two earls in 1588 and 1589 respectively, although he had to await the accession of James I to acquire any of the family titles.

Through the marriage of heiresses an ancient family could be considered not to have become extinct but, to use the Devon antiquary Thomas Westcote's term, to have been 'transanimated' into the husband's family. At a less-exalted level than that of the Sidneys, William Burton was able to show how his great-grandfather's marriage to an heiress had supplemented his family's lineage and helped to preserve the memory of two extinct families. The Burton pedigree could be traced back in the male line to James de Burton, a squire to Richard II, and, at the beginning of the sixteenth century, Burton's great-grandfather James had married Elizabeth, eldest daughter and co-heiress of John Herdwick. The Herdwicks had held Lindley since the thirteenth century, when William de Herdwick had married the heir general of the Rodviles. The Rodvile association with Lindley could be traced back to the Conquest. In contrast, John Smyth traced his pedigree back only the two generations necessary for gentry status. His second wife, however, could claim a link to the Berkeleys, through the marriage of her ancestor to the daughter and heir of a cadet branch of the family. Smyth considered this to be a source of pride, although, at the time of his marriage to Mary Browning, her clothier family was newly risen into the ranks of the parish gentry.[23]

Advantageous marriages could also enhance the lineage by creating links to other prominent families. Hence Shirley's pride in his father's marriage to Lady Frances Berkeley. The Berkeley lineage had similarly been enhanced by marriage. In the fifteenth century James, the nephew and heir male of Thomas, lord Berkeley, had married Isabel, the daughter of Thomas Mowbray, duke of Norfolk. Writing a history of the manor of Melton Mowbray, Smyth referred to this connection as 'noe small enoblinge of [the Berkeley] house and bloud'. At the same time, the marriage of Isabel's sister to Sir Robert Howard forged a link between the Berkeleys and the Howards that continued for two centuries and was reinforced by a number of subsequent marriages.[24] A claim to royal connections was particularly valued. Sir Simon Archer's father-in-law Sir John Ferrers claimed a common ancestry with James I through two great-grand-daughters of David I of Scotland. When Sir John rebuilt the staterooms of Tamworth castle, he adorned the great parlour with a frieze of painted shields, showing his descent from the Conquest. Three large shields in the place of pre-eminence over the mantelpiece supported his claim to royal blood. Sir Thomas Roe, the early Stuart diplomat, claimed descent from the same king through his grandmother Anne Hastings, as shown in a pedigree preserved among his family papers. Sir Edward Rodney could claim more recent royal connections. His mother was the niece of Jane Seymour and first cousin to Edward VI. Although his father died in debt, the Seymour connection took Rodney to Court in the train of the earl of Hertford, where he married Frances Southwell, a lady in waiting to Anne of Denmark. The wedding was paid for by the queen, and Rodney was knighted on the occasion by James I. All this was carefully recorded in his family history – as was his wife's descent from the dukes of Norfolk through her maternal grandfather Charles Howard, earl of Nottingham, Elizabeth's lord admiral. His ancestors may have lived in the 'middle rank of subjects, which is the most safe place', but his heirs had some grand connections.[25]

An interest in lineage and pride in ancestry was not limited to particular sections of the Elizabethan and early Stuart gentry, but was a general characteristic of this level of society. Felicity Heal and Clive Holmes have drawn attention to the flexibility of the puritan conception of the status hierarchy, based on grace, in the face of the gentry's continued obsession with lineage. Despite their stress on personal virtue, the godly did not disregard the significance of a long pedigree. In the brief account of her own life and the memoir of her husband, Lucy Hutchinson laid emphasis on both their pedigrees. She asserted that the Apsleys had been seated in Sussex before the Conquest, and wrote of her husband's parents as: 'two persons so eminently virtuous and pious in their generations, that to descend from them was to set up in the world upon a good stock of honour.' Burton's kinsman William Purefoy of Caldecote was one of the most prominent puritan gentlemen in Warwickshire. He was a close friend of lord Brooke, a parliamentarian in the civil war and a supporter of the execution of Charles I. As Dugdale recorded, Purefoy also rebuilt the manor house at Caldecote, 'where the Armes and matches of his Family are in severall pieces of sculpture very exactly represented.' He allowed Dugdale access to his papers, and in 1636 promised to approach lord Brooke on the antiquary's behalf. When lord Brooke was subsequently killed at Lichfield during the civil war, a local clergyman presented the widow of this puritan peer with his genealogy and biography, which demonstrated his 'antiquitie, noble extraction, and eminent vertues'. The list of contributors to the *Antiquities of Warwickshire* included several gentlemen – in addition to Purefoy – noted for their puritan sympathies, including Sir Thomas Lucy, Sir Edward Peyto and John Hales of Coventry, while Archer was himself known as a godly gentleman. Aside from their religious position there is nothing unexpected about the presence of these men among the contributors. It is probable that their assistance was motivated by the same factors as their social equals who held other religious views. Brooke's own failure to allow Dugdale access to his papers before his death almost certainly owed more to the antiquary's patent sympathies for the rival claimants to his estate than to any distaste for genealogical research or difference of religious complexion.[26]

Continuity of ownership of a family's ancestral estates was as important to their lineage as the length of their pedigree. The Shirleys were exceptional in having held the manor of Lower Eatington, Warwickshire since before the Conquest. This was, according to Dugdale, the 'only place in this County that glories in an uninterrupted succession of its owners for so long a tract of time'. At the end of the thirteenth century the family had adopted their surname from another of their manors in Derbyshire. These two manors remained of particular significance to the Shirleys, even after the family seat was established at Staunton Harold, Leics. in the fifteenth century. In the list of manors on the title page of the family history, the two ancestral manors were given pride of place. Showing a similar concern for ancient associations, when Thomas, lord Brudenell, acquired his barony, he took his title from his ancestral manor of Stonton Wyville, Leics., in preference to his family's seat of Deene, Northants. Similarly, Oliver St John chose the title viscount Grandison for his Irish peerage, utilising the name of the medieval family from which his family had inherited their estates at Bletsoe, Beds., and Lydiard, Wilts., to stress the continuity of the descent.[27] This sentiment in favour of continuity might influence the management of a family's estate, but it did not prevent the gentry from consolidating their land-holdings, selling off inconvenient parcels of land, or moving their residence to a more congenial site. Local histories tended to obscure the extent to which the active land market of the period had altered the structure of land-holding. In the arrangement of the *Antiquities of Warwickshire* Dugdale preferred to link a family's history to the manor that they had held for the longest period rather than that where they had established their seat. The pedigree of the Ardens is to be found not in the account of Park Hall where they lived, but with a manor they had held 'even from the Norman Conquest'. The Archer pedigree appears in the account of Umberslade, held by the family since the twelfth century, rather than Tanworth, which had been acquired as recently as 1604.[28] This bias was common among local historians. William Burton's great-grandfather had acquired part of the manor of Lindley through the marriage to Elizabeth Herdwick mentioned above. The family had established their seat there, and had consolidated their land-holding in the area through the acquisition of the manor of Dadlington. They had, however, retained their ancestral manor of Fauld, Staffs., where Burton was living when he wrote the *Description of Leicestershire*. In his *History of the Worthies of England*, Fuller included Burton among the worthies of Leicestershire, but emphasised that he had 'a more ancient Inheritance belonging to his name' in Staffordshire.[29]

Although the feudal system was in its final death throes by the end of the sixteenth century, the significance for a lineage of the possession of manors – as opposed to the mere ownership of land – was immense. The reciprocal relationship between feudal lord and tenant, which involved both privileges and duties, was an essential aspect of gentility. In 1623 George, lord Berkeley, came of age. The instructions given to Smyth (as his steward in Gloucestershire and Somerset) on the occasion, still survive. They required that, at the next manorial court for each manor, an agreement should be drawn up concerning their customs and privileges. Once the agreements were completed, they were to be conveyed to lord Berkeley: 'then I shall bee henceforth willinge to observe them on my parte, as I shall bee just and honorable, as fully as any of myne

Ancestors heretofore have done'.[30] The symbolic significance of the feudal bond remained strong. The emphasis on manors in local histories did not simply reflect the bias of the medieval records from Domesday Book through manorial court rolls to inquisitions *post mortem*. It also arose from the very real attachment of many gentry to the feudal ideals of their ancestors.

The importance of continuity of tenure to the lineage led many families to retain links to their ancestral estates, even after they had been lost or sold. The Newdigates of Arbury had reluctantly sold their ancient seat at Harefield, Middx., in 1585. In 1677 it was repurchased by Richard Newdigate, one of the contributors to the *Antiquities of Warwickshire*. During their 'exile' the Newdigates had continued to be buried in the parish church at Harefield, indicating the profound significance of the ancestral tie. The inscription on the funeral monument of John Ashburnham (d. 1671) at Ashburnham, Sussex, eloquently demonstrates the significance accorded to ancestral manors. In the reign of James I, his father's 'good nature and frank disposition towards his friends' necessitated the sale of Ashburnham, which according to the inscription had been in the family since 'long before the conquest'. Somewhat unusually in the case of families forced to the extremity of selling ancestral lands, his son was able to sufficiently recover their fortunes to petition the privy council to be allowed to repurchase the estate in little more than two decades – although it was only in 1640 that he managed to recover possession, just in time to have it sequestrated during the civil war. His pride in his achievement is clear from the importance it is given in the text of the inscription on his monument. It was perhaps in death that the visceral link to the ancestral acres was most visibly expressed. The body of Henry, lord Berkeley, was conveyed from his Warwickshire home back to Berkeley for burial among his ancestors, although his first wife was more conveniently buried in Coventry. Habington described a local gentleman as 'pyously removinge the corps of his father from London' for burial in Worcestershire. The Unton memorial picture in the National Portrait Gallery illustrates the carriage of Sir Henry Unton's body back to the family manor of Wadley for burial alongside his father and grandfather in Faringdon church, Oxon., after his death during an embassy to France.[31] The importance of manors with ancestral links – and the significance of the visual continuity of monuments to successive generations of a family – mean that collections of family tombs are frequently found in unexpected churches. The tombs of the Russells, earls and dukes of Bedford, are at Chenies, Bucks., rather than at Woburn, Beds, – despite the building of a crypt at St Mary's, Woburn, in readiness for their remains. Similarly, the Vernons of Haddon Hall, Derbys., lie in state at Tong, Shrops.

When county histories began to appear, the importance of continuity in pedigree and land-holding could cause concern to those gentlemen, whose families had settled outside their ancestral county. We can see this in a letter written to Dugdale in 1650 by William Bromley of Baginton. Bromley's family was originally from Staffordshire, and his father had purchased their Warwickshire manor as recently as 1619. A full exposition of their pedigree was outside the scope of Dugdale's book, and Bromley was concerned that they might appear 'as mushromes of a night's extraction'. To avoid this possibility, he asked, that Dugdale should include some reference to his Staffordshire descent. Consequently, Dugdale's text included a reference to Bromley's claim to be descended from Sir Walter Bromley of Bromley, Staffs., in the time of king John. Bromley also asked that Dugdale should mention 'our consanguinity with the Staffords (whose Cote we quarter) and our match with Mat. Widvile'. The *Antiquities of Warwickshire* recorded the Bromleys' relationship to both these prominent Staffordshire families.[32] Similarly, the genealogist Christopher Towneley noted under 'Lancashire' in his volume on the 'Arms of the Nobility and Pedigrees of the Northern Gentry', that 'I put these things following in this county though the[y] concerne Westmorland & Northumberland because the Traffords aimes [sic] to bring the Genealogie from thence'. By the mid-seventeenth century the Traffords had been an important Lancashire family for more than a century, but in lineage terms this was quite a short period, which did not reflect their status within the county hierarchy.[33]

A family's arms were 'theyre insygnes of gentry', the visible symbol of their lineage. Shirley believed his own family had derived their arms from an ancestor who acted as standard bearer to the duke of Saxony. Throughout his family history he drew attention to the constancy with which the Shirleys had borne the same arms. John Denton used his account of Cumberland to give a 'historical' account of how his family derived its armorial crest of 'a castle or tower sable, flames issuing out at the top thereof and a demi-lion rampant with a sword in his right paw issuing out the flames'. This crest was reputed to commemorate his ancestor's staunch support of the Baliols against the Bruces in the thirteenth century, when his stronghold was burnt beneath him. Dugdale's correspondent William Bromley was particularly concerned that the account of his family in the *Antiquities of Warwickshire* should mention the fifteenth-century Sir John Bromley, from whom he was lineally descended. Sir John had captured a French standard in battle, for which he had been granted an augmentation to his arms. The importance of this honorary crest to the Bromley lineage was recognised by Dugdale. He dedicated the map of Knightlow hundred to William Bromley, by the traditional method of including his arms on the engraving, and drew attention to the crest in the text. Such augmentations were not necessarily contemporary with the deeds alleged. Sir Piers Legh of Lyme, Ches., was awarded 'an Esocheon of Augmentation sable replenished with mollets silver, therein a mans Arme bowed holding in the hand a Standard silver' by William Flower, Norroy king of arms in 1575. The justification for this was his descent from a fourteenth-century Piers Leigh

Esq., who according to the grant was awarded the manor of Hawley, Ches., by Richard II in recognition of his service to the king and to his father the Black Prince at the battle of Crecy. Coats of arms, like pedigrees, could be manipulated to reflect or support current status.[34]

Coats of arms were particularly effective in providing a visual image of a family's alliances to other armorial families. On their marriage a couple's arms were grouped together heraldically by 'impalement'. Their shield was divided vertically, with the husband's arms placed on the right and the arms of his wife's father on the left. Impaled arms were borne only by the married couple, and were not passed down to their children. A permanent visual record of the alliance of the two families was created by the use of the impaled arms to decorate buildings, tombs, and a wide range of household objects. When Ralph Sheldon of Beoley and Weston died in 1613, he left to each of his married daughters a basin and ewer worth twenty-five pounds, to be engraved with 'the Armes of every of the husbandes of my said daughters joyned with mine'.[35] Impaled arms were particularly important on funeral monuments, such as that erected in 1632 by Sir Simon Clarke at Church Hanborough, Oxon., in memory of his grandmother Margaret, the daughter of John Mayny. The Mayny arms are shown impaled with those of Margaret's husband, and the monument also shows the impaled arms of Simon's mother (Edolph), his aunt (West) and his cousin's wife (Markham). Since none of these arms descended to Sir Simon, these important alliances were not recorded in his own quartered arms. The heraldry on the tomb of Burton's kinsman George Purefoy at Drayton, Leics., similarly recorded all three of his marriages, although only two of his wives were shown in effigy. The coats of arms on the tomb also recorded his third wife's former marriage to Sir Thomas Glover. The importance attached to impaled arms is reflected in the records of the College of Arms, where they appear both in copies of visitations and on funeral certificates. The funeral certificate of Sir Robert Gardiner, former lord chief justice of Ireland, was recorded by Henry Chitting in September 1620, some seven months after his death. It includes careful drawings of his arms impaled with those of each of his three wives. None of these marriages had produced living children, but Sir Robert's great-nephew and heir John Webb went to the trouble and expense of ensuring that they were fully recorded and illustrated on the funeral certificate.[36]

The practice of quartering arms created a permanent record of certain marriage alliances. When a man married an heiress, he placed her father's arms in a small escutcheon on his own shield, to symbolise his claim to represent her family in the absence of a male heir. Any children of such a marriage were able to quarter the arms of their mother's family alongside those of their father. When Burton's ancestor John Herdwick died in 1511, he left six daughters. The descendants of each of these daughters were entitled to quarter the

Figure 7 The tomb of Nicholas (d. 1589) and Elizabeth (d. 1587) St John
at Lydiard Tregoze, Wilts., erected 1592

arms of Herdwick, creating a visual link between Burton and his kinsmen among the Leicestershire gentry.[37] This visual cue could enhance a sense of kinship, which might otherwise be undermined by the passage of time. In late medieval documents the quartering of two coats is not unusual, but more elaborate displays were apparently rare before the Tudor period. By the end of the sixteenth century the practice of quartering had developed to extreme lengths. Shirley quartered fifty coats, George, lord Berkeley, laid claim to twenty and William, marquess of Winchester, twenty-three. At a less-exalted level the herald John Philipot was able in 1620 to marshal nineteen coats for the family of the Sir Heneage Finch, recorder of London, and managed twenty for his own family pedigree. It appears that the obsession with quartering was a reaction to the increased prevalence of armigerous gentry. As parish gentry and townspeople began to acquire coats of arms, elaborate quarterings provided a means of social differentiation. In a letter copied into a collection of pedigrees now in Hereford, Philipot wrote an account of his 'Notions and Testimonies' concerning the eleven coats quartered by the Coningsbys at the request of the family.[38] While Philipot clearly saw this use of his genealogical and heraldic expertise as a lucrative supplement to his income, not everyone approved of the prevalence of such extravagantly quartered arms. The *True Use of Armorie* observed that: 'except it be made in a pedigree or descent to lock up in an evidence chest, thereby to shew mens titles to their lands or the Alliences and kindreds of their houses ... I could wish that every man would content himself with his own peculiar coat of name, and not use above one quartered therewith at the most.'[39] Quartering remained popular throughout the period covered by this study, as evidenced by the escutcheons on numerous funeral monuments (see figures 7 and 11).

Collections of coats of arms were a frequent form of decoration in gentry houses. Although predominantly taken from churches, armorial collections often include notes on arms recorded in the homes of gentry families. In Leicestershire, for example, Burton collected notes at the homes of the Stares-mores of Frolesworth, the Waldrams of Oadby, and the Farnhams of Quorndon.[40] Such arms might represent the various marital alliances contracted by a family. There were also more extensive collections, which represented the local gentry community as a whole. In addition to adorning his tomb and the church walls at Sandon with his own family's arms, Erdeswicke set up the coats of the local gentry in the gallery of his house. Such displays were clearly linked to a family's sense of their position within the gentry community. In the case of catholics such as Erdeswicke, it was a way of visually expressing membership of the civil society from which they were distanced by religious differences. On a grander scale, the herald William Wyrley recorded three sets of arms in the earl of Shrewsbury's newly built manor house at Worksop, Notts. In the gallery were the arms of foreign and English nobles, in another room were the matches of the Talbot family, and finally there was a room containing the arms of the Derbyshire gentry. At Gilling castle the 433 coats of the Yorkshire gentry set up by the Fairfax family can still be seen in a frieze in the Great Chamber. The significance of such collections for expressing the gentry's sense of identity, and the importance that they attached to stability, continuity and traditional values was expressed clearly by Sir Robert Jermyn of Rushbrooke Hall, Suffolk. He displayed 139 coats of local county families with the inscription *qui sumus* (who we are). The importance of continuity was emphasised by his marshalling of the coats of 109 extinct families, labelled *qui fuimus* (who we were).[41]

As a taste for the classical increasingly asserted itself among the gentry as the seventeenth century progressed, heraldic display in homes and on funeral monuments became less fashionable. The armorial stained glass of the Peyto family, set up at Chesterton in the late fifteenth century, was destroyed during the remodelling of the house after the civil war, once it had been recorded for posterity in the *Antiquities of Warwickshire*. The Peytos were early converts to classicism, as shown by the development of their funeral monuments at Chesterton and their pre-war building projects. Among the provincial gentry as a whole, the desire to display family connections through heraldry did not die out, although it became less common as time progressed and seems to have become more directly related to important dynastic events. In Gloucestershire, for example, the Codrington family erected a display of at least fourteen coats – apparently to celebrate the marriage of cousins in 1651 which united two branches of the family. Ironically, the premature death of the husband before his father, leaving only daughters, led to the sale of the estate to a cousin shortly after the Restoration. The armorial stained glass eventually found its way to Combe in Wiltshire, where it provided a setting for the arms of the Houlton family.[42]

In seeking to understand the genealogical obsession of the Tudor and Stuart gentry, it is essential to appreciate the significance of lineage. To equate it simply with a pride in being able to trace one's pedigree back through countless generations is to underestimate the role of lineage within gentry society in this period. Lineage was what linked a gentleman to the land and to his community. It bound a family's members together, and linked them through a series of reciprocal ties to other gentry families, to their tenants and to the established hierarchy. All this was symbolised by their coat of arms, which provided a means to visually express both family pride and obligation. Local historians researching the pedigrees and land-holdings of gentry families needed to tread warily. If they cast doubt on a family's lineage, they were not simply in danger of arousing anger and a sense of injured pride. They could be accused of undermining the very fabric of society.

The importance accorded the collective lineage of the county gentry as demonstrated in their heraldic displays, was acknowledged by local historians and influenced the development of their works. Thomas Habington alleged that he undertook to write an account of Worcestershire, 'because it was objected by one that our countie conteyned fewe gentellmen of antiquity' and it was his intention to prove the charge wrong. Richard Carew described how the Cornish gentry could boast of their lineage rather than their current prosperity. He questioned 'whether any shire in England, of but equall quantitie, can muster a like number of faire coate-Armours'. At the other extreme of the country, William Grey believed that the northern gentry 'can produce more ancient Families, then any other part of England; many of them Gentry before the Conquest; the rest came in with William the Conqueror'. Conversely, in the *Perambulation of Kent*, William Lambarde acknowledged that the Kentish gentry were not generally of 'so auncient stocke' as their counterparts in other counties, since London provided a constant stream of courtiers, lawyers and merchants who settled in the county. To compensate for this perceived weakness, he stressed their learning, employment in the administration of the county and participation in other pursuits appropriate to gentility. There were various ways in which the lineage of county families could be demonstrated. Some antiquaries included lists of local families who traced their descent from the Conquest. Others included images of coats of arms, echoing the visual displays of their neighbours, or described them in the esoteric language of blazon. As we saw in chapter two, encroaching on the province of the heralds in this way was likely to bring rebuke, and there was also the danger of causing offence to neighbours, who might feel themselves exposed as newcomers or unfairly omitted. So, although antiquarian collections abounded in heraldic and genealogical information, local histories did not necessarily include all the material available to their authors, and tended to concentrate on medieval rather than modern families.[43]

The most immediately obvious manifestation of the influence of lineage on the development of local history is the overwhelming concentration on manors as the organising principle. There were practical reasons for this, given the importance of such records as Domesday and *Nomina Villarum*. Equally, these records assumed their importance, because of the concentration on manorial descents. It was by no means inevitable that the manor should dominate local history. As Thomas Westcote explained in his *View of Devonshire*, it was very difficult to trace the history of the majority of manors, which had often been dismembered, divided between several heirs or sold. Under different circumstances the parish might have emerged as the dominant unit of local history. It was the church rather than the manor house around which the life of the community revolved, and which linked the current inhabitants with the past generations buried within its precincts. If the Elizabethan clergy rather than the gentry had written the first local histories, the parish, archdeaconry and diocese might well have been more important than the manor, hundred and county. Reading Eamon Duffy's account of the sixteenth-century community of Morebath and its priest Sir Christopher Trychay, reminds us that local history could have developed differently. The priest who recorded such a rich impression of communal life in the parish accounts might have become the precursor of a generation of clerical parish historians. An analysis of why this did not happen is beyond the scope of this book, but as a result much that might have been memorialised within local histories was lost or preserved in fragmentary sources because the gentry wrote about what interested and concerned them.[44]

The evolution of William Burton's *Description of Leicestershire* provides a useful demonstration of how the gentry's obsession with genealogy influenced the development of local history. In the first edition, Burton organised the work as an alphabetical list of manors. As we saw in chapter two, Burton included pedigrees of extinct families to illustrate the descent of manors, but he limited the modern pedigrees he included to those of friends and kinsfolk. Despite this caution, he was censured by the heralds – with a number of whom he had a close working relationship – for trespassing on their territory. With this experience behind him, it might be expected that he would decline to include further pedigrees in the proposed second edition of his work. However, Burton clearly discovered that the disapproval of the heralds was not shared by his fellow gentry in Leicestershire, who wanted to see their own pedigrees in print. The final revised version of his text, dating from 1642, has innumerable pedigrees. The majority are drawn from the record of the 1619 visitation of Leicestershire, but many have been supplemented by additional or later information.

A significant example of how the interests of the gentry influenced Burton's revision of his text is that of the Skipwith family of Cotes. In 1622 Burton paid tribute to the 'good parts, his person, valour, learning, judgement, and wisdom' of Sir William Skipwith, but included no pedigree of his family. The association of the Skipwiths with Leicestershire had begun in the late sixteenth century, when Henry Skipwith of Ormesby, Lincs., married Jane, the widow of Francis Nele of Prestwold, Leics. Henry and Jane subsequently purchased the manor of Cotes, and in 1595 their son William purchased the manor of Prestwold. He became a justice of the peace and established the family seat at Cotes, where he lived until his death in 1610. In the 1590s Wyrley recorded that Cotes was 'the seat of Sir William Skipwith knight, a worthie gentleman whoe fetcheth his descent from the Auncient race of the Skipwiths in the countie of Yorke'.[45] The publication of the *Description of Leicestershire* coincided with Sir William's son Henry becoming a baronet. Having established their position through their wealth, personal merit and service to the community, the Skipwith family reinforced it through an emphasis on the traditional elements of lineage. The family provided Burton with the information required for the incorporation of their pedigree into the revised text. The descent of the family from the fifth son of Sir William Skipwith of Ormesby was emphasised in this pedigree, as it was on the monument erected to his parents by Henry, younger brother of Sir William Skipwith, at Tugby church in 1633. Sir William's own funeral monument was erected at Prestwold in 1631 in accordance with the will of his second wife Jane, daughter of Sir John Roberts of Woollaston. On it was inscribed the elegy written by the poet Sir John Beaumont two decades before. Jane bore her husband no children and does not appear on the Skipwith pedigree in Burton's revised text, which includes only the mother of his heir. However, the description of her husband's monument does acknowledge her part in its construction. To women such as Jane Skipwith, who were often ignored by heraldic pedigrees, the construction of funeral monuments was a means of inserting themselves into the genealogical memory of the families into which they married. In time this was reinforced by the inclusion of descriptions and illustrations of such monuments in local histories. The elaborate Skipwith monuments were erected as the family's status was reaching its zenith, as confirmed by Sir Henry Skipwith's service as a deputy lieutenant from the 1620s and as sheriff in 1636. The inclusion of detailed descriptions of the monuments and their heraldry in Burton's revised text were designed to underline the family's status within the wider gentry community.[46]

The correspondence between Burton and Sir Roger Smith of Edmondthorpe in 1632 further demonstrates the way in which members of the gentry – whose position was based on wealth and public service – recognised local history as a vehicle for reinforcing their claim to status through the traditional rhetoric of lineage. Sir Roger was a justice of the peace, who had purchased the manor of Edmondthorpe from Sir Henry Berkeley. Sir Henry was a descendant of the baronial Berkeley family and a friend of Burton's, whose pedigree was included in 1622. His wealth, however, was insufficient to support the status and lifestyle suggested by his lineage, and he sold his ancestral manor. Sir Roger Smith's position within Leicestershire society, by contrast, depended upon his wealth, his service as a magistrate and his reputation as a 'grave and religious' man. Yet he was also concerned to establish his family's claim to status based on lineage. Sir Roger represented a cadet branch of the Smiths of Withcock and, through his great-grandmother Katherine Ashby, claimed descent from the important medieval families of Burdet of Loseby and Zouch of Lubbesthorpe. Sir Roger had carefully examined the Burdet, Zouch and Ashby pedigrees in the *Description of Leicestershire* and he had discovered discrepancies, which he asked Burton to rectify: 'else it may stand as a bar and objection against the deriving of our pedigree from those families'.[47] His concern is evidence both of the authority Burton's published pedigrees had assumed, despite their errors and lacunae, and of the importance attached to them by members of the gentry.

Daniel Woolf has suggested that the *Antiquities of Warwickshire*, published some fifteen years after the last revisions to Burton's text, represents a move away from the late Elizabethan and early Stuart obsession with genealogy and sheer length of pedigree. It is certainly true that the pedigrees and illustrations of arms, seals and effigies in the book, which echo the contents of so many earlier manuscripts, are supplemented by biographical sketches. The account of Sir John de Astley to which Woolf draws attention, is, however, a comparatively rare example of extended biographical treatment in the work. More typical are the numerous accounts of manors passing from generation to generation, with the occasional mention of an ancestor who served as sheriff or fought in a particular war. This gradual move towards biography suggests that after a century of heraldic visitations and genealogical obsession the gentry had confidence in their collective identity and claim to continuity with their medieval forbears.[48] This increasing emphasis on biography is seen in the development of family history as a distinct branch of local history. Although John Smyth claimed with the *Lives of the Berkeleys* to have been the first to compose a genealogical history of a noble family, the idea was not unique to him. As we saw in chapter one, Thomas, earl of Arundel, who 'thought no other part of history so considerable as what related to his own family', had commissioned Sir Robert Cotton to write a history celebrating the greatness of his ancestors in 1613.[49] There were also a number of contemporary Scottish family histories which could contest the claim to originality with Smyth. The fair copy of David Hume of Godscroft's history of the Douglas family may have been completed shortly after the first draft of the *Lives of the Berkeleys*, but its preface suggests that it had a longer gestation reaching back to the mid-1590s.[50] As we have seen, family histories developed as a natural consequence of the trend towards increasingly detailed, narrative pedigrees that were being produced by the late fifteenth century. Moreover, the increasing importance of documents in litigation meant that the antiquary or the lawyer skilled in palaeography became an important member of noble households, and the family history provided such people with the means to curry favour with their patrons. Just as Smyth's *Lives of the Berkeleys* originated in the research required to settle the great lawsuit between the Berkeleys and the Lisles, the 'Great Books' of Anne Clifford's family history were the fruit of research carried out as part of her own battle to claim and protect the Clifford inheritance.

The earl of Arundel's commissioning of a history of the Howards by Cotton is often cited as evidence that genealogy mattered to the nobility of Jacobean England – and, indeed, it is a useful piece of evidence and I have used it in this way. Yet, we should also consider the significance of the project's failure to reach fruition. It was surely not for lack of interest on the part of the earl in promoting his lineage. His enthusiasm for purchasing Holbein portraits and the restoration of family tombs in Norfolk attest to the strength of his sustained interest. Neither was his social circle lacking in historians capable of the work. In addition to Cotton, there was John Selden, who published a catalogue of the classical inscriptions at Arundel House in 1628, and various antiquaries among the heralds of the College of Arms, including William Dugdale from 1638. Henry Lilly, who produced the 'Genealogie of the Princelie familie of the Howards', was a competent genealogist, but he was known predominantly as a manuscript illuminator. The book he produced consisted of 271 leaves of thick vellum, with 110 painted shields and numerous minatures of tombs, stained-glass windows and other artefacts. It is analogous to the great pedigree that Shirley produced before going on to compile his family history. The question we should consider is why wasn't the Howard pedigree a similar prelude to a family history?[51]

One reason might be that visual displays of lineage fulfilled different imperatives to family histories – and that the earl of Arundel lacked a sufficient reason to ensure the history was written. Visual displays of lineage appear to have been equally associated with success and failure. As we have seen, successful courtiers like Burghley and Shrewsbury and provincial, catholic gentlemen like Erdeswicke used heraldic displays as expressions of status. The production of family histories seems to be linked particularly to declining rather than to rising fortunes. It has been suggested that the flourishing of family history in Scotland was related to the pressures felt by the Scottish peerage after the union of the two crowns in 1603. In England they seem to be the product of more domestic concerns, arising from dynastic misfortune. Writing a family history was one of the ways in which representatives of a family attempted to preserve the lineage during periods of threat. It could have a practical purpose in reminding their readers of the claims that a family had on their loyalty or respect. Smyth began to write the *Lives of the Berkeleys* as a full-blown history rather than an extended panegyric for oral presentation, when the minority of George, lord Berkeley, had reduced the family's influence in Gloucestershire and the Midlands. Later the work was copied out and circulated among a select circle during the 1630s, when lord Berkeley suffered increasingly from poor health. At that time the management of the Berkeley estates passed initially to lord Berkeley's mother and, after her death, to his wife. Shirley similarly compiled his family history in the decade following the death of his brother, Sir Henry Shirley, who had been succeeded by a minor. Both works glorified their respective families, and showed how the lineage had survived and prospered despite trying times and periods of eclipse in the past. Arundel was rich, successful and had heirs. As a patron, he had many interests, and a family history might have seemed to involve more effort than it merited. Once Smyth had written the *Lives of the Berkeleys* – and we may be certain that Arundel knew of it – nothing less would have done for the earl.[52]

The civil war threatened the status and continuance of English families far more immediately than the union of the crowns in 1603 had threatened the Scots, and does seem to have spurred a similar development of family history. Had Arundel lived into the interregnum, Dugdale might have found himself employed completing a Howard family history rather than the *Monasticon Anglicanum* or the *Antiquities of Warwickshire*. If family history was the product of dynastic misfortune, the decline in his power, wealth and influence would have increased the earl's interest in written expositions of his lineage. From a less-exalted social level, Gervase Holles composed his account of his family during his exile after the civil war, when the future of his family was very uncertain. In it he expressed the hope that his lineage would survive and that, even if he did not live to see it, his son would have his rough copy transcribed on to vellum 'and the pedigrees and matches with their achievements hand-somly drawne and well painted as likewise the severall monuments; and so many pictures (in title and in oyle) of your ancestors and family as you can attayne to. And then it will last many generations, and appeare a treasure not unworthy the cabinet of you and your posterity'. If the family had perished, there would still have remained his manuscript account. The fragility of manuscripts makes one wonder how many similar attempts to preserve the memory of a lineage crumbled to dust or were consumed by fire or mice. It is, of course, possible that a Howard family history was produced for the earl of Arundel, but that it has been lost. Lilly's genealogy survived the upheavals of the civil war by chance. He apparently died before delivering his genealogy to the earl, and it remained in his family until after the Restoration, when it was purchased by the Howards. Given the temporary eclipses experienced by Arundel during the ascendancy of his great rival Buckingham, the existence of a family history would not necessarily undermine the thesis that family histo-ries were most frequently a product of instability and decline – much would depend on the date of production.[53]

The fragility of human life, demonstrated by the death of several children and the turbulent times in which he lived, influenced the Somerset gentleman Sir Edward Rodney to transform the results of his genealogical research into literary form and to preserve an account of his own life. He appears to have begun writing his family history as a guidance book for his son, since he was afraid that he would die before his son grew up. When his son died aged 22, Sir Edward revised the manuscript, and it became an elegy to Sir Edward's lineage. Sir Edward was thirty-nine when his fifth son, George, was born. This was the only one of his sons to survive infancy, although six daughters lived to maturity. Sir Edward initially composed the work so that George 'might have seen from example of his owne family what to follow and what to flee', but after George's death in 1651 he wrote a new dedication to his five surviving daughters. Two of these were already 'transplanted' into other families, and Sir Edward saw the fate of his lineage as enhancing those of the families his daughters joined. Significantly, he took no comfort from the continuance of his name in the offspring of his younger brothers, although his own father had inherited Stoke Rodney through the failure of a senior branch of the family. Rather he assured himself that it would be a 'great contentment' to his daughters' children:

> to have the greatest part of there bloud from a family which god hath blesed with so
> many desents as this tract doth mention; and all of them matcht into so many noble
> familyes; which though now it bee come to the period after a space of 500 yeares the
> comon periodd of kingdomes and all great familyes; is yet matter of thanksgiving

to god that it lasted so long; and that through so long a tract of time it hath not contracted any blemishes or spotts of infamy.

There was clearly a distinction in Sir Edward's mind between his own blood and lineage, which was inherited by his daughters and their children, and the name that would continue in his nephews. Such evidence helps us to understand how a possessor of a title or entailed estate, who valued his lineage highly but had no son, could yet fail to ensure that his heir male was sufficiently endowed to support the position he inherited. While their status and sense of identity was drawn from the extended family represented by their lineage, the gentry's emotional ties were to their immediate kin.[54]

The historian working in the Public Record Office or local archives among the myriads of people tracing their family trees might be tempted to think that an obsession with lineage has never gone away. And to an extent this is true. From Thomas Love Peacock and Jane Austen onwards, English novels have incorporated characters who are obsessed by their pedigree and see it as a signifier of status. Yet the nature of the obsession has evolved over time. In Anthony Trollope's *Doctor Thorne* (1858) the lineage is both rescued and overwhelmed by the combined power of money and sensibility, the forces of modernity. Today the interest is in genealogy, not lineage, and this is an important difference. People are interested if they discover an ancestor with a coat of arms, but they do not see heraldry as an expression of identity. They may make a pilgrimage to the village where their ancestors lived, but they do not believe that they share an almost mystical association with a particular piece of land. Although, as we have seen, the elements of lineage could be manipulated to reflect social reality, the upheavals of the seventeenth century ultimately proved too great for the concept to retain its force. In a society that had executed one king and deposed another, the decline of lineage as a bulwark of social status was inevitable. Before that decline, however, the gentry obsession with lineage had shaped the development of local history in a way that is still apparent today. Moreover, the growth in family histories – to which a personal memoir of the author was often appended – helped to shape the development of biography and autobiography, although a full exploration of that influence is beyond the scope of this book.

NOTES

1 Smyth, *Berkeley Mss*, vol. 2, p. 336.

2 Smyth, *Berkeley Mss*, vol. 1, p. 1; V. Sackville West, *Berkeley Castle* (Derby: English Life Publications Ltd., 1990), 30; J.J. Scarisbrick, *Henry VIII* (London: Methuen, paperback edn., 1981), pp. 482–3.

3 S. Adams, '"Because I am of that countrye & mynde to plant myself there": Robert Dudley, Earl of Leicester and the West Midlands', *Midlands History* 20 (1995), pp. 24–6, 29;

Toulmin Smith, *The Itinerary of John Leland*, p. 17; Sir Robert Naunton, *Fragmenta Regalia* (Washington, D.C.: Associated University Press, 1985), p. 49; Erdeswicke, *Staffordshire*, pp. 338–9; Dugdale, *Warwickshire*, p. 336; Staffs. C.R.O., D868/5, fo. 2; Sir Philip Sidney, 'Defence of the Earl of Leicester', *Complete Works*, A. Feuillerat (ed.), four volumes (Cambridge: Cambridge University Press, 1912–26), vol. 3, pp. 61–71.

4 Smyth, *Berkeley Mss*, vol. 2, pp. 381–91; *Smyth Papers*, vol. 1, p. 53; J. Broadway, 'John Smyth of Nibley: a Jacobean man-of-business and his service to the Berkeley family', *Midland History* 24 (1999), pp. 83–4; Surtees, *The History and Antiquities of the County Palatine of Durham*, vol. 3, p. 77–9.

5 B.L., Harley 4928, fo. 105v–6.

6 B.L., Harley 4928, fo. 108; the monument is illustrated in the great Shirley pedigree: Leics. C.R.O. P99.

7 L. Stone, *The Crisis of the Aristocracy* (Oxford: Clarendon Press, 1965), pp. 25–7; Heal and Holmes, *The Gentry in England and Wales*, pp. 34–7; Woolf, *Idea of History in Early Stuart England*, p. 116, 128–9; Woolf, *Social Circulation*, pp. 86–91, 137.

8 Differing views on the family are represented in L. Stone, *The Family, Sex and Marriage in England 1500–1800* (London: Weidenfeld and Nicolson, 1977) and R. Houlbrooke, *The English Family 1450–1700* (London: Longman, 1984); Heal and Holmes, *The Gentry in England and Wales*, chapter 2 gives an overview of the practical influence of the extended gentry family.

9 Northants. C.R.O., M(TM)604; FH269; FH270; Hants. C.R.O., 93 M86 W/2. A copy of the 'Grandison Book' is on display at Lydiard Tregoze, Wilts.; others are held by the Society of Antiquaries and the Swindon and Wiltshire Record Office.

10 Heal and Holmes, *The Gentry in England and Wales*, p. 11; J.F.R. Day, 'Primers of honor: heraldry, heraldry books, and English Renaissance literature', *The Sixteenth Century Journal* 21(1) (1990), p. 98.

11 There is an extensive literature on the significance of lineage: Heal and Holmes, *The Gentry in England and Wales*, pp. 27–30; M. James, *Family, Lineage, and Civil Society* (Oxford: Clarendon Press, 1974), pp. 108–11; M. James, *Society, Politics and Culture* (Cambridge: Cambridge University Press, 1986), pp. 308–415; R. Cust, 'Honour, rhetoric and political culture: the Earl of Huntingdon and his enemies', in S.D. Amussen and M.A. Kishlansky (eds), *Political Culture and Cultural Politics in Early Modern England* (Manchester: Manchester University Press, 1995), pp. 84–111; J.P. Cooper, 'Ideas of gentility in early modern England', in G.E. Aylmer and J.S. Morrill (eds), *Land, Men and Beliefs* (London: Hambledon, 1983), pp. 43–77; K. Wrightson, 'Estates, degrees and sorts in Tudor and Stuart England', *History Today* 37 (January 1987), pp. 17–22.

12 Smyth, *Berkeley Mss*, vol. 2, p. 440; Heal and Holmes, *The Gentry in England and Wales*, pp. 20–3.

13 This discontinuity is not found in all societies: see M. Sahlins, *Islands of History* (Chicago: University of Chicago Press, 1985), chapter 2 and the references in Woolf, *Social Circulation*, pp. 73–5. See also N. Llewellyn, *Funeral Monuments in Post-Reformation England* (Cambridge: Cambridge University Press, 2000), especially pp. 53–8, which discuss funeral monuments erected during their subjects' lives.

14 B.L., Additional MS 5410; William Dugdale, *The Antient Usage in Bearing of Such Ensigns of Honour As Are Commonly Call'd Arms* (Oxford, 1682), pp. 43–4; Smyth, *Berkeley Mss*, vol. 1, pp. 6–12; Carew, *Cornwall*, p. 65; William Grey, *Chorographia or a Survey of*

Newcastle upon Tine (Newcastle, 1649), hereafter Grey, *Chorographia*, pp. 43–4; Gerard, *Dorset*, p. 109. Woolf, *Social Circulation*, pp. 122–33 includes an interesting discussion on the length of pedigree, although I do not think he allows for the degree of conscious myth-building involved.

15 B.L., Harley 4928, fo. 26–9; S.B.T., D473/293, 36: my italics – 'merely' is used here in the sense of 'solely'.

16 Heal and Holmes, *The Gentry in England and Wales*, p. 36; Aubrey mentions a Digby family history, written by or on the orders of Sir Kenelm, Aubrey, *Brief Lives*, p. 99; I. Atherton, *Ambition and Failure in Stuart England* (Manchester: Manchester University Press, 1999), p. 25; Woolf, *Social Circulation*, p. 126.

17 Woolf, *Social Circulation*, p. 125; Northants. C.R.O., FH271; R. Trevelyan, *Sir Walter Raleigh* (London: Penguin, 2003), p. 95; Keen, *Chivalry*, pp. 32–3; F. Bacon, 'On truth', *Essays* (London: J.M. Dent & Sons, 1972), p. 3.

18 Holles, *Memorials of the Holles Family*, p. 3.

19 Holles, *Memorials of the Holles Family*, pp. 11–12.

20 College of Arms, Vincent 94, fo. 353; Wrottesley, 'A History of the Bagot family', pp. 93–4; Styles, 'Sir Simon Clark', p. 14.

21 S.B.T., DR37/vol. 46; B.L., Additional MS 34239, fos 3v, 6v.

22 Starkey, *Rivals in Power*, p. 216.

23 Burton, *Leicestershire*, pp. 173–9; Smyth, *Berkeley Mss*, vol. 1, pp. 48–50.

24 B.L., Additional MS 33588, fo. 36. Smyth originally intended to include the histories of the Berkeley manors in the family history, but later revised his plan and wrote them as separate accounts.

25 H. Norris, *Tamworth Castle* (Tamworth, 1899), pp. 15–29; Badminton Muniments, Fms/C3/2; B.L., Additional MS 34239, fos 6, 12v–3, 15–16.

26 Heal and Holmes, *The Gentry in England and Wales*, pp. 32–3; Lucy Hutchinson, *Memoirs of the Life of Colonel Hutchinson* (London: J.M. Dent & Sons, 1908), p. 29; Hamper, *Dugdale*, pp. 155–6; Woolf, *Social Circulation*, p. 91; Hughes, *Politics, Society and Civil War in Warwickshire*, pp. 71, 97, 122, 138, 300–1; Dugdale, *Warwickshire*, pp. 112–19, 375–7, 396–402, 799.

27 Dugdale, *Warwickshire*, p. 474; B.L., Harley 4928, fo. 1*; E.P. Shirley, *Lower Eatington: Its Manor House and Church* (London, 1869); J. Wake, *The Brudenells of Deene* (London: Cassell & Co., 1953), p. 112.

28 Dugdale, *Warwickshire*, pp. 576, 580, 549, 676.

29 Fuller, *The Worthies of England*, p. 134.

30 *Smyth Papers*, vol. 2, p. 54.

31 V. Larminie, *Wealth, Kinship and Culture* (Royal Historical Society, 1995), p. 60; Victoria County History, hereafter V.C.H., *Sussex*, vol. 9, pp. 126–30 traces the Ashburnham family association with the manor from 1166; Habington, *Worcestershire*, vol. 1, p. 161; Smyth, *Berkeley Mss*, vol. 2, pp. 387, 407; R. Strong, *The Cult of Elizabeth* (London: Thames & Hudson, 1977), pp. 84–110.

32 Hamper, *Dugdale*, pp. 241–3; Dugdale, *Warwickshire*, p. 153. Bromley's pedigree may be seen in J.P. Rylands (ed.), *Visitation of Cheshire* (London: Harleian Society 18, 1882), pp. 47–50.

33 Lancs. C.R.O., DDM11/71, unpaginated.

34 Denton, *An Account of the Most Considerable Estates and Families in the County of Cumberland*, pp. 93–4; Habington, *Worcestershire*, vol. 1, p. 192; B.L., Harley 4928, fos 11–24; Shirley, *Stemmata Shirleiana*, p. 6; Dugdale, *Warwickshire*, map between pp. 2 and 3, p. 153; T. Woodcock and J. Robinson, *Oxford Guide to Heraldry* (Oxford: Oxford University Press, 1988), pp. 69–70 – includes illustration of grant.

35 Before marriage a woman used her father's arms on seals, etc. Differencing did not apply to women, as they played no military role. See C.W. Scott-Giles, *Looking at Heraldry* (London: Phoenix House, 1962), pp. 43–5; Habington, *Worcestershire*, vol. 2, p. 15; E.A.B. Barnard, *The Sheldons* (Cambridge: Cambridge University Press, 1936), p. 39.

36 Styles, 'Sir Simon Clarke', pp. 17–8; Burton, *Revised*, Drayton; *Oxford Guide to Heraldry*, p. 121 – illustration of funeral certificate.

37 Burton, *Leicestershire*, pp. 174, 176–9; J. Fetherston (ed.), *Visitation of Warwickshire 1619* (Harleian Society 12, 1877), p. 254; A. Butler (ed.), *Visitation of Worcestershire 1634* (Harleian Society 90, 1938), p. 31. The number of Herdwick co-heirs is sometimes given as five, but there was a sixth daughter by a second marriage: B.L., Additional MS 31917, fos 87v–88.

38 Northants. C.R.O., FH 269 & 270; Hants. C.R.O., 93M86W/1; Herefs. C.R.O., B56/1, fo. 124.

39 B.L., Harley 4028, fos 4, 38v–9; Leics. C.R.O., P99; Smyth, *Berkeley Mss*, vol. 2, p. 426; Dugdale, *The Antient Usage in Bearing of Such Ensigns of Honour As Are Commonly Call'd Arms*, pp. 12–13.

40 B.L., Egerton 3510, fo. 48v.

41 M. Greenslade, *The Staffordshire Historians* (Stafford: Staffordshire Record Society, 1982), p. 26; Birmingham University Library, misc. 7/i/14, fo. 51; D. MacCulloch, *Suffolk and the Tudors* (Oxford: Clarendon Press, 1986), p. 119; Timothy Mowl, *Elizabethan and Jacobean Style* (London: Phaidon, 1993), pp. 21–2.

42 Dugdale, *Warwickshire*, p. 377; G. Tyack, *The Making of the Warwickshire Country House 1500–1650* (Warwickshire Local History Society, occasional paper 4, 1982), pp. 66–8; J.T. Cliffe, *The World of the Country House in Seventeenth-Century England* (New Haven: Yale University Press, 1999), pp. 15–16; 'A family connexion of the Codrington family in the XVIIth century', *Glos. Trans.* 18 (1893–94), pp. 134–41; Jane Badeni, *Past People in Wiltshire and Gloucestershire* (Malmesbury: Norton Manor, 1992), pp. 142–51.

43 Habington, *Worcestershire*, vol. 1, p. 35; Carew, *Cornwall*, pp. 63–4; Grey, *Chorographia*, pp. 41–2; Lambarde, *Kent*, pp. 6–7.

44 Westcote, *A View of Devonshire in MDCXXX*, p. 453; E. Duffy, *The Voices of Morebath* (New Haven: Yale University Press, 2001).

45 Burton, *Leicestershire*, p. 77; G.F. Farnham, 'Prestwold and its hamlets in medieval times', *Leics. Trans.* 17 (1932–33), pp. 2–84; College of Arms library, Vincent collection, vol. 197, fo. 43v.

46 Burton, *Revised*, Cotes, Prestwold, Tugby; F. Skillington, 'Sir John Beaumont of Gracedieu', *Leics. Trans.* 47 (1971–72), p. 46; College of Arms library, Vincent collection, vol. 127, fo. 420; Anon., *The Aristocracy, the State and the Local Community* (Henry E. Huntingdon Library and Art Gallery, 1987), microfilm reel 4, box 12: HA8535 and

HA8536 show Skipwith signing a letter to the Earl of Huntingdon as one of three deputy lieutenants in 1627.

47 Nichols, *History of Leicestershire*, vol. 3(1), pp. 520–1; Burton, *Revised*, Edmensthorpe, Withcock.

48 Woolf, *Social Circulation*, pp. 133–7.

49 Stone, *The Crisis of the Aristocracy*, p. 25.

50 D. Reid (ed.), *David Hume of Godscoft's The History of the House of Douglas* (Edinburgh: Scottish Text Society, 4th ser. 25 and 26, 1996).

51 D. Howarth, *Images of Rule* (London: Macmillan, 1997), pp. 254–9.

52 Glos. C.R.O., D9125, fo. 15; D8887/13608, fo. 68; *Smyth Papers*, vol. 10, fo. 63; B.L., Additional MS 33588, fos 58–9.

53 Holles, *Memorials of the Holles Family*, p. 5; see also G. Davies (ed.), *Autobiography of Thomas Raymond and Memoirs of the Family of Guise of Elmore, Gloucestershire* (London: Camden Society, 3rd ser. 28, 1917).

54 B.L., Additional MS 34239, fos 2v–3.

Chapter 6

Didactic history

O pening the preface to the *Antiquities of Warwickshire* Dugdale consciously placed his work within the didactic tradition of historical writing, by quoting from Raleigh's *History of the World*: 'It is History that hath given us Life in our Understanding since the World it self had Life and Beginning.' He described his purpose to be 'by setting before you the noble and eminent actions of your worthy ancestors, to incite the present and future ages to a virtuous imitation of them'. The work was a 'Monumentall Pillar', which like the monuments of ancient Rome would guide the living by reminding them of the heroic deeds and virtuous lives of the dead. In attempting to provide moral guidance to his contemporaries through the medium of history, Dugdale was pursuing a common aim of contemporary local historians. Smyth described the subject of the *Lives of the Berkeleys* as being of 'noble men and noble mindes'. These noble men were intended to act as models for the current and for future generations. The principal motivation for Smyth's initial compilation of the work was the provision of guidance to the young lord Berkeley, who succeeded his grandfather to the title in 1613 at the age of twelve. George Berkeley had been 'born generous and capable of vertue', but a man's honour or reputation 'is so delicate a thing as a small excess may blemish it, and acts of indiscretion may ruin it'. The lives of his ancestors were intended to instruct the young man in how to avoid the pitfalls surrounding him and to live up to the high promise of his birth. In a similar vein Sir Edward Rodney described writing his family history so that his posterity would not lack 'domestick examples to guide and direct their lives'.[1]

Although local historians thought it provided the principal justification for their endeavours, the didactic aspect of their work has attracted remarkably little attention. In a brief reference to the *Antiquities of Warwickshire* in *The Idea of History in Early Stuart England* Daniel Woolf mentioned Dugdale's citation of Cicero's *De Oratore* in his preface with reference to the historian's duty to uncover the truth. This he contrasted with the 'traditional' historian's citation of the work, which referred to the need to moralise and instruct. As we have seen, Dugdale was equally concerned with this didactic duty of the historian. Writing about the previous generation of antiquaries, F.J. Levy accepted at face value Lambarde's claim, that he was not writing history and by implication was not concerned with moral instruction. Such claims were a convenient means for antiquaries to free themselves from the confines of the rules for historical writing and to divert criticism. Moreover, the formal designation of a book affected who might license its publication. In 1638 Burton described the proposed second edition of his *Description of Leicestershire* as containing 'matters of antiquity, genealogy, and armory, which properly belong to the Earl Marshal, and history is the last part of the book'. Since publication was being organised by Sir John Lambe, the dean of Arches, Burton had no reason to fear any objection from the High Commission. Other local historians may have been wary of potential problems in obtaining a licence, if they acknowledged their work as history. Or their contacts in the College of Arms may have made a licence from the earl marshal easier – and cheaper – to obtain. Family historians, whose works remained in manuscript, had no compunction in calling their works histories, as the succession of generations provided a traditional narrative framework. Whatever the works covered by this study were called, I believe that they can only be fully understood if we appreciate that their authors were indeed writing in the didactic tradition.[2]

In Dugdale's opinion it was a natural human desire to wish to leave behind 'an honourable fame'. This desire led 'divers noble spirits to bold and high adventures'. The role of the historian was to record such deeds, in order that they might inspire later generations to emulate their ancestors. Shirley agreed, since there was 'nothing [so] capable to touch the soules & affections of generous persons then the Examples of Illustrious men.' When the examples were drawn from among a man's own ancestors, they were deemed to be particularly potent.[3] The importance that antiquaries attached to this role is significant for the development of local history, because it influenced the content of their works and their treatment of their sources. The historical content of their works was structured to represent the lives of the medieval nobility and gentry as idealised images of virtue and vice. As we saw in chapter four, in order to achieve this local historians could be led to lower their standards for the use of evidence, and to utilise sources which for other purposes they regarded with suspicion. Hence, the didactic tradition had a profound influence on the development of local history.

A belief in the didactic function of history originated in classical times. For historians such as Cicero and Tacitus, the purpose of history was to provide their readers with a guide to moral behaviour. As Tacitus explained, 'virtues should not be passed over in silence, while those responsible for wrong actions and words should be threatened with disgrace in the eyes of posterity'.[4] The late medieval chroniclers also had a moral purpose, for they took a theological view of history as part of the necessary guidance of the Christian man. During the Renaissance this medieval view of history as primarily educative was increasingly emphasised by the revival of classical learning. The didactic role of history was reinforced as European scholars sought to define and describe the model of civic virtue, which increasingly supplanted the earlier monastic ideal. This led to the literary content of histories being considered by many historians as more important than the evidential. If a work was to teach a moral lesson, it must first convince the reader. A persuasive, eloquent style of writing was the best guarantee of achieving that end.[5]

Local histories were written for a readership which exhibited a decided hunger for books providing instruction in civic virtue and personal conduct. Vivienne Larminie has suggested that, in this period, books on any subject were predominantly read for their guidance on moral questions, but some genres had such moral education as a central concern. Books of parental advice were very popular and may be traced back to classical models, pre-eminent among which was Cicero's *De Officiis*. Medieval Europe witnessed the development of the related genre of advice books for princes, written by advisers – or would-be advisers – who sought a quasi-parental influence. In the sixteenth century this medieval tradition was taken up by the humanists, producing works as different as Machiavelli's *The Prince* and Erasmus's *The Education of a Christian Prince*.[6] The early seventeenth century witnessed the publication of some extremely popular English examples associated with the Court. James I's *Basilicon Doron* was a combination of parental advice and guidance to a prince, written for his son Henry. It became a best-seller in England and circulated widely on the continent. Lord Burghley's advice to his son Robert was published in 1617, but appears previously to have circulated widely in manuscript form. It was frequently incorporated into the letters of advice, which many seventeenth-century fathers addressed to their sons. Sir Walter Raleigh's *Instructions to His Son and to Posterity* also enjoyed great popularity, reflecting the posthumous reputation of the author.[7] The widespread popularity of the genre of parental advice is suggested by the inclusion of models for such letters in Nicholas Breton's popular manual *A Poste with a Madde Packet of Letters* (1602). Those letters of parental advice which survive are almost certainly a tiny fraction of those which were composed. While many fathers adopted Burghley as their model, others such as Edward, lord Montagu of Boughton, composed more personal documents.[8] Nor was a young nobleman who had suffered the loss of his father, required to go forth into the world without the benefit of advice from his elders. Lord Berkeley did not only receive advice from Smyth in the form of the history of his family. Antony Stafford's treatise, a *Guide to Honour* (1634), was also written for his guidance.

The English public also provided a readership for the works developed by humanist writers out of the medieval tradition of courtesy books. Castiglione's *Il Cortegiano* appeared in an English translation by Sir Thomas Hoby in 1561, but it was widely read among humanists before this. Its influence has been seen in Sir Thomas Elyot's *Boke Named the Governour* (1531), and Roger Ascham recommended Castiglione's work as the model for the behaviour of an English gentleman in *The Scholemaster* (1570). As with the genre of parental advice the Elizabethan gentry were not merely the passive receptacles of the humanists' instruction in civility and morality. Sir Richard Berkeley was a leading member of Gloucestershire gentry society, and lieutenant of the Tower in Elizabeth's reign. Although he may have had contacts with humanist circles in London, he was a man engaged in practical politics and administration rather than scholarship. Nevertheless, he wrote a *Discourse of the Felicitie of Man* (1598), which repeated many of the commonplaces found in the humanist courtesy books. Smyth's expressed admiration for this work may owe something to the family association, but its intention and tone were undoubtedly congenial to him.[9] In the early seventeenth century such treatises on polite conduct proliferated. The close association between these works and the genre of parental advice is indicated by James Cleland's *Heropaideia or the Institution of a Young Nobleman* (1607). This work was dedicated to prince Charles and drew heavily on his father's *Basilikon Doron*. Henry Peacham's *Compleat Gentleman* (1622) was more encyclopaedic than previous works in the genre, but his introductory epistle indicated that he saw his work as firmly in the tradition of Elyot and Ascham. Peacham was to remain an authority on polite conduct for many years. Richard Brathwaite was a prolific writer of courtesy books, who was drawn from the same level of gentry society as Sir Richard Berkeley. A country gentleman, deputy lieutenant of Westmorland and justice of the peace, Brathwaite's *English Gentleman* (1630) and *English Gentlewoman* (1631) helped to propagate the humanist ideal of gentility to a wider audience.[10]

Histories, advices and courtesy books were all recommended to the gentry as sources of moral guidance. In 1577 the poet Gabriel Harvey included both Ascham and Castiglione in the list of books to be read by one of his pupils. When Smyth wrote to the young lord Berkeley following the death of his grandfather, he accompanied the advice in his letter with a copy of Speed's *History of Great Britain*. Four decades later the Gloucestershire gentleman William Higford, writing an advice book for his grandson, recommended the reading of *Basilicon Doron* alongside the works of Xenophon of Athens and Cicero 'for precepts of morality and virtuous education'. It is difficult to determine the extent to which such books were read, but they certainly found their way into the libraries of the gentry. Sir Francis Willoughby, the builder of Wollaton Hall, Notts., included eight volumes of advice in a library of around 250 books, while Castiglione, Elyot and Ascham all figure in the collections of university people who died while in residence at Oxford. Three surviving lists of the books taken by Smyth's son Thomas to Oxford in 1637–38 include various works of history, both English and classical, and Raleigh's book of advice. A generation later Pepys noted that Osborn's *Advice to a Son* (1656) was one of the three most read books in England.[11]

The subject of the didactic aspects of contemporary local histories matched that of parental advices and courtesy books: how a gentleman should conduct himself with honour. The predominant difference between the various forms lay not in their subject matter, but in their intended readership. Parental advice was initially written for a named individual – generally the writer's heir. Family histories might be addressed to the current head of a family, but concerned themselves more widely with all those who had an interest in maintaining the status and honour of the family. As we saw in chapter five, the writing of family histories was associated with times of dynastic crisis, such as the succession of a minor or the failure of the direct male line. At such times the authority and status of the families concerned were particularly vulnerable, and responsibility for the maintenance of a family's reputation was more widely dispersed than when its honour was concentrated in an acknowledged head. Urban histories addressed the civic elite, while the advice contained in the county histories was addressed to the local gentry. Both these forms also addressed a wider gentry readership beyond their local communities. It was for this wider readership that the courtesy books were written.

The efficacy of all the varied forms of advice depended ultimately on the acceptance of a shared view of what gentility involved. Despite the importance placed on lineage by local historians and many of their contemporaries, it was not the case that gentility was straightforwardly equated with the possession of a pedigree, ancient estates and a coat of arms. Habington described a cadet branch of the Croft family as 'retaininge but the name and blood of gentrie'. Although they could claim kinship ties with many prominent Worcestershire families, their lack of wealth and social position excluded this branch of the Crofts from the designation of gentry. Certain personal qualities were also expected of a gentleman. A thirteenth-century Lord Berkeley was recommended by Smyth for his prudent and modest nature. This lord stood as an example to vainglorious men, 'standing much upon their gentry and descent, as many bragadochioes doe, that have noething to comend them but their Ancestors names and Armes'. Lambarde maintained the orthodox position that gentility which came by descent 'if it be not accompanied with vertue, is but an emptie signe'. If pedigree could not compensate for lack of wealth, the reverse was not necessarily true. Sir Thomas Smith asserted in *De Republica Anglorum* (1583), that it was wealth and a reputation for gentility that were essential for acceptance as a gentleman in England. Provided a man's neighbours considered him a gentleman, he could acquire the requisite pedigree and arms through the services of a herald and become gentle in the eyes of the world at large. This no doubt reflected contemporary reality, although few commentators would acknowledge as much in their rhetoric. At the same time, many families were content to remain at the level of parish gentry, and never sought official recognition through a coat of arms. Smyth described the Harveys of Bradston as 'an ancient family reputed as gentlemen, and as may bee said, gentlemen by prescripcion in all their foresaid generations, yet never of coate Armour'. A gentleman was someone, whose wealth and leisure freed him from material concerns, enabling him to equip himself for the service of the state. He was Aristotle's ideal citizen, transported to provincial England. Although the passage of time has made it difficult for historians to identify the membership of a county's gentry with any precision, contemporaries appear to have had no such difficulty.[12]

While local historians attached great importance to the pedigrees of local families, they also warned gentlemen against relying solely on their birth to justify their position within society. Habington wrote of raising the name of Hacket from the dust to which time had consigned it, to teach 'the greate not to glory in theyre familyes'. As Peter Coss has demonstrated, gentility was not dependent purely on lineage, even before the economic and social upheavals of the sixteenth century. For the late medieval gentry, lineage was supplemented by a sense of social difference and by such characteristics as the holding of local office and of authority over the populace. During the sixteenth century the concept of gentility was modified – most noticeably by an increased emphasis on education, but not substantially altered. The Elizabethan and early Stuart gentleman's ideas of honour and correct conduct might have acquired a classical gloss, but they were still essentially the same as those which had informed the chivalric literature of their medieval ancestors. Through an examination of the concerns expressed by commentators such as local historians and advice writers, it is possible to distinguish what was required in order to be identified as a gentleman in this period.[13]

The ideal of gentility presented by local historians was very similar to that presented by the authors of conduct books and parental advices. They were all clearly drawing on a collection of shared beliefs, although circumstances and individual temperament might cause different writers to place greater or lesser emphasis on particular elements of gentility. Their purpose was less to instruct their readers in the meaning of gentility, than to remind them what being a gentleman meant in practice. Dugdale's complaint about 'poor Mechanicks', who 'by their activeness in the world ... get wealth, and assume the title of Esquire and Gentleman without controull, yea, and be allowed to do so', makes it clear that he wished to address the established gentry. When we consider Erdeswicke's reference to 'one of the Brookes, that takes himself to be a gentleman' and Habington's dismissal of William Edden's 'yeomanly petegree', it appears to be a common assumption among local historians that they were addressing the established rather than the aspiring gentry.[14] This is obviously in accordance with their emphasis on the importance of lineage, even if they denied its sufficiency alone to bestow gentility. The established gentry could be expected to understand the shared beliefs drawn on by local historians, even if they needed to be prompted to put those beliefs into practice.

In his account of the Worcestershire family of Littleton, Habington gave clear expression of what he believed was expected of gentlemen in public life:

> yf they would ryghtly consyder that God hathe bestowed on them lyvinges above the vulgar sort to the end they shoulde bee able in peace to governe and in war to defend them, which synce it cannot be don without the knowleadge of lawes and armes, howe muche are they to blame who, neglectinge thease, gyve themsealfes over to sportes (which are not altogeather unfytt beeinge used sometymes for recreation), or lyve idelly or wallowe in sensuality. You wyll answeare all are not called to be magistrates; but I replye all maye instruct theyre inferiour neyghbours, compose controversyes and learne how to defend themsealfes agaynst malignant adversaryes; and for tyme of war who are meeter to beare offyce in the feylde then our Gentellmen, and apter to bee soldyers then our servyng men.[15]

With its references to sports, idle living and suitable subjects for study, this passage also addressed the private life of the gentry. In this period the common perception of the household as the image of the Commonwealth in miniature meant there was little distinction made between the public and private roles of the gentry. In *Eirenarcha* (1581) William Lambarde emphasised the importance of a magistrate acting as an informal mediator among his neighbours to be as much a 'compounder as a commissioner' of the peace. The public duties of instructing inferiors and composing controversies were held to apply most importantly to a gentleman's own household and tenants. Similarly, a gentleman's private virtues of hospitality, charity and piety were important elements in establishing his reputation among his neighbours. The importance of community was also stressed. In criticising the Northumberland gentry, William Grey complained not only of their extravagance, but also of their abandonment of the locality: 'Since the union of both Kingdoms, the Gentry of this Country hath given themselves to idlenesse, luxury and covetousnesse, living not in their own houses, as their ancestors hath done, profusely spending their revenues in other Countries, and hath consumed of late their ancient houses.' Local historians commented on both public and private aspects of gentry behaviour within the context of local society.[16]

The elements of gentility stressed by didactic writers were remarkably consistent. In large part this was due to the uniformity of gentry education in this period, which propagated accepted ideas concerning honour and status. As we have seen, from the mid-sixteenth century, secondary education for boys was determinedly classical. Although the sons of nobles and catholics were more likely to be educated by private tutors than in the grammar and private schools attended by the majority of the gentry, they were all educated along the same lines in preparation for higher education. During the reign of Henry VIII the universities had developed as important centres of humanist learning, which extolled the ideal of the learned, responsible gentleman devoted to the service of the Commonwealth. It was this ideal which Habington extolled in the passage quoted above. The humanist influence on the education of the English gentry remained strong into the seventeenth century and helped to develop the accepted ideal of gentility.[17]

Local historians placed great emphasis on the importance of learning to the local gentry, as it was seen as an essential attribute of the good magistrate. As Habington's exhortation to the Worcestershire gentry makes clear, magistracy was considered to be the most important role of the gentry in times of peace. Burton described his friend, the poet Sir John Beaumont, as 'a Gentleman of great learning, gravity, and worth.' Beaumont had received an education typical of his class, attending both Oxford and the Inner Temple, but taking no formal qualifications. Dugdale similarly commended his kinsman Samuel Roper as 'a Gentleman learned and judicious, and singularly well seen in Antiquities', while Charles Neville, vice-provost of King's College, Cambridge, was 'that learned and truly noble gentleman'. In the *Lives of the Berkeleys*, Smyth criticised the adverse influence of their indulgent mothers on the education of lord Berkeley's father and grandfather. His grandfather, finding his education insufficient for his role as magistrate, was obliged to have his legal adviser appointed to the bench alongside him. Lord Berkeley had received a more formal education from an early age, on which Smyth may have had some influence. He was certainly involved in the arrangements for the education of the Berkeley heir in the 1630s.[18]

By reminding their readers of the cultural figures associated with their region, local historians further emphasised the link between gentility and education. Habington observed that Worcestershire 'hath bynne such a fountayne of flourishing witts, that the greatest county in the Realme can hardly compete there with'. Of these 'witts', Thomas Littleton, the author of the standard legal work on feudal tenures, was 'the greatest ornament of our Shyre, the Oracle of the lawe, the glory of Judges'. Thomas Allen, the mathematician of Gloucester Hall, Oxford, was claimed by Erdeswicke for Staffordshire on the grounds of his descent from the Allens of Buckenhall. Burton made extensive use of Leland to identify luminaries associated with Leicestershire, while other local historians used John Bale – whose main source had been Leland – for the same purpose. The poet Michael Drayton had been born in Warwickshire, but Burton claimed 'my near countryman and old acquaintance' for Leicestershire, on the grounds that it was his family's ancestral home. In the *Antiquities of Warwickshire* 'our late famous' poet was reclaimed for Warwickshire by Dugdale, who included Drayton's epitaph from Westminster Abbey in the account of his birthplace Atherstone. In his revised text of 1642 Burton advertised both his family's and his county's association with scholarship through the late rector of Segrave, his brother Robert Burton.[19]

The range of learning required by a good magistrate was quite extensive, and was not reflected by the formal syllabus of the universities. The digressive nature of local histories allowed their authors to include material on a range of subjects considered useful to a gentleman in his role as magistrate. The Yorkshire justice Sir William Wentworth advised his son to study 'lodgik, philosophie, cosmographie and especially historyes' to this end. The digressions in the *Description of Leicestershire* covered such subjects as embalming; sleepwalking; the effect of environment on health; giants; earthquakes; and volcanoes. Smyth's works included sections on numerology, husbandry and mineral resources. Somner's *Antiquities of Canterbury* included a digression on archery, reflecting his own interest in an activity which, despite the efforts of Charles I's government, had declined from a military skill to a sport. Such digressions from the main subject of a work were common in the literature of the period. They acted both to demonstrate the erudition of the author and to expose the reader to a range of subjects. In some cases readers may have been more interested in the digressions than the subject matter of the whole work. For the ease of reference of such readers, Thomas Philipot included a list of his significant digressions in the preface to *Villare Cantianum*. Somner's digression on archery also served a further purpose. It included an extract from John Bingham's *Notes upon Aelian Tacticks*, which had become 'somewhat deer and scarce'. In this way authors could make make salient extracts from obscure or expensive texts available to a wider readership.[20]

Although the emphasis of local historians was on the magistrate's service to the local community, great importance was also attached to service in the national sphere. In the published county histories this was most obviously expressed in the dedicatory letter to a national dignitary with local connections. The *Description of Leicestershire* was dedicated to Buckingham: 'whose sweet disposition and excellent gifts of Nature make manifest to the world, that his Majesty hath beene guided by his accustomed sharpe understanding and solid judgement, in choosing such a subject, most fit to receive his favors, and in imploying such a servant.'

Richard Carew's *Survey of Cornwall* was dedicated to Sir Walter Raleigh, who carried 'a large, both Martiall, and civill commaund' and was often 'a suitor, and sollicitor to others, of the highest place' on behalf of the people of the West Country. The importance of service on the national stage and in particular service to the king was reiterated in the body of the works. In his history of Worcestershire Habington praised the wit, spirit and learning of Francis Throckmorton, executed for his involvement in the attempt to liberate Mary Queen of Scots. The antiquary maintained that all agreed had Throckmorton enjoyed 'the sunshine of fortune as he had nothing but her deadly stormes, [he would] have bynne a meet counsellor for the most potent King'. In his work Dugdale emphasised how Sir Walter Aston's 'vast debts' had been caused by his service to James I as an ambassador to Spain. For this reason, selling his ancestral lands did not diminish his honour in the way that poverty caused by profligacy would have done. Habington considered Thomas Coventry, Charles I's lord keeper, such an ornament to Worcestershire that he expressed the wish that the family's newly acquired manor should be renamed in his honour.[21]

In his family history Shirley used the importance of service to the king to rewrite his brother's biography in such a way as to minimise Sir Henry's failure to achieve the local prominence he craved. In his account Shirley described how his brother was sent to Oxford to study the liberal sciences and then abroad to learn languages. Only when Sir Henry Shirley had 'adorned himselfe with all the qualities required in a compleate Gentellman' was he ready to return to England and attach himself to the court of the Prince of Wales: 'that glorious rising Sunne who by the attractive beames of his splendour drew all the bravest spiritts and most admirable wits to him'. According to Shirley the death of prince Henry led his brother to retire to the quiet life of a country gentleman. (Thus, he presented the reverse image to that suggested by the epitaph to Sir Dudley Digges at Chilham, Kent, who was portrayed as having abandoned the retired life he preferred at the king's command.) The implication that Sir Henry abandoned worldly ambition for the purer pleasures of scholarship is misleading. In the 1620s he was actively involved in the local politics of Leicestershire. He was, however, ultimately unsuccessful in his rivalry with the earl of Huntingdon. After his brother's death Shirley wished to preserve his memory as the inconsolable servant of prince Henry rather than as an unsuccessful local politician.[22]

Despite the significance attached to service to the king, the dominant theme of local historians was the importance of the gentry's service within their communities. Habington especially commended the industry of Arthur Salwey, a minor official in the Exchequer, who had recovered his family's declining fortunes to the extent that he and his son 'have sate on the supreme seate of Justyce in our shyre'. Dugdale held up Sir Clement Throckmorton as an example to the local gentry: 'a Gentleman not a little eminent for his learning and eloquence, having served in sundry Parliaments as one of the Knights for this shire, and undergone divers other publiq imployments of note'. This portrait failed to mention less-respectable aspects of Throckmorton's reputation, such as his association with deer poachers. William Chyld, who died in 1601, was described by Habington in terms wholly related to his public life: 'He served thys Shyre twyse as Shyreefe and long in Commission of the Peace; hee leaft a fayre estate and issewe whose name and bloud sittethe nowe on the bench of Justyce for thys county of Worcester.' The importance the gentry attached to their reputation for public service is reflected in the monument that John Washbourne, then aged eighty-four, erected in 1632 at Wichenford, Worcs. Washbourne dedicated the monument to his father, himself and his two deceased wives. It recorded that he 'hath been 60 years in the commission of the peace, and twice high sheriff of this County, and deputy-Lieutenant to four Lords Presidents of the principality of Wales and marches of the same'.[23]

By including an account of the public offices undertaken by successive generations of a local family, a local historian could create an impressive image of continued service. Dugdale's account of the Peytos of Chesterton traced the family back to the reign of Edward I, when a member of the family first appeared in the records as a coroner. This ancestor's son was a lawyer, who obtained the wealth 'which qualified his descendants the better for such great and noteable employments as th[e]y afterwards had in the world'. For several generations the Peytos served the king and their neighbours as collectors of the subsidy, knights of the shire and commissioners of the peace. Sir Edward Peyto, who died in 1643, was a puritan kinsman of Archer, who lent his support to the production of a county history. He was never a justice, and his frequent absences from the county in the 1630s; his wide intellectual interests; and his distinctive character made him an uneasy member of the Warwickshire elite. Peyto's son was less enthusiastic for the parliamentary cause than his father and was suspicious of the regime that followed. He died young during the interregnum, leaving a minor as heir. So, although they had supported the winning side in the civil war, the family was not in a position to capitalise on this, and their fortunes were at a low ebb in 1656. Dugdale's historical account of the Peytos was a way of asserting the family's undoubted right to membership of the Warwickshire elite.[24]

As Habington acknowledged in his exhortation to the Worcestershire gentry, not all were called upon to become magistrates. Yet, all gentlemen had a duty to maintain the peace and order of the local community. An important aspect of this duty was the expectation that a gentleman would act as an impartial arbitrator in disputes between his neighbours. For example, Habington commended the Worcestershire justice William Cokesey, who 'labored extraordinarily in quietinge controversyes'. Conversely, Smyth condemned Anne Berkeley, the mother of his first master, as 'a lady of masculine spirit', overbearing and contentious. He acknowledged her virtues, but deeply disapproved of the 'braules and jarrs' with her brother-in-law and the Poyntz family in which she became embroiled during her son's minority. For more than two decades Smyth himself acted as a mediator between local gentlemen and the entrepreneurial clothier Benedict Webb. In the *Description of the Hundred of*

Berkeley, Smyth also described how his mediation had brought to an end a local dispute between half-brothers over their inheritance. Gentlemen could also be expected to step in when disagreements between strangers threatened the peace of the local community. In his account of Stamford, Richard Butcher recalled how in 1594 Peregrine, lord Willoughby, had acted decisively to quell a brawl in an inn when he 'armed himself and his followers and on his warlike courser entred himself into the midst of the throng, and like a right valiant person and wise Commander pacified the uproare before any morall wound was given: so serving her Majesty by the procuring of her peace'. The preservation of the peace was a service owed by the gentry both to the local community and to the state.[25]

Through their interest in funeral monuments, local historians reveal how the ideal of public service influenced the visual culture of the period. Over the period covered by this study, the increasing importance of a gentleman's own character, his education and his service to the state in defining his status was reflected in the growth of funeral monuments celebrating the individual rather than the lineage (compare figure 7 with figures 10 and 11). Descriptions of such monuments are to be found in local histories and antiquarian notebooks alongside more traditional tombs. Although modern commentators identify these tombs as classical or Italianate, local historians described them in terms relating to the impression they were intended to convey, as fair, stately or dignified. Several well-illustrated examples may be found in Dugdale's *Antiquities of Warwickshire*, which introduced the use of engraved images of monuments to county histories. One is Fulke Greville's austerely classical monument in St Mary's, Warwick, the unusually simple epitaph of which described Greville as the servant of Elizabeth I, the councillor of James I and the friend of Sir Philip Sidney. Another is the funeral monument of Sir Thomas Puckering, in the same church, erected in accordance with his instructions and bearing the inscription he had written. Puckering, the son of Elizabeth's lord keeper, had been educated alongside Prince Henry and was described by Dugdale as 'a Gentleman much accomplisht with learning, and observation by travail in forrain parts'. On Puckering's death in 1637, Dugdale wrote to Archer, an executor, that the 'losse of youre deare friend ... I much bewayle, and soe hath all the country just cause to doe'. The predominant example of this genre recorded by Dugdale was the tomb of Sir Thomas Lucy at Charlecote, which celebrated him as an individual of learning and varied interests – an image which was also presented by an earlier portrait of him with his family. Lucy's tomb included a representation of him on his great horse and carvings of his classical texts, while the inscription praised not only his public service and personal piety, but also the welcome that he extended to scholars. The adoption of classical forms for monuments celebrating the individual should not necessarily be seen as a rejection of lineage. Classical monuments such as

Lucy's were often placed within the context of a collection of family tombs that visually conveyed a sense of continuity. At Lydiard Tregoze, Wilts., the monuments of the St John family provide a particularly striking example of a reverence for lineage and traditional forms in conjunction with the latest classical models. To the left of the altar is a triptych, originally created in 1615, but updated by later generations. This presents a commemorative painting of Sir John St John's parents and their progeny, surrounded by heraldic genealogical

Figure 8 The St John triptych at Lydiard Tregoze, Wilts.

Figure 9 The heraldic east window at Lydiard Tregoze, Wilts.

tables. It is surmounted by an image of Margaret Beaufort in the robes of
the duchess, representing the St Johns' claim to common ancestry with the
Tudors. To the right is the ornate, classical monument erected by Sir John for
himself and his two wives in 1634, when it represented the height of courtly
fashion. Between the monuments, the east window traces the descent of the
manor of Lydiard Tregoze through heraldic display. The chancel of St Mary's
church (see figures 8 to 10) shows how new styles sat juxtaposed with the old,
and the celebration of the individual was incorporated into an overall visual
celebration of the lineage.[26]

In his description of what was expected of the gentry, Habington equated
their role as magistrates in times of peace with that as military officers in
times of war. The widespread resonance of the military aspects of gentility
was evidenced by the continued popularity of traditional funeral monuments
depicting the deceased as a knight in armour. (Classical forms, although
increasingly popular, did not oust traditional forms before the Restoration.
The Tanfield monument at Burford, see figure 11, is representative of the transition.) It was natural that this resonance should be reflected in local histories.
Although England enjoyed a long period of peace preceding the civil war, the
majority of the English gentry had some contact with the reality of their military

Figure 10 The tomb of Sir John St John (d. 1648) and his wives
at Lydiard Tregoze, Wilts., erected 1634

role, albeit indirect. Shirley's father had served with the earl of Leicester in the
Low Countries in 1585, alongside more than forty other gentlemen from his
region. He was subsequently described by his son as famous 'for piety, cour-
rage and munificence'. Men who had served the king in arms also received
honourable mention in county histories. Erdeswicke recounted how Sir Ralph
Bagenholt had sold his lands to his tenants and spent the money, 'leaving

Figure 11 The tomb of Sir Laurence Tanfield (d. 1625) at Burford, Oxon.

his son, sir Samuel Bagenholt (now lately knighted at Cales, anno 1596) to advance himself by his valour, as he before had done'. Habington described Sir Matthew Carew as 'a Knight practised in wars abroad, and well beloved at home', while Gerard described Sir John and Sir Richard Bingham as deserving of 'especiall Remembrance' in his history of Dorset for their service to Elizabeth I in Ireland. Burton recorded in the *Description of Leicestershire* that two of his uncles, William and Anthony Faunt, had served in the Netherlands, where the former lost his life. As the genealogies recorded by Smyth included all the descendants of the Berkeleys, rather than just the direct male line, they reflected the large numbers of gentry sons who chose to follow a military career. These included three descendants of the family, who had lost their lives on the Isle of Rhé.[27]

The main emphasis in local histories was not on contemporary conflicts, but on the martial exploits of the medieval gentry. There was a great stress on single combat, which emphasised the personal courage of the knight. Dugdale drew attention to the valour of John de Astley, including engravings of his exploits to supplement the narrative account. In 1438 Astley had triumphed in a tournament in Paris before Charles VII. A few years later, he defeated Sir Philip Boyle in single combat, 'being gallantly perform'd on foot, with Battail-axes, spears, swords and daggers'. In consequence he was knighted by Henry VI.[28] By recording such careers, local historians emphasised the role of the individual and celebrated the pageantry and chivalry of medieval knighthood. Burton's ancestor John de Herdwick had been the steward of the nuns of Nuneaton and an unlikely military hero. Nevertheless in the *Description of Leicestershire* he was described as 'a man of small stature, but of great valour, courage, and strength'. He was associated with martial affairs by his descendant's identification of him as the man 'of whom the tradition goeth by an unknowne name' whose local knowledge enabled Henry VII to gain a tactical advantage at the battle of Bosworth. Smyth quoted from Michael Drayton's historical poem on Agincourt to illustrate the part played by lord Berkeley in the battle. Such poems perpetuated an image of battle as a clash between chivalric knights rather than representing the bloody confusion of reality.[29]

The military exploits of the crusaders also held a particular appeal for antiquaries. They carefully recorded tombs which they believed had belonged to crusading knights. In his description of the remaining tombs from the church of Dudley priory, Erdeswicke drew particular attention to the fact that two of the effigies were cross-legged, which was considered to be the mark of the crusader. Habington wrote of Worcestershire as being 'so often honoured with thease religious sepulchers'. In the long list of monuments in St Paul's given by Stow, that of the earl of Lincoln 'with his picture in armour, cross-legged, as one professed for defence of the Holy Land against the infidels' received particular attention. Significantly, Henry de Lacy had not been a crusader, although he had been active in Edward I's military campaigns in Wales, Scotland and France. Whatever he may have professed (as Stow would have been aware) de Lacy never acted upon it. William Grey showed a similar prejudice to Stow when he selected which funeral monuments to mention. In St Nicholas, Newcastle, he paid detailed attention only to those of Henry Percy, earl of Northumberland, and 'a warre-like Gentleman, lying with his legs a crosse'. The striking Jacobean monument to the mercantile Maddison family, with its numerous kneeling figures, was not described. Local historians also recorded the founding of chantry chapels and similar acts of piety by returning crusaders. In the life of Harding, founder of the Berkeley family, Smyth quoted an extract from the *Chronicle of Jerusalem*. He did not know whether the Harding mentioned in the chronicle was the same man. However tentative, the association of the family with the crusades was worth mentioning, and was intended to increase their honour.[30]

Among the martial virtues most praised by local historians was loyalty to the king, matching its importance in a civil magistrate. Geoffrey de Langley, Henry III's marshal of the king's household, was described by Dugdale as 'a man of extraordinary note: for I find him in the Catalogue of those great men who stood stoutly to the King against his rebellious Barons'. This stress on loyalty to the king raised some difficulties when recounting the history of families whose ancestors had failed in their allegiance. It was occasionally possible to justify this, on the grounds that the rebels had believed that they were adhering to the true heir to the throne. For example, as Perkin Warbeck had claimed to be the son of Edward IV, those who had supported him could be seen as justified in their rebellion. The Berkeley rebellions against Henry III, Edward II and Richard II could not be excused on these grounds. Smyth roundly condemned them, showing how they had damaged the prosperity of the family. In contrast, he praised the wisdom of their successors, who had come to terms with the Crown. The ostensibly successful political manoeuvring of Thomas, lord Berkeley, in his support of Henry IV against the legitimate king was, according to Smyth, punished not only by his failure to produce a male heir, but by the resulting four generations of 'blouddy and irksome controversies'. The idea that punishment was meted out by God on the descendants of rebels in this way was a commonplace among historians dealing with the reigns of the Lancastrians, Yorkists and Tudors.[31]

While the exploits of medieval knights loomed large in local histories, the military reality of their own period was less apparent. Among the proposed contents for the second edition of the *Description of Leicestershire* was an account of the contemporary martial state of the county, but this was omitted from the 1642 manuscript. Smyth did include the names of the local officers of the county militia in his *Description of the Hundred of Berkeley*. This was useful information for those who were to take over his responsibilities for safeguarding the Berkeley estates in Gloucestershire, particularly in the state of heightened tension that existed as Smyth was revising the text in 1639. In the *Antiquities of Warwickshire*, Dugdale made few references to the civil strife which had occurred during its composition. A reference to Sir Thomas Leigh's advancement to the status of baron 'in testimony of his stedfast loyalty' to Charles I, is a rare recognition of the influence of the wars on the local gentry. Dugdale's work was intended to promote harmony, not division among his neighbours. Supporters of either side could recognise the virtue in Sir Thomas Leigh's loyalty. More controversial subjects, such as the death of lord Brooke during the siege of Lichfield or Sir Edward Peyto's defiance in the face of the besiegers of Warwick castle, were better avoided. During the civil war, Newcastle had been taken by a Scottish army in the pay of parliament. To the royalist William Grey, the town had been undermined by treachery: 'the crowne of our heads is fallen, woe now unto us, for we have sinned', but these events received little attention in his work. The tendency of local historians to support the king might provide an alternative explanation of their reluctance to dwell on the war. However, there was no immediate change in emphasis when the royalists enjoyed the eventual victory after the Restoration.[32]

The traditional role of the gentry as benefactors of the Church was given significant emphasis in local histories. Since medieval times, those whom God had blessed with the riches of the world had been expected to protect and assist his servants in the Church. The role of the gentry as patrons of churches, benefactors to monasteries and employers of chaplains became incorporated within the definition of gentility. The importance of this part of the gentry's role could be emphasised by making it a reason for a local historian to include an account of a particular gentleman or family. Dugdale 'resolved to say something Historically of the before recited Earl of Mellent, in regard that by his pious gift of the greatest part of this village to the said Monks of Preaux, and his great possessions in this Shire, he deserves to be signally memorized.' The pious gifts of ancestors could also be used to praise the gentility of their heirs. In the *Description of Leicestershire*, Burton used the former benefactions of the Brett family to the priory of Chaucombe to praise their descendant, the countess of Middlesex. Since local historians generally avoided contentious issues, their works do not record the religious divisions between the gentry. Although there were some significant exceptions, the majority of local historians appear to have been religiously conservative, and all maintained the importance of respecting the piety of the medieval gentry, if not their theology. Local historians also stressed the respect that should be accorded to the physical fabric of church buildings and the responsibility of the gentry, particularly lay impropriators, for their maintenance. Hence, Gerard in his account of Dorset praised Sir Thomas Freke for rebuilding his parish church at his own expense 'contrarie to the Custome of these Times, who rather pull them downe, or convert them to prophane Uses' and Sir John Hannam, who 'if I mistake not, enjoyeth Revenues of the Church', for contributing to the repairing of Wimborne minster.[33]

The pious acts of the medieval gentry could also be used to criticise their descendants by unfavourable comparison. Gerard described chantry building as showing the ancestors of the Somerset gentry taking 'an extraordinary care in propagating God's service in that kind as they were taught'. Although based on what was to him discredited theology, he declared their memorials to be better than those of the contemporary gentry, who memorialised themselves through the names of their houses. In the same vein, Burton criticised the 'vaine and idle conceits of some novelists' who disparaged medieval memorials as idolatrous, and objected to the display of military banners and the like in churches. However, such disrespect for the monuments of the medieval gentry was not presented as a purely doctrinal issue. Burton also criticised the 'covetousnesse or necessity of some poore Clerkes or Sextons, or the want or poverty of some needy Curates', which also led to the destruction of memorials to remove the brass and other materials of value. It was recognised that such destruction was not necessarily driven by financial need, which provided an excuse of sorts. Tristram Risdon recorded how at Ashford, Devon, a tomb was 'violated in our memory by some in hope of gaine, but disappointed, carryed hence the lead wherin the dead was wrapt, who being men of some substance, it was observed afterwardes, theire wealth wasted, and none prospered'. The message for the gentry was that they should honour the memory of their ancestors, both by preserving their memorials and by supporting adequately the parish clergy.[34]

In their works, local historians upheld the ideal that a gentleman should act as a model of piety and conscientious religious observance. A gentleman's religious duties extended far beyond his own personal beliefs. As a magistrate he was expected to regulate the behaviour of his own household and to act as an example to the wider community. During Elizabeth's reign, the Berkeley household gained a reputation for catholic sympathies. In the *Lives of the Berkeleys*, Smyth recorded how archbishop Whitgift wrote to lord Berkeley: 'gravely advising him to take notice of the dispositions of his servants and his wives waiting woemen in matter of their conformity in religion; And how comely and honorable it would bee to see himself and his wife attended upon at service and sermons by his wholl family'. Habington drew on similar ideas about the role of the gentry in his description of Sir William Corteyn and his son as 'suche an example of bounty and pietie in beinge more like parentes than landlordes to theyre tenauntes, as all must needs prayse, and I wish all gentellmen would imitate'. Family historians had a particular interest in presenting their near relations as models of gentility and are, therefore, good sources for assessing what were considered the important characteristics of a gentleman. Sir Edward Rodney recorded how his father had held all the county offices 'proper for the best sort of gentleman' and described him as the epitome of gentility: 'Hee was of just stature six foote high or neere thereabouts, of a sound constitution of body, having beene seldome sick, hee was very temperate in his dyet, just in all his dealings, chaste in wedlock, a good Master to his servants, very hospitable and noble in his port and manner of living and generally an honest man and a good Christian'. *Mens sana in corpore sano*, indeed.[35]

For catholic antiquaries it was important to stress the constancy of the recusant gentry, while underlining their claim to continued membership of the gentry community. Habington stressed the piety of various Worcestershire recusants, such as Humphrey Pakington, who 'not ambitious of tytells but of virtewes, sereusly lyved and blyssedly dyed.' Such rhetoric could represent the enforced exclusion of catholic gentlemen from public life as a positive virtue. Shirley presented his father and elder brother as models of catholic piety in his account of the family, but this belied the reality. Sir George Shirley undoubtedly had catholic sympathies, but these conflicted with his desire to play a role in local society in keeping with his status. In the years preceding his death he was served by a protestant household chaplain. Although both Shirley and his brother were raised as catholics, Sir Henry had abandoned his allegiance by 1625, and his own sons were raised as protestants. Shirley's disapproval of such accommodation to the prevailing religious climate was demonstrated by his treatment of the Irton branch of his family in his history. Germaine Irton 'in a most unhappy hower, to the distraction of this ancient Branche ... degenerating from his stocke, fell from the Catholicke faith into the affection of Hearisie'. The father having abandoned the true faith, the son fell into a debauched life and the family estates were sold. Shirley himself steadfastly maintained his own catholic faith. In addition to the family history, he compiled a massive compendium, entitled *The Catholic Armorist*. Into this heraldic treatise he wove a defence of his religious faith and an account of those recusant families who had remained faithful during the years of persecution.[36]

The traditional image of gentility laid great stress upon hospitality, and this was echoed by local historians. Habington described the Savages of Elmley Castle, as 'honoured with Knyghthood, graced with the hyghest Offyces of this county, and beloved for theyre greate hospitality'. John Washbourne, whose funeral monument stressing his public service we encountered earlier, was he 'who contynewed longer Deputy Leyvtenant of the Shyre, Justyce of the Peace, and a good housekeeper of any in thys county'. Dugdale, similarly, recorded how Thomas Spencer of Claverdon 'for the great Hospitality he kept thereat was the mirrour of this County'. Sir John Beaumont's eulogy on the Leicestershire gentleman Sir William Skipwith commended his 'house as full and open as the air'.[37] As Henry, lord Berkeley spent comparatively little time in Gloucestershire, his visits were marked by significant ceremony. Smyth drew particular attention to the lavish celebration of Christmas on two occasions. The first was at Yate in 1559 and the second at Berkeley castle in 1604, which according to his steward became a fixed point for the calculation of dates within the Vale. When lord Berkeley was at Caludon during the Christmas season, it was the local gentry in the vicinity of Coventry who benefited from his hospitality. Of his Elizabethan ancestor Maurice Rodney, the family historian wrote: 'All that I can say of him is, that he was a great house-keeper, killing usually 12 great oxen in the 12 dayes [of Christmas] and that he was the first in this countye that gave livery cloakes to his men'.[38] A reputation for hospitality was an important element in maintaining a family's status, and it was incompatible with a magistrate's honour that he should acquire a reputation for meanness. While visiting Yorkshire in the 1590s, Wyrley described the impressive new house and garden built by Sir Henry Griffith at Agnes Burton. Griffith was a local justice of some standing and a member of the council of the North. Wyrley concluded his description with the observation, that 'the principall grace is the good hospitalitie thear gyven'. As well as being important to the status of a magistrate, such a reputation could assist a family to sustain its position through a period of decline. Hence, Erdeswicke described the Merevells of Throwley, Staffs., as 'a very ancient house of gentlemen, and of goodly living, equalling the best sort of gentlemen in the shire; though God hath not, for two or three generations, blessed their heirs with the best gifts of nature'. For the writers of parental advice it was important that hospitality should be tempered by moderation, as when lord Burghley cautioned that a man's housekeeping should be proportionate to his revenues. This same concern for moderation in expenditure – and in other areas of life – was echoed by local historians. According to Carew, the Cornish gentry:

> keepe liberall, but not costly builded or furnished houses, give kind entertainment to strangers, make even at the yeeres end with the profits of their living, are reverenced and beloved of their neighbours, live void of factions amongst themselves (at leastwise such as breake out into anie dangerous excesse) and delight not in braverie of apparrell.

Cornwall might be a long way from the Court in London, but its gentry had apparently inculcated the ideals of humanist civility.[39]

The requirement that the gentry should be charitable was inextricably linked in early modern minds with the duty of hospitality. Shirley described his great-grandfather as giving himself 'wholely to deeds of ardent charity, ample alms, and most free and noble hospitallity.' Habington commended the Sheldons of Beoley for their 'true virtue, hospitality and charity to the poore'. This reflects the traditional view of hospitality as the dispensing of food, drink and accommodation to all-comers, particularly to strangers and the poor. Hooker described William Alleie, an Elizabethan bishop of Exeter, among his many virtues as 'full of love, bountifull in hospitalitie, liberall to the poore, and a succourer of the needie'. In this interpretation, hospitality was a Christian responsibility and was not equated with the entertainment of one's social equals.[40] By the seventeenth century, charity was increasingly channelled through institutions and was focused on the deserving poor within the local community. It was the responsibility of the gentry to ensure that the community's charity was correctly used. The Cheshire justice Sir Richard Grosvenor advised his son to be 'charitable to the truly poor', but to 'drive from your gatts those lusty rogu[e]s and sturdy beggars that are able to earne their owne bread'. Habington accounted the clothiers of Worcester, who provided work for the poor, more charitable than those who relieved beggars at their gates.[41]

The traditional requirement that a gentleman should be hospitable to all and generous to those in need, was given additional importance by the acquisition of monastic lands by the gentry. The clergy had a vested interest in appealing to lay impropriators of monastic property to observe the pious uses for which their ancestors had originally donated the land. Local historians were among the most vocal of the clergy's secular allies, particularly Sir Henry Spelman in his *De non temerandis Ecclesiis*. A century after their dissolution by Henry VIII, the monasteries had become firmly associated in the minds of many commentators with great hospitality and acts of charity. Dugdale wrote that of 'their Hospitality to strangers, and great charity in dayly releif of poor people, I need not descend to particulars, our common Historians and the tradition of such, who were eye-witnesses thereof before that fatall subversion of those Houses, may sufficiently inform the world'. By contrast, William Grey thought the 'pride, covetousnesse, luxury, and idolatry' of the monks had been the cause of their downfall – there is no suggestion in his work that the monasteries had been a source of charity and hospitality. Yet, for many contemporaries the necessity of providing relief to the poor in Elizabeth's reign proved that the monasteries had been responsible for succouring the destitute in large numbers. Habington specifically enjoined the emulation of monastic hospitality and charity on the possessors of formerly monastic land. For gentlemen such as Dugdale, whose financial position meant that they clung perilously to their gentle status, the perceived economic burden resulting from the Dissolution weighed heavily. At the same time, Thomas Westcote balanced his sadness at the 'carcases' of the monasteries whose 'godly purposes' were no longer honoured, against an appreciation of the number of schools and almshouses that had been founded since their demise. Westcote here reflected the increasing emphasis on the channelling of charitable giving through institutions in the aftermath of the Reformation.[42]

The creation of institutions such as schools and almshouses provided opportunities for the provision of memorials recording benefactions, descriptions of which were recorded in local histories. These may be seen as the secular echoes of the stained-glass windows and carvings recording the gifts to the Church of earlier generations. For example, the schoolhouse erected by Sir Francis Nethersole at Polesworth bore the inscription *SOLI DEO GLORIA SCHOLA PAUPERUM*, but it was also decorated with coats of arms. The importance the gentry might attach to the commemorative possibilities of gifts to the community are seen in Gerard's account of Somerset, where he records various almshouses and their benefactors with approving comments. Describing the church at Ilminster, he reflected that the tomb of Nicholas Wadham (1532–1609) might fall to ruin as 'begins apace already', but his memory would be known 'as long as learning and religion remain with us' for his founding of Wadham College, Oxford, and of almshouses at Ilton, Somerset. In 1635 it was proposed that a new gaol to be built by public subscription in Northamptonshire should bear the names and arms of the founders: 'that posterity might see it was wholly performed by the liberality of the nobility and gentry resident within our own county'. On occasion, the word 'charity' was used to describe the donations that earlier generations made to the Church. This reinforces the impression that, while benefactions to the community largely replaced gifts to the Church in the post-Reformation period, the importance of such charitable giving as a measure of gentry status and as a means of memorialisation was unchanged. This is not to suggest that the medieval and early modern gentry lacked altruistic motivations for their charitable giving. Nevertheless, the form of their benefactions also served other purposes, and the development of local histories created an additional vehicle to advertise their generosity.[43]

The plethora of conduct books, advices and other guides to gentry behaviour that appeared in the sixteenth and seventeenth centuries is evidence of the changing role of the gentry within society. The image of the armoured knight – fighting abroad for king and Church, and at home keeping a hospitable welcome for all who came – remained strong. However, altered religious, economic, social and military realities made this image increasingly anachronistic. Local historians celebrated the traditional definition of gentility in their accounts of the medieval gentry, and continuity was an important theme in their works. Yet the dominant emphasis was on the gentry's role as magistrates and as guardians of the social hierarchy. The traditional qualities of gentility were increasingly interpreted in the light of the importance of this role, and were adapted to suit contemporary society. The didactic intentions of local historians are not as immediately apparent as those of writers of conduct books or parental advices. Their genealogical preoccupations and the structure of their works have obscured the educative nature of much of their material. The 'histories' of individual families have been recognised as establishing the importance of lineage, rather than as presenting models of gentility. Yet, when we examine their sources closely, it is clear that local historians were carefully selecting appropriate examples of virtue and vice. In his description of the misfortunes of the Smyth family of Shelford, Warwickshire, Dugdale was wholly dependent upon an account from someone who was not an eyewitness, an account which had been passed down to the next generation. While he was generally disparaging of such a source, Dugdale found the didactic value of this tale of an elderly husband murdered by his young wife and a family's future being squandered by an addiction to hunting, too great to omit it from his text.[44] The willingness of local historians to use sources such as oral testimony and chronicles, which they generally treated with suspicion, is evidence of the significance they attached to the didactic aspect of their work.

The enthusiasm of at least some members of the gentry for the efforts of local historians in this direction may be identified from their correspondence. Sir Francis Nethersole assured Dugdale that he sought 'no prayse from Men' for establishing the school at Polesworth. However, he made detailed suggestions as to what should be included in the *Antiquities of Warwickshire*, if Dugdale thought 'that the example and patterne of founding such a Schoole ... may by God's blessing do some good'. Gentlemen such as William Bromley and Roger Smith, whom we encountered in chapter four, were concerned not simply to have their genealogies correctly described, but also wished to see the martial, pious and other worthy acts of their families acknowledged in the histories of their counties. When Sir Aston Cockaine came to write a poem in praise of the *Antiquities of Warwickshire*, he did not laud it as a work of immense research and careful scholarship. For Cockaine it was primarily a celebration of the county gentry. He equated the work with the monuments and epitaphs of former generations, which had formed such an important source for its didactic content. The purpose of funeral monuments and of local histories in this period was equally to commemorate the dead and to exhort the living to emulate their example.[45]

NOTES

1 Dugdale, *Warwickshire*, pp. a3v, b1; N. Llewellyn, '"Plinie is a weyghtye witnesse": the classical reference in post-Reformation funeral monuments', in L. Gent (ed.), *Albion's Classicism: The Visual Arts in Britain, 1550–1660* (New Haven CT: Yale University Press, 1995), pp. 147–61; Smyth, *Berkeley Mss*, vol. 1, preface; vol. 2, pp. 426, 444; B.L., Additional MS 34239, fo. 4; see also Habington, *Worcestershire*, vol. 1, p. 35.

2 Woolf, *The Idea of History*, p. 240; Levy, *Tudor Historical Thought*, p. 140; Fussner, *Historical Revolution*, pp. 46–8, 180–2. Hughes, *Politics, Society and Civil War in Warwickshire*, p. 48 does recognise the significance of Dugdale quoting Raleigh; Nichols, *History of Leicestershire*, vol. 2(2), p. 843; Woolf, *Reading History in Early Modern England*, pp. 203–5.

3 Dugdale, *Warwickshire*, p. 325; The National Archives: Public Record Office, hereafter T.N.A.: P.R.O., SP9/9, fo. 231v.

4 Quoted in J. Boardman, J. Griffin and O. Murray (eds), *The Oxford History of the Classical World* (Oxford: Oxford University Press, softback edn., 1994), p. 636.

5 Q. Skinner, *The Foundations of Modern Political Thought*, two volumes (Cambridge: Cambridge University Press, 1978), vol. 1, chapter 8; Levy, *Tudor Historical Thought*, pp. 12–14; Woolf, *The Idea of History*, pp. 10–13, 142–3.

6 Larminie, *Wealth, Kinship and Culture*, p. 149; J.E. Mason, *Gentlefolk in the Making* (Philadelphia: Philadelphia University Press, 1935), chapter 3; Cicero, *On Duties*, ed. M. Griffin and E. Atkins (Cambridge: Cambridge University Press, 1991), pp. xvi–xxi; Skinner, *The Foundations of Modern Political Thought*, vol. 1, pp. 213–15. Courtesy literature and manners are examined at length in A. Bryson, *From Courtesy to Civility* (Oxford: Clarendon Press, 1998).

7 J.P. Sommerville (ed.), *King James VI and I Political Writings* (Cambridge: Cambridge University Press, 1994), p. xv; L.B. Wright (ed.), *Advice to a Son* (Washington, D.C.: Folger, 1962), pp. 9–13, 17–32. For the use of Burleigh's advice, see F. Raines (ed.) 'The history and antiquities of the Isle of Man', *Stanley Papers Pt 3* (Manchester: Chetham Society 70, 1867), pp. 43–6; 'Letter book of Sir John Holles', *HMC Portland Mss 9* (1923), pp. 4–7; R. Cust (ed.), *The Papers of Sir Richard Grosvenor* (Manchester: Record Society of Lancashire and Cheshire 134, 1996), pp. 26–38; H. Love, *Scribal Publication in Seventeenth-century England*, p. 202 n. 53.

8 L. Stone, 'Lord Montagu's directions for his son', *Northamptonshire Past and Present* 2(5) (1958), pp. 221–3.

9 Mason, *Gentlefolk in the Making*, chapter 2; F.W. Conrad, 'The problem of counsel reconsidered: the case of Sir Thomas Elyot', in P.A. Fideler and T.F. Mayer (eds), *Political Thought and the Tudor Commonwealth* (London: Routledge, 1992), pp. 75–107; D. Englander, D. Norman, R. O'Day and W. Owens (eds), *Culture and Belief in Europe 1450–1600* (Oxford: Blackwell, 1990), pp. 76–84; Smyth, *Berkeley Mss*, vol. 1, p. 264 – Sir Richard's work was published under the name of Barckley.

10 Mason, *Gentlefolk in the Making*, chapter 5; D. Bush, *English Literature in the Earlier Seventeenth Century* (Oxford: Clarendon Press, 2nd edn., 1962), pp. 24–6; Heal and Holmes, *The Gentry in England and Wales*, pp. 18–19.

11 Curtis, *Oxford and Cambridge in Transition*, p. 134; *Smyth Papers*, vol. 3, fo. 8; vol. 5, fos 32–3, 35; William Higford, *Institutions: or, Advice to His Grandson* (1658; reprinted London, 1818), pp. 51–2; A.T. Friedman, *House and Household in Elizabethan England* (Chicago: Chicago University Press, 1989), p. 31; Mason, *Gentlefolk in the Making*, p. 69.

12 Habington, *Worcestershire*, vol. 2, p. 319; Smyth, *Berkeley Mss*, vol. 1, p. 124, vol. 3, p. 117; Lambarde, *Kent*, p. 454; Heal and Holmes, *The Gentry in England and Wales*, pp. 6–19, 29–30; J.P. Cooper, 'Ideas of gentility in early-modern England', pp. 43–77; J. Morrill, *The Nature of the English Revolution* (London: Longman, 1993), pp. 195–200; S. Shapin, *A Social History of Truth* (Chicago: Chicago University Press, 1994), chapter 2; A. Sharp, 'Edward Waterhouse's view of social change in seventeenth-century England', *Past and Present* 62 (1974), pp. 27–46; J. Broadway, 'To equall their virtues': Thomas Habington, recusancy and the gentry of early Stuart Worcestershire', *Midland History* 29 (2004), pp. 1–24.

13 Habington, *Worcestershire*, vol. 2, p. 7. See also Smyth, *Berkeley Mss*, vol. 1, p. 124; P. Coss, 'The formation of the English gentry', *Past and Present* 147 (1995), pp. 38–64; Keen, *Chivalry*, chapter 8, pp. 249–50.

14 Dugdale, *Warwickshire*, p. 336; Erdeswicke, *Staffordshire*, p. 376; Habington, *Worcestershire*, vol. 1, p. 436.

15 Habington, *Worcestershire*, vol. 1, p. 238.

16 Heal and Holmes, *The Gentry in England and Wales*, p. 59; R. Cust, 'Honour and politics in early Stuart England', pp. 61, 92; P. Clark, *English Provincial Society* (Hassocks: Harvester Press, 1977), p. 119; Grey, *Chorographia*, pp. 44–5. Work on defamation and slander in the period indicates that the overlapping of public and private extended beyond the gentry: J.A. Sharpe, *Defamation and Sexual Slander in Early Modern England: the Church Courts at York* (Heslington, York: Borthwick Institute of Historical Research, University of York, Borthwick Papers 58, 1980).

17 K. Wrightson, *English Society 1580–1680* (London: Hutchinson, 1982), pp. 191–3; R.

O'Day, *Education and Society 1500–1800* (London: Longman, 1982), pp. 95–7; Curtis, *Oxford and Cambridge in Transition*, chapters 4–5; M. Todd, *Christian Humanism and the Puritan Social Order* (Cambridge: Cambridge University Press, 1987); M. Todd, 'Seneca and the Protestant mind: the influence of Stoicism on Puritan ethics', *Archive for Reformation History* 74 (1983), pp. 182–99.

18 Burton, *Leicestershire*, p. 120; F. Skillington, 'Sir John Beaumont of Gracedieu' *Leics. Trans.* 47 (1971–72), pp. 43–50; Dugdale, *Warwickshire*, pp. 50, 121; Smyth, *Berkeley Mss*, vol. 2, pp. 287, 394, 426; *Smyth Papers*, vol. 2, pp. 71, 73; vol. 9., p. 111v.

19 Habington, *Worcestershire*, vol. 1, p. 238; vol. 2, p. 130; Erdeswicke, *Staffordshire*, p. 17; Burton, *Leicestershire*, pp. 39–40, 85, 91; Dugdale, *Warwickshire*, p. 791; Burton, *Revised*, Segrave.

20 J.P. Cooper (ed.), *Wentworth Papers 1597–1628* (London: Camden Society, 4th ser. 12, 1973), p. 18; W. Somner, *The Antiquities of Canterbury* (London: Royal Historical Society, 1640), pp. 76–9. Heraldic treatises were often similarly excursive: Day, 'Primers of Honor', p. 99.

21 Burton, *Leicestershire*, p. 55; Carew, *Cornwall*, p. 3; Habington, *Worcestershire*, vol. 1, p. 174; vol. 2, p. 131; Dugdale, *Warwickshire*, p. 763.

22 B.L., Harley 4928, fo. 109v–10; D. Fleming, 'Faction and civil war in Leicestershire', *Leics. Trans.* 57 (1981–82), p. 28.

23 Habington, *Worcestershire*, vol. 1, pp. 381–2; J.H. Gleason, *The Justices of the Peace in England 1558 to 1640* (Oxford: Clarendon Press, 1969), p. 214; Dugdale, *Warwickshire*, p. 496; R.B. Manning, *Hunters and Poachers* (Oxford: Clarendon Press, 1993), p. 166; Habington, *Worcestershire*, vol. 1, pp. 65, 502; R.E.M. Peach, *Notes and Records of the Washbourne Family* (Gloucester: privately printed, 1896), p. 22: the inscription has since been removed.

24 Dugdale, *Warwickshire*, pp. 374–80; Hughes, *Warwickshire*, p. 138.

25 Habington, *Worcestershire*, vol. 2, p. 150; Smyth, *Berkeley Mss*, vol. 2, pp. 252–4, 266–78; vol. 3, p. 196; E. Moir, 'Benedict Webb, clothier', *Economic History Review* Second Series, 10 (1957) pp. 256–64; Butcher, *The Survey and Antiquities of the Towne of Stamford*, pp. 24–5.

26 Llewellyn, 'Claims to status through visual codes', pp. 157–60; Llewellyn, 'Plinie is a weyghtye witnesse', p. 151; Dugdale, *Warwickshire*, pp. 352, 361, 366, 402; G. Jones, 'Thomas Puckering's tomb – the original contract', *Warwickshire History* 2(5), (1974), pp. 37–40; Hamper, *Dugdale*, pp. 163–4; Anon., *Charlecote Park* (London: National Trust, 1995), pp. 11–13; Heal and Holmes, *The Gentry in England and Wales*, pp. 59, 267, 293; Hughes, *Politics, Society and Civil War in Warwickshire*, p. 45; A.M. Minardiere, *The Warwickshire Gentry 1660–1730* (M.A. dissertation, University of Birmingham 1963), p. 78; Archer, *Correspondence*, fo. 46.

27 Llewellyn, 'Claims to status through visual codes', p. 155; B. Donagan, 'Halcyon days and the literature of war: England's military education before 1642', *Past and Present* 147 (1995), pp. 65–100; Adams, '"Because I am of that countrye & mynde to plant myself there": Robert Dudley, earl of Leicester and the West Midlands', Appendix 2; B.L., Harley 4928, fo. 104v; Erdeswicke, *Staffordshire*, p. 493; Habington, *Worcestershire*, vol. 1, p. 323; Gerard, *Dorset*, p. 81; Burton, *Leicestershire*, p. 105; Smyth, *Berkeley Mss*, vol. 1, p. 266; vol. 2, pp. 186, 233.

28 Dugdale, *Warwickshire*, p. 73 (illustrated on preceding pages).

29 Burton, *Leicestershire*, pp. 173–4; Smyth, *Berkeley Mss*, vol. 2, p. 11.

30 Erdeswicke, *Staffordshire*, pp. 340–2; Habington, *Worcestershire*, vol. 2, p. 209; Stow, *London*, p. 298; Grey, *Chorographia*, p. 14; Smyth, *Berkeley Mss*, vol. 1, p. 9.

31 Dugdale, *Warwickshire*, pp. 136, 742; Smyth, *Berkeley Mss*, vol. 1, pp. 101–3, 123–4, 274–8, 358; vol. 2, p. 36.

32 D. Williams, 'William Burton's 1642 revised edition of the Description of Leicestershire', *Leics. Trans.* 50 (1974–75), p. 32; Smyth, *Berkeley Mss*, vol. 3, *passim*; Dugdale, *Warwickshire*, p. 173; Grey, *Chorographia*, p. 38.

33 Dugdale, *Warwickshire*, p. 417; Heal and Holmes, *The Gentry in England and Wales*, chapter 9; Burton, *Leicestershire*, p. 238; Gerard, *Dorset*, pp. 103, 114.

34 Gerard, *Somerset*, p. 89; Burton, *Leicestershire*, p. 97; B.L., Additional MS, 36748, fo. 88.

35 Smyth, *Berkeley Mss*, vol. 2, p. 377; Habington, *Worcestershire*, vol. 2, p. 257; B.L., Additional MS 34239, fos 14v–5.

36 Habington, *Worcestershire*, vol. 1, p. 264; T.B. Trappes-Lomax, 'Roman Catholicism', V.C.H. *Leics.*, vol. 2, p. 57; A.C. Lacy, 'Sir Robert Shirley and the English Revolution in Leicestershire', *Leics. Trans.* 58 (1982–83), pp. 25–35; Shirley, *Stemmata Shirleiana*, p. 89; B.L., Harley 4928, fos 127–8; *The Catholic Armorist* survives in several fragments. The major part is among the papers bequeathed by Sir Joseph Williamson to Queen's College, Oxford (Queen's College MS 141–3); a further fragment is in the T.N.A.: P.R.O.: SP 9/9. I am grateful to Richard Cust for telling me about this work.

37 Habington, *Worcestershire*, vol. 1, p. 502; vol. 2, p. 71; F. Heal, *Hospitality in Early Modern England* (Oxford: Clarendon Press, 1990), pp. 13, 24–5; Dugdale, *Warwickshire*, p. 497; Skillington, 'Sir John Beaumont of Gracedieu', p. 46.

38 Smyth, *Berkeley Mss*, vol. 1, p. 264; vol. 2, pp. 287, 370; vol. 3, p. 411; Heal, *Hospitality in Early Modern England*, p. 74; B.L., Additional MS 34239, fo. 10v.

39 College of Arms, Vincent 197, fos 157v–8; Habington, *Worcestershire*, vol. 1, p. 502; Erdeswicke, *Staffordshire*, p. 483; Wright, *Advice to a Son*, p. 9; Cooper, *Wentworth Papers*, p. 14; Higford, *Institutions*, p. 6; Carew, *Cornwall*, p. 64.

40 B.L., Harley 4928, fo. 97; Habington, *Worcestershire*, vol. 1, p. 70; Hooker, *A Catalogue of the Bishops of Excester* (London: H. Denham, 1584), entry 46; F. Heal, 'The idea of hospitality in early modern England', *Past and Present* 102 (1984), pp. 66–93.

41 Heal, *Hospitality in Early Modern England*, pp. 129–32, 176–8; Cust, *The Papers of Sir Richard Grosvenor*, p. 32; K. Thomas, *The Perception of the Past in Early Modern England* (London: University of London Creighton Trust Lecture, 1983), pp. 17–19; Habington, *Worcestershire*, vol. 2, pp. 426–7.

42 Dugdale, *Warwickshire*, pp. 147, 813; Grey, *Chorographia*, p. 18; Habington, *Worcestershire*, vol. 2, p. 362; Westcote, *A View of Devonshire in MDCXXX*, pp. 145–6.

43 Dugdale, *Warwickshire*, p. 803; Gerard, *Somerset*, p. 136; J. Wake, *The Brudenells of Deene* (London: Cassell & Company, 1953), p. 113; Habington, *Worcestershire*, vol. 1, p. 457; vol. 2, p. 319.

44 Dugdale, *Warwickshire*, 37–8.

45 Hamper, *Dugdale*, pp. 241–3, 306–7, 481; Nichols, *History of Leicestershire*, vol. 3(1), pp. 520–1.

Chapter 7

◆

Local history and the physical world

The evolution of local history in England was closely linked to developments in surveying and map-making. Saxton's atlas of county maps appeared three years after the publication of the *Perambulation of Kent*, while the second edition of Lambarde's work coincided with the production of Symonson's highly detailed map of the county. Within a few short years, towards the end of the sixteenth century, the county made its appearance as both a cartographic and a historical subject. Seeing a county represented by a map gave visual form to what had previously been an abstract idea. The county was only one of the spatial communities to which the medieval gentry belonged – and not necessarily the strongest of those communities – but in Elizabeth's reign it was given a potent, visual form.[1] Had the Church maintained its medieval monopoly on education and caused the first atlas to contain maps of dioceses and archdeaconries, the development of local history might have taken a different course. Instead, the break with Rome and the dissolution of the monasteries radically changed the built landscape of England, and it was this altered topography that was recorded in the first widely available, detailed maps. The advent of maps available to the gentry coincided with an increasing contact with and awareness of the world beyond their immediate localities. In this period a higher proportion of the gentry travelled away from their native counties on a regular basis. They went to the universities and inns of court to be educated. They spent time in London: pursuing legal cases, attending parliament, or simply for pleasure. Their experiences inevitably increased their spatial awareness. Over time an appreciation of geography was married to the gentry's well-established sense of history. This made them aware that they were men 'of a place as of a time' and provided fertile ground for the development of topographical history.[2]

Unlike cartographers, who were restricted by a limited symbolic language, local historians enjoyed a considerable degree of freedom in their description of the world around them. Whereas other areas covered by their works were controlled by the availability of documentary evidence, their physical environment was there to be observed and described. Moreover, topographical writing was a new discipline, with no established criteria concerning what should be included and how it should be handled. The extent to which local historians interested themselves in topography varied widely. Some antiquaries were largely desk-bound and studied local history almost entirely from documents. Others, such as Thomas Habington, made extensive journeys to record the heraldry in local churches, but recorded little of the countryside through which they travelled or its secular buildings and landmarks. By contrast, Thomas Gerard counted each of the sixty stone steps up the hill behind Weymouth from where he gained a fine view of the town and harbour, while Richard Carew scrambled among the ruins of Restormel Castle.[3] Urban historians were obviously concerned with contained and accessible topographical units, but they too varied in how much of a physical sense of the urban landscape they conveyed. In 1641 Burton included a detailed account of the topography of Leicestershire in his plan for the revised version of his county history, and this appears in the rough draft. When the draft was neatly copied by a scribe, this section was replaced by a description of rural pastimes. Whether this was a personal decision, or the result of the reaction from fellow antiquaries who read the manuscript, such as Dugdale and D'Ewes, is unclear.[4]

Despite the different levels of their interest in topography, early local histories provide useful material which helps us to understand how the gentry of the period related to their environment. Although they were working without established conventions to inhibit them and enjoyed the comparative freedom provided by the descriptive power of language, the image of their environment presented by local historians is strikingly similar to that of the cartographers. The principal limitations on antiquaries were those imposed by their own attitudes and those of their readers. Local historians were drawn from among the educated social elite. This same class provided the main market for the early county maps. Consequently, the picture of the Elizabethan and early Stuart world we gain from both sources is that of the world as seen from the perspective of the educated gentry.

This chapter is concerned with a number of areas related to the topographical content of local history. Firstly, it explores the parallels between its development and the appearance of the early county maps and town plans. I shall examine the ways in which the two forms reflect a similar view of the environment that they describe, and how the perspective of the gentry – as the primary consumers of both – shaped their content. Secondly, I shall consider the thesis advanced in the 1970s by Margaret Aston, that the physical ruins of monastic buildings and the nostalgia they evoked were a significant factor in the subsequent flowering of antiquarian activity.[5] I shall go on to examine how the classical bias of the humanist education received by the gentry influenced their relationship to the physical world, and I will show how local historians were predisposed by their education and by the available literary evidence to interpret archaeological remains as Roman in origin. Finally, I shall show how, despite their limitations, local historians in this period took the first tentative steps towards the development of archaeological research on a scientific basis.

Figures such as Lawrence Nowell, John Norden and John Speed, as we saw in chapter one, are important in both the development of English maps and local history. In addition, there were numerous individuals who showed an interest in both the visual and documentary representations of their counties. Speed's map of Rutland in *The Theatre of the Empire of Great Britain* was provided by John, lord Harrington of Exton, who also provided material for the county commentary. Maps, if included at all, were a minor feature of early county histories – but, as with *Britannia*, over time they increased in importance. In 1576 Lambarde's *Perambulation of Kent* had included a map of the Saxon heptarchy; in 1596 this was supplemented by a map of the beacons of Kent. Sixty years later Dugdale's *Antiquities of Warwickshire* included a map of the whole county, and detailed maps of the four hundreds. Local historians who circulated their works in manuscript did not include maps, but would have expected their readers to possess at least a copy of Saxton's or Speed's map of their own county. The provision of maps was one of the last stages in the process of publishing a county history, and to an extent (as today) was controlled by the costs of reproduction. Their increasing prevalence as an element in county histories is evidence of the importance attached to them by authors, printers and readers.

William Burton combined a keen interest in cartography with his antiquarian studies. While a law student, he produced a more elaborate version of Saxton's map of Leicestershire, with the addition of eighty new place-names, a map which was published in the 'Anonymous' series by Jodocus Hondicus of Amsterdam in 1602.[6] Burton's reference in the *Description of Leicestershire* to his observations 'with the helpe of a prospective glasse' suggests his amendments to Saxton's map were in part based on his own surveys. This conjecture is borne out by his brother Robert's observation in the *Anatomy of Melancholy*: 'What more pleasing studies can there be than the Mathematicks, Theorick or Pratick parts? As to survey land, make mapps, models, dials etc., with which I have ever much delighted myself.'[7]

Accurate equipment for surveying was becoming increasingly available, and scientific instruments were becoming an important part of the furniture of gentry studies. In 1595 Smyth purchased for lady Berkeley 'a globe, Blagraves mathematicall Jewell, a quadrate, Compass, Rule, and other instruments'.[8] Burton included additional material from textual sources on his map of Leicestershire, such as the boundaries of the six hundreds. This map was later used by Speed in his *Theatre*, with the addition of a town plan of Leicester, and Burton included a scaled-down version in the *Description of Leicestershire*.

As county histories developed in depth and scope and the accompanying visual images became more elaborate, local gentlemen continued to be involved in the production of maps and other drawings. The map of Kineton hundred in the *Antiquities of Warwickshire* was corrected for Dugdale by Archer's kinsman Richard Verney, who also provided drawings of funeral monuments. In 1638 Dugdale suggested that the production of views of Warwickshire towns, castles and other notable features should be undertaken by Archer's eldest son. The young man had a 'dextrous hand' and such drawings were 'a great pleasure to any ingenious mind', something that could 'be performed with delight as a recreation'. Skill at drawing was a desirable attribute for a cultured gentleman. William Higford advocated 'limning' and 'pourtraying with the pencil' as 'parts becoming a gentleman'.[9] However, providing visual images gradually became increasingly professionalised. When published in 1656, Dugdale's work incorporated views of the most important towns, castles and gentry seats of Warwickshire executed by the topographical artist Wencelaus Hollar. Dugdale's initial use of Hollar may have originated from a wish to give employment to an old acquaintance, since both men had been clients of the earl of Arundel before the civil war and Hollar was newly returned to England when the engravings were commissioned. However, the continued use of Hollar by Dugdale, Elias Ashmole and others indicates how his images were recognised as enhancing antiquarian works. The engravings significantly increased the cost of printing, but they enhanced the book's appeal to Dugdale's gentry readership and helped to gain support for the undertaking before publication. In 1654 Archer informed Dugdale that his 'Cosen Peytoe did borrow your Cuttes to shew them to my Lady Verney, the better to drawe her on, to contribut towardes you about Compton'. At the same time, the visual apparatus of maps was increasingly used to acknowledge the role of the gentry as patrons of local history. In 1579 Christopher Saxton included the arms of his patron Thomas Seckford on each of the maps he produced. In 1656 Dugdale similarly used the maps in his county history to acknowledge those who had contributed significantly to his endeavours. The map of Warwickshire paid tribute to Archer's vital contribution to the project as a whole (see figure 12). The maps of each hundred were dedicated to members of the local gentry, whose papers he had used extensively.[10] The choice of the maps for this form of dedication from among all the engravings in the volume is indicative of their importance to the educated gentry.

In the seventeenth century, topographers, cartographers and landscape artists attempted to convey similar information through different media, and their methods often overlapped. In the *Art of Describing*, Svetlana Alpers drew

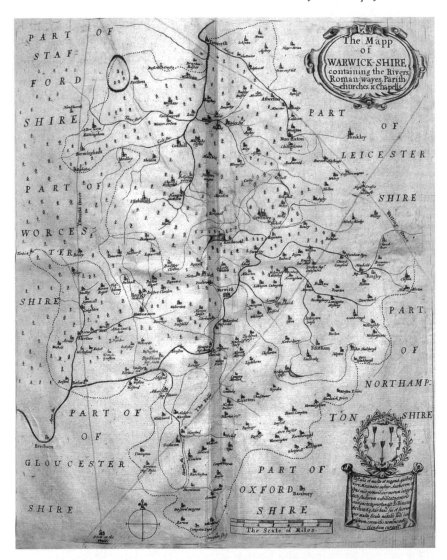

Figure 12 Map of Warwickshire from the *Antiquities of Warwickshire*,
dedicated to Sir Simon Archer

attention to the relationship between cartography and the development of
Dutch landscape painting. She suggested that the seventeenth-century Dutch
would have been confused by the divisions between art and maps recognised
by modern art historians and cartographers. When maps were understood to
be a form of picture and when pictures were as important as text in conveying
meaning, the distinction was less apparent. The earliest of the 'realistic' Dutch

landscape paintings translated the conventions of map-making into art. Rather than presenting the bounded view of the located observer, these panoramic landscapes adopted the bird's-eye view familiar from contemporary maps. Leah Marcus in turn related this visual approach to landscape to the pastoral poems of the early Stuart period, contrasting the 'cartographic perspective' of Drayton's *Poly-Olbion* to the single reference point of the country-house poems of Jonson and his successors. The genre of topographical city views, represented by Braun and Hogenberg's *Civitates Orbis Terrarum* (1572–1617), was also taken up and transformed by Dutch artists. (The *Civitates Orbis Terrarum* was a popular work; Burton referred to it in the *Description of Leicestershire* as a book to which his readership would have easy access.)[11] The relationship between cartographic and topographical images may be seen in various representations of English castles, houses and gardens in this period. The images are presented from a bird's-eye view, enabling the artist to display all their features on a two-dimensional surface.[12] Speed's town plans adopted the same method, so that, for example, the different styles of the English cathedrals may be identified. Symonson's 1596 map of Kent distinguishes churches with spires from those with towers, while Thomas Watts' map of Wisbech hundred in Cambridgeshire (copied in 1657 from an earlier version of 1597) shows the details of churches, manor houses and windmills. Maps and landscape images also incorporated verbal material, drawn from the province of the topographers and historians. Speed's atlas not only included town plans, but also such non-cartographic information as the descriptions of towns and their administrations; pictures and descriptions of significant battles; the arms of the nobility; drawings of Roman remains and of significant buildings; and portraits of the kings of England. Like Burton on his map of Leicestershire, Speed included the boundaries of the administrative sub-divisions of the counties. This supplementary material has been used to identify the county gentry as the market to which Speed's maps were directed. The same people were the intended readership for local history.[13]

Drawing on the example of Dutch cartographers, Alpers drew attention to the increasing amount of historical information that was included on maps in the form of short texts and illustrations. She saw this development as illustrative of how the dominance of narrative history was being challenged by the thematic study of the past based on a wider range of evidence. To record history in maps with accompanying illustrations and text, was to place the alleged facts within a verifiable geographical rather than chronological framework. Similarly, contemporary paintings, such as Sir Henry Unton's memorial portrait and Anne Clifford's 'Great Picture', combined images and texts. Although these texts would have been impossible to read when the paintings were displayed on a wall, they added authority to the images. A parallel may be drawn here between contemporary maps and the increasing use of drawings of seals, documents and funeral monuments on contemporary pedigrees. As the textual exegesis of the pedigree became ever more prominent, the pedigree book began to replace the illuminated roll, and in time the family history evolved. Similarly, as the commentary to maps became more extensive, it became necessary to provide a separate narrative. The visual context of the narrative remained important, however, because of its relationship to the physical world. By placing their works within the known geography of their counties and relating the accounts of individual manors to each other by the inclusion of topographical details, local historians lent authority to their works. This complemented their emphasis on the use of documentary evidence and extensive research.

The principal features depicted on the early county maps were also those which attracted the attention of historically minded gentlemen: rivers, market towns, castles, gentry houses, parks, parish churches and forests. Lists of such features often occur in antiquarian notebooks. Archer's notes include lists relating to Warwickshire derived directly from Speed's map. Burton incorporated such lists in the general description of the county at the beginning of his book, but he introduced a historical dimension by including lists of former religious houses and of towns no longer possessing a market.[14] Urban historians similarly concerned themselves with the physical monuments that attracted the attention of the early town topographers: the walls, gates, bridges, churches and market crosses. From both the urban histories and the maps it is clear that monastic buildings remained an important part of the landscape in towns in the generations after the Dissolution. By contrast the sites of former monasteries are significant on county maps only when taken over by the gentry for secular use. However, while map-makers attempted to convey the appearance of churches, windmills and other features of the built environment, local historians largely eschewed physical description. The architectural information recorded by William Worcestre in the late fifteenth century did not become a feature of early modern local histories. For Worcestre's successors, features such as markets, parks and religious houses had the advantage of providing plentiful documentary evidence, and records rather than observations were the cornerstone of their scholarship. They were concerned less with the physical evidence that a particular town held a market, than with the documentary evidence granting the right to host a market. Since local historians used Domesday and the fourteenth-century *Nomina Villarum* as the basis of their county gazetteers, they included many places which had subsequently been depopulated or enclosed. Such places were not included on maps, and occasionally there was considerable doubt as to where they had been located, but they did find their way into local histories.

Since county maps and histories were produced for the gentry, it is not surprising that their houses should feature prominently in both. There were practical reasons for members of the central government wanting the location of gentry houses included on the maps they sponsored. For example, in 1585 Sir Amias Paulet was concerned, when assessing the suitability of Chillington as a prison for Mary, queen of Scots, to find that the most ardent protestants among the local justices lived some distance from the house. Such an assessment was far easier to make with the assistance of a map, as was ensuring that justices were evenly distributed across a county.[15] The houses of the gentry were also significant indicators of the wealth and importance of a county. In this respect local historians had an advantage over the cartographers. They were able to record not only the number and location of gentry houses, but details of their age, size, building materials and architecture. Although a cartographer could surround a county map with pictures of the most significant houses, the space available was limited. Local historians were able to take note of far more houses, and their works stand as a testament to the vitality of gentry building activity in the Tudor and early Stuart period. Unfortunately, since their interest was predominantly in conveying an impression of the size and status of houses, local histories are of limited use to architectural historians as they predate the widespread introduction of engravings.[16]

In 1624 Sir Henry Wotton described the importance of their houses to the Jacobean gentry: 'Every mans proper Mansion House, being the Theater of his Hospitality, the Seate of Self-fruition, the Comfortablest part of his owne life, the Noblest of his Sonnes Inheritance, a kinde of private Princedome; Nay to the Possessors thereof, an Epitomie of the whole World.'[17]

Local historians bore witness to the importance of building as an indicator of status to the Elizabethan and early Stuart gentry, as they recorded the number of new and modernised buildings to be found in their localities.[18] For many houses in Staffordshire, Sampson Erdeswicke mentioned only the name of the owner or the fact that it was built on a former monastic site. Of the score or so houses for which more information was provided, over half were recently built or substantially repaired. Of these, Erdeswicke described the newly built house at Wilbrighton as 'a proper gentleman's house of brick' and what is now Biddulph Old Hall as 'a very state-like and fair new house of stone'.[19] In his *Description of Leicestershire* Burton made less mention of local gentry houses than Erdeswicke, but demonstrated the importance of buildings to gentry status by incorporating a drawing of his seat at Lindley in the frontispiece of his book. The inclusion of views of several prominent local houses among the illustrations of Dugdale's *Antiquities of Warwickshire* further emphasised their significance as indicators of gentry status.

The boldest declarations of status through building in the Elizabethan and early Stuart period were made by the proxy palaces and 'prodigy' houses built by noblemen and courtiers, such as Theobalds, Longleat, Holdenby and Castle Ashby. Wyrley was impressed by the grandeur of the 'magnificent' house at

Worksop built by the Earl of Shrewsbury in the 1580s, although he did not like its situation. The importance of such prodigy houses was acknowledged by Dugdale, who referred to Sir Francis Willoughby as building 'that stately House at Wollaton in Com. Nott. being the most eminent piece of Architecture in all those parts'. The only comparable house in Warwickshire was Aston Hall, built by Sir Thomas Holt between 1618 and 1635. Dugdale recorded that Holt: 'advanced to the dignity of a Baronet; Of whom I may not omit to take this further notice; viz. that by him there was a faire Parke inclosed here, and a noble Fabrick therein erected, which for beauty and state much exceedeth any in these parts.'

The juxtaposition of the mention of the augmentation to Holt's rank and the building of his house demonstrate the way in which the two were linked in the antiquary's mind. It was in recognition of the importance of Aston Hall as an expression of its builder's status that his biographical details were mentioned in the same entry. Following Dugdale's usual practice, these details should have appeared in the entry for Holt's ancestral manor of Duddeston.[20]

The early local historians did not describe gentry houses in detail, but concentrated on the material used and the status of the buildings. The most detailed description given by Erdeswicke was that of the home of the Astons at Tixall: 'a fair house, the first height from the ground very well wrought of stone, the rest of timber and plaster; but it is since beautified, or defaced, (I know not which to say) with a goodly gatehouse of stone ... being one of the fairest pieces of work made of late times, that I have seen in all these countries.'

This emphasis on building materials and status was supplemented by reference to demesnes and parks. For example, in Staffordshire again, Enfield was 'a goodly manor and a park ... where Thomas Grey, late of Enfield, built a very proper brick house'. When referring to medieval houses, Erdeswicke almost invariably mentioned these features, as if to show that the failure to build a new house was not due to poverty and did not reflect adversely on the status of the family mentioned. Hence, in the neighbouring manors of Throwley, Blore and Okeover in the north-east of the county, there were: 'a fair, ancient house, and goodly demesne'; 'a goodly ancient house and park'; and 'another fair old house, and a park, and goodly demesnes'. This approach was copied by later local historians, who continued to describe the houses of the gentry in terms of the wealth and status displayed through their ownership. The description of funeral monuments in their works similarly emphasised their grandeur and impact, rather than giving detailed descriptions or passing artistic udgements.[21]

Where a local history was critical of a house, it was invariably because the builder had offended against the accepted standards of gentry behaviour. A Leicestershire gentleman owned a house near Utcester in Staffordshire, which was called Blount Hall. As Erdeswicke remarked, a 'man would think that it should, by the name, be the ancient seat of the Blounts'. Leland had indeed recorded that 'some say that this is the antient seat' of the Blount family. Erdeswicke disapproved of what he saw as an unjustified attempt to augment a gentleman's status. Accordingly, he described Blount Hall as 'a house of no great account' built by a gentleman who was 'a little glorious'. Having visited many of the houses they described, local historians were aware of how uncomfortable and inconvenient many impressive houses were as family homes. Wyrley assessed Worksop Manor in Nottinghamshire, the work of the architect Robert Smythson, as follows: 'At this Wirkensoppe Georg Earle of Shrewsburie hath built a magnificent house, what seat I utterly dislyke, for that the prospect is upon a dampish marrsh towardes the south, and it suffereth great penurie of water, and that which is brought to the house cometh with great difficultie.'

This contrasts sharply with Gerard's description of Raleigh's house at Sherborne, which James I had given to the earl of Bristol: 'whether that you consider the Pleasantnesse of the Seate, the Goodnesse of the Soyle, or the other Delicacies belongeing unto it, it rests unparralleled by anie in these Partes'.[22] Whether Wyrley would have been so forthright in his opinion of Worksop outside his own notebook is doubtful. Local historians were generally mindful of the importance of such houses as symbols of gentry wealth and status. In the *Antiquities of Warwickshire* Dugdale moved not towards more accurate descriptions, but towards a greater emphasis on wealth and status – through the inclusion of engravings of such prominent houses as Aston Hall and Compton Verney.

Castles were particularly important as indicators of status because of their associations with royalty and nobility. Medieval castles, designed for fortification and a communal style of living, required large amounts of capital expenditure to make them suitable for contemporary, aristocratic life. In many cases the expenditure was deemed excessive, and the castle owners moved to more appropriate accommodation. At Restormel in Cornwall, Carew found the castle, formerly 'a Palace, so healthful for aire, so fayre (in regard of those days) for building and so strong for defence' in a sad state of decay: 'for the Parke is disparked, the timber rooted up, the conduit pipes taken away, the roof made sale of, the planchings rotten, the wals fallen downe, and the hewed stones of the windowes, dowres & clavels, pluct out to serve private buildings'.[23] By the late sixteenth century the Berkeley family lived at Caludon near Coventry, where Henry, lord Berkeley, remodelled his house at far less expense than would have been required to make Berkeley castle comfortable. However, he continued to visit Berkeley regularly every two or three summers, where he kept great state. Smyth recalled how, having left Caludon accompanied by around fifteen attendants, lord Berkeley would arrive at the castle surrounded by three to five hundred friends and tenants. Following his appointment as lord lieutenant of Gloucestershire, lord Berkeley also spent the Christmas season at the castle in 1604. His occupation of his ancestral home at this time underlined the importance of his appointment to his family's status. In 1635 Elizabeth, the wife of George, lord Berkeley, took over the management of his estates and began to undertake repairs to the castle. Smyth wrote approvingly to lord Berkeley of the repairs to 'the mantion seate of your honor', and his views were echoed by lord Berkeley's sister: 'as shee is a true and affectionate frend to my brother, soe is shee also a lover of his posteryty, as she does amply expresse in her care of his estate, and in the paines shee takes in repayringe that old castle, so much for his honor.

Despite the repairs to the castle, lord Berkeley did not take up residence. On his infrequent visits to Gloucestershire, he seems to have preferred to stay with his steward.[24] Nevertheless, the significance of a medieval castle as a source of family status was also attested by John Denton in his account of Millom, Cumb. Although the castle was threatened with ruin, it was still occupied, the family:

> holding themselves content, that the old manner of strong building there, with the goodly demesne and commodities which both land and sea afford them, and the stately parks full of huge oaks and timber woods and fallow deer, do better witness their antient and present greatness and worth, than the painted vanities of our times do grace our new upstarts.[25]

While Berkeley and Millom castles stood as symbols of their owners' former importance and of their continuing claim to status, for others the acquisition of a castle enabled them to display their current wealth and power. Erdeswicke recorded how John Dudley, duke of Northumberland, 'in his greatness' coveted and succeeded in acquiring Dudley castle. He repaired the fabric and erected new buildings in this monument to his power. The situation of the castle, 'mounted loftily on a very high mountain', made it a particularly potent symbol. Dudley's son Robert was given Kenilworth castle shortly before being created earl of Leicester. In the *Antiquities of Warwickshire* Dugdale included not only three views of the castle, but also a plan of the building which Leicester turned into a palace fit for a queen at a reputed cost of £60,000. Kenilworth had been slighted after the battle of Edgehill on the orders of Parliament, by blowing up the outermost wall of the keep and breaching the wall of the outer ward. Hollar's engravings, which were based on earlier drawings, do not show this damage – to do so would have reduced the value of the castle as an indicator of the prestige of Warwickshire. Leicester's brother Ambrose Dudley was given Warwick castle in 1562 and restored a range of buildings there sufficiently to entertain the queen at Warwick in 1566 and 1572. Thereafter he appears to have neglected the castle. In 1601 Sir Fulke Greville described it in a letter to Sir Robert Cecil, as having 'been a common gaol these ten or twelve years; the wall down in many places hard to the ground, the roof open to all weathers'. His son was granted the castle in 1604 and, following his father's death, began restoring it as his main country seat. According to Dugdale, Greville spent more than £20,000 on its restoration and made it 'a place not onely of great strength, but extraordinary delight'.[26]

Dugdale's account of Greville's restoration of Warwick castle drew attention to the 'most pleasant Gardens, Walks and Thickets' with which he adorned it. The garden was an important element of late Elizabethan and Stuart gentry houses, and consequently attracted the notice of local historians. It was an important sign of gentility and status to have a house surrounded by a formal garden, rather than to have it jostled by a farm and outbuildings. Burton drew attention to the house of his friend Sir John Beaumont, at Gracedieu – a former nunnery. He explained that the nuns had arranged the walled garden to resemble the Biblical Gethsemane, but sadly did not include a detailed description. Wyrley described Burton Agnes in Yorkshire, the home of the hospitable Sir Henry Griffith, as 'lacking not the grace of a bewtifull garden'. The family portrait of the Lucys of Charlecote, Warwickshire, painted around 1628, shows a glimpse of their garden through the open door behind Sir Thomas Lucy's chair. Like their elaborate costumes, the expensive carpet, the book on the table, the dogs and the hawk on its perch, the garden in the background is a symbol of the family's economic, social and cultural status. Cornelius Johnson's portrait of the Capel family, painted around 1640, also shows a formal garden in the background – possibly that of the family seat at Little Hadham, Herts. The importance of their gardens to gentry ideas of status was more fully realised in the country-house paintings that became fashionable in the late seventeenth century. These invariably portrayed the house not in isolation, but surrounded by its formal gardens.[27]

One advantage enjoyed by historians in describing the physical manifestations of gentry status was their ability to show them increasing over time. For example, Dugdale's description of the home of his neighbours the Fishers of Great Packington used the additions to the estate of each generation to reflect the growing economic and social status of the family. John Fisher, a Shropshire gentleman, 'built the whole of the body of the present Fabrick' in 1574. The house, like many built in the Arden area of Warwickshire in the sixteenth century, was constructed of timber rather than of the higher-status stone or brick. John Fisher's son 'made a Park of the Outwood', increasing the status of the property by the addition of this symbol of gentility. His son Sir Robert Fisher was created a deputy lieutenant in the 1630s. He 'raised that large Pool Eastwards from the House, built the Lodge in the Park; and much adorned his Seat with other places of delight, and had issue severall sons and daughters'. Here Dugdale implicitly linked the family's economic, social and reproductive success. All might be interpreted as reflecting divine favour on the family.[28]

Other features of county maps and local histories were also included, predominantly because of their interest to the educated gentry. Although the gentry no longer formed a martial caste, the military exploits of their ancestors were an important part of a family's claim to honour. Local battles were, therefore, an essential part of the gentry's self-image. From the early county maps of Saxton onwards the sites of battles such as Bosworth were included, and the majority of counties were associated with a battle of sufficient importance to rate a vignette from Speed. It was inevitable that descriptions of such battles, in which the ancestors of the local gentry had played an important part, should become an essential element of local histories. For Habington the battle of Evesham was 'allmost the greatest of importance that ever concerned the state of England', and that it had occurred in Worcestershire enhanced the prestige of the county and its gentry. As we have seen, Burton was particularly proud of the role he claimed for his ancestor in the battle of Bosworth. The range of oral sources that Smyth drew on for the account of the late fifteenth-century battle of Nibley Green shows that it remained an important cultural milestone to the local villagers and gentry alike. In his autobiography Dugdale recorded how in February 1643 he, a 'skylfull Surveyor', and some other gentlemen, went to Edgehill. There they drew up a plan of the battlefield, recording how the armies had been drawn up, the cannon placed, the dead buried and so forth. Although the battles of the civil war were too recent and potentially controversial for inclusion in Dugdale's county history, this experience would have helped him to a greater understanding of the accounts of medieval battles.[29]

Hills, the most prominent of local landmarks, appeared on county maps and were celebrated in local histories. Burton described Bardon Hill, as 'the most noted landmark of these parts. The Top whereof affords a pleaseing prospect into the neighbouring Countries and is easily discernable att 40 miles distance'. His interest in natural history led him to digress on how hills were created, quoting as his main authority the German mineralogist and metallurgist Georg Agricola. The height of a local hill was clearly a source of pride. Smyth declared the beacon at Stinchcombe in the vale of Berkeley to be comparable for height and prospect 'with any of those in Palestina, Italy, in the Isle of Man, of Hainborrowe in Cornwall, so greatly celebrated with Geographers'. On a clear day he claimed that you could see seven counties, as well as the cities of Gloucester, Bristol, Worcester and Hereford. For Habington, the authority of the Beauchamp earls of Warwick was symbolised by their chase, situated on the commanding heights of the Malvern hills. Erdeswicke described Blythbury as being 'on a good rough steep hill' and regretted that the gentry family resident there had moved their seat to the kinder environment of the valley. St Michael's Mount in Cornwall 'looketh so aloft, as it brooketh no concurrent, for the highest place' and was a place of religious and strategic significance. Carew described the approach to the mount and the garrison and chapel there. Having ascended the mount, the visitor was faced with 'a bad seat in a craggy place', known as St Michael's chair, 'somewhat dangerous of accesse, and therefore holy for the adventure'. As Carew was one of the more active of the early local historians, he presumably clambered up to this high point rather than admiring it from below.[30]

It has been suggested that the early modern mind regarded mountains as bleak and barren, and that the cursory treatment of hills through their pictorial representation by 'mole-hills' in the maps of the period reveals a lack of interest. It is true that Erdeswicke described the uplands of north-eastern Staffordshire as 'a cold wild country', where no gentleman would choose to seat himself. In contrast, Smyth described the village of Nibley as 'not more pleasantly seated on a comely hill then a healthfull, then which none in the county or scarce in the kingdome standeth in sweeter aire'.[31] In coastal counties in particular the beacons were important features, and consequently drew the attention of local historians such as Lambarde and Carew. Habington described the Malvern hills in some of the vivid descriptive prose, which occasionally brings his work to life and suggests a real interest in the subject:

> beinge of themsealves highe, yet seeme higher because they rise out of a deep vale wheare the river Severn increasing fyrst by Teme and then by Avon makethe a watry waye towards the Seas. Thease, holly scituated on the southsyde of our Country, doe with theyre steepe backe lyke the rydge of a house bound in some places from Herefordshyre. They mounte about Malvern itselfe in high rockes, leavinge in fore-passed ages underneathe a world of trees, overshadowinge bushy thicketts.[32]

It was extremely difficult to portray relief accurately until contour-lines were invented in the eighteenth century, and the effective treatment of local relief did not develop until the nineteenth century. The simplistic representation of hills on the early maps seems to have been due to lack of technique rather than lack of interest.

The clearest deficiency of the early county maps to modern eyes is the lack of roads. Similarly, local historians make little mention of the roads running between the various towns and villages they record. Roman roads were habitually mentioned, but as links with the classical past rather than as arteries of communication. By contrast, tables containing information about roads did appear in works such as Grafton's *Abridgement of the Chronicles of England* (1570) and Stow's *Summary of the Chronicles of England* (1575). The reason for the neglect of roads by cartographers and local historians was presumably cultural. As some of the most dedicated travellers of the period, these were precisely the people who could have provided accurate and detailed information about local roads. The collection of church notes by local historians and their visits to each other and to their neighbours required them to become intimately acquainted with the routes of roads and the state of their upkeep.

Their correspondence provides a rich source for the state of local roads. For example, in February 1629 Burton sent Archer detailed instructions on how to reach Lindley. The next month he promised to visit Archer himself, 'when the ways shall growe fairer (for that I am a bad traveller)'. Two months later he was still deterred from travelling by the foul weather, which made the woodland roads unpleasant. This close acquaintance did not persuade the majority of antiquaries that roads were a fit subject for inclusion in local histories – rather the reverse, since the poor state of many roads did not reflect well on a locality. Roads did appear on the maps included by Norden in his county histories. This seems to reflect Norden's background as an estate surveyor, which gave him a different, more practical perspective compared with the majority of local historians. Norden may also have included the roads on his maps because this information was useful to the central government, whom he attempted to interest in his project.[33]

Although the Romantic worship of the natural world would have been completely alien to the seventeenth-century mind, hills, rivers and other natural phenomena did have a special significance as the work of the Creator. Roads, on the other hand, were not part of God's Creation. Nor did they have identifiable founders, builders or owners, like houses, parks and parish churches. To include roads on county maps would, therefore, neither have drawn attention to the glory of God, nor enhanced the prestige of any individual, family or corporate body. This interpretation of the reason for their neglect by local historians is supported by the nature of the few references to roads (apart from those built by the Romans) that do occur. Habington's description of the road running through the village of Broadway, for example, provided no useful information for the traveller. Instead, it used the road to point out the features of the countryside, particularly those aspects of the landscape where God had favoured Worcestershire. The road was 'the Broad and highe waye from the Shepherdes' coates, which on the mounted woldes shelter themsealfes under the hylles from the rage of stormes downe to the fruytfull vale of Evesham, or rather of England'.[34]

The absence of roads from maps, and the use of rivers for navigation in topographical works might suggest that travel by water was more common than by land in the late sixteenth century. Outside London, however, rivers were rarely used for passenger transport. The use of rivers by topographers derived from their symbolic significance as primordial arteries, which had flowed through the countryside since the time before it was populated by Man. Although roads were omitted, contemporary maps do bear witness to the importance of land transport by their inclusion of bridges. The gentry were frequently involved in disputes over responsibility for the upkeep of bridges, and this issue became particularly acute in the aftermath of the destruction caused by the civil war. The accounts of medieval lawsuits concerning responsibility for bridges, included in the *Antiquities of Warwickshire*, accordingly had contemporary significance.

The arrangement of topographical works by following the route of rivers began with Leland's *Cantio Cygnea* and was promoted by Camden in *Britannia*. As we saw in chapter one, Erdeswicke, in a letter to Camden attached to a copy of his work, acknowledged that he had chosen to follow the rivers in direct imitation of *Britannia*. Michael Drayton adopted the same method for *Poly-Olbion*, which was subtitled 'A Chorographicall Description of Tracts, Rivers, Mountaines, Forests and other Parts of this renowned Isle of Great Britaine'. It was the works of God, not the temporary constructions of Man, that were Drayton's concern in his chorography.[35] By the early seventeenth century the use of the rivers to provide navigation within a topographical work was an established convention. The use of Camden as a model for the structure of a manuscript history was not always preserved by subsequent copyists or editors, but can often be inferred by features in the text. The original of John Denton's account of Cumberland has, for example, been lost, and William Gilpin, the recorder of Carlisle who copied it in the late seventeenth century, admitted to reordering the manors and townships into their respective baronies. Denton's use of the rivers to navigate his subject is, however, suggested by evidence such as the start of the account of Thwaites: 'Thence along down the river of Dudden stands the manor of Thwaites'. In 1622 Burton chose to arrange the *Description of Leicestershire* alphabetically, but clearly came under pressure to change this for the revised edition. He justified his persistence with the alphabetical order: 'because the Rivers and Brookes in this Country are few and the Townes many and that I should be forced theerby to a greate Landlopeing'. Thomas Philipot justified the alphabetical order of his *Villare Cantianum* on the pragmatic grounds that it removed the need for an index. The practical difficulties of navigating by the rivers in a detailed study, as suggested by Burton, led to modifications of the approach by local historians, but there was no wholesale abandonment in favour of the alphabetical and the idea of the journey remained important. In his account of Devon, Risdon wrote:

> many waies might be used, as taking the hundreds or Tithings for my guydes; by the Course of its Rivers, or by the Archdeaconryes as they are lymitted: But ... I purpose my setting forwardes in the East parte of the County and with the Sun to make my gradation into the South houlding course about the River Tamar ... And lastly take notice of such memorable thinges as the Northe parte affoard.

The influence of Camden and Drayton was reinforced by Dugdale's decision to arrange the *Antiquities of Warwickshire* according to the rivers and the Roman roads. In this he echoed the development within county maps, which began to show Roman roads long before modern highways were included. Although the Roman roads were still important for travellers in the seventeenth century, their inclusion was not on practical grounds. Such roads were significant because they provided a link with the country's classical past. Dugdale was particularly fortunate in this respect, as Warwickshire was crossed by no fewer than three of the great Roman roads: Watling Street, the Fosse Way and Icknield Street.[36]

Although there was a close relationship between the county maps produced in this period and the verbal descriptions of local historians, there were important differences. The scale of the county maps and their lack of sophistication in symbolic representation meant that the amount of information they could meaningfully portray was limited. The antiquaries had far greater freedom of expression, and they were able to notice details of the local topography which were beyond the scale of the cartographer. The use of verbal descriptions also allowed local historians to speculate about the origin of certain landscape features, such as tumuli and the remains of ancient hilltop forts. The cartographers included well-known archaeological sites, but their treatment was uncertain. The red horse of Tysoe, Warwickshire, was mentioned by Camden in the 1607 edition of *Britannia* and described by Dugdale as 'the proportion of a Horse in a very large forme; which, by reason of the ruddy colour of the earth, is called the Red Horse, and giveth denomination to that fruitfull and pleasant Countrey thereabouts, commonly called the Vale of the Red Horse'. The red horse appeared among the allegorical figures adorning the maps accompanying Drayton's *Poly-Olbion*, but does not feature on the more conventional maps of the period. Stonehenge was a monument of such significance that it attracted the attention of cartographers and antiquaries alike. John Speed noted its location at Amesbury on his map of Wiltshire, included a drawing in one corner and gave a brief account of its origins based on Geoffrey of Monmouth in a panel below. This material was so important to him that it dominates one-third of the space devoted to the county. Aubrey, the Wilshire antiquary, was less impressed by Stonehenge than by Avebury, which 'does as much exceed in greatness the so renowned Stoneheng, as a Cathedral doeth a parish church'. Camden used the similarity of the two sites to dismiss the idea that Stonehenge had been magically transported from Ireland by Merlin. Yet Avebury did not appear on Speed's map. Camden also thought Stonehenge was too irregular to be Roman work, although Inigo Jones idealised it as a piece of classical architecture. Although his *Stonehenge Restored* (1655) is the work of an artist, not a local historian, it does serve to demonstrate the greater scope antiquarian writers enjoyed in exploring and celebrating such monuments. The visual language of the cartographers was inevitably more limited than the verbal language of the topographers – and Speed's map of Wiltshire shows the frustrations of this limitation.[37]

In the introduction to the *Antiquities of Warwickshire*, Dugdale wrote that Henry VIII's dissolution of the monasteries 'gave the greatest blow to

Antiquities that ever England had, by the destruction and spoil of many rare Manuscripts, and no small number of famous Monuments'. The religious changes of the sixteenth century, by providing incontrovertible evidence of the mutability of human institutions, undoubtedly helped to stimulate the development of a more acute historical sense. The extent to which the ruins of monastic buildings contributed to this is more difficult to gauge. In the preface to *Britannia*, William Camden described the grief and curiosity that monastic ruins evoked in him when young. The link between anxiety about the loss of the material culture of pre-Reformation England and the growth of anti-quarianism has recently been reiterated. Yet, the neatness of this conjunction requires us to question it critically. The dissolution of the monasteries and the iconoclasm of the early Reformation provide a convenient, immediate explanation for the growth of antiquarianism – but, as we have seen, there were many other factors at work, including the increased education of the gentry, their greater mobility and access to documentary evidence. To the newly educated gentry the Dissolution could be equated with the barbarian assault on Rome – both were destructive events marking the end of an era and leaving visible monuments to later ages. Dugdale drew on this parallel, writing of the 'barbarous generation' responsible for the destruction of the monasteries. Other local historians presented a more positive interpretation of the Dissolution as a cleansing fire. Contemplating the destruction of the religious houses in Canterbury, Lambarde was able to 'pitie and lament this generall decay, not onely in this Shyre, but in all other places of the Realme also', while at the same time:

> considering the maine Seas of sinne and iniquitie, wherein the worlde (at those daies) was almost wholy drenched, I must needes take cause, highly to praise God that hath thus mercifully in our age delivered us, disclosed Satan, unmasked these Idoles, dissolved their Synagogs, and raced to the grounde all monuments of building erected to superstition, and ungodlynesse.

Since the Dissolution provided such a convenient explanation for the urban and rural decline that they observed, there was no incentive for local histo-rians to seek other, less immediately obvious, explanations. So the economic problems in towns and cities such as Canterbury, Coventry and Leicester were attributed to this one cataclysmic event. The loss of pilgrims and of the charitable activities of the monasteries provided a convenient explanation for economic decline. The ruins thus contributed to nostalgia for the past, rather than to the growth of historical understanding.[38]

Visible scars had been left on the urban and rural landscape by the Dissolu-tion, but the physical ruins attracted comparatively little interest – except as symbols of decline. The early modern mind did not regard ruins as picturesque as later generations were to do, but considered them eyesores which 'deformed' the landscape. Smyth celebrated the removal of the remaining stones of a local priory to provide building material for Berkeley castle, replacing the ruins with 'plaine and fruitfull meadowe ground'. The fate of formerly religious sites clearly generated conflicting reactions. For example, Habington praised the Elizabethan bishop of Worcester, who had the suppressed chapel of Wyke razed to the ground, 'least any parte thereof should bee left to be wickedly despised or deformed with ruines'. Yet, elsewhere he described how Cleve-lode, formerly a chapelry within the parish of Madresfield, 'complaynethe of her mother who suffered her Chapell to vanishe awaye, her bowells rent upp and dedicated to the Idoll Ceres'. The constant opinion, however, was that ruins were undesirable eyesores. In the 1640s lord Herbert of Cherbury visited Tintern Abbey, which was subsequently to become one of the most celebrated of Romantic ruins. Herbert, however, visited the spot specifically to inspect the tomb of one of his ancestors, which he found 'wholly defaced and ruined'. This was no sightseeing trip to view picturesque ruins. Similarly, Weever recorded that the curious went to the site of the Augustinian abbey of Lasnes, Kent, to examine coffins that had been found there. Monastic ruins were interesting for the tombs and heraldic carvings they contained, but not yet as sites in their own right. In this respect they differed little from the parish churches that local historians visited to collect their church notes – many of these churches being themselves in a sorry state of decay.[39]

The gentry had, of course, been the primary beneficiaries of the release of land represented by the dissolution of the monasteries, and their attitude to the event was coloured by this. Even catholic antiquaries had to face the reality that their families and friends had acquired monastic property. Where buildings had continued to some extent to serve the same purpose, this could be presented as an expression of continuity. Hence, Sir Thomas Shirley described his ancestor's acquisition of the priory church at Breedon as a means of preserving the sanctity of the building:

> And all the places of Sepulture, for this religious and devoute Stocke of Shirley being profaned by the Lamentable demolition of the Religious Howses in England, hee purchased the Priorie Churche of Bredon of kinge Henry the Eighte, after the Suppression, for a Buriall place for himselfe and all his Successours forever.

The reuse of material from monastic buildings that had been partly demolished by Henry VIII's commissioners and allowed to decay thereafter could be interpreted as a positive act of improving the environment. Hence, the 'old fabrick' of the church and monastic buildings at Arbury, Warwickshire. was demolished in Elizabeth's reign and there was 'built out of their ruins a very fair structure'. Similarly, in Dorset a 'faire Mansion House' belonging to Sir John Strangewayes had replaced the monastic ruins at Abbotsbury. What was regarded as beyond the pale was the removal of materials from a sound building, leaving a ruin in its wake. Hence, in Newcastle upon Tyne a monastic building was initially turned into a magazine, but, after the accession of James

I, was 'begged of a Scot'. He sold the lead from the roof and some of the stone and timber, 'so that this stately fabrick is almost wasted and only a receptikle to birds of prey'. With satisfaction Grey recorded that the lead thus sold sank during transportation, which 'has been the end of many sacrilegious purloined goods, transported by sea'. The sacrilege here seems to be that of destroying a building that the town found useful rather than having a necessarily religious connotation, since Grey was a protestant who described the Dissolution as the result of the 'pride, covetousnesse, luxury and idolatry of these clergy'. The association of this trespass against the community with a Scot suggests that the local and national resonances of this event were stronger than the religious.[40]

The reaction of the English gentry to the ruined monuments to Henry VIII's dissolution of the monasteries was far more complex than simple nostalgia – and in the closing years of the period covered by this study it was complicated by their reaction to the destruction caused by the civil war. Dugdale's fulminations against Henry VIII's commissioners have to be considered in the light of the very few references to the damage caused by the rival parliamentarian and royalist armies. Sublimation seems to have been as important a factor in Dugdale's attitude to mid-Tudor events as nostalgia.

An outstanding feature of local historians' representation of their world was the importance of the country's Roman past. As we saw in chapter two, the emphasis of the education system made works of classical history more familiar to many gentlemen than the English chronicles. When Dugdale wished to draw attention to the scholarly nature of his work, he chose to compare it with classical histories. He described his extensive use of public and private records as 'imitating Polybius, Livie, Suetonius and Tacitus, who made speciall use of the publique Records of Rome'. Each of these authors would have been familiar to Dugdale's gentry readership. By invoking them at the start of his work, Dugdale was implicitly associating Warwickshire with this classical inheritance. Similarly, William Grey linked his work to both classical and national historians: 'Greece had his Homer. Rome his Virgil. Our Britons had their Gildas. Saxons had their Beda. England had of late his learned Camden, and painfull Speed' – so Newcastle was to have its Grey.[41]

Although each edition of Camden's *Britannia* included more Anglo-Saxon and medieval material, it remained a monument to the importance of the country's Roman past to the educated elite of England. It was a matter of national and local pride to rescue remnants of classical civilisation from the obscurity into which time had cast them. In 1599 Camden visited Cumberland with Sir Robert Cotton, where they encountered John Senhouse of Netherhall, who had been collecting altars, statues and inscribed stones found on his land for some twenty years and using them to decorate his house and garden. Senhouse was a man who believed in education – his third son was sent to

Oxford and entered the church, ending up as bishop of Carlisle – and it was the classical education they received that encouraged 'well learned' members of the gentry to appreciate the value of Roman artefacts. As Camden remarked in *Britannia*, the known interest of men like Senhouse in such objects meant that they were brought to his notice by the 'unskilful and unlettered' men who found them, and were preserved rather than being broken up and reused as building stone or rubble. It seems that Camden's work could also be used almost like a catalogue to locate portable Roman remains. In 1607 Nicholas Roscarrock, the Cornish writer of saint's lives who lived with lord William Howard at Naworth Castle, wrote to Camden to correct a description of a stone which Camden had seen at Thoresby and described in *Britannia*. Howard 'hath it now with a great many more in his garden-wall at Naworth, where he would be glad to see you to read them'. Cotton's library included not only an invaluable collection of manuscripts, but also artefacts such as Roman coins and inscriptions, many of which were acquired on trips such as that he took with Camden. He was also a friend of Howard, who informed him in 1608 that he had located 'at least 12 stones, most of them faire inscriptions that you have not yett heard of'. The notes of Roman inscriptions supplied by Reginald Bainbrigg of Appleby to Camden also found their way into Cotton's collection. In turn Cotton provided Speed with four illustrations of Roman altars to adorn his map of Northumberland. Burton was himself a collector of Roman coins, and in 1607 he went to inspect a hoard found buried beneath Watling Street – the day after the news of the find reached him.[42]

The paucity of literary evidence concerning the Roman occupation of Britain enhanced the importance of physical remains. Only John Stow writing his *Survey of London* had the benefit of significant written sources to aid his description of the locality's early history. The significant Roman remains at Leicester, which included a temple dedicated to Janus and a bath-house, enhanced the city's prestige for Burton and by association that of the whole county. They also encouraged him to relate all the evidence of early occupation of Leicestershire to the Roman period. Similarly, the vicinity of the Roman station at Manceter led Dugdale to assume that the iron-age fort at Oldbury originated from the same period, and its proximity to Dorchester supported Gerard's assumption that Maiden castle was originally a Roman summer camp.[43] Dugdale associated the finding of prepared flints at the Oldbury site with the weapons of the 'native Britains', but did not recognise this as evidence that they had built the fort. Part of the reason for the almost invariable ascription of antiquities to the Roman period was surely that there was some literary evidence to support it. The dismissal of Geoffrey of Monmouth's British history had left a vacuum, which antiquarian ingenuity had not yet filled with Celts and Druids. The Romans were at least known to have existed, and had produced the earliest written accounts available to local historians. It was the Roman historians who were predominantly used to demolish Geoffrey by men such as John Twyne, who supplemented the written accounts with archaeological evidence from surviving buildings, coins, inscriptions and tombs. Twyne, a contemporary of Leland's and one of the distinguished line of Kentish antiquaries, also made use of topographical observations when producing a theory of Britain's earliest settlement – about which the Roman sources were silent. The authority of Camden also influenced local historians. If Camden said that sites such as Oldbury, Maiden Castle and the hill-fort at Cadbury, Somerset, were of Roman origin, local historians would require significant evidence before they would contradict him.[44]

The Roman sources provided a starting point for understanding local landmarks, but they were not accepted blindly. In the mid-seventeenth century the assumption then current was that ancient tumuli covered the mass burials of Romans – or possibly Danes – who had fallen in battle. This theory was advanced by Camden and Weever, based predominantly on the evidence of Tacitus, but it was not universally accepted. In a letter to Dugdale the herald Edward Bysshe wrote: 'I meete not with any thing that comes any way home to your demand concerning the burying of Soldiers in the field. What you meete with in Mr Camden and Weaver, is more then any thing I can yet find will justifie.'

Despite Bysshe's doubts, Dugdale repeated the accepted theory in the *Antiquities of Warwickshire*: 'That these Lowes, or artifically raised heaps of Earth, were antiently made to cover the Bodies of such as were slain in the field, in the time of the Romans, we have the testimony of Tacitus'. At this point Dugdale's evidence was predominantly literary and he had undertaken little fieldwork. However, he was clearly not content to leave the matter there. Dr Thomas Browne suggested in his correspondence with Dugdale, begun in 1658, that the only way to discover the true origins of tumuli was the practical experiment 'of subterraneous enquiry by cutting through one of them either directly or cross-wise'. Dugdale had earlier reached the same conclusion. In 1653, while working on the earl of Denbigh's pedigree, he sought to persuade him to have a tumulus at Monk's Kirby 'to be dig'd downe to the levell earth'. At the bottom of the tumulus he expected there to be 'some Urnes, or at least bones and coles'. Monk's Kirby was a significant location, since Dugdale's kinsman Samuel Roper had already found the remains of walls and Roman bricks by excavating on his own land there. Excavation was not, of course, a foolproof method of discovering the truth. On the Isle of Wight the antiquary Sir John Oglander undertook excavations of barrows and concluded that the remains were indeed Roman. It was, however, a practical approach, and it might seem strange that local historians were generally slow to follow Oglander's example. This may have been due in part to a lack of inclination or skill or to problems of land ownership. Dugdale's ability to investigate the tumuli at Monk's Kirby was dependent upon the earl of Denbigh – presumably none were located on Roper's land there. While working on the *History of Embanking and Draining* (1662), Dugdale learnt from the mathematician and surveyor Jonas Moore that some urn burials had been found at Soham, Cambs., although not in association with a tumulus. Since the landowner was Dugdale's 'very good friend' he resolved to ask that further excavations be conducted, but he was in a position only to suggest and not to initiate such archaeological fieldwork. Perhaps equally significant in discouraging excavation was the way in which barrow-digging in the Tudor period had become associated with treasure hunters. To disturb Roman graves was presumably as reprehensible to many antiquaries as stripping the brass off medieval tombs, a practice described by Weever as an 'inhumane, deformidable act'. Nevertheless, there were clearly attempts to instigate archaeological excavations in a systematic manner to answer specific questions among local historians in the 1650s, showing that they were influenced by the developments in scientific investigation which led to the formation of the Royal Society.[45]

Local historians did not ascribe all earthworks to the Roman period – but it was generally assumed that the ancient Britons had left no monuments. So, if an earthwork was not considered Roman because of its irregularity or the lack of supporting finds such as inscribed stones or coins, it might be interpreted as Danish, Saxon or even later in origin. For example, Smyth ascribed a medieval origin to two iron-age hill-forts within the hundred of Berkeley. One was known as 'Beckets-burie', suggesting the fortification resulted from the conflict between Henry II and his archbishop. Nearby Uley Bury was reputedly the work of Earl Godwyn.[46] The peripheral situation of the vale of Berkeley in Roman Britain made the Romans unlikely builders of extensive fortifications there. Earl Godwyn on the other hand was associated with Berkeley through the scandalous stories of the twelfth-century historian Walter Map. As predominantly the historian of a family reputed to have arrived in the country at the Conquest, Smyth was less interested in the Roman past than many of his fellow antiquaries.

The importance of physical remains in supplementing literary evidence encouraged local historians to carry out their own observations and elementary archaeological investigations of local sites. Although on the whole they did not excavate, they conducted careful surveys. In his *View of Staffordshire*, Erdeswicke described a hill-fort, to which the name Borough was attached, suggesting that it was the site of an ancient town. The surviving remnant of his history of Cheshire contains a detailed description of the thirteenth-century Beeston castle. One of the earliest of Archer's letters on antiquarian matters includes a description of an earthwork at Cheswick in Tanworth parish. Although Camden did carry out his own fieldwork, his identification of places mentioned in the Antonine Itineraries was often based on literary evidence, reported finds and maps. One such identification was between the Antonine Vernometum and Burrough in Leicestershire. This was subsequently confirmed by Burton's fieldwork. He surveyed the site and concluded:

> (that which maketh most for the proofe) in that very place there riseth up an Hill, with a steepe and upright ascent on every side but South eastward; in the top whereof appeare the expresse tokens of a Towne destroyed, a double trench, and the very tract where the wals went, which inclosed about 18. Acres within.

In the first edition of *Britannia*, Camden had associated the Roman station of Ratae with Ratby, Leics., but had in later editions altered this opinion to identify Ratae with Leicester. In 1622 Burton accepted Camden's revised opinion, but following his own investigation of the area around Ratby he decided that this was indeed the site of the Roman station. On a commanding area of high ground covering around a hundred acres at Ratby, from where you could observe the Antonine site at Burrough, he found trenches and ramparts indicating the existence of an oblong fort of around six acres. In his revised text he asserted that an actual visit to the site would have persuaded Camden to agree that Ratby was indeed Ratae.[47]

Local historians also took advantage of the occasional opportunities for archaeological fieldwork created by agricultural and building work. As a comparatively young man in Elizabeth's reign, Habington observed a stone coffin, which was found in a Worcestershire field during ploughing. Half a century later he described the coffin and its contents in some detail and conjectured that its occupant had been an important Dane. This he based on his observation that the coffin was laid north–south, suggesting a non-Christian burial, and on the local earthworks, which he interpreted as the remains of 'warlike fortifications'. His conjecture was supported by his researches into local place-names, which suggested that the Danes had maintained winter quarters in the area. The Little Crosby hoard of Anglo-Saxon coins, which Daniel Woolf has written about extensively, was found by a sharp-eyed boy, who was driving cattle across the edge of the Catholic burial ground. He spotted a coin lying on the surface of ground, which had been disturbed by a recent burial. (William Blundell was concerned to insist upon the coins being visible on the surface and to involve only his own household in their collection, so that they would not count as treasure trove belonging to the king.) When unusually dark earth was spotted, while digging for marl on Archer's land in Warwickshire, it was interpreted by some to be the site of a large mass grave. The finding of an iron spearhead and potsherds suggested to Dugdale that it might have been a significant Mercian settlement. Meanwhile, the 'old foundations of buildings, Roman Bricks, and coines' found in Alcester revealed the length of settlement there despite its absence from Domesday. In the 1630s one of William Somner's Kentish neighbours came across 'a strong and well couched arched piece of Roman Tile or Brick' while digging a cellar. Somner 'for curiosity sake' took one of the bricks to add to his collection of Roman remains, some of which he had found in his own garden.[48]

It is clear that the finding of archaeological remains aroused considerable interest both among local historians and the wider gentry community. Leland recorded that a brass pot full of Roman coins was found 'within living memory' in south-west Cornwall, while digging out a fox. Coins, intrinsically valuable for their metal content as well as of archaeological interest, were especially interesting to landowners when they were found on their land. In 1655 William Blundell informed his cousin James Scarisbrick of Scarisbrick, Lancs., then at St Omer, that 'Hugh Worthington, your tenant, hath found a few days since, in the ground about his home, divers scores of most ancient Roman pieces'. Blundell's antiquarian interest in the coins is evident from the way in which he described several of them, but there was also a question of property rights associated with such potentially valuable finds. Less intrinsically valuable archaeological finds also aroused interest. In 1608 Burton was told by 'a gentleman of our country' of a fourteenth-century coffin dug up at St Paul's, and wrote to the herald Nicholas Charles for details. Knowledge of such finds spread widely through the networks of antiquarian correspondence. When some unusual bones were found in a Worcestershire churchyard, Habington was able to compare them to a similar find made near Gloucester. Thomas Philipot, describing a collection of Roman funeral urns in Newington, Kent, could relate them to similar, recent finds at Coggeshall, Essex and at Bath. The general interest in such relics of the past is evidenced by Smyth's report that what was presumably a mammoth's tooth had in the sixteenth century been displayed by the Bassett family in the parlour window of their manor house. Smyth had heard this story from a variety of sources, although the identification of the tooth as human led the antiquary to doubt the reliability of his information. Weever recorded the finding of a corpse filled with lead at Newport Pagnell in 1619. Some of the bones were kept in the church 'there to be shown to strangers as reliques of admiration'. The remainder were taken away 'by Gentlemen neare dwellers, or such as take delight in rare Antiquities'.[49]

Renaissance humanism had been largely concerned with the rediscovery of Greek and Latin scholarship from newly found or reinterpreted manuscripts. It was natural that the successors of the early humanists should endeavour to understand the physical remains that they found by reference to those texts. It was having read Vitruvius that enabled Burton to recognise a Roman bathhouse when he saw one. It was not that local historians were blind to the possibility of a non-Roman origin of physical remains. As pioneers in archaeological examination, it was difficult for them to interpret physical remains in the absence of literary evidence. Moreover, it was the importance of the country's Roman past to the educated gentry which encouraged much of the antiquarian investigation of their physical surroundings.[50]

None of the surviving itineraries of John Leland cover Norfolk, but among his notes was a reference to information provided by Sir John Dickon concerning the excavation of cremated human remains in earthenware pots at Kenninghall, Norfolk. The coincidence of the site with the location of the duke of Norfolk's new house suggests that the find occurred as part of the building work. While Roman coins and pottery were frequently ploughed up in fields, it was building works and the digging of clay for brick-making that led to the most extensive archaeological finds. The Roman cemetery at Spitalfields described by John Stow in the *Survey of London*, for example, was found when the land was used as a brick-field.[51] In Norfolk, which experienced a Tudor and early Stuart building boom and had an established tradition of brick-making in addition to a history of extensive human habitation from neolithic times, the circumstances were particularly favourable for the stimulation of archaeological interest through the accidental discovery of remains.

As a consequence of *Hydriotaphia*, Thomas Browne's treatise on urn burial, and his later 'Concerning some urnes found in Brampton-field in Norfolk, Anno 1667',[52] we are well informed about the early history of archaeology in Norfolk. The treatise was occasioned by the digging up of around fifty funerary urns in a field in Old Walsingham. The urns were found in a dry, sandy soil within three feet of the surface and close together. Browne, who was well known for his interest in natural history and antiquities and who had a cabinet of curiosities in his Norwich home, was sent a sample of the find by a friend. Near the same spot was found an area of around six square yards where charcoal and other evidence of burning was found, leading Browne to conjecture that this was the site of the funerary pyres. The proximity of the site to the Roman fortification at Brancaster led Browne to suspect that the remains were Roman, although there were no coins within the urns to confirm this as there had been at Spitalfields. Through his account of the evidence for cremation among the ancient Britons, Germans and Danes we gain a greater understanding of why antiquaries were so ready to ascribe archaeological finds to the Romans. The extensive literary evidence left by the Romans, combined with the hoards of coins and identifiable remains at known Roman sites such as Brancaster, provided a solid foundation for research. In an age when scientific evaluation of archaeological finds was in its infancy, the meagre evidence concerning the early inhabitants of Britain meant that antiquaries could do little more than speculate about their culture and customs. The cache of urns found in Brampton, near Sir Robert Paston's house at Oxnead, were undoubtedly Roman, as confirmed by the inscriptions found on several and the coins included among their contents. If this later find led Browne to reconsider his belief that the Walsingham urns were Roman, he does not mention it.

The Kenninghall and Walsingham urns were not the only such finds that emerged in Norfolk. There had been other urns discovered at Caistor and at South Creake, while ten had been found on land belonging to Robert Jegon at Buxton. This last find was, as Browne noted, not near any recorded garrison, although he tended to the view that the urns were in themselves likely evidence of Roman occupation of the site. Some of the finds from Buxton were preserved by Sir William Paston, who was well known locally for his interest in antiquities. After the cache of urns at Brampton (described by Browne in his 1667 account) was discovered, Paston's son and heir Sir Robert organised the digging of part of his park which adjoined the site. The results, as described by Browne, were disappointing, as it seemed that the stratification of the site had been disturbed by earlier digging. This dig is one of the earliest deliberate exploratory excavations in the history of archaeology. It is significant that its instigator was a member of the Royal Society; the systematic choice of site is indicative of the development of an increasingly scientific approach to antiquities after the Restoration.

As an antiquary, Browne stands at the crossroads between the study-bound scholar described by Robert Burton, seeking answers among the 'rubbish of old writers' and the new experimental natural scientists, imbued with the spirit of Francis Bacon.[53] These diverging approaches can be seen in Browne's two works on urn burials, which were written about a decade apart. *Hydrotaphia* includes some short descriptions of the finds. It also mentions how they determined that certain items were made of bone or ivory rather than wood, as they sank in water and would not burn. The bones were examined sufficiently to determine that there was no evidence of a single urn containing more than one cremated body. The vast majority of the text is, however, concerned with literary sources and placing the Walsingham urns within a cultural context. By contrast, the Brampton account contained a far more systematic and detailed description of the urns, their location, appearance and contents. A similar development of scientific method may be seen in Somner's *Chartham News* (1669), a posthumously printed pamphlet recording the finding of bones during the excavation of a well. Somner's account of what he identified as the remains of a hippopotamus combined physical description with careful topographical observation. In the *Pseudodoxia Epidemica*, Browne had criticised those scholars who preferred to believe what they read rather than troubling themselves to leave their studies and make their own observations. As we have seen from William Worcestre in the fifteenth century, there had been local historians who did go and see, make measurements and even dig in the search of knowledge. In Browne we have the beginning of a more scientific approach not just to going and seeing, but to recording and interpreting.

As we have seen, in 1642 Burton replaced a detailed account of Leicestershire's topography intended for his second edition with a description of rural pastimes. The most important of the 'Pleasures & Divertisments' Leicestershire provided were according to Burton 'Hunting & Hawking the usuall recreations of the Country Gentlemen'. This change to Burton's original intentions is indicative of how he perceived his readership as attaching importance to these pastimes. The topography that the local gentry were predominantly interested in was that which pertained to their own interests. Hence the inclusion of deer parks on the county maps of the period, features which represented an important visual symbol of a county's wealth and the status of its leading gentry. When we examine Speed's map of Leicestershire, Burton's description of the well-stocked parks of the county becomes yet more significant. All but one of the parks shown are within two hundreds in the west of the county. In comparison with its neighbours, Leicestershire was poorly supplied with deer parks. This was to some extent acknowledged by Burton, who castigated the 'frugality' of those owners who had converted deer parks to other uses. Yet the honour of Leicestershire was upheld by the 'Noble Proprietors' of the parks at Ashby, Donington, Gerondon, Bradgate and Bagworth, who 'amply stored' their parks with red and fallow deer.[54] By this assertion, Burton attempted to rectify the impression conveyed by the maps that Leicestershire was not a good county for hunting. It is impossible to separate the topographical interests of Elizabethan and early Stuart local historians from their sense of local pride. They were never purely objective observers of the world around them. The features included on county maps and described in the histories reflected the gentry's concern with their own status and with the history of their own and related families. Hence the inclusion of gentry houses, parish churches, deer parks and medieval battlefields. The humanist education received by the majority of the gentry led to an interest in classical antiquity, and so the visible remains of the Roman past were also included. Hills and rivers found a place as significant features of God's Creation. The non-Roman roads had no founders, no association with particular families and were not part of the landscape created by God. If county maps and local histories had been created for purely practical reasons, the roads would have been included. Their exclusion indicates the cultural preoccupations of the cartographers and topographers and the interests of their gentry readership.

Local historians in the period covered by this study were the products of a culture which valued literary evidence above the physical, and their observation of the world was shaped by the assumptions they derived from that literary evidence. The classical emphasis of gentry education and the survival of literary evidence relating to the Roman past led local historians to misinterpret the physical remains they examined. The disinterested study of nature, science and antiquities was to be the work of later generations. Nevertheless, the origins of this development may be seen in the way in which local historians began to carefully observe, measure and describe archaeological remains. They brought to the examination of archaeological sites the meticulous care which they devoted to the study of heraldic glass and monuments.

They were among those that laid the foundations of what was to develop into the scientific study of archaeological remains.

NOTES

1 Symonson was a surveyor at Rochester, whose map, on a scale of almost two inches to a mile, was used by Richard Kilburne to measure the location of parishes in his *Survey of Kent* (1659). The importance of the county as an abstract entity to the English gentry has been exhaustively explored: see C. Holmes, 'The county community in Stuart historiography', *The Journal of British Studies* 19 (1980), pp. 54–73.

2 V. Morgan, 'The cartographic image of "the country" in early modern England', *Transactions of the Royal Historical Society*, 5th Series 29 (1979), pp. 129–54; Cliffe, *The Yorkshire Gentry*, pp. 20–4.

3 Gerard, *Dorset*, p. 35; Carew, *Cornwall*, p. 138.

4 Compare the introductions of Staffs. C.R.O. D649/4/2, and Burton, *Revised*; Williams, 'William Burton's 1642 revised edition of the Description of Leicestershire', pp. 30–6.

5 M. Aston, 'English ruins and English history: the Dissolution and the ruins of the past', *Journal of the Warburg and Courtauld Institutes* 36 (1973), pp. 231–55.

6 Burton, *Leicestershire*, To the Reader; B. Gimson and P. Russell, *Leicestershire Maps* (Leicester: Edgar Backus, 1947), pp. 4–5.

7 Burton, *Leicestershire*, p. 43. Robert Burton is quoted in S. Piggott, *Ruins in a Landscape* (Edinburgh: Edinburgh University Press, 1976), p. 111.

8 D. Smith, *Antique Maps of the British Isles* (London: Batsford, 1982), p. 154; John Speed, *The Counties of Britain* (London: Pavilion, 1988), pp. 12, 149; Morgan, 'The cartographic image of "the country" in early modern England', p. 135; Mendyk, '*Speculum Britanniae*', pp. 60–1; Smyth, *Berkeley Mss*, vol. 2, p. 385.

9 Hamper, *Dugdale*, pp. 179–81, 185–6, 257–8, 287–9; Dugdale, *Warwickshire*, p. 425; Higford, *Institutions*, p. 99.

10 G. Tindall, *The Man Who Drew London* (London: Chatto & Windus, 2002); Hamper, *Dugdale*, p. 279; Dugdale, *Warwickshire*, preceding pp. 1, 3, 267, 487, 637.

11 S. Alpers, *The Art of Describing: Dutch Art in the Seventeenth Century* (London: John Murray, 1983), chapter 4; L.S. Marcus, 'Politics and pastoral: writing the court on the countryside', in K. Sharpe and P. Lake (eds), *Culture and Politics in Early Stuart England* (London: Macmillan, 1994), pp. 139–59; Burton, *Leicestershire*, p. 119; J. Hale, *The Civilization of Europe in the Renaissance* (London: HarperCollins, 1993), pp. 30–3.

12 For example, see the picture of Kenilworth castle c. 1620 in Mowl, *Elizabethan and Jacobean Style*, p. 74; Stone and Stone, *An Open Elite?*, plates IV–VIIB.

13 D. Smith, *Maps and Plans for the Local Historian and Collector* (London: Batsford, 1988), pp. 33, 89.

14 S.B.T., DR473/293, fos 1–8v; see also B.L., Lansdowne 860B, fo. 42v, Northants. C.R.O., FH84–7; Burton, *Leicestershire*, pp. 4–6.

15 Wrottesley, 'A History of the Bagot Family', p. 77; Morgan, 'The cartographic image of "the country" in early modern England', p. 138.

16 Sir Robert Atkyns, *Ancient and Present State of Gloucestershire* (1712 – reprinted Wakefield: EP Publishing, 1974) is significant for the inclusion of over sixty engravings of gentry houses by Johannes Kip, which provide a rich visual record not matched by the accompanying text.

17 Quoted in M. Airs, *The Tudor and Jacobean Country House* (Stroud: Alan Sutton, 1995), pp. 1, 23.

18 For the importance of building, see Airs, *The Tudor and Jacobean Country House*; C. Platt, *The Great Rebuildings of Tudor and Stuart England* (London: UCL Press, 1994).

19 Erdeswicke, *Staffordshire*, pp. 4, 175.

20 Birmingham University Library, misc/7/i/14, fo. 51; Dugdale, *Warwickshire*, p. 639, 767–8; Tyack, *The Making of the Warwickshire Country House 1500–1650*, pp. 61–6.

21 Erdeswicke, *Staffordshire*, pp. 68–70, 380–1, 483–7; M. Briggs, *Goths and Vandals* (London: Constable, 1952), pp. 46–9.

22 Erdeswicke, *Staffordshire*, pp. 514–5; Toulmin Smith, *The Itinerary of John Leland in or About the Years 1535–1543*, vol. 2, p. 168; Birmingham University Library, misc 7/i/14, fo. 51; Gerard, *Dorset*, pp. 124–5.

23 Briggs, *Goths and Vandals*, pp. 40–2; Carew, *Cornwall*, p. 138.

24 Smyth, *Berkeley Mss*, vol. 2, p. 370; vol. 3, p. 411; *Smyth Papers*, vol. 5, fo. 30; vol. 9, fo. 86; vol. 10, fos 67, 111.

25 Denton, *An Account of the Most Considerable Estates and Families in the County of Cumberland*, p. 9.

26 Erdeswicke, *Staffordshire*, pp. 336–7; Dugdale, *Warwickshire*, pp. 160–6, 343, 572; Tyack, *The Making of the Warwickshire Country House 1500–1650*, pp. 55–6.

27 Burton, *Leicestershire*, p. 119; College of Arms, Vincent 197, fo. 157v; Anon., *Charlecote Park* (London: The National Trust, 1995), pp. 11–13; R. Strong, *The Renaissance Garden in England* (London: Thames and Hudson, 1979). The Lucy portrait is also attributed to Johnson.

28 Dugdale, *Warwickshire*, p. 724; Tyack, 'The making of the Warwickshire country house', pp. 49–50; J. Thirsk, 'The fashioning of the Tudor–Stuart gentry', *Bulletin of the John Rylands University Library of Manchester* 72 (1990), pp. 69–85: pp. 79–80.

29 Habington, *Worcestershire*, p. 80; Hamper, *Dugdale*, p. 20.

30 Burton, *Revised*, Bardon Park; Burton, *Leicestershire*, pp. 28–9; Smyth, *Berkeley Mss*, vol. 3, p. 349; Habington, *Worcestershire*, vol. 2, p. 110; Erdeswicke, *Staffordshire*, p. 246; Carew, *Cornwall*, p. 154.

31 J.B. Hartley, 'Meaning and ambiguity in Tudor cartography', in S. Tyacke (ed.), *English Map Making 1500–1650* (London: The British Library, 1983), pp. 22–45; Erdeswicke, *Staffordshire*, pp. 479–80; Smyth, *Berkeley Mss*, vol. 3, p. 261.

32 Habington, *Worcestershire*, vol. 2, p. 110.

33 V.A. LaMar, *Travel and Roads in England* (Washington D.C.: Folger, 1960); Archer, *Correspondence*, fos 21, 26, 33; Mendyk, *'Speculum Britanniae'*, pp. 60–6.

34 Habington, *Worcestershire*, vol. 2, pp. 34–5.

35 S. Schama, *Landscape and Memory* (London: HarperCollins, 1995), pp. 320–32; Dugdale, *Warwickshire*, pp. 175, 179, 222, 225, 292; B.L., Harley 1990, fo. 10.

36 Denton, *Cumberland*, p. 14; D.J.W. Mawson, 'Another important copy of John Denton's manuscript', *Transactions of the Cumberland and Westmorland Antiquarian and Archaeological Society* 78 (1978), pp. 97–103; Burton, *Revised*, opening of The Second Book; Dugdale, *Warwickshire*, pp. 60–1, 142, 666, 784; B.L., Additional MS 36748.

37 P. Newman, *Gods and Graven Images* (London: Robert Hale, 1987), pp. 62–71; Dugdale, *Warwickshire*, p. 422; Woolf, *Social Circulation*, pp. 213–17.

38 O.D.N.B., C. DeCoursey, 'Society of Antiquaries (act. 1586–1607)'; Dugdale, *Warwickshire*, sig. b3v, p. 492; Lambarde, *Kent*, pp. 267–8.

39 Habington, *Worcestershire*, vol. 1, p. 166; vol. 2, p. 136; Dugdale, *Warwickshire*, p. 509; Smyth, *Berkeley Mss*, vol. 3, p. 259; I. Ousby, *The Englishman's England: Taste, Travel and the Rise of Tourism* (Cambridge: Cambridge University Press, 1990), p. 11; Weever, *Ancient Funerall Monuments*, p. 41.

40 B.L., Harley 4928, fos 99r–v; Dugdale, *Warwickshire*, p. 784; Gerard, *Dorset*, p. 31; W. Grey, *Chorographia* (Newcastle: F. Graham, 1970) – a facsimile of the 1883 edition (edited by Joseph Crawhall), including Grey's manuscript additions, pp. 52–3.

41 Dugdale, *Warwickshire*, p. b1; Grey, *Chorographia*, 'To the candid reader'.

42 Woolf, *Social Circulation*, pp. 224–5; A.L. Rowse, 'Nicholas Roscarrock and his Lives of the Saints', in J.H. Plumb (ed.), *Studies in Social History* (London: Longmans, Green & Co., 1955), pp. 14–6; G. Ormsby (ed.), *The Household Books of Lord William Howard of Naworth Castle* (Durham: Surtees Society 68, 1878), pp. 412, 469–87; Haverfield, 'Notes on Reginald Bainbrigg of Appleby, on William Camden and on some Roman inscriptions', pp. 343–78; Speed, *The Counties of Britain*, pp. 138–9; Burton, *Leicestershire*, pp. 131–3, 161.

43 Burton, *Leicestershire*, pp. 160–1; Dugdale, *Warwickshire*, p. 788; Gerard, *Dorset*, p. 72.

44 A.B. Ferguson, 'John Twyne: a Tudor humanist and the problem of legend', *Journal of British Studies* 9 (1969), pp. 24–44; Piggott, *Ruins in a Landscape*, pp. 55–76.

45 Dugdale, *Warwickshire*, pp. 3, 50; Hamper, *Dugdale*, pp. 232, 286–7; Camden, *Britannia*, p. 98; Weever, *Ancient Funerall Monuments*, 'To the Reader', p. 6; S. Piggott, *Ancient Britons and the Antiquarian Imagination*, p. 120; G. Keynes (ed.), *The Works of Sir Thomas Browne*, four volumes (London: Faber, 1964), vol. 3, pp. 84–7; vol. 4, pp. 302–27; Warwickshire C.R.O., Z65/4; Piggott, *Ruins in a Landscape*, pp. 13–14; K. Thomas, *Religion and the Decline of Magic* (London: Penguin, 1991), pp. 279–80; M. Hunter, *Science and the Shape of Orthodoxy* (Woodbridge, Suffolk: Boydell Press, 1995), pp. 181–200.

46 Smyth, *Berkeley Mss*, vol. 3, pp. 77, 193.

47 Erdeswicke, *Staffordshire*, pp. 116, 556–8; Archer, *Correspondence*, fo. IV; Burton, *Leicestershire*, p. 62; Burton, *Revised*, Ratby.

48 Habington, *Worcestershire*, vol. 1, pp. 135–6; Mendyk, *Speculum Britanniae*, p. 110; Woolf, 'Horizons of early modern historical culture' in Kelley and Sacks, *The Historical Imagination in Early Modern Britain*, pp. 95–7, 101, 103–6; Dugdale, *Warwickshire*, p. 568; W. Somner, *Chartham News* (London: T. Garthwait, 1669), p. 5.

49 Chandler, *John Leland's Itinerary*, p. 66; Gibson, *Crosby Records*, pp. 280–1; Warwickshire C.R.O., CR1598/1; Habington, *Worcestershire*, vol. 2, pp. 47–8; T. Philipot, *Villare Cantianum* (London, 1659), pp. 249–51; Smyth, *Berkeley Mss*, vol. 3, p. 193; Weever, *Ancient Funerall Monuments*, p. 30.

50 Burton, *Leicestershire*, p. 161; S. Piggott, *Ancient Britons and the Antiquarian Imagination* (London: Thames & Hudson, 1989), pp. 13–35.

51 Chandler, *John Leland's Itinerary*, p. 317; Stow, *London*, p. 152.

52 Browne, *Religio Medici*, pp. 92–148.

53 Burton is quoted in Piggott, *Ancient Britons and the Antiquarian Imagination*, p. 15; for Browne's relationship to Baconism, see Basil Willey, *The Seventeenth-Century Background* (London: Routledge & Kegan Paul, 1986), chapter 3.

54 Burton, *Revised, General Introduction*.

Conclusion

This study has attempted to show that within the wider context of early modern antiquarian writing there exists a miscellaneous collection of county, urban and family histories, topographical writings and other related works that justifies the use of the term local history. It is an anachronistic term to apply to this period, but I have tried to show how it is essential to understanding the full significance of the different works in these various sub-genres. The works considered here form part of the long continuum of the development of local history, as we understand the term today. Periodisation is the bane of historians and the definition of terms such as 'the gentry' is potentially controversial. Yet, I do believe that these works can be identified as articulating the concerns and preoccupations of the English gentry, from the generation who first received a grammar-school education after the Reformation, to those who completed their education before the outbreak of the English civil war. Historical periods are never precise, of course. John Leland has much in common with William Camden, and Robert Thoroton's *Antiquities of Nottinghamshire* (1677) has more in common with the *Antiquities of Warwickshire* than with later works. Yet, there is something sufficiently distinctive about the century preceding 1660 to merit the attention that it has received here.

There were a number of factors that came together in the mid-sixteenth century to challenge the gentry's sense of cohesion and continuity. The most dramatic was the Reformation, which divided the contemporary gentry into protestants and catholics and separated the protestants from the religious beliefs and practices of earlier generations. The dissolution of the monasteries released a vast amount of land on to the market and created a fluidity in land ownership which disrupted traditional patterns and introduced new entrants into the provincial gentry. The abolition of enforced celibacy led to the creation of clerical dynasties, which also changed the complexion of provincial society. At the same time the increasing use of the gentry in the civil administration of the country brought them into more regular and direct contact with central government. In contrast the traditional military role of the gentry declined as the sixteenth century proved more peaceful than the fifteenth, and the value of professional soldiers was increasingly appreciated. It was into this changed society that the heralds were sent to ensure that the traditional hierarchy of civil society was maintained and that symbols of gentility were not usurped by those who had no right to them by birth. It was a task that was as doomed to failure as the attempts to enforce sumptuary laws had proved.[1] One side-effect of the heralds' activities was to draw the provincial gentry's conscious attention to their lineage and the evidence that could be used to confirm or deny their status. This was a vital factor in shaping the development of local history in England.

The activities of the heralds stimulated the gentry's interest in their past, but it was the increased provision of education that enabled them to become more than passive consumers. The education that equipped them to act as local administrators and to pursue their lawsuits also enabled them to become historians. As local gentry communities experienced structural and cultural changes, their members enjoyed increasingly regular contacts with the wider world, both directly through visits to London, provincial cities or university towns, and indirectly through books. The consequent awareness of local particularities encouraged enthusiasm for local history among the gentry. The emphasis on genealogy and the meaning of gentility in local history reflects the gentry's attempts to establish the continuity of gentry identity across the gulf of the Reformation in reaction to the changes they experienced. Local history helped to connect them to their medieval ancestors.

In their topographical writings local historians, like cartographers, described the landscape from the perspective of the landed gentleman. The subsequent evolution of maps was driven by their practical applications. Although roads were not featured on early county maps, they were added on reprinting or as the counties were resurveyed. The 1730 edition of the *Antiquities of Warwickshire* merely supplemented the existing text, but replaced the simple maps of the first edition with more sophisticated, newly surveyed versions.[2] The rapid evolution of maps to maximise their utility stands in contrast to the comparative stagnation of local history. Gerard's *Survey of Dorsetshire* was finally published in 1732 without amendment; such delayed publication did not occur in cartography.[3] Topography constituted the aspect of local history that had the most potential to break free from the mould imposed by the structure of gentry society. Manorial boundaries did not appear on the landscape, and the examination of the physical environment took the local historian back beyond the range of written evidence and recorded ancestors. The potential for rapid evolution in local history was reduced by the development of archaeology as a field distinct from local history. The monumentality of a printed history compared to the more disposable maps also ensured that the past weighed heavily upon later generations of local historians. As recently as 1967 H.P.R. Finberg wrote: 'An overpowering interest in the class to which the historians themselves belonged, or would have liked to belong, has cast a genealogical blight over English local history from which it is only now beginning to recover.'[4]

Genealogy, heraldry and the descent of manors remained staples of local history long after they had lost their centrality to the self-identity of local historians and their readers.

The Elizabethan and early Stuart gentry saw themselves as socially differentiated, but not divorced, from the remainder of the population. They produced works that reflected their own perspective on the world. It was a wider perspective than their medieval ancestors had enjoyed, incorporating a new world across the Atlantic, but still recognisable. An invisible thread joined the Jacobean gentleman portrayed in anachronistic armour on his funeral monument to his ancestors at Crécy, Poitiers and Agincourt. In the mid-seventeenth century the world of the gentry was turned upside-down and, while normalcy was apparently restored in 1660, the invisible thread had been broken. The gentry who were educated after the civil war were influenced by the growth of natural philosophy, which presented them with a new paradigm, incomprehensible to their forebears. There followed not evolution but revolution, when old assumptions were overturned.

Looking ahead to a county history written just half a century after the Restoration, Sir Robert Atkyns's *Present and Ancient State of Gloucestershire* (1712) recorded a gentry that appeared to have separated itself from the rest of the community. The descriptions and engravings of funeral monuments remained, but they were increasingly classical in form, with Latin inscriptions incomprehensible to the majority of the congregation. The use of heraldry was restrained. It was not that the uneducated had understood the esoteric language of heraldry, but they had been able to recognise the symbols of different gentry families and so appreciate the interrelatedness of the ruling class. The separation of the gentry was concretely expressed in the physical distance maintained through their houses, increasingly surrounded by substantial parks and other barriers. Atkyns incorporated engravings of sixty-four gentry houses in his work, visually identifying their owners as a distinct class. Earlier works had scattered engravings of coats of arms throughout their pages, mingling medieval with modern, and extinct with current. Atkyns massed the coats of the Gloucestershire gentry on to eight pages at the beginning of the volume, underlining the impression that this was a distinct and separate community. Such changes represent a significant change in the gentry's perception of their place in the world and their sense of the past, which has been the subject of this study.

NOTES

1 J. Youings, *Sixteenth-Century England* (London: Penguin Books, 1984), pp. 110–29.
2 Smith, *Maps and Plans for the Local Historian and Collector*, pp. 72–6, 88–90.

3 Gerard, *A Survey of Dorsetshire Containing the Antiquities and Natural History of That County With a Particular Description of All the Places of Note, and Ancient Seats, and a Copious Genealogical Account of Three Hundred of the Principal Families. Published From an Original Manuscript, Written by the Reverend Mr. Coker of Mapowder in the Said County* (London: J. Wilcox, 1732)

4 H. Finberg, 'How not to write local history', in C. Kammen (ed.), *The Pursuit of Local History* (Walnut Creek, CA: AltaMira Press, 1996), p. 193.

Appendix: the major figures and works used

Name	Dates	Local associations	Works/description
Arthur Agard	1540–1615	London	Record-keeper
Thomas Allen	1542–1632	Staffordshire, Oxford	University tutor and antiquary
Sir Simon Archer	1581–1662	Warwickshire	Antiquary
Richard Bagot	1541?–97	Staffordshire	Genealogist
Reginald Bainbrigg	1545–1613	Westmorland	Schoolmaster
Sir John Beaumont	1582–1627	Leicestershire	Poet and antiquary
William Belcher	d. 1609	Northamptonshire	Antiquary
William Bell	1538?–98	Worcestershire	Antiquary
Sir Robert Berkeley	1584–1656	Worcestershire	Antiquarian lawyer
William Blundell	1560–1638	Lancashire	Antiquary
William Blundell	1620–98	Lancashire, Isle of Man	*A History of the Isle of Man*
Sir Wingfield Bodenham	*fl.* 1640s	Rutland	Antiquary
Edmond Bolton	1575–1635?	London	*Elements of Armories*
Sir John Borough	d. 1643	London	Record-keeper and herald
Robert Bowyer	1560?–1621	London	Record-keeper
William Bowyer	d. 1570	London	Record-keeper
Thomas Browne	1605–82	Norfolk	*Hydriotaphia – Urne Buriall*
Thomas, lord Brudenell	1578–1663	Northamptonshire	Antiquary
William Burton	1575–1645	Leicestershire, Staffordshire, Warwickshire	*The Description of Leicestershire*
Richard Butcher	1583–1665?	Stamford	*Survey and Antiquitie of the Towne of Stamford*

Name	Dates	Local associations	Works/description
Sir Edward Bysshe	1615?–1679	Surrey	Herald
William Camden	1551–1623	London	*Britannia*, Herald and schoolmaster
Richard Carew	1555–1620	Cornwall	*The Survey of Cornwall*
Nicholas Charles	1582–1613	Warwickshire	Herald
Walter Chetwynd	1598–1669	Staffordshire	Antiquary
Henry Chitting	1580–1638	Suffolk	Herald
Sir Simon Clarke	1579–1652	Warwickshire	Antiquary
William Claxton	1525–1600	Durham	Antiquary
Humphrey Colles	d. 1640	Warwickshire	Feodary (officer of the Court of Wards)
Robert Cooke	d. 1593	London	Herald
Sir Robert Cotton	1571–1631	Westminster, Huntingdonshire	Antiquary and founder of library
John Denton	d. 1617	Cumberland	Account of the estates and families in Cumberland
Sir Edward Dering	1598–1644	Kent	*Account of the Weald*
Sir Simonds D'Ewes	1602–50	Suffolk	Antiquary and autobiographer
Sir Kenelm Digby	1603–65	Warwickshire	Polymath
Sir John Doddridge	1555–1628	London	Antiquarian lawyer
Roger Dodsworth	1585–1654	Yorkshire, Lancashire	*Monasticon Anglicanum*
Michael Drayton	1563–1631	London, Warwickshire	*Poly-Olbion*
William Dugdale	1605–86	Warwickshire	*Antiquities of Warwickshire*, Herald
Sampson Erdeswicke	d. 1603	Staffordshire, Cheshire	*A View of Staffordshire*
Charles Fairfax	1597–1673	Yorkshire	*Analecta Fairfaxiana*
Henry Ferrers	1550–1633	Warwickshire	Antiquary
Thomas Fuller	1608–61	Northampton-shire, Dorset	*Worthies of England*
Richard Gascoigne	1579–1661	Yorkshire	Genealogist
Thomas Gerard	1592–1634	Dorset, Somerset	*A Survey of Dorsetshire*, *Description of Somerset*

Name	Dates	Local associations	Works/description
Robert Glover	1544–88	Kent	Herald
Arthur Gregory	d. 1603	Warwickshire	Antiquarian lawyer and feodary
William Grey	1601–74	Newcastle	*Chorographia or a Survey of Newcastle upon Tine*
Edward Gwynne	d. 1645	London	Genealogist and collector
Thomas Habington	1560–1647	Worcestershire	*A Survey of Worcestershire*
John Harestaffe	*fl.* 1610s–1630s	Derbyshire	*Chronicle of the Vernons*
William Harrison	1534–93	London	*Description of Britain*
Sir Christopher Hatton	1605–70	Northamptonshire	Antiquary and patron
Townshend Hereford	*fl.* 1630s	Herefordshire	Genealogist
Philemon Holland	1552–1637	Coventry	Schoolmaster and translator
Gervase Holles	1606–55	Lincolnshire	*Memorials of the Holles Family*
John Hooker als. Vowell	1526–1601	Exeter, Devon	*Description of Exeter*
William, lord Howard	1563–1640	Cumberland	Antiquary and patron
Roger Kemys	d. 1610	Gloucestershire	Antiquary
Richard Kilburne	1605–78	Kent	*Survey of Kent*
Daniel King	1616?–1661?	Cheshire	*Vale Royal of England*
St Loe Kniverton	d. 1625	Derbyshire, Nottinghamshire	Antiquarian lawyer
William Lambarde	1536–1601	Kent	*The Perambulation of Kent*
John Layer	1586–1641	Cambridgeshire	Antiquary
William Le Neve	1592–1661	Norfolk	Herald
Scipio Le Squyer	1579–1659	London	Record-keeper
Sir Hamon L'Estrange	1605–60	Norfolk	Theologian and historian
Henry Lilly	c.1589–1638	London	Herald

Name	Dates	Local associations	Works/description
Henry Lyte	1529–1607	Somerset	*Light of Britayne*
Thomas Lyte	1568?–1638	Somerset	Genealogist
John Norden	1548–1625?	London	*Middlesex, Hertfordshire*
Laurence Nowell	1530–c.1570	Lancashire	Antiquary
Sir John Oglander	d. 1655	Isle of Wight	Antiquary
John Philipot	1589?–1645	Kent	Herald
Thomas Philipot	d. 1682	Kent	*Villare Cantianum*
Sir William Pole	1561–1635	Devon	Antiquary
Henry Purefoy	*fl.* 1560s	Leicestershire, Warwickshire	Antiquary
Thomas Raymond	1575–1642	Somerset, Gloucestershire	Feodary
John Redding	*fl.* 1620s–1650s	Northampton-shire, London	Antiquarian lawyer
Robert Reyce	1555–1638	Suffolk	*Breviary of Suffolk*
Tristram Risdon	c.1580–1640	Devon	*Peritinerary of Devon*
Sir Edward Rodney	1590–1657	Somerset	*Memorials of the Rodney family*
David Rogers	*fl.* 1609–37	Chester	Expanded *Breviary of Chester*
Robert Rogers	d. 1595	Chester	*Breviary of Chester*
Samuel Roper	d. 1658	Warwickshire, Derbyshire	antiquary
Nicholas Roscarrock	1548?–1634	Cornwall, Cumberland	Hagiographer (writing about the lives of the saints)
William Ryley	d. 1667	London	Record-keeper and herald
Henry St George	1581–1644	Cambridgeshire	Herald
Richard St George	1545–1635	Cambridgeshire	Herald
Robert Sanderson	1587–1663	Lincoln	Clerical antiquary
John Selden	1584–1654	London	Legal antiquary
Sir Thomas Shirley	1590–1654	Huntingdonshire, Leicestershire, Derbyshire, Warwickshire	*Genealogical history of the Shirleys*

Name	Dates	Local associations	Works/description
William Smith	c.1550–1618	Cheshire	*Vale Royal of England*
John Smyth	1567–1641	Gloucestershire, Leicestershire	*Lives of the Berkeleys Description of the Hundred of Berkeley*
William Somner	1598–1669	Kent	*The Antiquities of Canterbury*; Anglo-Saxon dictionary
John Speed	1552–1629	London	*Theatre of the Empire of Great Britain*
Sir Henry Spelman	1562–1641	Norfolk	*History of Sacrilege*
John Stow	1525–1605	London	*The Survey of London*
James Strangeman	d. 1595	Essex	Antiquary
Thomas Talbot	1535?–1595?	London	Record-keeper
Silas Taylor	1624–78	Herefordshire	Antiquary
Francis Thynne	1546–1608?	Gloucestershire, London	Herald
Nathaniel Tomkins	1599–1681	Worcester	Clerical antiquary
Christopher Towneley	1604–74	Lancashire	Antiquary
John Trussell	*fl.* 1630s–1640s	Winchester	*Touchstone of Tradition*
John Twyne	d. 1581	Canterbury	Schoolmaster
Sir Roger Twysden	1597–1672	Kent	Antiquary
William Vernon	1585–1667	Cheshire, Lancashire	Antiquary
Augustine Vincent	1581?–1626	Northamptonshire	*Discoverie of Errours*, Record-keeper and herald
John Vincent	1618–71	Northamptonshire	Antiquary
William Webb	*fl.* 1580–1620	Cheshire	Antiquary
John Weever	1576–1632	Lancashire, London	*Ancient Funeral Monuments*
Thomas Westcote	1567–1637	Devon	*A View of Devonshire*
William Wyrley	1562–1618	Leicestershire, Staffordshire	*True Use of Armorie* (although anecdotal evidence suggests that this was Erdeswicke's work), Herald

Index

Note: page numbers in *italics* refer to illustrations